The Chisholm Trail

BY SAM P. RIDINGS

EDITOR'S NOTE

A noble book, rich in anecdote and character.

J. FRANK DOBIE

This frontier classic is a comprehensive history of the world's greatest cattle trail, the Chisholm Trail, which ran from San Antonio, Texas, to Abilene, Kansas — approximately eight hundred miles. It is one of the best books written about the cattle drives of our western frontier and the colorful characters associated with them, including Charles Goodnight, Charles A. Siringo, Joseph G. McCoy, and various gunslingers and Indian chiefs.

Before the Civil War, Texas cattle were driven to the large markets of the North through Missouri. However, the longhorns carried ticks that transmitted disease to other livestock, and consequently Missouri farmers stopped the herds from passing through the state. It became difficult to get cattle to the markets in the North.

During the Civil War, Texas ranchers went off to serve the Confederate cause. Few of the cattle they left behind were slaughtered in their absence, it not being possible to transport the longhorns out of Texas given Union control of the Mississippi River and the fact that destination Northern states were not part of the Confederacy. The herds grew so large that the animals sold for only four dollars a head in Texas, compared with the forty dollars a head paid in the North and East. Clearly there was money to be had in moving cattle northward.

When the Kansas Pacific Railway extended to Abilene after the war, cattleman Joseph G. McCoy saw his chance. Sam P. Ridings, author of the current work, writes that McCoy

> built shipping pens at Abilene, sent messengers out to meet [the herds], and advertised Abilene generally as the great shipping point on the new Kansas Pacific Railway. On account of the efforts, energy, and labor of young McCoy, Abilene became famous throughout the West as the northern terminus of the Chisholm Trail.

Six million cattle and an equal number of mustangs traveled the trail (named for Jesse Chisholm, a trader) in the years of its most active usage. During the two or three months required to traverse the entire route, drovers crossed rivers, canyons, and mountains and dealt with Indian ambushes, cattle rustlers, and stampedes.

Sam P. Ridings (1868–1942) was a prominent Kansas attorney who spent six years studying the Chisholm Trail. According to reviewer J. Frank Dobie, Ridings went "over the land, lived with range men, studied history" before he wrote. Dobie called Ridings' work "a noble book, rich in anecdote and character."

This edition of *The Chisholm Trail: A History of the World's Greatest Cattle Trail* is an exact facsimile of the first edition of 1936.

Les Adams
Chairman, Editorial Board

BIRMINGHAM, ALABAMA
OCTOBER 9, 2012

The Chisholm Trail

SAM P. RIDINGS

This picture is inserted in consideration of the fact that the reader of any book of this character should consider the same a conversation with the author; and ,by being able to see a picture of the person with whom such conversation is had, it should add to the interest of the same. How much more can you appreciate a broadcast on your radio if you know what the broadcaster looks like? In this publication, the writer is speaking to you, telling you what he saw, heard, and knows of the old trails, cow-camps, plains, and frontier of over fifty years ago.

The Chisholm Trail

A HISTORY OF THE WORLD'S GREATEST CATTLE TRAIL

TOGETHER WITH A DESCRIPTION OF THE PERSONS, A
NARRATIVE OF THE EVENTS, AND REMINISCENCES
ASSOCIATED WITH THE SAME.

By

SAM P. RIDINGS

Skyhorse Publishing

First Skyhorse Publishing edition 2015
Special Contents © 2012 Palladium Press

Skyhorse Publishing books may be purchased in bulk at special discounts for sales promotion, corporate gifts, fund-raising, or educational purposes. Special editions can also be created to specifications. For details, contact the Special Sales Department, Skyhorse Publishing, 307 West 36th Street, 11th Floor, New York, NY 10018 or info@skyhorsepublishing.com.

Skyhorse® and Skyhorse Publishing® are registered trademarks of Skyhorse Publishing, Inc.®, a Delaware corporation.

Visit our website at www.skyhorsepublishing.com.

10 9 8 7 6 5

Library of Congress Cataloging-in-Publication Data is available on file.

Cover design by Anthony Morais
Cover photo credit Thinkstock

Print ISBN: 978-1-63220-266-6
Ebook ISBN: 978-1-63220-768-5

Printed in the United States of America

DEDICATION

To my wife, Nettie L. Ridings, and to my three children, Pauline Breeden of Kemmerer, Wyoming, Capt. Eugene W. Ridings of the United States Army, and Marie Cooke of Merigold, Mississippi, this volume is affectionately dedicated by the author.   —S. P. R.

PREFACE

It is the universal attitude and characteristic of the men who traveled the old trails of the West to have a very great desire for the name and correct location of the same to be perpetuated. Such is more important in their minds than the preservation of the history of their own families or of their ancestral homes. This is the paramount feeling that has impelled the production of this volume. There are others as hereinafter set out.

As the ranks of the men, who traveled the plains and the frontiers of over fifty years ago, grow thinner year by year, the writer has discovered that, when friends induce him to talk of happenings and historical events of the Old West, they become very much interested. This is true, even though such narratives seem very commonplace to the writer and were considered of very little importance when they happened.

A record of some of the events and historical matters dealt with in this volume, in the opinion of the writer, should be preserved for the consideration of future generations, and no such record of many of the same has been recorded or retained. This being true, this history will be lost unless written by someone. If the efforts of the writer will result in placing some of the same in the history of the age in which they belong, this volume has served its purpose, and the labors of the writer have not been expended in vain.

In this production it is impossible to deal extensively and in detail with the various subjects herein touched upon. It is only the purpose of the writer to give a general consideration of each of these matters, and if the reader is further interested in any of them, he or she is advised to seek a work devoted exclusively to the subject desired. Persons generally have been so busy with the other affairs of life, that they have not had their attention called, even in a general way, to most of the historical matters herein referred to. The writer in producing this work has dealt with the subjects that he considers the reader would desire to gain information in reference to, and while in some particulars it may appear that he has departed somewhat from his subject, he has written what he considers would be of interest to his readers.

In either reading or writing the writer abhors the constant use of the personal pronoun "I," and for that reason this volume is, as far as possible, written in the third person, and he has attempted to eliminate entirely the personal pronoun of the first person singular.

It is through no idea of self-aggrandizement or financial gain that this volume is produced. Personally, the writer has done nothing which would place his name among the historical characters of the country. His services have been very commonplace, and have only been a very small part of the one great aggregation. His only ambition is to record the history of the worthy deeds of others. As a business venture, the writer will be highly gratified if he receives in return the actual expenditure made in this venture.

This publication is not only in fact a venture, but an experiment. The writer has written many volumes of legal briefs, which judges were under legal obligation to read, but in putting forth a publication that people in general can be induced to read, is a real departure, and he enters upon the same with fear and trembling, that is, as near as he ever trembled at facing any undertaking. He, therefore, asks that his critics will deal leniently with him. As an inducement to obtain this result the writer will say: That everything contained in this volume is true in substance as historical recitals; that is, they are as accurate as possible for any human agency to make them.

The author started writing this volume some five or six years ago, but halted when he discovered that his memory, after so many years, could not be relied upon without verifying the accuracy of the same. This proof he has made at the expense of a great amount of effort and research. He now feels that he can, without hesitation, present this work to the public with a recommendation as to its truthfulness and accuracy. With this assurance the writer submits this volume to the consideration of those interested in frontier history.

Sam P. Ridings

Medford, Oklahoma, 1936.

CONTENTS

ILLUSTRATIONS

The Chisholm Trail

VOLUME I
AND
VOLUME II

THE CHISHOLM TRAIL

CHAPTER I.

NECESSITY FOR THE TRAIL

At the time of the breaking out of the war between the states in 1861, the Indians who remained in the Northern portion of the United States, east of the Mississippi River, and who had not been killed by the white invaders, had settled down on quiet reservations. The remaining portion of the Northern Indians had, prior to this time, retreated westward before the white man's rifle as it cleared the way for the white man's plow. These retreating Indians had made their last stand either in or at the foot of the Rocky Mountains and on the plains to the east of the same. The white man's cottages of logs, rock, and the sod of the prairie dotted the eastern portion of these plains, while the steel rails of the transcontinental railways were being extended further west and were preparing to reach out onto these plains.

In the Congress of the United States, at this time, the different factions were staging a battle incessant to determine whether the states which were to be carved out of this northern plains country were to be free or slave states. Both the Oregon and the Santa Fe trails extended westward from the Missouri River, the eastern boundary of Kansas. Each of these trails wound its way to the west, as devious as the trail of a serpent, and each crossed these northern plains. The Santa Fe trail terminated in the heart of the continent at Santa Fe, New Mexico. The Oregon trail found its way to various points on the Pacific coast.

The foregoing describes the situation generally in the North. In the Southern portion of the United States, in the years preceding the war between the states, the fearless Davy Crockett had gone forth from his home in Tennessee to fight for the independence of Texas, and with his companion, Thimblerig, had cut loose from civilization at Nacogdoches, and, threading the forest wilderness, and swimming the rivers, had reached the old Alamo Mission, where now stands the beautiful City of San Antonio, Texas. There, fighting a forlorn hope, these soldiers of the frontier had died, together with Bowie, Bonham, Travis, and their other Texas companions. These brave defenders of Texas liberty had fallen when massacred by the ruthless invading Mexican Army, led by the more ruthless Santa Anna.

The hardy and fearless pioneers of Texas had rallied under the battle cry of, "Remember the Alamo"; and under the leadership of the rugged, intrepid, and sagacious Sam Houston had conquered Santa Anna and his Mexican Horde at San Jacinto. This conquest had been made in one of the most remarkable and decisive battles that the world has ever known. The flower of the Mexican Army had been driven back across the Rio Grande, and the power and control of the Mexican Government completely torn down and annihilated for all time in the country to the east of that river. Thenceforth the flag bearing the lone star floated over the great empire of Texas, and soon above it waved the Stars and Stripes.

Also, prior to this national conflict, the Indians in the Southern portion of the United States, living east of the Mississippi River, who belonged to the Five Civilized Tribes, comprised of the Cherokee, Creek, Choctaw, Chickasaw, and Seminole, had been taken forcibly by the armed forces of a Christian and civilized Government, and placed on separate reservations in what is now the eastern portion of the State of Oklahoma. There had also, prior to the time stated, been ceded to the Cherokee Indians a strip of land fifty-eight miles wide immediately west of the Cherokee Reservation, immediately south of the southern boundary of Kansas, and extending west as far as the United States' possessions at that time reached, which location was then undetermined. This strip of land was said to be an outlet for the Cherokee Indians to the west from their reservation for hunting purposes. This was known as the Cherokee Outlet and later as the Cherokee Strip. The Cherokee Indians, as all people know, were not hunters. This land was never utilized by them, and this country until long after the Civil War was unoccupied. The land included in this outlet had really been considered worthless; hence the generosity of Congress. Regardless of the early impression of this country, it is now well known that it contained some of the finest, most valuable, and fertile land in the United States.

All this vast stretch of country, north of the Red River, prior to and for many years after the Civil War, was unoccupied and remained a veritable wilderness, over which roamed lawless bands of Western or Plains Indians, buffalo and other native wild animals. Onto this country, during that time, occasionally ventured intrepid explorers, traders, and outlaws, some of whom returned therefrom, while others left their bones upon the plains. Thus extended westward these two advances of civilization, while between them lay a vast domain, extending from the Red River on the south to central Kansas on the north. This intervening country, several hundred miles in width, was as void of civilization and protection of government as the jungles of South America.

Such was the situation in the West when active warfare between the states was entered into at the firing of Fort Sumter. The entire Nation was thereafter engaged in Civil War for the four years ensuing. During these four years, and up to the year 1866, the energy, power, and wealth of both the

North and the South were exerted and spent in this civil conflict. During these years extensions of the frontiers and advancing the same were forgotten. Following the final capitulation of the Confederate Army at Appomatox, the armies of the North and the armies of the South left their bivouacs, cantonments, and forts, and returned to their former homes. Soon thereafter the men and women of the North took up their march to the west, singing both in spirit and in words:

> "We will cross the prairies as of old
> Our fathers crossed the sea,
> To make the West as they the East
> The homestead of the free."

In the South the men of Texas, joined by the Eastern and Northern men, pushed their herds westward, through thickets and woodland, across the glades and prairies to the Rio Grande. The trails left by the retreating Mexicans served as cow-paths, which were followed by the advancing herds. These pioneers left the line of their march marked with homes and ranches.

During the Civil War it had been impossible to send cattle out from the State of Texas. That State was a part of the Confederacy, and cattle during that period were not sent to States in possession of the Federal Army. During most of the war, the Mississippi River had been in the possession of the armies of the North, and for that reason no cattle could pass from Texas down or across to the east side of that river. During all these years the cattle of Texas multiplied, until the most accurate statistics show that at the close of the war there were over 3,000,000 cattle on the farms and ranches of that State. While this number purports to be accurate, we know that it cannot be exact. It has been said that the cost of rearing a steer to maturity in Texas at that time was fifty cents, and this was the cost of branding it. There was no market for these cattle, and they were practically without value.

Following the close of the war some of these cattle were driven east to the Mississippi River, and shipped by boat to New Orleans and other points down the river, but the demand for them in this direction was soon satisfied. The people of the South, if they had the opportunity, were generally without means to buy any great amount of meat. In 1866 some cattle were driven across the desert to the Pecos River, and up that river to New Mexico and as far as Santa Fe, but the demand in these localities was meager as compared with the supply. The states to the north and northeast needed these cattle, and were able and willing to pay good prices for the same if it was possible to transport them to the localities of the demand. Reasonable prices for these cattle would have made the citizens of the State of Texas wealthy beyond their most exaggerated dreams.

In the year 1866 many Texas cattlemen, and also purchasers from the North, drove herds north across the Red River, thence taking a northeast course across the country of the Five Civilized Tribes, in what is now eastern Oklahoma, attempted to cross either the State of Missouri or the State of Arkansas, and thus reach the markets or railways. Almost without exception these undertakings ended in utter failure and disaster. The Five Civilized Tribes were engaged in farming, thus dependent on their crops for support; and the interference with these farming enterprises and the difficulty of handling these wild range cattle in a farming country was the first great difficulty encountered. The greatest trouble, however, arose upon reaching the States of Missouri and Arkansas. On the borders of and within both of these states, where these market bound herds must cross, were large numbers of men discharged from both armies, who sought the course of least legitimate efforts to provide means for living. Members of this class were ready to take up any means possible, re-

Mobbing cattle drover from Texas and stampeding herd in Missouri in 1866—McCoy.

gardless as to whether it was legal or not, to obtain money. If it could be done under the pretense of being for a commend able purpose, it would cause them less trouble.

Members of this lawless element would stop these north bound herds, claiming that they were interested in preventing the spread of what was then termed the Spanish fever, a disease later known as the Texas fever. In most cases these parties would levy blackmail on the drovers, requiring them to pay certain sums of money before they would be permitted to proceed on their journey. In case the drivers in charge of the herds refused to meet the demands of these lawless men, they were whipped and robbed, and all of their belongings and their cattle taken away from them. For the reasons stated there was not a successful drive of cattle north from Texas during the entire year of 1866. The season closed with this record, and no market had yet been found for the herds of Texas.

In the year 1866, there was organized at St. Louis, Missouri, a railway company under the name of "The Kansas Pacific Railway." The purpose of this company was to extend a line of railway west from the Missouri River. In 1866 or the spring of 1867 this company boldly pushed its railway westward onto the Great Plains. It took its course up the valley of the Kaw River from Westport, now Kansas City, Missouri, to Topeka, Kansas, and pushed on to Manhattan, Junction City, Abilene, Salina, and Ellsworth. Abilene, Kansas, was the nearest location, on a direct line, north on the prospective route from Texas to make the cattle drives and reach this new railway. A young energetic cattleman from central Illinois, by the name of Jos. G. McCoy, recognizing the opportunity of establishing this location as a shipping point, and preparing to care for the herds coming from the south, built shipping pens at Abilene, sent messengers out to meet them, and advertised Abilene generally as the great shipping point on the new Kansas Pacific Railway. On account of the efforts, energy, and labor of young McCoy, Abilene became famous throughout the West as the northern terminus of the Chisholm Trail.

In the spring of 1867 the people of Texas learned that this new line of railroad was being built across the plains country to the north. The only question that then remained was the possibility of making the drive and breaking a trail across the several hundred miles of intervening wild and uncivilized country, which was not only exposed to the ordinary dangers of a wild country, but was also exposed to the assaults of the Western or Plains Indians, who for years had been on the war path. Many were the ranchers of Texas who stood upon the south bank of the Red River and looked anxiously to the north across this country; then returned to their ranches, afraid to venture over it. This feeling was brought about largely from a knowledge of the well advertised difficulties encountered and results of the attempted drives to the north the preceding year. Such was the necessity for a broken trail to guide the herds from Texas across this wild, exposed, and dangerous land.

There were no historians stationed along the routes of these trails of the West ready to record the deeds of these hardy plainsmen, and much of this early history is therefore lost to future generations. From the best recorded facts that can be gathered, and from the best existing information, it appears that it remained for a Californian, small and insignificant in appearance, but who had met and overcome all the difficulties and adversities of the plains and frontier, to make the first successful drive over this route. His name was Col. O. W. Wheeler. More will be said in future pages of this remarkable man and the drive he made.

Inasmuch as we are dealing at this time with the resources of the State of Texas and its capacity for producing the great herds that were ready to be thrown onto the northern markets, it is well, at this time, to observe the character and resources of this country, and to submit a general description of the same.

This great State has included within its boundaries over one hundred and seventy million acres of land, with all kinds and characters of surface, soil, and climate. The writer has traveled over all parts of the State of Texas, and from such personal observation considers it, when taken as a whole, one of the greatest States, if not the greatest State, of the Union of States. If the State of Texas was entirely segregated from the rest of the world it could come nearer subsisting, or could subsist longer and with less difficulty, than any other known territory of the same size. Over most of the State, except the extreme eastern portion, is found some specie of what is known as the mesquite grass. This grass is especially adapted for grazing at all seasons of the year.

The beauty of the State of Texas is unsurpassed. In most of the southern portion of the same the Spanish moss[1] trails down from the trees and is swayed by the gentle breeze. Also in the southern portion of the State, in the early days, the long-

---

[1]Spanish moss is so familiar to persons living in the South that it is not necessary to describe the same, but persons living in other portions of the country usually know very little in reference to it. This moss is a parasitic growth found in large areas of the South, including southern Texas. On higher ground it is seen covering the trees in bunches, but in lower ground it grows much longer, trailing down from the trees and swinging gracefully in the wind. Along bayous or wooded lakes these fine stems or vines grow many feet long, giving to the timber a sort of dismal and dreary appearance. These long bunches of moss are gathered by the natives and placed in piles to decay until nothing but the fiber, which is the greater portion of the same, remains. This fiber is washed and spread or hung out in the bright sunlight. The color of the fiber at first is gray, but the effect of the bright light on the same is to turn it a glossy bright black. It is then placed in bales of about eight pounds each and shipped to market. This fiber is used for upholstering. All buggy cushions were upholstered with the same, and it is in general use for similar purposes yet. It is an article familiar to all persons, but few of them know where it comes from or what it is produced from.

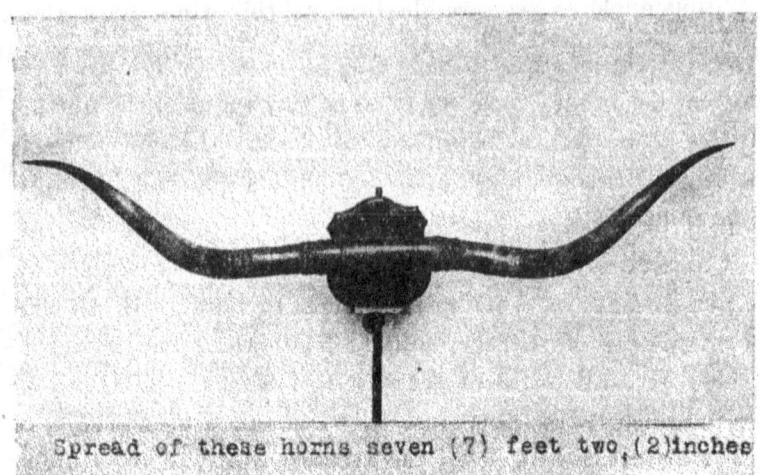

Spread of these horns seven (7) feet two, (2)inches

This set of horns was brought from Southern Texas during the cattle days, and is now owned by and kept in the Stock Exchange Bank at Caldwell, Kansas.

horned cattle, the descendants of the herds driven by the Moors into old Spain, roamed through the dark chaparral thickets, wild as the deer with which they associated. These were the first cattle introduced into this country, and were brought here by the early Spanish explorers and settlers. In the central portions of the State the cattle grazed through the ragged mesquite thickets, where the grapevine cacti twines around the trees. Here also extends the long stretches of prairie dotted with great bunches of broad-leaved cacti with the long and dangerous spines, around which the cattle cropped with great caution; the native mesquite grass. This cacti is generally known as the prickly pear, and during the early springtime these huge bunches are covered with large yellow bloom. These blooms encircle leaves as large as a palm-leaved fan.

In the eastern portion of the State is found the towering long and short-leaved pine, in the forests of which twilight reigns a greater portion of the day. Out in the western portion of the State extends the broad plains, generally known as

Llano Estacado. Here the "man-cactus"[2] rears its head and stands like a lone sentinel on the plain. On the south the Gulf of Mexico washes the borders of the State, and along its beaches is almost perpetual summer. In the extreme northern portion, while the summers are long, during the winter months the chill winds and often the blizzards blow down from the north.

It has been heretofore stated that, in the days preceding the Civil War, the long-horned breed of cattle was found in the State of Texas. In making this statement the writer desires to impress the significance of the same as to the size of the horns of these cattle. The illustration appearing herein, while large, is not by any means the largest coming out or found in that country. The horns on these cattle were so large that in this day and age they are beyond conception. This is the more remarkable from the fact that they generally lived in a timbered country or among brush. These cattle in early days, when they were hunted, would hide in the chaparral thickets[3]

---

[2] There are perhaps more varieties of cacti than of any other plant. It grows in different localities in all shapes, sizes, and forms. In portions of Texas, even further north than Palo Pinto County, one variety grows in the mesquite timber in the form of a vine, which entwines the trees just as a grapevine. In the Staked Plains country one variety grows on the plains, standing straight some six or eight feet high. These cacti often grow isolated and long distances from each other, and when seen from a distance they look very much like a man standing out alone on the plains. Hence, they are called "man-cactus."

[3] The chaparral thickets of southern Texas consist of an evergreen oak together with all other sorts of bushes and vines, often including cacti, interwoven. Frequently when going through these thickets large vicious rattlesnakes sound the traveler a warning. This vegetation is as near impenetrable as could seemingly be made. The cattle and other animals would make trails or cow paths through the same. When the cattle would come out of these thickets to graze on the adjacent prairie the cowboys would watch and rope and tie as many of them as they could before they could return and hide. They would then drive a herd or bunch of tame cattle along, and release these tied animals and drive them away with the tame cattle. There were some of these tied animals which would not leave with the tame cattle, and would persistently attempt to return to the thickets. The cowboys would again rope them and sew their eyes shut by taking thread and sewing the eyelids together over their eyes, so that the animals could not see to run to the thickets. They would then follow along with the tame cattle, and when sufficiently far away the thread would be cut in the stitches and permit the animals to regain their eyesight. The cowboys of those days thought no more of roping and tying one of these wild and ferocious animals than we would of catching a chicken or turkey.

and come out during the night to graze, and return to their hiding place shortly after daylight.

The writer desires here to register a protest, on behalf of the old time southern long horned cattle, on account of the almost universal misrepresentation of this long suffering breed, from the hideous pictures which have been made and published illustrating them with long horns sticking up in front of their heads in a curve the shape of inverted teeth of a hayrake. If this departed race of cattle could know that they had been described thus, there would be a universal rattling of old bones, and, on sight of one of these pictures, there would be a general stampede.

The picture herein set out of the horns of one of these ancient cattle is an exact outline of all of them. There was but very little difference in the shape of these horns. They extended almost straight out at right angles from the head, with but a small graceful curve in them. It is a shame to disfigure these cattle with the sort of horns that most of the artists have placed on them.

In the extreme eastern portion of the State were found a breed of cattle with shorter horns. These cattle were known, in the earlier days of the cattle industry, as the Southeastern cattle. The descendants of these cattle are still found in portions of eastern Texas, Louisiana, and Arkansas. While ranching and cattle raising is still a large portion of the business and industry of the State of Texas, it is now systematized, and instead of the ancient longhorns are found the fat classy Herefords. The old days with all their excitement, danger, and thrill have passed away. The affinity of all persons for the land of their nativity is natural, but it always seemed to the writer that this characteristic was more pronounced in Texans than most other persons. During the cattle drives up the trail, it was a common remark by cowboys and cowmen from southern Texas that when they returned to where they could see the Spanish moss swing down from the trees they would be satisfied and would remain there. It is a fact that can be ascertained from observation, even at the present time, that there are fewer native Texans who emigrate to other localities than from any other state.

Jesse Chisholm, former scout and plainsman, for whom the Trail was named. —Courtesy of Oklahoma State Historical Society.

CHAPTER II.

JESSE CHISHOLM

The cattle trail, known as the Chisholm Trail, was the greatest one of its kind in the history of the world. Its length varied according to the different periods of time during its existence. In its inception it extended and was traveled all the way from San Antonio, Texas, to Abilene, Kansas, a distance of approximately eight hundred miles. The early herds going north over this trail crossed the Red River at various points, but when well established it crossed that river, left the State of Texas north of the City of Ringgold, and entered the State of Oklahoma below the mouth of Cache Creek and south of the City of Waurika, near the line between the present Cotton and Jefferson Counties, Oklahoma. It then took its course north. In later years it straightened out, gradually working west, until it followed near the present line of the Chicago, Rock Island and Pacific Railway and the route of the Meridian Highway, known as Government Highway 81, and crossed the north line of the State of Oklahoma south of the City of Caldwell, Kansas, the exact location being about eighty rods east of the point where Highway 81 crosses the state line between Kansas and Oklahoma. The trail ran from this point north to Abilene, Kansas. From Caldwell to Abilene it varied but sixteen miles from a course due north, Abilene being sixteen miles further east than Caldwell.

This cattle trail was named for Jesse Chisholm, and was so known throughout the entire West. The reason for this will hereafter appear. Two things are peculiar in this regard. One of them is that while Jesse Chisholm was one of the prominent and noted characters of the frontier and old West, he was not a cowboy or cattleman. It has been truthfully said, that the only cattle he ever drove were yoked to his wagons. The second is that he never traveled this trail except from the present City of Wichita, Kansas, to its crossing on the Cimarron River, where the present City of Dover, Oklahoma, now stands, a distance of less than one hundred and fifty miles.

Considering the times and surroundings in which he lived and died, Jesse Chisholm was truly a remarkable man. His life was spent without any idea on his part, that he would ever be known as a historical character, and he died without considering that he was, or ever would be, known as other than an ordinary trader. Much of the history of this remarkable man has been lost. Some that remains is legendary, but many written records are preserved proving his activities, worth, and standing. The following are some of the high points of his life. There are many others, but in this brief sketch they cannot all be included.

Jesse Chisholm was a mixed blood Indian, being something less than a half-blood Cherokee. He was born at the old home of the Cherokees in the East. The exact date and location of his birth are uncertain, but from the best information obtainable he was born in the State of Tennessee in about the year 1806. His father was a white man of Scottish descent, and his mother was a mixed-blood Cherokee. The exact proportion of Indian blood of his mother is uncertain. The only record we find as to this fact is that her name was Rogers, and that her family were mixed-blood Cherokees. His mother was a sister of Talihina Rogers, whose first name is often given with other variations, but who married General Sam Houston. The Rogers family were evidently quite intelligent, as its members reached a degree of considerable prominence among the Cherokees.

It is a well known fact that the Cherokees, aside from being a well civilized and cultured people, produced men in their tribe who could and did compete favorably with the ablest statesmen of our Government. History reveals that the Rogers family moved from their home in the East, among the first emigrants of their tribe to remove to Arkansas, settling in their new home in the year 1816. Homes in Arkansas had been, prior to this time, guaranteed by the President of the United States for such of the Cherokees as would remove to the same. This was done by a letter written, granting such permission and guarantee, by President Jefferson, dated January 9, 1809, which was approved by treaty of 1817.

It is very probable that Jesse Chisholm's father and family removed to Arkansas at the same time, as we find them located there soon afterward. The Chisholm family became prominent in the Arkansas settlement of the Cherokees. In the treaty concluded July 8, 1817, between the National Government and the Eastern Cherokees and the Arkansas Cherokees, we find among the Arkansas Chiefs who signed this treaty the names of James Rogers and John D. Chisholm. The relative standing of these two men among the Indians and their intelligence can be judged from the fact that Rogers and Chisholm were the only ones among fifteen chiefs signing this document who could write their names. The remaining thirteen all signed by mark. Rogers was selected from the tribe in Arkansas as a representative of the Government, and sent east to assist in procuring the consent of the balance of the Cherokees who had not moved, or as many as possible of them, to move to the Indian Territory.

The first recorded account of Jesse Chisholm and his activities is in 1832. It will be borne in mind that at the time of the removal of his family to the West Jesse Chisholm was only about ten years of age, and at the time stated, in 1832, he was about twenty-six years of age. Even at this early age he was engaged in laying out and establishing trails. The Choctaw Indians procured the National Government to construct a road for them over the rough country between Fort Towson and the Arkansas River. This was done that these Indians might receive their supplies sent to them by the Government from the Arkansas River to the north instead of the longer route by way of the Red River on the south. From the character of the country over which this new trail was to pass selecting a route for the same was a very important and difficult matter. This trail extended one hundred and forty-seven miles over this wild rough country. This route was selected, laid out, and surveyed by Robert Bean and Jesse Chisholm.

The important points, marking the life and character of Jesse Chisholm, were good judgment, his retiring and unassuming disposition and character, absolute trustworthiness, fidelity and honesty in his dealings, and his never assuming authority or forcing his judgment or services upon anyone until the same was solicited or sought. He was a wise counselor, a safe adviser, and was held in high esteem by all who dealt with him. This was especially true of the Indian tribes of the entire Indian Territory, and extended even to the wild Apaches.

Jesse Chisholm having come West as a mere child, and being a keen observer, by the time he reached manhood knew the country of western Arkansas and the Indian Territory perhaps better than any other man. He had a fine memory and fine intellect, and it is said that he could speak well and converse in fourteen different Indian languages. His services were always much sought after as a guide and interpreter.

Jesse Chisholm married the daughter of a trader by the name of Edwards. His father-in-law operated a store near what was then known as Fort Holmes, which was located at the mouth of the Little River, near the present site of Bilby,

Seminole County, Oklahoma. This store and location, at one time known as Fort Edwards, was at first on the north side of Little River, but afterward was removed to the south side of the river and remained there during the important period of its operation. This trading post in 1849 and 1850 had the reputation of being the most important one on the trail between Fort Smith and Santa Fe. At the time of the Beale expedition to the west, hereinafter referred to, Edwards was still operating this post, and Jesse Chisholm was living in the southern portion of what is now Seminole County, Oklahoma. His home was near the Canadian River, and was almost on the transcontinental route laid out by the Beale expedition. Chisholm's home at that place was said to be the outermost point of civilization.

Jesse Chisholm had but one child, a daughter, Mrs. Jennie Chisholm Davis, who lived a few years ago in southern Okfuskee County, Oklahoma. Her postoffice address was Paden, Oklahoma. During his travels Chisholm rescued, or procured the release of, many prisoners taken and held by the Comanche Indians. Among them was a white boy, who was a small lad when obtained from the Indians. While this boy was perhaps never legally adopted, he remained with Chisholm and took his name, and was known as George Chisholm. He followed the footsteps and example of his foster father, was a scout of considerable note, and served in that capacity during the Civil War. Jesse Chisholm's father-in-law's name was James Edwards. Edwards was a white man who intermarried with a Creek woman. Thus Jesse Chisholm was a mixed blood Cherokee, while his wife was a mixed blood Creek.

Jesse Chisholm succeeded his father-in-law in the operation of this store at the mouth of Little River, and as his success grew and increased his influence extended until he became known as the most successful and influential trader on the

Southern Plains. The Apaches, Kiowas, Comanches, and other Plains Indians came long distances to his store to trade. In order to better handle this trade he established posts further to the west. He operated one near the present town of Asher, Pottawatomie County, Oklahoma; another near Lexington, Cleveland County, Oklahoma; also one at Council Grove, which location is about six miles west of Oklahoma City. It is a well known fact to all persons familiar with the frontier at that time, that salt was one of the most sought after articles of consumption. This fact was soon realized by Jesse Chisholm, and he was early interested in the production of salt in what is now the State of Oklahoma, and produced the same at a number of points in the Indian Territory. One of these was in Blaine County, prior to the Civil War.

One evidence of the shrewdness and far seeing business judgment of Jesse Chisholm was, that, after the railway extended west from the Missouri River, he early saw the importance of connecting himself with the trade that was increasing from the north. He had previously established a trading post on what is known as Chisholm Creek, which location is now within the corporate limits of the City of Wichita, Kansas. He spent much time at this post and gave it a great deal of attention. Also he often made trips to the north and east, from there going as far as Fort Leavenworth, Kansas. In the intervening time, after the establishment of this trading post until his death, he studied and familiarized himself with this northern trade, and, had it not been for his untimely demise, he would have profited very much from the same. Chisholm Creek was named for him. His connection with the trading post at that point, and his connection with the increasing trade from the north, brought about the locating and laying out of this trail which bears his name. This trail will perpetuate his name longer than anything else he left behind.

Jesse Chisholm had perhaps more power and influence with all the Indian tribes of the Indian Territory than any other man. He was sought out as a friend by them, being one in whom they could confide, and with whom they could counsel. He was a safe adviser in time of need and in time of distress. At the time of the breaking out of the Civil War he counselled and advised neutrality on the part of all of the Indian tribes in the Indian Territory. Today we can appreciate the wisdom of his counsel. His advice in this regard would have been accepted by all of the Indians, had not both parties to this conflict brought about conditions which made it impossible for the Indians to follow this course. The participation of these Indian tribes in this controversy between the different portions of the Nation was followed by the dire results that Chisholm had foreseen.

Jesse Chisholm himself remained absolutely neutral during this conflict, and at the close of the war he was sought out and sent by the Federal Government as a representative to the Indian tribes, or at least some of them, in making or concluding treaties with the Government. His dealings and services at these times and in these matters were fair and always satisfactory to both parties. His influence for good was felt in this wild country more than that of any other man, and for good reason did the Indians of the Indian Territory view his death as a calamity.

He died in what is now Blaine County, Oklahoma. At the time it occurred he was on one of his trading expeditions, and was looking after his interests in this portion of the country. His death occurred in March, 1868, at the age of about sixty-two years. His photograph, a copy of which is reproduced herein, is the only known picture of him in existence. This was taken in the later years of his life, and perhaps not long before his death. It is said that it was taken at Leavenworth,

Kansas, perhaps in the summer preceding his death, when it is claimed that he made one or more trading trips to that place. This picture would indicate a man much older than Chisholm really was at that time, but he had never acquired the art of posing for a picture. He was buried near where he died, on the North Canadian River in southeastern Blaine County, Oklahoma. He died suddenly; it has been said or presumed by some, from pneumonia, but others have claimed from indigestion. His grave was lost for many years, but was located a few years ago by Jos. B. Thoburn, who at that time was Curator of the Oklahoma State Historical Society, and who has done more to preserve the history of the State of Oklahoma than any other man.

It is really difficult to find any portion of the frontier which Jesse Chisholm did not visit during the period of his active life. It seems he was constantly on the move to or from some Western point. There was a small settlement of Cherokees in Mexico, and in the spring of 1842 George Guess, better known as Sequoyah, the inventor of the Cherokee Alphabet, set out from the Cherokee Nation with his son and a few companions to cross the intervening wild country to this place. After many perils and wild adventures he, his son, and one companion reached this settlement. Sequoyah, however, never lived to return to his home, but died in Mexico in 1843.

Jesse Chisholm was sent to investigate the fate of Sequoyah, or at least did so. A report setting forth the journeyings, wandering, and difficulties of this Sequoyah party was published in the Cherokee Advocate, a Cherokee publication, on the 26th day of June, 1845. There was also furnished with this article a statement as to the death of Sequoyah, witnessed by Jesse Chisholm, which statement reads as follows:

> "Warren's Trading House,
> Red River, April 1st, 1845.

We the undersigned Cherokees, direct from the Spanish Dominions, do hereby certify that George Guess, of the Cherokee Nation, Arkansas, departed this life in the town of Sanfernando in the month of August, 1843, and his son (Chusaleta) is at this time on the Brasos River, Texas, about 30 miles above the falls, and intends returning home this fall.

Given under our hands day and date above written.

> Standing Rock, his x mark.
> Standing Bowles, his x mark.
> Watch Justice, his x mark.

Witness:

Daniel G. Watson

Jesse Chisholm."

There had been a great amount of agitation, in which it was sought to procure the Government to establish a southern route for travel, which would run from Fort Smith, Arkansas, to California. Several attempts were made, much of this route laid out, and a great amount of improvement in the way of building bridges and grading crossings on streams done on the same. The first expedition launched in this enterprise was commanded by Capt. R. B. March in 1849, the second by Lieut. A. W. Whipple in 1853, and the third by Lieut. E. F. Beale. Beale was in 1858 ordered to survey a route from Fort Smith westward for a wagon road and stage line, which would continue to the Colorado River. He also made and submitted an estimate of the expenses for building a railroad from Fort Smith to Antelope Hills, this being approximately the western line of Oklahoma. This cost he placed at $9,311,900. He started on this mission on the 29th day of October, 1858, and was engaged in carrying out this enterprise for about one year.

The first requirement of Beale on this trip was to find an efficient guide to accompany him. He first sent a messenger to procure the services of Black Beaver,[1] who was then living at or near Camp Arbuckle on the Canadian River, which could not have been far from the home of Jesse Chisholm at that time.

Black Beaver objected to taking this trip, and stated as a reason for his refusal that the Comanche Indians were at war with the Government, and the expedition would be compelled to cross the country occupied by this tribe; that it was late in the fall, the grass was in good condition to burn, and the Comanches would burn the same, leaving the expedition without food for their stock; thus it ending in disaster. This would perhaps have been the result of the enterprise, had it not been for the fact that the weather during most of the time this expedition was in progress was such that the grass would not burn.

Jesse Chisholm was then requested to accompany Beale as a guide, and he at first made the same objection that Black Beaver had made. In fact, the services of both of these noted scouts and guides were sought, but Black Beaver could not be persuaded to go. Chisholm finally agreed to and did accompany the party. They pushed their course up the Canadian River, past the Cross Timbers, past the Wichita Mountains, and onto the Great Plains. Most of this was done in mid-

---

[1] Black Beaver was a member of the Delaware tribe of Indians. He was born in Illinois in 1806. He was a contemporary of Jesse Chisholm, and led many expeditions both for private parties and for the Government. On these trips he traveled the then Indian Territory, Colorado, and the country to the southwest into Mexico. He also made a number of trips as far west as the Pacific Ocean. He commanded a company of Delaware and Shawnee Indians in the service of the Government during the Mexican War. At the breaking out of the Civil War it was apparent that the scattering garrisons of Federal Soldiers in the Indian Territory would be exposed to the combined forces of the Southern Army, and these garrisons were ordered to assemble and travel north to Fort Leavenworth. Which they did. In making this trip Black Beaver guided them. He led this command into the Cherokee Outlet near the point where the Chisholm Trail crosses the southern boundary of the same, and followed almost the line of the same to the southern boundary of Kansas. This was four years before Jesse Chisholm laid out his trail. For this service Black Beaver suffered loss by confiscation of his property at the hands of the Confederacy, for which he was never compensated by the Federal Government, except to a very small percent of his actual loss.

winter, and all under very adverse circumstances. The hardships of the party were many and great, their suffering was severe, and they were exposed to an unusual severe winter, but Beale rendered an enthusiastic report of the trip and of the conditions which he found. His men had built bridges, cut down banks to afford crossings, and completely constructed a road adequate for their wagons to travel over. The report, made by Beale, and presented to Congress, had nothing but praise for the route. The life of Jesse Chisholm was simply a succession of these trips, trials, adventures, and dangers. He thought nothing of them. To him they were simply a part of the day's work. If we had a graphic description of these adventures written today they would entertain the readers of Western History for generations to come.

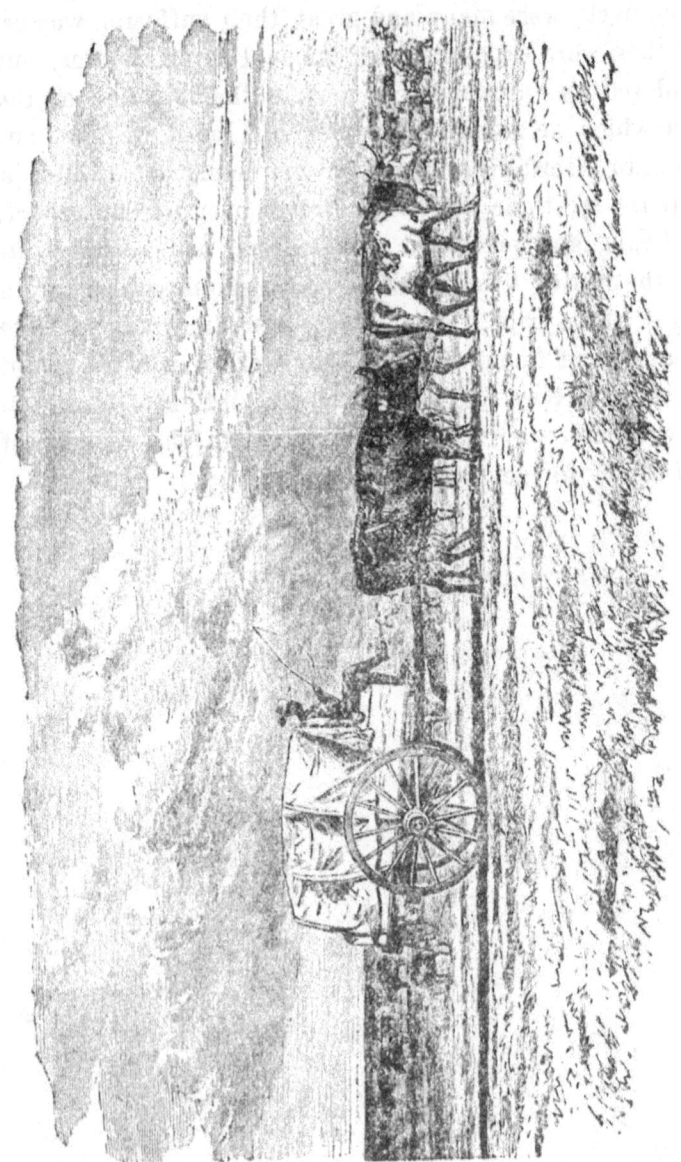

Camp wagon used on the early drives up Chisholm Trail.—McCoy.

CHAPTER III.

THE EARLY TRAIL

The original Chisholm Trail was established in 1865, and was used to reach the Indian tribes in the Southwestern country. Before the railway extended west from Kansas City or Westport, that location, as well as the ones on the border of the frontier to the north of it, had become important trading points and bases of supply for the western country, which included the Plains tribes of Indians. From Jesse Chisholm's store on Chisholm Creek these supplies for the Southwestern Indian tribes could be disbursed; hence the necessity of a trail on which to carry them to the consumers.

The trail, as originally laid out, extended from this supply store on Chisholm Creek to the vicinity of the present location of Anadarko, Oklahoma, or a distance of approximately two hundred and twenty miles. When the cattle herds came up from Texas in 1867, they followed this trail from the crossing on the Cimarron River, now Dover, Oklahoma, to near the present site of Wichita, Kansas, passing just west of this location and going on north to Abilene. Thus, it is seen that approximately one hundred and fifty miles of Jesse Chisholm's trail was adopted as a part of the cattle trail from Texas. In return, however, for the use of the trail the cattle drivers named the entire trail "The Chisholm Trail." The old trail, subsequent to 1865, was extended from Anadarko to Fort Sill. After 1867, when the cattle drives began, the cattlemen, in order to distinguish the trail continuing on south from the Cimarron River to Anadarko, which was a part of the original trail, designated that portion of the same as "The Trader's Trail." This was so named for the reason that that portion of the trail was used by the freighters and traders, and in order to distinguish it from the cattle trail, which left the Trader's Trail on the townsite of the present City of Dover, crossing the Cimarron River at the mouth of Kingfisher Creek, about one and a half miles to the east of the other trail, and then passed to the east of the present City of El Reno, Oklahoma. This cattle trail, the entire distance from San Antonio, Texas, to Abilene, Kansas, was known as the Chisholm Trail, and was so designated by the cattlemen from the time when the first herds passed over it in 1867 until it was finally closed in 1889 by the flood of immigration and the homesteader's plow.

While this trail was universally known and went down in history as the Chisholm Trail, yet few cowboys and persons in general knew for whom it was named, and few persons knew to what Chisholm it referred, why it was named for him, or who he was. Many persons even yet, who are quite well informed, do not know the origin of the name, and some contend that the trail was named for John Chisum, who was once a Texas cattleman living at Paris, Texas, later in Concho County, Texas, and still later in New Mexico. As will be observed in future pages John Chisum never traveled over this trail, never claimed to have anything to do with it, nor to know anything about it. When the initial herd went over the Chisholm Trail, John Chisum was crowding his first outfit to, and establishing his ranch in, New Mexico.

There is no one now living who knows, nor is there any record left showing the exact course taken in making this first drive over the route of the old Chisholm Trail. In determining the same we have only the record left by Jos. G. McCoy in his Historic Sketches of the Cattle Trade of the West and Southwest, published in 1874. McCoy was the man who put Abilene on the map and determined the northern point of the cattle trail. In his book he only gives us a general statement of the location of the cattle trail in 1867, and thereafter, from the Kansas line north to Abilene, but nothing so far as to the location and route further south. We do have, however, a definite designation made of the route of this trail across the Cherokee Outlet or Cherokee Strip as it existed in the year 1872. This record is authentic. It was made by the United States Government and shows the location of the trail over each one hundred and sixty acres of land crossed by it in going over the Outlet at the time of the Government survey of the same. This route is given herein in the last chapter of this work.

From the south line of the Cherokee Outlet on south to the crossing of the Cimarron River there could be no change in the route, as it passed most of this distance through the only opening there was in the black jack timber. This timber extended for miles on either side of the trail.

Referring to this original trail as laid out by Jesse Chisholm from the present site of Wichita to the southern line of the State of Kansas, it appears that after leaving Chisholm's store on Chisholm Creek it bore south and slightly west, passing a short distance west of the present City of Wellington, Kansas, and on in approximately the same direction, crossing the Chikaskia River north and east of the present City of Caldwell, Kansas. The writer, when a boy, heard it said that after the City of Wellington was established, it being east of the trail, the citizens of Wellington plowed a furrow branching off from the trail and going to the town of Wellington, and placed signs at the intersection directing the traffic through the newly established town. From the Chikaskia River the trail bore southwest in about the same general direction, and reached the south line of Kansas about two miles south and slightly east of the present City of Caldwell, at a point about eighty rods east of the highway and railway tracks.

After crossing the Kansas line the trail still bore south and somewhat west, passing to the west side of the railway at a point about one-half mile over the state line, and following the exact line of Highway 81 for about three miles. It then crossed to the east side of the railway, passing about one half mile to the east of Renfrow, Oklahoma. Next it bore due south for about four miles, passing east of the breaks on the head of Polecat Creek, south of Renfrow. It crossed Polecat Creek about two miles east of the railway and Highway 81. It then took a southwest course, crossing the section line running east on the north line of the City of Medford, two miles east of that city. From the last mentioned point, it ran about due southwest, crossing exactly over the townsite of Jefferson, Oklahoma, and going south from there, crossing the Salt Fork River on the east side of the railway bridge, thence south, varying to the west, crossing the townsite of Pond Creek a short distance west of the railway and Highway 81. It continued south and west just west of the railway until after it crossed the county line into Garfield County. It then crossed to the east side of the railway, passing about one-half mile east of the railway at Kremlin, Oklahoma, and continued on the east side of the railway, varying from one-quarter to three-quarters of a mile, until it reached a point between North and South Enid, when it crossed to the west side of the railway. At North Enid it was three-quarters of a mile east of the railway. It crossed the townsite of Enid, passing apparently over the Government Square. It then bore somewhat more to the southwest, and at a point one and a half miles south of Enid it was three-quarters of a mile west of the railway.

The trail then dropped back east, crossing to the east side of the railway two and one-half miles south of Enid. It soon, however, returned to the west side of the railway and followed the same course, near the present track of the railway, on south across the townsite of Waukomis. The lines of the trail and railway vary but little in this course, frequently crossing each other, one crossing being on the townsite of Waukomis. The trail and railway continued on almost the same line south. At the town of Bison, near which was the old camping ground of Buffalo Springs, the trail crosses the townsite west of the railway, and leaves the Cherokee Outlet near the center of the south line of Section 36, Twp. 20 N. of Range 7 West.

The trail in later years varied somewhat from the original route taken. Also there may have been some variation after the establishment of the trail in 1865 and before the line was marked by the Government in 1872. When this survey was made the cattle trail had been established, and the line marked followed it. In later years the trail between Renfrow and Medford, Oklahoma, varied further to the west of the original, and passed over the townsite of Medford. At Jefferson, the trail used by wagon travel, by stage lines, and by some cattle drivers passed one mile east of Jefferson. This route was taken in order to avoid crossing both Pond Creek and Osage Creek, and effecting the crossing of Pond Creek below the point where the two creeks came together. In this course the trail passed around and on the south side of the large pond on the south side of Pond Creek.

This pond extended in a semi-circle for almost three-quarters of a mile around a bend in Pond Creek, on the south side of the creek and a short distance east of the railway. The creek was named for this pond. Also the original townsite of Round Pond was named for the same, the name having been transferred from the old station. This pond has now been drained, and is only a dry depression. In the early days, within the memory of many, it was a large deep pond filled with fish. Also, in later years, there was somewhat of a variation of the trail at Skeleton Creek, where the City of Enid is now located.

At this point the later trail passed further to the east. The old Skeleton Ranch was located some distance east of the railway, and a well known camping place was at the springs in the east portion of the City.

Continuing with the route of the trail from the south line of the Cherokee Outlet, where we left it, it followed what is now the line of the railway south to the City of Hennessey, Oklahoma, crossing that townsite west of the railway. It then took its course south through the natural opening in the black-jack timber, on the east side of Turkey Creek, to the present City of Dover. On the townsite of Dover the trail divided. The cattle trail went to the southeast, crossing the Cimarron River just below the mouth of Kingfisher Creek, one and one-half miles below the railway and Highway 81. The original trail or Trader's Trail continued south, crossing the Cimarron River just east of the railway and wagon bridge on Highway 81. It then followed almost the exact line of the railway on south, crossing the townsite of Kingfisher, and on to Okarche.

From Okarche it bore southwest, leaving the route of Highway 81, and going further west to Caddo Springs, where was afterward established and still is maintained the Cheyenne Indian School and the present station on the railway known as Concho. At Caddo Springs a beautiful spring gushed from the ground, from the waters of which many a weary traveler and his tired animals quenched their thirst. It then continued southwest, crossing the North Canadian River at almost the same point that the 98th Meridian crosses the same. Afterward, in 1869, at this point was established the Darlington Agency, it being the official agency for the Cheyenne and Arapaho Indians. From here it continued on south, crossing the South Canadian River west of Union City and Minco, to Anadarko, and afterward extended to Fort Sill.

In reference to the location of the cattle trail coming up from the south and before reaching the crossing of the Cimarron River, it is difficult to give an exact location of the same until in later years, for the reason that it was some time before it had a definite location. In the first drives this trail after leaving Red River bore much to the east of a direct line of travel. This was done for the purpose of following a portion of the way the old trails made by drivers in preceding years, whose destination was further to the northeast, and also to enable these pioneers in some cases to follow for some distance a trail left by soldiers returning from, or during, the recent war. Perhaps the greatest cause of such deviation was to avoid the western or plains Indians, who at that time were continuously on the war path. In the beginning the main object was to get a trail broken, and then the travel could follow the same general direction. This they did, but in the future it gradually dropped back to the west, making a more direct route. Finally the trail was a well established route, following generally the present line of the Chicago, Rock Island and Pacific Railway from its crossing of the Red River on north.

It will be borne in mind, that until long after the laying out of this trail there were no established stations along the same. The Pond Creek Ranch was one of the first permanent locations on the trail, it was not established until long after the trail, and was first known as the Sewell Stockade. This ranch stood about one hundred and fifty yards east and a little south of the water tank on the railway south of the present town of Jefferson, Oklahoma. Darlington Agency, on the north bank of the North Canadian River, was established in 1870, and Fort Reno in 1874. The marks of the old trail are even yet plainly visible at points along the route of the same. They can still be seen near the Kansas-Oklahoma state line, at the crossing of Pond Creek, and the tourist on Highway 81 can see them just south of Hennessey, Oklahoma, as well as at many other points.

The cattle trail after entering the State of Kansas, as stated, passed a short distance west of the present City of Wellington, when it bore north, crossing the Arkansas River west of the City of Wichita, and went on to Abilene. During the driving and shipping season of 1867, the first year of the cattle drives from the south, there was much variation in the routes taken in Kansas. The next season the persons interested in the drives procured a surveyor to run an exact line from Abilene to the point where the trail left the Indian Territory. This line was laid out and markers, consisting of piles of sod, were erected to guide the drovers straight to Abilene. It is probable also that furrows were plowed to mark the route of the same. The writer has heard this was done.

This trail was traveled all the season in later years by freighters and other conveyances, including stage coaches, after the agencies and forts had been established. The travelers had no hotels or inns to accommodate them, they were compelled

Old time Concord stage coach, similar to those used on the Chisholm Trail.

to carry their own equipment, and camp in the open. The stage coaches changed horses and continued their travel all night, obtaining meals at the stage stations. The camping places on the trail were at any point where wood, grass, and water could be found. This was usually on any of the streams. In the winter season wood was the most sought after, and in the summer water and grass.

In the summer buffalo and cow chips were easily obtained and were ample fuel for the camper. The principal camping points on the trail were in their order, traveling south; the Nenesqua River, Slate Creek, near the present site of Wellington, Kansas, Chikaskia River, Bluff and Fall Creeks, near the Kansas and Indian Territory line, Pond Creek, near the present site of Jefferson, Oklahoma, Wild Horse Creek, south of the City of Pond Creek, Skeleton Creek, near the present City of Enid, Buffalo Springs, near Bison, Turkey Creek, on the east bank of which the trail ran from Hennessey to Dover, Oklahoma, Red Fork Ranch, now Dover, Kingfisher Creek at the present location of the City of Kingfisher, Caddo Springs, and Darlington Agency, after its establishment in 1870. Stage stations and ranches were maintained in later years at the following points in the Indian Territory: Polecat Creek, Pond Creek, Skeleton Creek, Buffalo Springs, Bull Foot, Red Fork, Kingfisher, Fort Reno, and at other points temporarily.

The writer first knew this trail as a small boy. Wichita, Kansas, at that time was the terminus of the railway, and all commodities for consumption in the settlements beyond that point were hauled by wagon or, as it was termed at that time, "freighted." The writer had been over this trail from Wichita to Pond Creek Ranch many times prior to the fall of 1881. After about the year 1876, the settlements in southern Kansas cut off the cattle drives from Texas, as they could not enter or cross the cultivated farming country. Caldwell was located in Kansas, just north of the state line.　Wellington, some twenty-five miles north and east of Caldwell, was located and established as the county seat of Sumner County.　It was then a small town of scattering buildings on the hill north of Slate Creek.　The trail at that time was used as a traders' trail exclusively, except for the small number of native cattle which were driven over it.　It did not follow the section lines, but maintained its usual course directly across the prairies.　It crossed the Chikaskia River about four miles east and about two and one-half miles north of Caldwell, at what was then known as Ryland's grove.　The Atchison, Topeka, and Santa Fe Railway built into Caldwell in 1880, and the trail that far south, for all purposes, was closed forever.

After the trail crossed Fall Creek and Bluff Creek, a short distance southeast of Caldwell, it ascended the long hill south of these creeks, crossing the line into the Indian Territory near the top of the grade, about two miles south of Caldwell.　In later years, from a point a short distance south of the state line, the traveler could look to the north down upon the City, and for miles over the farms, farm houses, and cultivated fields. Further to the south on the trail this view was soon lost.　Often when passing over this trail, in early days the writer has paused to observe this view; and while doing so, has pondered upon the fact, as to how many travelers upon this cattle and trader's trail have from this point looked back upon civilization for the last time for many months or years, and many of them forever; and how many wayfarers upon this trail coming up from the south, dirty, dusty, travel stained, and travel worn, after hundreds of miles on the plains, have been gladdened by the first sight of civilization that they had had perhaps for many months or many years.　Persons who have never spent months or years on the plains or on the extreme frontier, cannot appreciate what civilization or settlements mean on his return, to a traveler who has done so.

The writer traveled over this trail to the south from Caldwell in 1881. He was then a small lad, and its wonders still remain vivid in his memory.

The trail at that time, from a point where it reached the high ground, just south of the Kansas line, on to the creek of Pond Creek, a distance of twenty-three miles, passed through a continuous prairie dog town. The barking of these little denizens of the prairies was incessant along the entire route. With each bark the tail of the barker would give a quick jerk, and its barking apparatus and tail seemed to work in entire unison. All the other stretches of upland along the route were covered with prairie dog towns. The trail at that time was also used as a cattle trail. During the shipping season many herds daily passed over the same. The main portion was beaten as hard as the concrete of the highway that now parallels it. This had been done by the millions of hoofs that had trampled it.

The prairie dog owls, about the size of a quail, were seen on all sides, perched upon the prairie dog holes. These owls would sit there apparently dozing, with one of their big eyes shut and the other half closed. When one sought to approach them, they would either drop into the prairie dog holes or rise and fly away, seemingly as light as a feather. Occasionally the vicious buzz of a rattlesnake, a sound familiar to every traveler upon the western plains, would be heard. Then its spotted body either slid into a prairie dog hole or coiled into a circle, with its head and blunt nose protruding upward in the center. Its body coiled around and encircled its head for protection of the same, from this position, when the stranger came close enough, the body of the snake would straighten out like a spring that had been compressed, its mouth opening wide automatically raised the long fangs lying down along its jaws, and it would, if close enough, sink these fangs into its victim. On the extreme end of these snakes' tails were carried rattles. When disturbed this tail began quivering, and these rattles started a continuous and monotonous buzzing.

It was always said that any person, even though he had never seen or heard a rattlesnake before, would instantly know what it was upon first sound. The sound had a vicious menacing meaning that no one could mistake. All the animals feared these snakes as much as men. Many prairie chickens in large bunches would be seen along the trail. These birds were then extremely tame, and would rear their heads in an inquiring way, as if seeking to ascertain what the rights of such travelers were in this untamed country. Occasionally, a bunch of wild antelope would be seen some distance away. Almost invariably, they would circle around the traveler in order to get the scent, and from that they would know what sort of a creature was invading their country. The white bristling hairs on the rear portion of these fleet-footed animals would glisten in the sunlight. On all sides were seen the unmistakable signs which told the traveler, that he was in a land that had not yet been brought under the hand of Civilization.

After crossing Pond Creek, and passing around the large pond on the south side of the same, for which the creek had been named, the trail reached the old Pond Creek Ranch, one of the oldest landmarks on the same. Here the open well of brackish water, equipped with a wheel and bucket to bring the water to the surface, supplied the thirsty sojourner with sufficient water to quench his thirst and that of his team or horse. To the south of the old ranch, at this time, were first seen by the writer the two graves of luckless cowboys, who had less than ten years before died in encounters with the Indians, and who had been buried as they had lived, "on the lone prairie."

About one mile to the south from the Pond Creek Ranch was the crossing of the Salt Fork River. The crossings of the Salt Fork, Cimarron, and the South Canadian rivers were the three worst crossings to be negotiated on the trail. All of these rivers flow over a bed of sand, and all of them, being long rivers, are subject to extensive rises, during which time they remain impassible for long periods of time. During these rises, the force of the swift water causes the bed of the river to shift, and for some time after the water subsides this sand is unsettled and loose. Persons or animals crossing it will sink into the same. This is called quicksand. All of these rivers, also the Red River, and the North Canadian to some extent, have this soft sand in them after a period of high water. Freighters were sometimes caught with their wagons and teams in this quicksand. Often it would be so bad, that they would be compelled to unload their wagons, carry their freight out, and take their wagons apart, carrying them out piece at a time.

It was a well known fact among travelers on the trail, that horses were worse to bog in this quicksand than any other animals. While mules bogged, on account of the small size of their hoofs they could withdraw their feet from the sand better than horses. Cattle having cloven hoofs, while withdrawing from the sand, the hoof would close up and were withdrawn with ease. In crossing these rivers after a flood time, when possible, a bunch of cattle were driven across first. These cattle could easily go through the quicksand, and their going through the same would settle it until teams and wagons could easily pass over. There have been many wagons lost in all of these streams. These parties had attempted to cross while the water was deep. Before they could get their wagons out they had sunk into the sand until the water had risen covering them, and they could not be removed. At low water time, in all of these rivers, portions of these wagons could be seen sticking up above the water.

Going on south the trail passed the grave of Pat Hennessey, at the present site of the City of Hennessey. It was located about twenty feet west of the roadway, on the side toward the bank of Turkey Creek. Several flat rocks rested on the top of the grave. This was the condition about seven years after the death and burial of Hennessey. The grave was not enclosed, and around the same in places the grass had not grown. There were many persons who stopped to view this grave, and this may have been caused from their trampling the grass. Most every stagecoach that passed this grave stopped for its passengers to view the last resting place of this pioneer.

At Caddo Springs the Cheyenne school had been established, and its buildings which were there at that time still stand. The present growth of trees around the same were not

Cheyenne School at Caddo Springs as the same appeared in 1880.

there when the writer first knew it. About two and one-half miles from this point to the southwest was located the Darlington Agency, with its large and extensive storehouses standing on the north bank of the North Canadian River. Further on to the southwest, on higher ground, stood Fort Reno. Over this fort the National Flag was flying high and waving in all its glory. It always gladdened the heart of the traveler. The fort then consisted of primitive buildings, which were later replaced by more modern structures. From here the sound of the cannon at sunrise and sunset echoed far against the distant hills, proclaiming to the wild Indians the power of the white man, and that civilization was crowding in upon them.

Some ten or twelve miles from this fort to the south the teams of faithful horses, steady mules, and plodding oxen slowly dragged the wagons of the freighters through and over the long stretches of sands across the Canadian River and over the long sandy bottom on the south side of the same. Over this sand in flood time the Canadian River carried a torrent of water. The scenes as heretofore set out were such as were found along this primitive highway, the old Trader's Trail, when the boys, who are now old gray-haired men, traveled over it. Such were the scenes of childhood in the west, and such will never be seen again.

CHAPTER IV.

JOHN CHISUM

There has been a vast amount of discussion and purported argument on the part of a few persons, advancing the claim that John Chisum opened the Texas cattle trail to Abilene, and that it was named for him, but unfortunately most of these persons did not know who John Chisum was, or how he spelled his name. Some of these arguments, apparently made in candor, have been so unfounded as not to occasion any attention. The great trouble in collecting history of this kind is, that there are so many old gentlemen, absolutely honest in their intentions, who want to advance their long set opinions as to the same, and some who claim to have personal information are so positive, claiming they could not be mistaken, when there are some forgotten facts which change the results of their conclusions entirely. One eminent writer expressed the matter very accurately by saying, that he encountered so many honest old men who had "elastic memories."

The writer knows of but one credible authority which states that John Chisum first traveled this trail. The writer of that article never talked with John Chisum, but obtained his information from other sources. Edward Everett Dale, Dean of the History Department of Oklahoma State University, in his excellent work entitled, "The Range Cattle Industry," published in 1930, simply gives both contentions. He cites, in favor of the John Chisum contention, the only credible authority there has ever been published in favor of that argument. This authority is the McArthur manuscript. This manuscript deals with the early cattle industry, and gives the information of the writer as it had come to him, not from John Chisum personally, but from some other source which he deemed authentic.

Cattle pens and Drovers Hotel at Abilene, built by the McCoy brothers.—McCoy.

The McArthur manuscript sets forth, on pages 152 and 153 of the same, in substance, that John Chisum in 1866 crossed the Red River at the northwest corner of Cooke County, Texas, followed Mud Creek to its source, crossed the Washita River at Elm Springs, and went north to the Canadian River, following the Kingfisher Creek valley to the Cimarron River, thence north to the Salt Fork River, and on north, crossing the Kansas line at Caldwell, and the Arkansas River at Wichita, Kansas, continuing north past Newton to Abilene. Without in any way attempting to detract from the McArthur manuscript as an authority, and particularly not attempting to discredit the author, as he was a very able man, the writer will say, that it takes but one statement to effectually dispose of the contention made in this authority, and that is that there was no Abilene, Kansas, until the year 1867. Abilene was a station on the Kansas Pacific Railway, which was built west from Kansas City. It had no existence until the road was built, and the road was not started west from Kansas City until the spring of 1867. If Abilene had been established, he could not have shipped cattle from that point until the railway arrived and the loading pens had been built. That was not until late in the summer of 1867.

There could have been no other purpose in driving cattle to Abilene, or to any other point in Kansas, than to have shipped them east. The Indian tribes of western Kansas were on the war path at that time, and it was almost impossible for an emigrant train to get through, much less a herd of cattle, so there could have been no intention of driving them in that direction. The statement is made in this article that this herd was driven to Abilene, and as Abilene was the northern shipping point the evident purpose is to show that the cattle were shipped at that point, and they could not have been shipped without a railroad to ship them on. John G. McCoy, who built and owned all of the first cattle pens at Abilene, says that the first herd from the south arrived there late in the year 1867, and belonged to Col. O. W. Wheeler and his associates. The McArthur manuscript is evidently in error as to the year, and, being wrong as to the year, it cannot be correct.

John Chisum could not have traveled over this trail in 1867, for the reason that he was on his way to New Mexico with a large herd of cattle at that time. On this trip he traveled across the desert to the Horse Head crossing on the Pecos. In 1866 he was preparing and arranging to make this drive in 1867, and was gathering a large bunch of cattle with full intentions of changing his residence from Concho County, Texas, to New Mexico.

A very important consideration, in determining the establishment and the naming of the Chisholm Trail, is that the trail has always been known and designated as "The Chisholm Trail," while John Chisum did not spell his name "Chisholm," but spelled it "Chisum," thus the spelling of the name itself would determine who was intended.

The most convincing fact that has been presented, and one which would determine the matter, if there was no other, is as follows: In 1866 Charles Goodnight, who was operating a ranch in Palo Pinto County, Texas, drove a herd of cattle southwest from his ranch to Concho County, then west across the desert to the Horse Head crossing on the Pecos River, and up that river to New Mexico. John Chisum was preparing, in 1866, to do this same thing. In 1867 Goodnight and Chisum joined their herds and drove over this route to New Mexico. These two great western characters were together for years, and knew each other better than most brothers. In 1927 Hubert Collins, who was a very good friend of the writer, was preparing his book entitled "Warpath and Cattle Trails," and wrote to Goodnight making inquiry as to John Chisum's connection with the Chisholm Trail. Collins received a reply from Goodnight, and sent a copy to the writer. Hubert Collins is now deceased, Charles Goodnight is also dead, but the original of this letter is still in possession of the persons having the papers of Hubert Collins, and the writer still has the copy. This letter to Collins refers to a number of other things, but so far as it pertains to the matter referred to, reads:

"Chisum never crossed Red River with a cow in his life and told me so but he did follow the Goodnight Trail to *Bosque Grande* on the Pecos River below old Fort Sumner in 1867 and continued driving over that trail for several years. I handled all of his drives for three years and know what I am talking about."

This letter, signed by Charles Goodnight, is dated at Clarendon, Texas, July 23, 1927.

Further, it will be borne in mind, that in 1866 John Chisum was not located in northern Texas. In 1857 he moved from Paris, Texas, and in 1866 and 1867 was located in Concho County, Texas. This point was about as far from the Chisholm Trail as he could get and still remain in Texas. He would, at this time, have had as little interest in opening this trail as any cattleman in Texas.

In order to further clarify this matter, and not in the least detract from the character and standing of John Chisum, who was a very important western character and a very honorable man, we will set out herein a short review of his life and activities, showing some of the high points in the same.

John Chisum was born in Tennessee in the year 1824. In 1837 his parents moved their family west, settling south of the Red River, near where is now located the City of Paris, Texas. He had three brothers, Pitzer, James, and Jefferson. After John Chisum was well established in New Mexico, these three brothers joined him there, and assisted him in handling his vast herds, as they grazed over a western empire. John Chisum grew to manhood in the new location of his family in Texas. He was a sober, industrious young man, and having acquired a considerable amount of real estate, laid out and platted on his land the town of Paris. In addition to his town platting venture, he launched out as a builder and contractor. He took the contract for and built the first court house in Paris, and also many other important buildings of that period.

John Chisum, even in his early years, and extending through his entire life, was a shrewd, farseeing, cautious, and fair dealing business man. Scrutinizing carefully all the history possible of the life of this man, the writer will say that he has not found an act of dishonesty in the same. His one great enemy, Major L. G. Murphy, never made such a charge against him. In 1854, when about thirty years of age, John Chisum first entered into the cattle business. For some time he held his herds around Paris, and for a few years drove cattle to Shreveport, shipping them by boat to the Mississippi and down the same to market. In 1857, in order to obtain a location where his cattle business could better expand, he moved to Denton County, Texas, and, with the same object in view, in 1863, he moved on to Concho County, and there established an extensive ranch, where his herds roamed over a wide range and increased until 1867. The dream of John Chisum was ever for expansion of his holdings and for building greater his interests. For this purpose he was looking westward, a course which he never abandoned, and which finally ended at the foot of El Capitan Mountains of New Mexico.

In the year 1866, Charles Goodnight drove his herd westward from the Concho, across the hundred miles of barren, waterless desert to the Horse Head Crossing on the Pecos, and up that river to New Mexico. This same year, John Chisum was gathering his herds and marshalling his equipment for the same drive. In the summer of 1866 and the spring of 1867, John Chisum's cowboys guided their mustangs over the glades and prairies of this portion of Texas. The long skirts of their *tapaderas* [1] trailed through the mesquite as they gathered together the herds, that were to enter into the aggregation, which was to constitute the extensive caravan on the journey to New Mexico.

As early as was convenient in the year 1867, this well equipped outfit trailed its course from the Concho to the westward. The country over which this trip was to be made was wild. Few white men had traveled over the same, and death in some violent form lurked at all points on the route. The wild Indians of the plains and mountains were hostile, and were ever ready to plunder the unprotected traveler. Spanish spurs jingled on the heels of John Chisum's riders, the best of pistols swung at their waists, and the most effective rifles of that day were strapped on their saddles. A string of wagons, each drawn by mules, carried all the needed supplies of the entire outfit, while the long string of wild gaunt Spanish cattle strung out in traveling fashion onto the desert, heading westward for the Pecos River. After taking their course over almost one hundred miles of waterless desert this combination of animals and men reached the Horse Head crossing on the Pecos, and the wild and famished animals plunged into the water.

Thus John Chisum moved westward and up the Pecos, passing the site where now stands the beautiful City of Roswell, New Mexico. He continued his course northward with his ten thousand head of cattle, his horse *Remuda*, and mule drawn

---

[1] *Tapaderas* is of Spanish or Mexican derivation. It is perhaps composed from the Spanish words *tapa*, meaning cover, or from the verb *tapadura*, being the act of covering. These tapaderas were heavy leather, which covered the front of the saddle stirrups and extended down in long pointed leathers at the sides, reaching almost to the ground. They were so named by the Mexicans and southwestern cowboys and were worn on the saddle stirrups in riding through brush or high grass, or to protect the feet in a storm.

wagons, until he reached a point about forty miles south of Fort Sumner. Here in a large grove of cottonwood trees he located a ranch, which he named *Bosque Grande.*[2] Here he fought all the wild elements of the frontier, and finally conquered them. He remained at *Bosque Grande* about five years, when he moved his ranch down the Pecos, locating at a point about five miles south of the present City of Roswell. This was a lovely location, which he named South Springs. Here he built a veritable frontier empire. He was not only the Cattle King of the Pecos, but of the entire West. His brands, at that time, marked more cattle than that of any other man in the United States. His buildings were large and commodious, and his word was law up and down the Pecos. Here he reigned in western style, with all the pomp and splendor of a Feudal Lord.

John Chisum is well known throughout the West, even to this day, on account of the peculiar marks and brands of his cattle. These were known as the "long-rail" and "jingle-bob." The long-rail was a long bar brand,[3] extending along the side of the animal, being burned with a branding iron, but of such a length that it could not be burned off or destroyed with a frying pan brand.[4] The jingle-bob was a peculiar slit in the ear of an animal. When properly slitted, it would cause one portion of the ear to drop down, and the other portion would stand upright. This mark was easily recognized when cutting out cattle on a roundup.

While John Chisum was a man, all of whose characteristics were of peace and good will toward all mankind, he is better known in history as one of the leaders of one faction in the Lincoln County War. A narrative of the life of John

---

[2] *Bosque Grande* is a Spanish name which Chisum applied to his ranch. The English meaning is *big grove.*

[3] A bar brand is a straight horizontal line burned on an animal.

[4] A frying pan brand is a large spot burned on an animal by a large flat iron such as the bottom of a frying pan, which would destroy and burn off a brand over which it burned.

Chisum is not complete without at least a short statement as to this conflict.

Lincoln County, New Mexico, at the time of the Lincoln County war, comprised in its borders one-fifth of the area of the Territory of New Mexico, including what is now about five counties. The village of Roswell had been started at that time. It was located five miles north of John Chisum's ranch at South Springs. The town of Lincoln, some fifty miles to the west, was the county seat of Lincoln County. Roswell was in the valley of the Pecos, while the town of Lincoln was over in the range of the Capitan Mountains. Major L. G. Murphy, who had been a major in the Regular Army, had been mustered out of the same at Fort Stanton, some nine miles west of the town of Lincoln. Murphy had engaged in the mercantile business at Lincoln, and also carried on a number of other enterprises. He became very wealthy and powerful in New Mexico. He was crafty, grasping, and tyrannical. He had been educated for the priesthood, but had strayed far from its precepts. He was well educated, and used it to his advantage. He became a big political power in New Mexico, and the oppressive use of this power brought on the Lincoln County war. This war not only drenched the mountains and valleys of New Mexico with blood, but caused one governor of the then Territory of New Mexico to be removed from office, and echoes of this war were heard in the White House at Washington and in the Halls of Congress.

Murphy had a ranch west of the town of Lincoln, but he moved it over southeast of Lincoln, nearer to that of John Chisum. It is claimed he was stealing John Chisum's cattle, and in so doing relied on the sheriff, whom he had elected, to protect him. Whether Murphy or his men actually did any of the stealing is not certain, but in any event persons from whom he bought some of Chisum's cattle were convicted for stealing them. At this time a highly educated, extremely religious, and conscientious attorney by the name of Alexander A. McSween had settled in Lincoln, and was attorney for Murphy. Murphy hired him to defend some of the parties arrested for stealing Chisum's cattle, and McSween having, as he stated, discovered that these men were guilty, refused to further defend them. This was characteristic of McSween. He was a man who never shot a gun in his life, never took a drink, and carried his Bible in his saddle pockets when attending court away from Lincoln.

McSween's withdrawal from the employ of Murphy brought about a friendship between him and John Chisum. John Chisum, McSween, and an Englishman by the name of J. H. Tunstall associated themselves together in a number of business enterprises at Lincoln, among which was a bank and a general store, which were operated in competition with Murphy. Tunstall also owned a ranch several miles southeast of Lincoln. This Englishman had working for him as one of his cowboys a quiet little lad of about eighteen years. He was a smiling, good natured young cowboy. His hands and feet were as small as those of a lady, and whenever occasion permitted he dressed very neatly in western style. This boy had been born in New York City, but, when only a few years of age, had gone with his family to seek their fortune in the West. His father had died, and was buried at Coffeyville, Kansas, and his mother had made the journey further west with her two children.

Here the boy had drifted onto the cattle ranges, though young in years, had become an expert cowboy, and was working for his friend Tunstall. This lad's name was William H. Bonney, but he is better known as "Billy the Kid." Every sentence and paragraph of the history of the Lincoln County war is punctuated by the crack of his pistol. Had he been granted a pardon, as the other participants in the Lincoln

County war were, and had stopped when the war was over, he would have been a hero. But such was not the case, and he is known as a western desperado. Even as it is, he still lives in song and in spirit in New Mexico. Ask an old Mexican in that country, "Usted savy Guilleymo Bonney?" (Do you know William Bonney?) His face will light up, and he will reply, "Si, Bele the Keed." In the minds of these old residents, Billy the Kid still rides over the Capitans, across the hills and valleys of New Mexico, and down to old Fort Sumner. Billy the Kid was a friend of John Chisum, and a frequent visitor at South Springs Ranch.

Murphy had elected a cowboy by the name of Brady to the office of Sheriff of Lincoln County. Murphy, having the sympathy of the Sheriff's office, had sued McSween and Tunstall, and had an attachment issued for their property. An organized band of about twenty deputies, sworn in by Sheriff Brady, armed themselves, and after first being filled up with whiskey, served at Murphy's saloon, went out under the guise of serving this attachment, and met and killed Tunstall. This was done in a drunken orgy. They met him on the road, killed him and his horse, and laid them down side by side, with Tunstall's coat under his horse's head, and his hat under his own head, as if they had lain down and gone to sleep. Billy the Kid, kneeling at the side of his fallen friend, with tears flowing, swore a solemn oath that he would kill every man who had helped to murder his benefactor. He performed his work in that regard well. He was killed when twenty-one years of age, and, it is said that, not counting Indians and Mexicans, he had acccounted for twenty-one men.

The Lincoln County war continued with fighting and bloodshed, until it culminated in the killing of Sheriff Brady by Billy the Kid, and in the three days' battle in Lincoln, in which McSween's house was surrounded by officers and some sixty deputies acting in the interest of Murphy. In this battle McSween never fired a shot, but prayed most of the time, and was killed grasping his Bible. The McSween house was burned over the heads of the defenders, but Billy the Kid let all the inmates run out, and helped them all he could in their attempt to escape. Then he picked up a splinter, lit a cigarette, and drawing his hat down tight on his head, threw the door open and rushed out, killing two men, and escaped without a scratch. Billy the Kid was a one-gun man, but it is said that on this occasion he carried a pistol in each hand.

Billy the Kid was convicted for killing Sheriff Brady, and sentenced to be hung, but a few days before that event was to take place, he killed his two guards and escaped. He could have left the country and escaped entirely, but he returned to Fort Sumner, where he was eventually killed by his one-time friend Pat Garrett. The Lincoln County war ruined Murphy. Before the event of the Three Days Battle, Murphy, bankrupt and sick, retired to Santa Fe and died there before the result of the battle and McSween's death reached him. He was the one-man power on the side opposed to Chisum, Tunstall, McSween, and Billy the Kid, and with his death the contention ended, as his followers lost interest.

Pat Garrett was elected Sheriff of Lincoln County, arrested Billy the Kid before his conviction and sentence, and after his escape followed him, and finally killed him under circumstances in which Garrett stated he had the advantage. Pat Garrett's description of Billy the Kid is the most apt of any that the writer has seen. A portion of the same reads as follows:

"Billy the Kid was a likeable fellow. He was quiet and never bragged. There wasn't any fuss or bluster in him. He was not quarrelsome, he never hunted trouble. If you had never met him before or heard of him you would have thought him a mild, inoffensive sort of a boy. You certainly would not have taken him for a fighter or a killer. I never saw him mad in my life and I hardly remember him when he was not smiling; but he was the most murderous youth that ever stood in shoe leather, and he was game all the way through. When I was elected sheriff, he and I broke friendship. When I started in to hunt him down, I hoped to capture him, I did not want to kill him."

The injustice and oppressive methods used by the Murphy faction in the Lincoln County war were circulated throughout the west. Some parties censured Samuel B. Axtell, then Territorial Governor of New Mexico, claiming that he should have used different methods in handling the situation. President Hays concluded that it would be best to remove Governor Axtell and appoint someone far from either faction to take his place and handle the final adjustment of the situation. The President thereupon removed him, and appointed in his place his friend, General Lew Wallace. Governor Wallace pardoned all the participants in the war, except Billy the Kid. He held a personal interview with Billy the Kid, in which he informed him that he would also pardon him for all his offenses, except the killing of Sheriff Brady, and if he would stand trial on that charge and was convicted he would pardon him for it also. Billy the Kid was suspicious, and thought if he was once disarmed he would be killed by his enemies. He refused the Governor's offer, and returned to his old life, with the result as stated.

In justice to Billy the Kid, it is necessary that the persons judging him put themselves in his position. He had not been trained in the finer arts of civilization, he had been reared on the prairies, and the only law that he knew was that dealt by his ready gun, in the use of which he had become an expert. He knew that Murphy was in the wrong, and he knew that the deputies of Sheriff Brady had killed his friend. He considered the act a ruthless murder, and blamed the sheriff for the deed. The only retribution that he knew or wanted to know was tragic and sudden death to the persons whom, he had concluded, were implicated in the killing.

John Chisum, Tunstall, and McSween were not fighting men, but fate had placed them at the head of one faction in this bloody conflict. McSween's character has been detailed heretofore. Tunstall was a quiet inoffensive Englishman. John Chisum was a shrewd, pushing business man, who did not have time to have trouble with anyone. What the three leading characters lacked in the power of defense, protection, or inclination to avenge their wrongs was made up by Billy the Kid. He literally shot himself to fame, and then shot himself to destruction.

After the close of the Lincoln County War, John Chisum continued to live at South Springs ranch. His herds increased, and he grew wealthy beyond any dream that he had when locating in New Mexico. It is estimated that at one time one hundred thousand head of cattle wore his brands. He turned over to Mrs. McSween several hundred head for money he owed her husband. She removed to Three Rivers, some fifty miles southwest of Lincoln. Here she prospered and was known as the Cattle Queen of New Mexico. She sold her ranch at Three Rivers to Albert B. Fall, afterward United States Senator from New Mexico and Secretary of the Interior in the President Harding Cabinet. The old South Springs ranch was for many years the most famous throughout the entire West. Here all persons, whether friends or strangers, were always welcome to come and go at will. The ranch was operated on the true western plan. There any person came and remained as long as he desired, and was always welcome, with no price paid for such entertainment by anyone. The table at South Springs Ranch remained set at all times, ready for all comers.

John Chisum, in contrast to most western men, never carried either pistol or rifle on any occasion, except in early days when he was fighting Indians. During the entire Lincoln County war he never carried a weapon. To do so was not according to his disposition. John Chisum died in 1884, some several years after the close of the Lincoln County war. He died at Eureka Springs, Arkansas, where he had gone for his health, and was buried at Paris, Texas, the place of the beginning of his activities. His niece, Sallie Robert, formerly Sallie Chisum, was his housekeeper at South Springs Ranch. She was the daughter of his brother James Chisum, and died at Roswell, New Mexico, in 1934. From the arrangement and plans made by John Chisum, South Springs Ranch became one of the beauty spots of the West. After his death, it was purchased and is still owned by H. J. Hagerman, well known railroad builder and once governor of New Mexico. To the students of western history, however, the spirit of Uncle John Chisum still lingers around South Springs.

Col. Oliver W. Wheeler, who in 1867 broke the Trail from the Red River to the Red Fork Ranch, a distance of almost three hundred miles.—McCoy.

CHAPTER V.

COL. O. W. WHEELER

Many persons fairly familiar with western history have never heard of Col. O. W. Wheeler; others only know him, or know of him, as a successful cattleman and cattle dealer. All cattlemen in the days of the Old West were prominent and important. If not, they were relegated to a position where they did not rank with that fraternity. The Chisholm Trail was a well broken thoroughfare, coming up from the South to the shipping points in the North, over which the herds of the cattlemen were driven. So far as these men were concerned, it made no difference whose herd broke the trail, nor did it make any difference as to the difficulties encountered in breaking the same. It was the usefulness of the trail, and that alone, which was considered by them.

The trail must have a name, and so it had been named the same as the portion which had been broken as a wagon trail, and which extended from Wichita to the Cimarron River. All of these cattlemen knew they traveled up the Chisholm Trail, but few of them knew why it was so named, and fewer knew who Chisholm really was. Cattlemen were too busy in those days to inquire as to who first drove a herd over the trail, or as to any other historical matters. History, at that time, was not in the course of study of these men. Only since it has been important from a historical point of view, in order to correctly record these facts for the information of future generations, have these matters been seriously considered. Due to this situation, after the lapse of so many years, the unfortunate thing is, the difficulty encountered in procuring the correct information.

This is particularly true in case of Col. O. W. Wheeler. He was known as one of the leading cattlemen on the frontier. He attended to his own business—had a plenty of it; bothered no one, and made no display of himself. Cattlemen, who were his contemporaries, knew that he had driven the first herd in the difficult task of breaking the cattle trail through the Indian Territory from the Red River to the Cimarron. That, however, made but little difference. His rating and standing as a cattleman was vastly more important, but time has reversed the relative importance of these matters. The only authentic written history produced at the time, or near enough to the time that it may be considered correct, states without question that Col. O. W. Wheeler guided the first herd across this wild and unconquered country, on the route of the Chisholm Trail from the Red River to the Cimarron.[1]

It is the purpose to record here the important facts that the writer has been able to learn connected with the life of the remarkable character whose name appears at the head of this chapter. Col. O. W. Wheeler was born in the State of Connecticut in about the year 1826. It is understood that his family were well-to-do farmers and stockmen in his native state. He was not only taught to handle stock on the home farms, but was sent to school and trained in the higher institutions of learning. He was given a fine education and well equipped for a successful business or professional career. The hand of Fate, however unforeseen, has a habit of playing surprising tricks on us "mortals here below." In this case, as often happens, the subject of this sketch was turned aside from an apparently clear and unobstructed pathway, leading to a successful future, and ushered face to face with darkest despair, and eventually directed in a course which ultimately led to a greater success than the original would have brought.

---

[1] Historical Sketches of the Cattle Trade of the West and Southwest, by Jos. G. McCoy, the pioneer western cattle shipper, printed in 1874, page 261.

In 1850, Wheeler did not have the prefix of "Colonel" to his name; that was acquired years later by dangerous experiences on the western prairies. He was, however, a promising young man, ready to enter a successful career in the East. It was suddenly discovered, at this time, that he was a victim of the most dreaded and malignant malady known in the part of the country in which he lived. This was tuberculosis of the lungs, and was considered as sure a sentence of death as if he had stood upon the scaffold with the hangman's noose about his neck. Instead of being crushed by this judgment and condition, it only imbued him with a spirit of bravery and fearlessness, which characterized his future carrer and brought him success upon the Western Plains. Here he was always known as a man devoid of fear under all circumstances. He was a man, not only small in stature, but frail and slender. Men who knew him stated without hesitation that in the frail frame of this man was housed more determination, perseverance, unwavering fearlessness, and infallible business judgment than any other man they ever knew. His accomplishments are more remarkable on account of the disadvantages against which he was compelled to contend and under which he labored. The state of his health during most of his life materially handicapped him, as he never grew to be extra strong.

Just preceding this unfortunate circumstance in the life of young Wheeler, nuggets of gold had been dug up in Sutter's mill-race on the Pacific coast, and other like discoveries had followed in a wide area in the State of California. This had electrified the entire world, turned the course of thousands of adventurers to the West, and started them across the plains. Also, thousands of other people with families joined the long caravans, the wagons of which were dragged slowly across the vast plains country, while the wondering Indians looked down on them from the hilltops with amazement.

Wheeler concluded he would not die without an effort to regain his health by change of climate, and, to overcome his affliction, he sought the gold diggings of California. On account of his debilitated condition, he feared the rigorous and extensive journey across the plains. For this reason he traveled by water and crossed the Isthmus of Panama. In the spring of 1851 he turned his back upon his childhood home, and with little hope of ever returning alive, took passage on a mail steamer for the Isthmus. The only means of crossing the Isthmus, at that time, was by going by canoe up the Chagres River, and thence by pack mules to the harbor at Panama on the Pacific side. In crossing the Isthmus a form of tropical fever, known as the Panama fever, which was the curse of that country, seized upon him. This, with his usual perseverance, he overcame, and finally landed in California after being thirty-two days on the voyage.

When he arrived in California, it was only two years after gold had been discovered there, and the excitement that pervaded the country can well be imagined. This thrill permeated the very atmosphere of the country to which this invalid had been suddenly transplanted. This condition seemed to improve his health from the very beginning, and he soon went to work in the mines. However, his strength not being sufficient to engage in this sort of labor, he was compelled to give it up. He then went to Sacramento and took a position in a mercantile business. He was very much adapted to dealing in livestock and trading; taking up this vocation he purchased a limited number of horses and cattle, and went out into the mountains and desert to meet and trade with, or sell to, incoming emigrants, whose stock was worn out by the long journey across the plains and desert. In this, he not only made considerable money, but from the nature of the life and business in which he was engaged, his general health became much improved. The ravages of the disease from which he had suffered, however, left its marks upon him, and he always presented an emaciated appearance. Had it not been for his fearless and fiery disposition, which overcame it, he would have been considered an insignificant looking individual.

He thereafter entered into greater enterprises. He successfully followed the business of freighting to the mining camps. He bought a mercantile establishment and sold it at a profit; he speculated in a large bunch of sheep with great gain; he went south to Los Angeles, bought cattle and drove them north, and still made money. While in southern California he purchased an extensive and well equipped cattle ranch, which within a year he sold at great profit, keeping a portion of the cattle. Wheeler had now become an experienced and confirmed cattleman. He drove his herds northward and established a meat market in San Francisco, which consumed forty head of cattle daily.

After ten years' absence, Wheeler returned to his native Connecticut, apparently a well man. On this trip he crossed the plains for the first time. His experience in the mountains and on the trail had, however, taught him well the ways of the Indians, and he soon became an expert in dealing with them. On his return to the West, he bought a herd of horses and prepared to drive them over the trail to California. This was in 1861, and most of the Western Indians were on the war path, roving the plains at will, killing every person possible, and waylaying every caravan they could find. It was necessary, in order to cross the plains at that time, to assemble a large aggregation of wagons and men for mutual protection. This was done, when there were gathered together Wheeler's large herd of horses, with his men and outfit, and several hundred wagons of emigrants with over one thousand head of their loose stock. The number of persons constituting this caravan has not been preserved, but there must have been from six to eight hundred. Wheeler was elected commandant of this extensive organization, and was designated as "Colonel," a designation by which he was known the remaining portion of his life. This was, perhaps, the largest number of persons who ever crossed the plains in one body.

Led by this intrepid little frontiersman, the caravan moved out on its long and tedious journey. The Indians swarmed around them, and many times threatened to overpower them. For days and weeks their wagons, teams, and herds moved slowly but steadly forward. From the way this outfit was handled, the Indians well knew that some experienced hand was guiding it, and also they knew full well the penalty of any rash act on their part. It is said that in this entire trip there was not lost an animal or man because of the Indians. They arrived in California in due time, well and happy. Wheeler sold his horses at a big profit. He then returned to the cattle business, which was now to claim him for the balance of his life. He bought cattle in southern California, drove them north, and sold them in the mining camps at a profit. Wheeler had come to California to the gold mines, but he now made more money than the gold diggers, and procured it without taking it from the ground. He drove his stock as far north as Nevada, following this business until the spring of 1867.

In 1866, there was an extensive drought in southern California, and it was necessary to sell all the cattle in that producing portion of the State. The result was that, in the spring of 1867, cattle could not be had in southern California, which was the main source of the supply in the West. Wheeler knew that the State of Texas was overflowing with cattle, and there was no market for them, so he conceived the idea of driving a large herd from that State across the plains to California. In this enterprise, he associated himself with two reliable and enterprising men, a Mr. Wilson and a Mr. Hicks.

Early in the spring of 1867, these three men crossed the plains by the southern route, going by the way of El Paso, Texas, and arrived at San Antonio in that State in due time. Because of his experience on the plains and being a natural leader, Colonel Wheeler was the acknowledged head of this enterprise. Let us here observe the magnitude of the undertaking that lay ahead of this party. Not a herd had crossed the Indian Territory up to this time, except the herds of 1866, which had gone to the northeast and met disaster. The trail to Abilene, Kansas, the route he was compelled to follow, was not only unknown, but no definite route existed, and it was unexplored by white men; the bands of soldiers who had ventured out onto and attempted to cross it had been led by experienced guides. The task of exploring this route and driving a large bunch of cattle across it seemed impossible to accomplish successfully; the Government was trying hard, but with little success, to subdue the wild Indian tribes of the plains.

It was the plan of Col. Wheeler to drive his herd direct across the Indian Territory to Abilene, Kansas, which was just being established on the new Kansas Pacific Railway, and then west across the plains, over the route he had followed before, to California. The hazard of the undertaking was doubled several times by the uncertainty of the conditions that were to be encountered in the progress of the undertaking, and by the extent of the unforeseen difficulties that they would encounter. They prepared to meet and overcome all these, whether they were plains Indians or other formal enemies.

These parties procured twenty-four hundred head of as fine cattle as could be bought in Texas. They also bought over one hundred head of unexcelled cow-horses, and hired fifty-four of the best cowboys who could be found in Texas. These men were not only qualified as cowboys, but as Indian fighters as well. This outfit was furnished with the best saddles, and as complete an equipment as could be procured. Each man was armed with a new Henry Rifle,[1] the last word, at that time, in Indian fighting guns. These weapons in the hands of experienced users were very effective in Indian fighting. They also carried a number of needle guns or buffalo guns for long range. Each man had swung at his belt from one to two of the latest model, large caliber Colt revolving "six-shooters." They were a formidable array. *Conchos*[3] glistened on the head stalls of their bridles, their long leather *tapaderas* trailed down from their stirrups, their large Spanish spurs dragged the ground and jingled a merry tune as they walked or rode. New stiff *chaparajos*[4] adorned the legs of every rider. Each wiry mustang jumped and snorted at every move of the rider. On the right side, looped by a string to the saddle horn, hung the ever present lasso (*reata*), made of good rawhide. From the left side, with the loop on the handle around the saddle horn, hung the cowboy's quirt, less than three feet long, but the only whip he ever used. Thus equipped this bunch of cowboys trailed out twenty-four hundred head of long-horned southern cattle from

[1]The Henry Rifles, used at this time, were first made in 1866. They were manufactured by New Haven Arms Company. They were lever action repeating rifles, working on the same plan of the 1873 Winchester Rifles. They were of .44 caliber, rim fire, and shot sixteen times. For short range they were the most effective repeating rifles made before the 1873 model .44 center fire Winchesters.

[3]*Conchos* were bright glistening metal disks usually the size of an inch or two inches in diameter, fastened onto the head stall of a bridle. They were doubtless so named from the Spanish *Concha*, meaning shell. They were evidently originally made from shells.

[4]*Chaparajos* is the name given to the leather coverings for the legs worn by cowboys. They buckled at the top around the waist, and protected the legs in brush, rain, or from cold. The name so given to them is of Mexican derivation, perhaps being a combination of the Spanish word *chapa*, meaning a metal cover for adornment, or a rough cover, and the word *rajar*, a coarse cloth or material. It may be taken from the Mexican word *chaparro*, meaning brush, as they protected the legs of the riders from the brush. The derivation of this word is doubtful. It is a well established word on the frontier, but it is claimed that it is not derived from the Spanish, but belongs to the Mexican entirely. It is pronounced chap-a-ra-hos. In present usages in English the abbreviated form of the word is used, and these coverings are simply called "chaps." In early days they were largely known as "leggins."

their native pastures, which they would never see again. Jos. G. McCoy in his book, to which reference has heretofore been made, and which comprises the principal written history of these early drives, written within a few years afterward, on page 261 states:

"No more complete outfit or better herd of stock ever left Texas. This herd was the first to pass through the Indian Nation and break the trail over which the drive of 1867 came."

This outfit left San Antonio in the early summer of 1867. They crossed the Colorado River at Austin, and the Red River near where the drives of the preceding year had passed on their disastrous journeys, but soon left these old trails and bore to the west of the same, breaking a trail across the unknown country. The storms gathered, the lightning flashed, the thunder roared, the rains poured, and the cattle stampeded, but they were gathered again and trailed to the northward. It proved to be the wettest and most disagreeable season to drive cattle that was known during the life of the trail. The outfit swam strange rivers, creeks that were swollen into large streams, and traversed flooded lands, but ever kept their course to the northward. It is generally known that in driving in this sort of weather, cattle do not do well. The grass is washy and soft, and the cattle do not take on fat. Such was the case with this herd.

Colonel Wheeler knew many of the obstacles that he might encounter, as well as the advantages. One of these was the disposition of the wild plains Indians to the westward, and, for that reason, he kept his course to the east of a direct line. He passed about fourteen miles east of the present City of El Reno; headed to the northwest, striking Kingfisher Creek near the present City of Kingfisher, and then followed that creek northward on the east side of the same to its mouth, where it empties into the Cimarron River. This point is about one and one-half miles below the crossing of that river by the railway and Government Highway 81. It is a strange fact, but nevertheless true, that this point always remained the crossing of the Chisholm Cattle Trail until the same was forever closed. After crossing the river at this point Wheeler went up the same on the north side for about one and one-half miles, where he struck the Old Chisholm Traders' Trail, which had been laid out by Jesse Chisholm in 1865. Thus was broken the great cattle trail from San Antonio to the known trail on the north side of the Indian Territory. The only purpose of Wheeler was to find the most direct route to his objective, which at that time was a point in the vicinity of the newly established town of Abilene, Kansas. From there he would travel westward across the plains, as he had done before.

Another herd of cattle crossed the Red River, driving north, at about the same time the Wheeler herd crossed. This herd belonged to a man by the name of Thomson, which, if it took the same course as the Wheeler outfit, followed him. It was not driven by its owner all the way to Abilene, but was sold in the Indian Territory to some eastern speculators, who took it on to Abilene. The route taken by the Wheeler drive passed a short distance to the east of the established Chisholm cattle trail of years to come, over which the millions of cattle traveled to the northern markets.

After reaching the established Chisholm Trail, the Wheeler outfit continued northward on the same. The rains continued to pour, the rivers and creeks rose in proportion, but this herd trailed on north over the finest land and the finest range that could be found. It crossed the Kansas and Indian Territory line just south of the present City of Caldwell, and went north to Abilene. The season had not only been disagreeable and hard on the drivers, but the Asiatic cholera had broken out all over the western and plains country, persons on all sides were falling victims to this dreaded ailment, and dying in great numbers. To make matters worse, the plains Indians were still on the war path, were killing every helpless traveler and settler possible, were stealing and running away stock on every occasion, and creating consternation in general on the trails crossing the plains country.

Wilson and Hicks did not have the daring spirit of Wheeler, and, when they reached Abilene, after taking all the existing conditions into consideration, refused to continue on their journey westward. Wheeler begged, and then abused them, but it was all to no avail. They were more afraid of the cholera and the Indians than they were of his abuse, and they refused to continue. Wheeler was so disgusted with the situation that he declared he would never again enter into partnership with anyone, and this declaration he never violated. Their cattle were held on grass for some time, and then shipped to market with fair profit.

Wheeler had learned that the cattle business in the central west held more promise for the future than it did in his home State of California, and he cast his lot with the plains cattle business from that time on. When his partners would not continue their journey with the herd across the plains, Wheeler wanted to winter the cattle in Kansas, but his partners would not agree to that, and when they were shipped Wheeler bought another bunch of fifteen hundred head on his own account, wintered them in Kansas, and drove them to Quincy, Illinois, the next season, where he placed them on pasture, together with many more that he bought at a low price on account of the fear of the Spanish fever. When the scare subsided he had a large herd of domesticated fat cattle, which he sold for a small fortune. He then went to Texas and bought a herd of five thousand head, which he drove to Nevada.

While this herd was traveling northward he bought and shipped six thousand more head to Chicago.

Wheeler's judgment in cattle ventures was so unerring that it appeared his observation could penetrate the future. When the market was good Wheeler's cattle came in by the thousands. Then he would cease shipping and stand as an idle observer, while others would lose without fail. He would then come forward and make money with each venture. In 1870 Wheeler drove from Texas and disposed of twelve thousand head of cattle. In 1871 he brought up the trail seven thousand head. In his drives he learned, the same as all other trail drivers did, that it was best to drive in smaller herds than was done at first. About twenty-five hundred head was the most convenient number to include in one drive. In 1872, Wheeler sold at one time five thousand head of cattle for $125,000.00, but in 1873 he foresaw the break that was coming, and did not drive or buy. But few cattlemen were so lucky in avoiding the catastrophe of 1873.

Wheeler continued his operations at Newton, Wichita, and other points. He was in Kansas City in 1874. Here we lose track of him, and, from this time on, we have been unable to learn of any of his dealings or his life. Whether he fought out his battle on the Pacific Coast, further west, or where he went, no one seems to know. We do not know where his remains rest. In any event, he left a record for wise dealing and unerring judgment in the cattle industry in the plains country. The greatest achievement of his life will ever go down in history as his trip across the unmarked and uncharted country, when he rode at the head of his herd and broke the trail from the Red River to the Cimarron across the Indian Territory.

Whether this cattle trail should be named the Chisholm Trail, in honor of the great and unassuming plainsman who traveled it from the Arkansas River in Kansas to the Cim-

arron in Oklahoma, or whether it be named for the fiery little
warrior who drove the first herd over it from the Red River
to Abilene, Kansas, we are not to say.   The trail has been
named, not by us, but by the men who first traveled it, and
that name has been perpetuated by the stern-faced, sun-tanned
drovers, and picturesque and hardy cowboys who rode the same
for two decades after Col. Wheeler first trailed his herd over
and broke the trail. We concur in the act of these men, and
long may the memory of this old highway and the deeds of the
men who rode it live in history, story, and song through generations yet unborn.

In describing this trail during the years of its use, when
millions of southern cattle traveled up the same, we desire to
tell you in the words of a man who spent many years of his
life on it, an old friend of the writer, Charles A. Siringo. We
quote from his book "Reata and Spurs" on page 26:

"On reaching the City of Austin, on the Colorado River,
two hundred miles from its mouth, at the town of Matagordo,
we struck the Chisholm Trail proper. From here north to the
line of Kansas, a distance of about seven hundred miles, it was
one continuous roadway, several hundred yards wide, tramped
hard and solid by the millions of hoofs which had gone over
it. It started in at a ford three miles below the City. All
smaller trails from the different Gulf coast districts merged
into this great and only Chisholm Trail."

While Siringo fixed the south terminus of the Chisholm
Trail at the ford near Austin, where the trails from all points
south converged, the main branch extended southwest from
Austin to San Antonio, and it is generally considered that the
Chisholm Trail extended from San Antonio to Abilene.   In
any event, few of the men are still living who trailed the herds
over the same in the days of its activities, and their numbers
are growing less each year.

Charles Goodnight, the father of the cattle industry in the Panhandle.

CHAPTER VI.

CHARLES GOODNIGHT

Charles Goodnight never traveled the Chisholm Trail, did not know Jesse Chisholm, or for whom the trail was named. He did know that it was not named for his friend John Chisum. It has been necessary, in order to eliminate the confusion as to the naming of the trail, to give a short history of the life of John Chisum. This is well, however, as all persons should know more than they do about this historical character. The same is true as to Charles Goodnight, except that it is necessary to connect him with the Chisholm Trail for an entirely different reason. While Charles Goodnight knew nothing about the Chisholm Trail, yet the course of his life and the part he played in the West had more to do in changing the route and stimulating later activities on the trail, during a portion of the period of its life, than that of any other man.

Charles Goodnight never operated in the cattle business east of his first established ranch in Palo Pinto County, Texas. This ranch was about forty miles west of Fort Worth, and between the cities of Weatherford and Mineral Wells, Texas. He is properly designated as the father of the cattle industry in the Panhandle of Texas. He not only established the cattle industry in that portion of the State, but up to the time of his death, which occurred in 1929, when he was 93 years of age, he was the acknowledged leader of that business in all western Texas. He kept pace with all improvements and developments in it, sought out the best breeds of cattle adapted to the country, and the best methods of handling them.

Prior to the year 1880, the railways had extended into eastern and central Texas, and thus reached and handled a large portion of the cattle that would have otherwise traveled up the Chisholm Trail. From this portion of the State of Texas, prior to the advent of their railways, Dodge City, Kansas, had been the principal shipping point after 1875. The Chisholm Trail, from the then terminus of the railroad at Wichita to the southern line of Kansas, had been closed by the settlements. The cattle which came up to Dodge City took what was known in those days as the Western Cattle Trail or Texas Cattle Trail. This was the name given this trail on the maps at that time. This trail started northwest of San Antonio, and entered the Indian Territory approximately sixty miles west of the Chisholm Trail, in what is now Tillman County, at a point north of the present City of Vernon, Texas.

The settlements south of Wichita closed the Chisholm Trail to the Indian Territory line in about 1876. The railway was built into Dodge City in 1872. It immediately became the greatest headquarters in all the West for buffalo hunters. Dodge City is located fifty miles north of the then Indian Territory line, and directly west of Wichita, Kansas, but from the fact that it is about one hundred and sixty miles west of Wichita, the settlements south of Dodge City did not interfere with the trail between it and the Indian Territory until several years afterward, when the settlers pushing westward had reduced the plains to homes and farms that far west. Dodge City designated itself during this time as the "Cowboy Capital." It lived up to its name until the farmers closed the trail south of it to the Indian Territory line in the early eighties.

In 1880 the Atchison, Topeka, and Santa Fe Railway built south to Caldwell, Kansas, and the Indian Territory line. The Chisholm Trail came to life once more, and millions of cloven hoofs each year traveled over it again. In 1880 the "Cowboy Capital" was moved to Caldwell, and remained there until it was lost by the extension of the Chicago, Rock Island and Pacific Railway in 1889. The foregoing conditions have been detailed at length, and, if the reader will bear them in mind, it will readily be seen the effect that the efforts and results obtained by Charles Goodnight had on the Chisholm Trail, even though he never personally used the trail.

Charles Goodnight in the early days of the cattle industry in the West was a powerful, energetic, intelligent, resourceful, and fearless young man, about thirty years of age. Taking all of these attributes into consideration, there was nothing left to constitute all the requirements for success. He was a native of Illinois, born in 1836. When he was nine years of age his family moved to Texas, settling at Milam. Here he lived until he was nineteen years of age, at which time he went further west into Palo Pinto[1] County. Raising and handling cattle was the principal industry in the State of Texas at that time. While this country is spotted, yet, to take it as a whole, it is a good cattle country. There is a sufficient supply of grass, and the hills, the mesquite and blackjack thickets furnish an abundance of protection for stock in all kinds of weather. Young Goodnight eventually engaged in the cattle business, and threw all his energy and efforts into the same. In order to procure the initial capital to install himself and gradually get into the cattle business he first freighted by ox team, hauling supplies from San Antonio and Houston to the settlements and ranches in Palo Pinto and other counties to the northwest. The starting at any time is difficult for a young man without means, but Goodnight kept increasing his holdings until he established himself well in the cattle and ranching business.

---

[1]*Palo Pinto* is Spanish, and being literally translated means spotted post or tree. The meaning of *palo*, which literally means post or tree, has been varied and corrupted considerably, and is often used to mean place or location, as in Palo Alto, which means high place or high point or tree. The land in Palo Pinto County, Texas is very spotted, as all know who have visited that part of the State of Texas. This name was perhaps given to the county on account of this spotted condition of the land, or from some trees growing thereon.

One of the principal qualifications required of the settlers in the portion of Texas where Charles Goodnight was located at that time was to be a reputable Indian fighter. In this business Goodnight also qualified and grew to be an expert. During the Civil War he enlisted and served in the ranks of the Texas Rangers. His duties during this period of four years were to hold back the hostile Indians on the plains, and prevent their excursions and depredations on the frontiers of Texas.

After the close of the Civil War, Goodnight returned to his neglected ranch and cattle interest in Palo Pinto County. He found himself and partner, who was associated in the business with him, possessed of a vast number of cattle, estimated by him at 7,000 head. Under the conditions, as they existed there at that time, these cattle were a liability instead of an asset. Their numbers were increasing, there was no available market for them, nor was there any prospect for a market in the future. The nearest point, considered by Goodnight, to reach a market for any of his herd was in the settlements of New Mexico. There were so many other herds nearer the markets to the southeast, east, and northeast that it was impossible to think of competing with them. In order to reach New Mexico, he would be compelled to go north over the Staked Plains, or to the west across the desert to the Pecos River, and up that river. The route to the north, even in the country bordering on the Staked Plains,[2] swarmed with all the different bands

---

[2] The Staked Plains is the English designation and meaning of the Spanish name originally given to these plains. The Spanish name is and was "*Llano Estacado*." The plains were so named from the fact that a trail which was afterward used as a stage route was laid out across the same near the route followed by Charles Goodnight and the Goodnight trail. This route was laid out in 1846 by General Pope, was used as the southern route to California, and ran west to El Paso, Texas. After this route was traveled, in order to keep the right course across the desert, when the wind blew the dust and sand over the trail, stakes were set to mark the route. Thus it was called Staked Plains, or in the Spanish "*Llano Estacado*." These plains comprise a large scope of usually sandy, arid, country extending across the western part of Texas. It is also stated, that this name originated with the early Spanish explorers, but if so, it must have been applied for the same reason as stated.

of the wild Plains Indians, including the murderous Apaches. No civilized thing could exist among these hordes of bloodthirsty, scalp-hunting savages. On the other hand, in the route to the west to the Pecos, there lay between him and that river almost one hundred miles of scorching desert. Not one drop of water was to be found in this one hundred miles. This desert portion of the trail is actually ninety-six miles long.

Goodnight selected the desert route rather than the northern and Indians. He was the first man to drive a herd of cattle over it, or to demonstrate that such a thing could be done. This was ever afterward known as the "Goodnight Trail." It extended from Concho County, Texas, to Fort Sumner, New Mexico. In solving this problem for the disposition of the cattle in this portion of Texas, Goodnight exhibited the characteristics for ingenuity and boldness, which ever made him a leader and famous on the frontier. There was a Government post at Fort Sumner, in eastern New Mexico. Thousands of Indians received the supplies furnished them by the Government at this point. Colorado was settling. Many persons had been induced to go to this Territory in search of gold and adventure. Extensive settlements had grown up at Denver, Colorado City, Pueblo, and other points. The Indians and settlements needed beef, and Texas had it to spare.

No person before Charles Goodnight had ever dared to dream of driving a herd of cattle across the desert country from the Concho to the Pecos, but Goodnight not only dreamed it, but mustered his men and herd to travel over it. He determined that the route he would take should strike the Pecos at the "Horse Head Crossing"[3] on the same. When the season

---

[3] The Horse Head Crossing of the Pecos River was located on the route laid out on the trail by General Pope in 1846. This trail crossed the Pecos River at the Horse Head Crossing. The origin of the name or the reason for so naming it is uncertain. It is claimed by some, that it was so named on account of the bends in the river resembling a horse's head. This is hardly justified, for the reason that no bend exists in the river at this point, and the banks are so steep and of such a nature that it

was far enough advanced that his cattle were in good condition to take to the trail, and stand the strain of this trip over the desert, he started out on his famous drive in the spring of 1866. His outfit consisted of such equipment as was necessary in making a trip of this kind. The cattle were in the first place selected so that the strongest and ones better suited for the hardships of the journey were procured. The best of horses, strong and well trained, were chosen. Above all, the men were selected, not only for their capability in handling the herds and enduring the hardships of the trip, but for their efficiency as Indian fighters.

They were well armed, most of them were ex-Confederate soldiers, well-trained in the use of their weapons, and were not afraid. For three days this aggregation of ox teams drawing the wagons, these thousands of crowding, bawling, and finally moaning, staggering, long-horned cattle, a large horse *remuda*, together with dozens of lank, fearless, and hardy cowboys, steadily took their course to the westward across these sandy waterless plains. They stopped only for an hour or so at a time, and this at long intervals. They traveled over the burning sands day and night. Many of these hardy cattle dropped in their tracks and were left behind. The rest moved on slower and slower, moaning as they traveled along.

Finally they passed through Castle Mountain Gap Canyon for about four miles, and when they emerged, the river some ten or more miles away could be seen. The cattle went wild, the horses took fresh life, and the drivers forgot that they

---

is not probable that the river has changed its course. It has also been claimed, that the surveying party which laid out the trail lost their horses there, but such would not account for the naming it as stated. The most reasonable solution of the matter, and the one that the author adopts, is that it was a custom on the plains, as all old plainsmen know, to mark water holes, fords, springs, and any location that was difficult to find, by placing a buffalo head or other marker on high ground or in a conspicuous place, where it would be seen when nearing the place sought. In this case a skull or horse's head was set up to mark the proximity to the crossing. Persons giving directions to others traveling over the route would direct them in accordance with the marker set up.

had had no sleep, except in the saddle, for three days. To more clearly understand this trip, and the feeling on reaching the Pecos, it is best to quote a short description of the same in the words of Charles Goodnight himself, as follows:

"In my first drive across the 96 mile desert, I lost 300 head of cattle. We were three days and nights in crossing and during that time we had no sleep or rest, as we had to keep the cattle moving constantly, in order to get them to water before they died of thirst. I rode the same horse for three days and nights, and what sleep I got was on his back. When the cattle reached the water they had no sense at all. They stampeded into the stream, swam right across it, and then doubled back before they stopped to drink. During this trip the steers got as gentle as dogs."

The Pecos River for miles above and below the Horse Head Crossing has steep banks, and it was only at places where there were depressions along the banks or paths going down to the water that the cattle could get down, and for that reason they would spread out for miles up and down the river. From the Horse Head Crossing of the Pecos, the herd wound its way up the river for hundreds of miles to Fort Sumner, New Mexico. Here Goodnight sold his entire herd of cattle on the hoof at eight cents per pound. In the route he had taken he had driven his herd over six hundred miles, but the returns were sufficient to prove the correctness of his judgment.

The following year, 1867, this same trail was followed by Charles Goodnight, John Chisum, and Oliver Loving. Chisum concluded, that if it was profitable to drive the cattle across, and there was such a demand for them, it would pay to raise them in New Mexico. Therefore he located and established his famous ranch in that year at *Bosque Grande,* south of Fort Sumner. During the succeeding years Goodnight and Loving were in partnership in their drives across this same route. They were also associated with John Chisum.

Several years later on one of their drives, as they neared this crossing of the Pecos, Loving rode ahead to reach the river and provide for reception of the herd. He was ambushed and wounded by the Indians, who were hidden near the river. One of Loving's companions rushed back and told Goodnight, who was back with the herd, what had happened. Goodnight made diligent search for his partner, but failed to find him, and they gave up the search, supposing the Indians had killed him. He had, however, survived and hidden, and was found badly wounded and almost starved five days later by some Mexicans. They took him to Fort Sumner, where Goodnight found him on his arrival. Loving, however, contracted blood poison from his wound, and died a few days later. All the early drivers on the Goodnight trail had much trouble with the Indians, and lost many men and cattle on this account.

In his original cattle enterprise in Palo Pinto County, Goodnight had been in partnership with a man by the name of Sheek. Goodnight and Loving had realized $80,000.00 on their cattle driving enterprise. On his return to Texas in 1870 Goodnight turned over one-half of this sum, or $40,000.00, to Loving's widow. He divided the remaining portion with Sheek, leaving him only the sum of $20,000.00. This, however, was not all of his worldly possessions at that time. He had previously invested in a ranch in Colorado, which held more promise for the future than his investments in Texas.

Goodnight was at this time thirty-four years of age, strong and ambitious. He sold out his interests in Texas, and cast his lot in Colorado. Before he left for his future home he was married to Miss Mary Ann Dyer. In the selection of a wife, he used the same business judgment he had in his other affairs of life. This wife was his companion, associate, adviser, and home maker for fifty-six years, until death separated them. Much of the time she rode a Spanish mustang, the same as the cowboys, into the cow camps and on the roundups, by the side of her husband. Charles A. Siringo in his "Reata and Spurs" says of Mrs. Goodnight:

"When spring came, I was called in from the plains, and put in charge of a roundup crew, consisting of a cook and twelve riders. Our first roundup was on the Goodnight range, at the mouth of Mulberry Creek. Here we had the pleasure of a genuine cattle queen's presence. Mrs. Goodnight, a noble little woman, a dyed-in-the-wool Texan, attended these roundups with her husband."

Mrs. Goodnight was perhaps as well known throughout all the western country for her loyalty and fidelity to the cattle industry as her husband. She belonged to a family of ranchers who prospered. Her brothers as well as her husband were among the progressive cattlemen who helped to advance that industry in the Panhandle country.

When Charles Goodnight removed to Colorado, he sought to enter into a line of business which would be less strenuous, dangerous, and exacting, than the life he had been living up to that time. He therefore entered into the banking business, but kept his ranch in Colorado, and operated the same in connection with his other business. The fate of the banking business within a few years after 1873 is National history. This fate, as we all know, was not due to a lack of management, foresight, or business acumen on the part of the operators, but was one of those unforeseen rocks that lie beneath the uncharted waters of the financial world, that will wreck any ship regardless of the qualifications of the pilot or master. In this wreck Goodnight lost all he had invested in the bank, and lost his ranch. When he adjusted his affairs, all he had left was 1600 head of cattle, but while Fate had apparently played him a mean trick, the future proved that it was to his advantage. Had it not been for this disaster, Goodnight would

Artist's view of the Goodnight and Dyer Ranch in the Paloduro Canyon.
—McCoy.

simply have been a western banker, and would not have been known as the father of the cattle industry in the great empire of the Panhandle country, and would not have made the fortune which he gathered from this business.

In addition to the several hundred cattle which he had left from the wreck, Goodnight had other assets in his physical vitality and mental ability to undertake anything. He also had a wife ready to share any adversity with him, and had three brothers-in-law, all of whom were well versed in the cattle business, and rugged pioneers like himself. Charles Goodnight knew Texas, from the black soil of the central portion of the State west to the Rio Grande. He had long traveled over the Staked Plains and the country bordering on the same. He recalled the broad plains of the Panhandle country, even when it was covered with scalp-seeking redskins. He recalled the beautiful range country of the Palo Duro Canyon[4] on the headwaters of the Red River, known as the Paloduro. The State of Texas had issued land scrip and sold the same. This entitled the holder to select and take the number of acres of land belonging to the State of Texas specified in each certificate. This had been issued and sold, many years prior to 1870, in order to induce settlers to take up land in Texas and improve the State. Holders of this scrip had taken up most of the land on the Paloduro. Owing to conditions this land could be bought for a very small amount. The draw backs which caused the land to be cheap also faced the persons buying. These were the conditions which the settler was compelled to meet: The Cheyenne

---

4 The Palo Duro or Paloduro Canyon is a large plain surrounded almost all the way round the same by a high bank, and is almost a natural enclosure. It is located southwest of Amarillo, Texas, in Deaf Smith County, perhaps thirty miles from Amarillo. It is on what is known as the Paloduro Creek, which is on the head waters of the Red River. The word is Spanish. The meaning of the words in Spanish are as follows: *Palo* translated literally means post or tree. *Duro* is an adjective, and means firm, hard, rough, or durable. In Spanish it means hard wood, but the name is applied to a bush growing in the Panhandle country, for which the Canyon and Creek are named. This enclosure in this canyon has been referred to as being the finest grazing land in the United States. This name is sometimes spelled "Paladora."

Indians to the north had been placed upon their reservation and quieted; the Comanches of the plains had been quieted and moved upon their reservation with the Kiowas; but the wild Apaches still roamed the wide expanse of the open country for hundreds of miles around, and they continued to harass and make life hazardous in all this country until the close of the year 1877. The buffalo still roamed at will over the Panhandle country, and these natives of the prairies cropped the curly mesquite and buffalo grass from hundreds of miles on one of the finest grazing countries in the world.

Charles Goodnight with his usual foresight saw the day in the near future when these Indians and buffalo would be compelled to abandon this country, and saw the vast wealth that lay in the cattle business on the same as soon as the cattle could be established thereon. With this idea in mind he drifted his herd into the northern Panhandle[5] country in the summer of 1877. He did not have the means at this time to enter into the cattle business to the extent that he desired, and in order to carry on the same on a larger scale he entered into a partnership with a Scotchman by the name of Odair. They not only made arrangements to go south into the Palo Duro Canyon, but also to buy large tracts of land there, and to buy a large number of shorthorn bulls to turn with their cattle and improve the breed of their herds. These cattle were the ancestors of the herds that in future years wound their way over the country to the eastward and poured onto the Chisholm Trail, and into the shipping points at the end of the same. In carrying out their plan they bought large tracts of land over the

---

[5] Panhandle refers to what is known as the Panhandle of Texas. It is used to designate that portion of the State of Texas which extends northward and which separates Oklahoma from New Mexico. It was so named by the early day plainsmen on account of its similarity to the handle of a frying pan when attached to the balance of the State of Texas. The strip of land on the north side of the same, connecting the State of Oklahoma with New Mexico, has also been designated as the Panhandle of Oklahoma, but the pan handle as used in this article refers to the Panhandle of Texas.

country, and spotted it so that large interests could not afford to come into the country and molest them in their locality, on account of the scattered condition of the remaining land.

Following out their plan, in the winter of 1877, or in the spring of 1878, Goodnight and his outfit moved south to the Palo Duro, and established his famous ranch of that name. He was also the first to introduce the Hereford cattle in the Panhandle. These cattle were the greatest improvement ever made on the herds of the plains. They are the last word in the breeds of cattle in the cattle industry, not only in the Panhandle, but also in the entire State of Texas. These millions of cattle from the Panhandle, in future years, cut wide and dusty trails over their route eastward, passing near Mobeetie, Texas, and Fort Sill, Oklahoma, and joining the Chisholm Trail usually near the South Canadian River. This connection with the Chisholm Trail was made at several points. The life of the Chisholm Trail was revived, as the cowboys from the Panhandle, accompanied with their horse *remudas* and chuck wagons, drove millions of cattle up the same to the railways at Caldwell, Hunnewell, and other markets on the Kansas border.

Goodnight rode the range and with the roundups, and prospered. He grew wealthy beyond his most exaggerated dreams. He saw the broad expanses of wilderness over which he had roamed subdued by the modern hand of Civilization; he saw the steel rails of the railroads eventually laid almost to his door; he lived to see untold millions of dollars realized from oil produced by modern methods on the very land over which he had ridden for years; he saw tall stately buildings rise, and one of the modern cities of the world rear its head at Amarillo,[6] Texas; all at his very doorstep.

---

[6] The word Amarillo is Spanish and means yellow. It is usually pronounced in English as spelled, but the Spanish pronunciation of the same is entirely different. In Spanish it is pronounced *am-a-reo*. The "*LL*" in Spanish words is one of the things very difficult for an English speaking person to correctly pronounce.

Goodnight has to his credit the preservation of a large herd of buffalo, and he also crossed the buffalo with native cattle. These, however, did not produce highly satisfactory animals. It has been said that the establishing of his buffalo herd was the idea of Mrs. Goodnight. She took some motherless buffalo calves, which they had captured alive, and reared them. From this start grew the thriving and extensive herd of buffalo which were owned by Goodnight, and which were and are famous throughout the West.

Charles Goodnight was also the founder of the Goodnight College, located at the City of Goodnight, in Armstrong County, Texas. The City of Goodnight is located about sixty miles southeast of Amarillo. He operated this school himself for several years, and then gave it to the City as a high school building. Goodnight and his wife moved to the little City of Goodnight in 1887. Here they lived quietly and contentedly until they were separated by the death of Mrs. Goodnight in 1926. During this time he looked after, in a general way, his extensive interests, carrying into effect his useful ideas to advance the cattle industry, not alone in his community and State, but in the entire Nation. He is credited, and doubtless justly so, with originating the idea of a serum treatment, which consisted of inoculating domestic animals subject to the Texas or Spanish fever, and thus rendering them immune to that fatal disease. He originated this idea from the fact that he observed that a domestic calf which had suckled a mother suffering from the disease never contracted or died from the same.

Mrs. Goodnight had lived the life of a pioneer western woman, which she enjoyed. She had lived with, shared all the hardships of the plains, ridden at the side of her husband, and been his companion. That he missed her, no one can doubt. He had lived, been reared, and moulded in the hard school of the frontier. This life had taught him to take the world as it was dealt to him and never complain. The proud spirit of this old plainsman and benefactor of the West, however, gradually drooped after her death, and he finally succumbed. He died at Tuscon, Arizona in December, 1929, three years after the death of his wife, and at the age of ninety-three years. Thus one by one the pioneers of the plains, who have survived its hardships and dangers, go down before the never failing cycle of Time, and are laid to rest in the land that they helped to subdue and win to civilization.

Courteously yours
Jos. G. McCoy

Joseph G. McCoy, founder of the cattle shipping industry at Abilene.

CHAPTER VII.

JOSEPH G. McCOY

The efforts of no one man brought about the establishment and development of the great Chisholm Trail which reached the magnitude and importance it held when at its zenith of usefulness. The efforts of some men associated with it were directed to the purpose of developing the trail. Such men were McCoy, Col. Wheeler, and dozens of their contemporaries. Both of the men named and Jesse Chisholm were interested in laying out and establishing portions of this long trail. Other men contributed largely to the development of the same, but did it on account of their activities and efforts in extending their business at other points. Such was the case with Charles Goodnight. All of these persons and the many others contributing their part deserve credit and are entitled to have the results of their efforts recorded as a part of the history of this once great enterprise. Joseph G. McCoy did more than any other one man to establish the early drives over the Chisholm Trail route, did more to stimulate them after the trail was broken, and to establish Abilene as the terminus.

We have heretofore seen the result of the Civil War on the cattle conditions of Texas. It will be recalled that during the war the armies of both the North and the South consumed all the cattle in the eastern portion of the country, while the Federal Army held control of the Mississippi River and prevented the passage of any cattle from the west across the same, and thus bottled up the cattle of Texas, where they remained and increased to a superabundance. Joseph G. McCoy had pondered over this matter, and he also had seen the result of the attempted drives of cattle from Texas in the summer of

1866, when approximately 260,000 head crossed Red River in an attempt to travel to the northeast to reach a market. He had considered the results of these drives, all of which were failures. This question entirely absorbed him, until he devoted himself exclusively to the cause of obtaining and establishing a northern market for these cattle.

The Kansas Pacific Railway extended west from the Missouri River onto the plains country reaching as far as Salina, Kansas, in the spring and summer of 1867. The fact of the intention, on the part of this company, to build a road at this time had been well known since the fall of the preceding year, throughout the United States, and especially in Texas. The people of Texas were not only interested, but many cattle dealers of the north were watching this development, in order to engage in the business of buying and driving cattle north from Texas. It was a certainty that a great market would be established at some point on the railway, where connection was made with these drives, but the designation of this point, the establishment of the market, and a safe and orderly method of handling the cattle when they reached their destination was due to only one man, and that was Joseph G. McCoy.

Joseph G. McCoy was a native of Springfield, Illinois. He and his two brothers were there engaged in the cattle business together on a large scale. Joseph was the youngest of the three. Their business extended over a large part of the State of Illinois. In the fall of 1866 Joseph G. McCoy was about thirty years of age, and was well experienced in the buying, selling, and handling of cattle. As soon as the Kansas Pacific Railway Company had its line of road well on its way to the west, young McCoy began to formulate his plans for the establishment of the market for these southern cattle. He went to the offices of the railway company in St. Louis, Missouri, and laid before them his plan for the building of pens, yards, and

Abilene in 1867, when the first herd coming up the Chisholm Trail reached the same.—McCoy.

equipment in general for the handling of these herds of cattle at some appropriate location along their line. He failed to interest the officers of the company, and they declared his plans visionary. He then traveled over the route of this railway and inspected the different points along the line. Junction City was an established station on this route, and he attempted to interest the citizens of that town in his enterprise, but failed to do so. He finally agreed and contracted with the railway company to arrange and build the necessary equipment himself, and the company agreed they would pay him one dollar for each car of cattle loaded from these pens.

McCoy selected Abilene, Kansas, as the most logical point for the building of the pens and making connection with the northern drives. No better point could have been chosen. Abilene was almost on a due line north of the point where the herds would leave the Indian Territory, a very suitable country as to the lay of the land existed around the point selected, and there were no settlements to the south of this point to interfere with the driving of the cattle to reach the loading pens. There was really nothing but a station at Abilene, but that made no difference; they could build the town, but they could not make the physical conditions around the same. Abilene was located about twenty-four miles northeast of Salina, and about twenty-seven miles southwest of Junction City.

The site of his future operations being selected, McCoy sent for his two brothers to join him, and they all devoted themselves to the task of preparing the place for the reception of the herds. This was no small task. There would have been no trouble in building the pens and arranging the equipment for handling ordinary domestic cattle, but in making this equipment they must construct the same sufficiently strong to resist all the viciousness and strength of these wild frenzied cattle from the plains, which were as untamed and ferocious as the buffalo reared on these prairies. This was not all they must do. There were several herds on their way trailing north from Texas, intending to reach the railway at some point, they knew not where.

The McCoys procured the services of experienced plainsmen, hired them to go south into the Indian Territory and meet these herds, and direct them on to Abilene. This they did, and it was not long until the wild cattle from the plains of Texas were stampeding across the townsite of Abilene, and the cattle pens and loading chutes were in full operation. The drives of 1867 were, as before, an experiment, but, unlike the former experiments, they were a very great success, with the exception that the weather conditions were bad. None of the cattle reached Abilene until late in the season. Only 35,000 head of cattle were shipped from this point in the summer of 1867.

Although the season of 1867 had not been a desirable year for the handling of cattle on account of the excessive rainfall and the rankness of the grass, which caused the cattle to remain thin, the McCoys were encouraged with their progress so far and the prospects for the future. They built a three story frame hotel building at Abilene; they enlarged their facilities for handling the drives of coming years, and sent representatives throughout the State of Texas, advertising the route, facilities, and advantages of shipping from Abilene. They also inserted advertisements to the same effect in the papers of Texas, and sent circulars throughout the State, containing the advertisements of the trail and market.

As a result of the efforts of these men, 75,000 head of cattle came up the Chisholm Trail from Texas in the season of 1868; during the season of 1869, 350,000 head of Texas cattle came to the northern shipping points over this trail; during the season of 1870, 300,000 head came up the same to market, and in the year 1871 the maximum of the drives was reached.

During this season 600,000 head were driven up the Chisholm Trail. The trail at this time was a well broken thoroughfare, and the dangers of traveling the same, except those inherent in the business and from the elements, had disappeared.

To show the precision and thoroughness of the methods adopted by the McCoys in preparing to handle the vast herds coming up from the south, and to arrange for the convenience of the drivers and dispatch of the business, the following will well illustrate: The original trail, in its course through Kansas, crossed the Arkansas River at Wichita. If a line be drawn direct from Caldwell, Kansas, the point where the trail left the Indian Territory, direct to Abilene, the destination, it will be seen that the direct line will run a few miles west of Wichita. This few miles they concluded made the drive that much longer. Accordingly, in the spring of 1868, a surveyor was employed by the McCoys, and at their direction and expense a straight. and direct route from Caldwell to Abilene was run. This was all done so that the trail would not only be direct, but well marked, and the route could be seen for a long distance ahead.

Soon after the advent of the railway, the settlers began to crowd in immediately to the south of Abilene. The trouble then began. These settlers organized and prepared to make war on the cattle drivers and stop the herds from crossing their farms. This trouble would not only injure, but might prove disastrous to the cattle shipping business. In order to forestall this result, the McCoys contacted the leaders of this organization, and finally made satisfactory arrangements through them with the settlers whose farms were being crossed by the cattle drives. These settlers were to be paid, by the McCoys and the drovers, certain sums of money, and the cattle permitted to be driven to the shipping point over a certain strip of country extending from the open range.

In 1870 the two older brothers of the McCoys became disgusted at the lack of consideration and co-operation extended to them by the railway company in this shipping enterprise, and also on account of the failure of the railway company to pay to the McCoys large sums of money due them for the cars of cattle loaded, according to their contract. For this reason they sold their interest, in the business they had built up, to Joseph G. McCoy, and the two older brothers, withdrawing from the partnership, left Abilene. The McCoys had enlarged their holdings and facilities until they were extensive and complete for the period and location. The business was continued by Joseph G. McCoy, who had prospered until he had been buying considerable numbers of southern cattle for the purpose of wintering them on the plains of Kansas. This had been found to not only be possible, but very profitable. In the summer of 1870 young McCoy bought a large herd of these cattle, and procured range to winter them. To help finance this enterprise, he was expecting to use this considerable sum of money coming to him from the railway company.

In what is here related as to what had taken place in the dealings of the McCoys with this railway company and in those which followed, the writer is casting no reflection on this railway, but the same is solely chargeable to some of the officers of the road. This inefficiency, short-sightedness, and lack of business judgment were discovered in a few years, and a reorganization made, removing these officers, and this branch of the railway was placed in more efficient hands. This contract with the McCoys was not reduced to writing, and the railway may have had a sinister motive in not having this done. Among people of the West, in early times, especially among cattle dealers, men seldom reduced their agreements to writing, and the words of all men were considered as good as the best bonds. In these times, a man who was found wanting in this respect was soon stung out of the hive, considered as an outcast and a criminal, and fit only to associate with horse thieves.

The railway had delayed these payments as long as it could, and finally in the fall of 1870, when McCoy needed this money to conclude his cattle enterprise, and made demand on the company for the same, it not only refused to pay, but repudiated the contract, and, above all, became insulting. This company also owed McCoy large sums of money which he had expended from his personal funds at their request and for their benefit in the East in resisting the passage of laws in Illinois and other states which would forbid the shipping of western cattle across their borders.

All other means having failed, McCoy was compelled to bring suit against the railway company. The case was filed in the District Court at Junction City, Kansas. Upon the trial, in 1871, judgment was rendered for McCoy in the full amount of his claim. The case was appealed by the railway company to the Supreme Court of Kansas, and was finally decided by that tribunal in 1872. The opinion was written by Judge Brewer, is entitled Kansas Pacific Railway Company vs. Joseph G. McCoy, and is reported in Kansas Reports, Volume 8 at Page 538. By the terms of this decision the judgment of the lower court was affirmed and the railway company ordered to pay the full amount of the judgment.

The relief, however, had come too late. The blow had long since fallen on the head of this luckless promoter. He had fostered and established at Abilene the greatest cattle market there was at that time in the world. It had brought millions of cattle from their native plains in the South to Abilene, and had helped to open the great cattle thoroughfare extending for over eight hundred miles across hills, plains, and prairies. He fell a victim to the very power he had benefited. On account of the hard winter of 1870-1871 and the failure to get his money from the railway company, McCoy was driven to desperation and financial ruin. His creditors closed in upon him and he lost a fortune. His interests and holdings were sold at a sacrifice. He saw all that he had planned and built up in years of labor shattered on the rocks.

We might here note, that few men, who by their foresight, perseverance, and efforts have established large enterprises and rendered, produced, and bestowed the greatest and most lasting heritage upon mankind, have ever realized the benefits resulting from their labors and efforts. Many of them have only received abuse and condemnation from the persons benefited.

The season of 1871, however, ended the life of Abilene as the leading market for southern cattle. Some of the herds, in order to avoid the fast advancing settlements, shifted to Ellsworth and other shipping points to the west. Finally the settlements became too extensive to drive through, and with the season of 1871 the trail from the south was closed as far as Newton, Kansas. This was the history of all the cattle towns located any distance north in the State of Kansas. Abilene, Ellsworth, Great Bend, Newton, Wichita, and Dodge City all had their day, which still exists in the history of these towns. Caldwell, Hunnewell, Arkansas City, and Kiowa, all being on the State line between Kansas and the Indian Territory, survived until the extension of the railways to the south ended their lives as shipping points.

The Atchison, Topeka, and Santa Fe Railway Company extended its line to the westward and reached Newton, Kansas, in 1871, Dodge City in 1872, Wichita in 1872, and Caldwell in 1880. Each of these towns in turn became the principal shipping point for southern cattle, being at the terminus of the railway. In 1871, when the line extended to Newton, Joseph G. McCoy, in conjunction with other parties, established shipping pens and yards at that point. During the short time that it held the terminus of the railway, Newton made good its opportunities. It is said that during this brief period it was the most high-rolling cow-town there ever was in the West. Newton as a cattle shipping point was short-lived, as the railway built on twenty-six miles into Wichita the following year, 1872. Wichita reigned supreme as a shipping point for three or four years, when the settlements to the south closed the northern drives for it.

When the railway built into Wichita, Joseph G. McCoy followed the shipping business there, operated pens, and bought and sold cattle at that point for a couple of years, and then removed to Kansas City, Missouri, where he continued to work with the commission companies and other lines of the cattle business. In 1874 he wrote and published his book entitled, "Historic Sketches of the Cattle Trade of the West and Southwest." This book gained in popularity as an authentic history, not only of the cattle business, but also of the history of the country in the primitive times when he operated. Its importance increased with time, and for a while it was almost impossible to buy one of the volumes. Many of them sold for fifty dollars each, and higher. In 1932 this book was reprinted by the Rare Book Shop of Washington, D. C. Volumes of it are now available at a reasonable price, and the reading of the same, by all persons interested in Western History, is recommended.

In 1889, at the time of the opening for settlement of the Original Oklahoma Country, usually designated as Old Oklahoma, Joesph G. McCoy settled at Reno City, a town immediately north and west across the North Canadian River from the present City of El Reno. This town has entirely disappeared. McCoy soon moved with the rest of the settlers of Reno City to El Reno. His ability was soon recognized in this new land, and in the first election held in this country, which was in the fall of 1890, he was the Democratic nominee for delegate to Congress from the Territory of Oklahoma in the fifty-second Congress. He was, however, defeated by David A. Harvey, the Republican nominee. He subsequently returned to Kansas City, Missouri, where he continued to carry on in the work to which his life was devoted, the cattle business.

He died in Kansas City October 19, 1915. While his greatest efforts and devotions have been lost sight of in the turmoil and strife of the world, his book remains as the paramount monument of his life. His efforts were devoted to and spent in his endeavor to further the cattle industry of the West and Southwest, for which he worked and wrote. Whatever the results have been, we know that his endeavors, his labors, and his sacrifices for the cause for which he strove were great, and that he lived and died without realizing the proper and adequate returns therefrom. Such has been the fate of many men, but history should record and the world now appreciate these efforts in accordance with his labor and his sacrifices.

W. E. Malaley, taken while he resided at Hennessey, Oklahoma.

CHAPTER VIII.

WILLIAM E. MALALEY

In dealing with the history of the Chisholm Trail, there are necessarily involved the names and a brief account of the lives and activities of the men connected with the trail, not only the establishment and laying out of the same, but also connected with and contributing to the life and usefulness of it. In this regard so many men participated in and devoted many years of their lives to the business which developed and supported the trail, that it is impossible to deal with all of them or even mention them. There has been included herein a brief history of only a few persons whose efforts were foremost in matters connected with the establishing and developing of the trail or business supporting the same.

It is equally not only important, but necessary, in order to give a complete history of the trail, to give some idea of the lives and works of a few persons who were materially connected with the country supporting the same at the time it was used, and these efforts and valuable services on the frontier, which should be remembered, would be lost to history if not preserved by some one. Among the foremost ranks of this latter class of persons was William E. Malaley.

When the last gun was fired over the last battle field of the Civil War, and its echoes had died away, a change immediately came over the people of the entire Nation; a change which turned into a totally different course the energies, efforts, and aspirations of the entire populace of both the North and the South. For four years the struggles for supremacy in battle had been the great object of not only the soldiery, but of the people in general. Upon the close of the war all these labors

and exertions were lifted from the shoulders of the people, their
minds were relieved from these worries, and they were given
an opportunity to engage their labors and intellect in other
fields. Therefore, they immediately looked about them to survey the conditions and the world in general. The soldiers of
both armies were released, and it became necessary for them
to seek homes, either permanent or temporary, for themselves.
Some returned for a time at least to their former abodes, and
others sought new homes suited to them according to the
changed conditions which existed.

On account of the younger and more active men of the
country having been for so long engaged in the war, the progress of the settlement of the frontier had been delayed and
sadly neglected. Thus it is not unusual, but a natural result,
that a vast number of young men who were released from both
armies came to the frontier, and either took up homes or engaged in the cattle business. Many of the ex-soldiers from the
North went south to Texas, and worked and rode side by side
with the boys against whom they had fought only a few years
before.

During the war the cattle of the Southwest had increased
and run wild, and the owners of a large portion of the same
were unknown. While these cattle had but little value at the
time, in 1867, the Chisholm Trail was opened and communication established between the Southwest and the East and Northeast. Cattle immediately became valuable, and the business
flourished beyond conception. These were the days when the
man with the branding iron and rope, who knew how to use
them, flourished. The maverick[1] belonged to some person, and

---

[1] To all persons in the West and Southwest the word "maverick" is significant,
is or has been a household word, and it is unnecessary to define the same, but to
others, it has no meaning without explanation. A maverick is an unbranded animal,
generally referring to the cattle class. Tradition has it, that the word originated as
follows: In the Gulf coast country in Texas, in the days long before the Civil War,
there lived a cattleman by the name of Maverick, who either because of his humane

that person was the one who placed a brand upon it. These cattle could not be misappropriated, because no one knew who the owners were. The energies of some of these active young men, who were transplanted in the West, were exerted and their talents used for the advancement of the country and the subjugation of the frontier to law and order, resulting in unlimited good, while the efforts of other active minded ones were devoted to pillage and plunder; and to harassing, annoying, and preying upon law-abiding citizens. The result of the energies of this latter class was to retard and hold back civilization.

Into this maelstrom of humanity, came William E. Malaley, a young soldier, fresh from the Federal Army. The position that he occupied among this mass of people scattered over the Western Plains evidenced the confidence and trust that the Government placed in him. He carried a commission as United States Marshal, having special jurisdiction over the western Indian Territory and the Panhandle of Texas. He was at this time just coming into his prime of active young manhood. He was intelligent, cautious, shrewd, and, while unassuming, fearless; but his greatest attribute was that he was trustworthy and implicitly honest.

William E. Malaley was born at Randolph, Alabama, January 1, 1850. His father was a typical son of the South, and a slaveholder, who conducted a mercantile establishment at Randolph. Young Malaley's immediate family consisted of his father, mother, one sister, and himself. Just prior to the beginning of hostilities in the Civil War, the elder Malaley, his wife, and the daughter all died within a very short time, and the son William E. was left alone when a little over ten

---

ideas or for some other reason refused to mark his cattle by burning brands upon them, and let them run without marks or brands, and all of these cattle were designated as "Mavericks," as belonging to Maverick, and the name became generally known and applied to all unbranded cattle.

years of age. The orphaned son was taken in care by a brother of his father. This uncle and young Malaley could never get along, and disagreed from the start. The boy always contended that the uncle treated him in a brutal manner, beat, and abused him. If this is not a fact, it can hardly be understood why he could not live harmoniously with this lad, as William was always considered one of the most agreeable men. In any event a great prejudice grew up in the mind of this boy toward the uncle; a prejudice which lasted a lifetime so far as William was concerned.

The result of the disagreement between the uncle and young Malaley was, that the boy before he was twelve years of age, and just at the time of the breaking out of the war, ran away from the home of his foster father. He took his course among strangers; into an unknown country, an unknown world, and in doing so directed the same to the northward. His former associates and boyhood friends had enlisted in the Confederate Army, and it may be that the youth sought safety from his uncle beyond the lines of the Federal Army. In any event, his course was directed to the Northern Army, and as soon as he could reach its lines he sought to enlist. On account of his age, he was barely twelve years old, they refused his offer, but he did obtain a position as a messenger boy. It is doubtful whether he was ever, on account of his youth, permitted to enlist and enroll. He remained with and served with the 11th Indiana Cavalry until they were mustered out at the close of the war.

When the war closed Malaley had no home to return to, and he accompanied his friend and associate, Lieut. Stover, to the latter's home at Wabash, Indiana. He remained there but a short time, when, being seized with the impulse common to ex-soldiers, he sought his fortunes on the western frontier. He first landed in Kansas, then drifted south to Texas, and from there into the Indian Territory, where he was engaged for a time handling stock for the Indian Agent at the Darlington Agency. He, however, soon engaged in the cattle business for himself, and it was during this time that he was appointed as United States Marshal for the territory stated. His duties as Marshal were not only to apprehend and capture white violaters of the law and to subdue their lawlessness, but it also devolved upon him to assist in keeping down disturbances among the Indians and to protect white persons in the Indian Country from violence at their hands. It will be remembered, that at that time there was no post at Fort Reno, and but a meager bunch of soldiers was kept at Fort Sill and Fort Supply. The nearest available body of soldiers of any size was at Fort Leavenworth, Kansas. So it was to this point that Agent Miles journeyed to seek soldiers for protection upon the breaking out of the Cheyenne War in 1874.

Stone Calf, one of the two leading chiefs of the Cheyennes, had taken part of the tribe and left the agency, and in the latter part of June, 1874, it became apparent that either a massacre or an Indian War was imminent, and Malaley was called to the Agency for consultation. It was deemed best that Miles and an escort should go to Fort Leavenworth for reinforcements, and that Mrs. Covington, daughter of Brinton Darlington and wife of J. A. Covington, one of the parties in charge at the agency, together with their infant daughter Katy, and other ladies at the agency, should be removed to the settlements out of the danger zone. Accordingly, on the morning of the 4th of July, 1874, they started up the Chisholm Trail on this journey. The party consisted of Agent John D. Miles, J. A. Covington, Sarah (Darlington) Covington, his wife, Katy Covington, their daughter, a babe in arms, Marshal William E. Malaley, a lieutenant, two or three soldiers, and a few other persons. The party journeyed all day, and stopped that night at the Red Fork Ranch on the north side of the Cimarron River. Some of them were conveyed in an army ambulance and a buggy, while others traveled on horseback. The trail, for some eight miles north after leaving Red Fork Ranch, was skirted by blackjack timber, and, on account of the danger from marauding Indians, they traveled very cautiously on this morning.

About nine miles north from the ranch which they had left, and soon after leaving the timber along the trail, while skirting the east bank of Turkey Creek, they came upon the remains of Pat Hennessey and the evidence of the massacre that had recently taken place. The party went on to Buffalo Springs, a distance of about six miles, where they found a number of travelers congregated. After the body of Hennessey was buried the party pushed on to Wichita, Kansas. Agent Miles went on to Fort Leavenworth to procure aid, while Malaley returned to the Indian Territory to assist in suppressing the conflict with the Indians. At this time there were two efficient United States Marshals assigned to this district, one being Ben Williams, a Quaker installed by Brinton Darlington, and the other Malaley. Williams at this time was among the Arapaho Indians, living with them to hold them from entering the war against the Government.

The duties of Malaley, connected with his livestock business, compelled him to give up his position as Marshal. This he did shortly after the Indian uprising of 1874 was subdued. He then threw all his energies and ability into making a success of the cattle business. He at times was associated with many of the leading cattlemen of the Cherokee Strip. He had interests and was closely connected with Major Drum of Kansas City, Missouri, who was President of the Cherokee Strip Livestock Association. He had a large ranch southeast of the present City of Medford, Oklahoma. Many were his herds that traveled from the Panhandle of Texas across to the Chisholm Trail and up the same to his ranch or to market. While his cattle raised clouds of dust on the trails his brand, the running W, marked the cattle on many hills and valleys. The world had not only smiled on him; it had cast its blessing and had given him what all men desired, wealth and power.

In later years Malaley became a close friend of the writer. He first knew him in the early eighties. He was then a man in the prime of life. He was not a man of large dimensions nor was he a man of imposing appearance. He was of medium size, but from the effects of his outdoor life, he was strong and active. He was at this time much more robust than in later life. He was very unassuming, both in dress and in demeanor, and associated with his cowboys as any other cow hand, sharing all their hardships with them. He was known all over the Cherokeee Strip as the best rider in the cattle country. It was a familiar saying, that any cowboy who tried to ride a bad horse and was thrown would remark, "Billy Malaley could not ride that horse"; and if the rider did not make the excuse someone else would make it for him, even if he did it in a joking way.

Malaley was at this time taken into the counsels of the big cattle interests of the West and Southwest. His advice was considered conservative and sound, and was sought by many men. He rose to and held a position of trust, confidence, and power among the cattle barons of the country. His greatest asset was his reputation for extreme honesty. Anyone dealing with him knew that no trick or fraud was concealed beneath the surface in the transaction. He was an officer of the Cherokee Strip Livestock Association from the time of its organization. He made several trips to Washington City in the interest of the Association.

There are, however, unseen rocks beneath the smoothest surface of any financial waters which any business man ever launches his bark upon. This is true regardless of the utmost caution that the navigator may use. Never was this better exemplified than in the life of Mr. Malaley.

The part of the Indian Territory known as the Cheyenne-Arapaho Indian reservation was located in the western portion of the territory, immediately south of the Cherokee Outlet, and was bounded on the east by the Unassigned Lands, on the south by Greer County and the reservation of the Kiowa-Comanche and Wichita Indians, and on the west by the Panhandle of Texas. This Cheyenne-Arapaho reservation embraced approximately 4,300,000 acres. Almost all of the same was fine grazing land. On this land there were about 3,500 Indians, of which about two-thirds were Cheyenne and one-third Arapaho. Up until the early years of the decade beginning with 1880, this land had remained idle, and the extensive growth of grass on the same grew up, died, and was burned. No one received any benefit therefrom. In the first part of this period enterprising cattlemen drove small herds into this country, and by giving influential Indians cattle for the privilege, pastured them thereon.

In the early part of January, 1883, the principal chiefs of the Cheyenne-Arapaho Indians met, and directed the Indian Agent in charge, J. D. Miles, to enter into a contract for the leasing of the entire country to seven cattlemen, as follows: Edward Fenlon, William E. Malaley, Hampton B. Denman, Jesse S. Morrison, Lewis M. Briggs, Albert G. Evans, and Robert D. Hunter. Of these parties, according to the lease, Fenlon was to have 570,000 acres, Malaley 570,000 acres, Denman 570,000 acres, Hunter 500,000 acres, Evans 457,000 acres, Briggs 318,000 acres, and Morrison 140,000 acres. The lease was to extend for ten years, and contained all other necessary provisions for the protection of both parties. They were to pay for this privilege the sum of $86,000.00 per year, payable semi-annually. This would be an unexpected income, and would go that far toward the support of the Indians.

This lease was entered into and met the approval of Agent Miles, or rather it was supposed that it was entered into, as it was agreeable with all parties concerned. These cattlemen brought extensive herds into this country and stocked it well. According to the terms the lessees had a right to cut timber for posts on the land, and could fence the same with wire fences. All this was done. Other cattlemen who had gotten no part of this valuable grazing land, some of them intermarried white men, who lived on portions of this country and wanted to use the same for grazing, kept causing trouble and interceding with the Indians to cause more trouble. This agitation was carried on until the matter was taken up by the Government at Washington, and the Attorney General rendered an opinion holding that the Indians had no right to enter into the lease, and held the same void.

President Cleveland finally issued a proclamation to have all cattle removed from the country. The lessees named in the lease above referred to at that time had in this country something over 210,000 head of cattle. General Sheridan was sent to take charge of affairs and report to the officers of the Government as to the conditions. Sheridan arrived in July, 1885, made his investigation, and reported that a portion of the Cheyenne tribe, the number being about 1200, was dissatisfied with the leasing contract. The writer desires to state here that in his opinion this statement is correct, and also that this is the total number mustered by the agitators, including the squaw men who had helped to originate and advance the trouble. This is not all these Indians did. Great numbers of them made a business of hunting and killing the cattle of the ranchmen, and it is claimed were encouraged by some squaw men so to do, since no prosecutions or punishment could be meted out to them for such acts. This statement does not apply to all the squaw men, as some of them were in favor of the leasing. However, the writer was in this country during this time and formed his opinion from being on the ground. He could, also, name some of the instigators, but to do so would avail nothing to anyone at this time.

Sheridan further reported that the employees around the agency were in favor of the leases and considered it for the best interests of the Indians, that all proceedings had been reported or taken place at the agency, and that Agent Miles' name appeared in connection therewith. Much censure in connection with this matter has been directed at Agent Miles by some writers. All of this originated from the agitation of the persons above referred to. It is always easy to find argument for persons who want to be critical. In this censure it has been stated that Malaley and some of the other parties taking these leases were well known by Miles and the insinuation made that he either wanted to favor them or was paid for his influence.

All men who knew Agent Miles knew that his character and honesty were unimpeachable. In all things he tried to do what was for the best interest of the Indians. The dissatisfied element referred to turned against him, but it was not from any fault of his. The Indians were receiving for this rental almost twenty-five dollars per year for each man, woman, and child on the reservation. They wanted to lease the land, and it was perfectly natural that if they did so, Agent Miles would prefer that they lease it to persons of known integrity who would carry out the terms of the lease and who were able to do so. The Indians also preferred to lease to persons they knew. They desired that persons they knew and whom they trusted would be interested in the leases and would see that the Indians were not defrauded. It is noteworthy that the report of Sheridan does not cast any insinuation or make any charge of wrongdoing on the agent or the lessees. The writer having known and associated with Malaley many years, stands ready to denounce any assertion of dishonesty on his part. The source of this trouble was well known at the time. It was jealousy on the part of some cattlemen, an effort to obtain preference by certain squaw-men, and the power of certain others in authority whom they persuaded to help them.

Sheridan's report stated that each of the leases had been fenced, that all the ranchmen had complied with their agreements, and had paid the rentals promptly, also that the Indians had caused much loss and damage by killing the ranchmen's cattle. Before this report had reached the President, he had issued his proclamation that all the ranchmen, together with all their cattle, horses, and other property, be removed from the Cheyenne-Arapaho reservation within forty days. William E. Malaley owned much the larger portion of these interests. Only persons familiar with the handling of livestock can realize the vast number of cattle that 210,000 head is. This amount at that time, when thrown upon the market, together with the other current marketable cattle, was sufficient to overrun the demand and scuttle the price in the entire United States. Beside this, the majority of these cattle were totally unfit to be marketed. It was impossible to find range or a place to remove them. The pastures of the Cherokee Strip to the north were stocked to their capacity. In vain representatives of the cattlemen went to Washington and plead for more time. Even with the utmost effort it was impossible to gather and drive these cattle beyond the borders of the reservation within the time given, and the gathering and driving continued until late into the fall and winter of 1885.

While the cattle were being removed from this country, the Indians did not seek to bring on any difficulty with the cowboys, unless the Indians were in position to have an unlimited amount of advantage. The fact was that they feared the cowboys very much. During the visit of Sheridan at the fort, he told a joke on his soldiers, which was in substance as follows: He said a big Cheyenne came up to him one day and asked him if he was the boss of the fort; he told the Indian that it was under his command, and asked him what he wanted. The Cheyenne stated to him, that he wanted to buy that biggest cannon at the fort. Sheridan told him that he could not sell it to him for the reason that he wanted it to kill his soldiers with. The Indian turned in disgust, and said he did not need it to kill soldiers, he wanted it to kill cowboys; that he could kill soldier with a club.

The conditions that existed in this country immediately before and during this time have never been described accurately by anyone. The writer was there and knows. He would not even attempt to and could not give it full force and effect. These Indians who had been aroused by the intermeddlers referred to were roving at will over the country, carrying Sharpe .45-70 and Winchester .44 rifles. In one hand they carried the ever present long ramrod, not using it, however, as a ramrod, but grasping their hand around and resting their gun over it when firing. They would drop down on one knee and fire in this manner. Their arrogance was the most disgusting and overbearing that could be imagined. There was only one person who could duplicate it, that was another arrogant Indian. In this statement no reflection is cast upon any Indian from the fact of his being an Indian. Indians are the same as all other persons, and members of their tribe are the same as those of the white man, often and in many cases not as bad. These Indians referred to belonged to the vicious class.

The writer has often wondered, if there were not many boys who went into this country, at that time, who never came out. He saw one time at least, when he thought of his own boyhood home, which he never expected to see again. These Indians had a bad habit of locating the camps of freighters, cattlemen, and travelers, and running off their horses. If the owner had the good fortune to ever find his stock, the Indians would claim that the animals had strayed and were taken up by them. They would demand large sums of money, usually forty or fifty dollars, for their services and trouble, and the unfortunate victim was compelled to pay it. This was evidently a trick learned from the white man. At the time stated the writer caught them in the very act. Trouble ensued, if that will explain it. The result was that no one was hurt, but they did not get the horses. These renegade Indians made no pretense of doing anything but hunting for cattle, and they killed them on sight just for the fun of seeing them fall.

Malaley's cattle were crowded out of the country, and taken wherever he could drive them. Some were taken north onto the T5 Range in the Cherokee Outlet. The market started going down, and it is a well known fact among cattlemen of this time, that the throwing of this vast amount of cattle on the market started the slump, which never let up until it ended with the crash some two years later. Malaley lost a fortune, not only one, but several. Through it all, he only smiled and said nothing. During the many years thereafter, that the writer knew him, he never heard him utter one word of censure or abuse against the ones who helped to crowd this loss upon him. There was censure due, and many of the men who helped to ruin Malaley financially also ruined themselves. Billy Malaley was a wise man, but the best plans of the wisest sometimes fail. The best illustration of these conditions was expressed by a man caught in the crash, and who stated it as follows: He said, when he was making money he made it so fast that he had to look behind him and see if someone was not putting it into his pocket, but when he commenced losing it, he had to look behind him to see if someone was not taking it out.

The fate of Malaley was largely brought about by the removal of the cattle from the Cheyenne-Arapaho reservation. He would, doubtless, have survived the crash that followed very well had it not been for this misfortune. As it was he went the route of many others of his contemporaries, and, like most of them, he was never able to retrieve his lost fortunes.

From a moral point of view, Billy Malaley was a man without a peer. He was sober, industrious, and one of the most agreeable and congenial men the writer ever knew. One of his most outstanding characteristics was his lack of ostentation. He never tried to make a show of himself, and detested any sham or assumption. His dress was always of the simplest pattern. He seldom ever carried a gun on the range, and when he did it was usually his Winchester rifle. While living at Hennessey, the citizens, knowing his standing as a plainsman, induced him to have his picture taken with a Colt .45 six-shooter and a Winchester rifle, and knowing him as he did, the writer has always wondered how they were able to persuade him to submit to this process. A copy of this picture is inserted herein. After leaving the range and entering upon the life of an ordinary citizen, Malaley would have been the last man whom any stranger would have selected as being a noted frontier character.

When Old Oklahoma was opened for settlement in 1889, Malaley settled at Hennessey. This town was built on the east bank of Turkey Creek. The grave of Pat Hennessey, whose remains, in 1874, Malaley and his party had found tied to his wagon and burned, and whom he had buried, was on this townsite. At the time he lived at Hennessey the writer was living at Pond Creek, some fifty-five miles north. The old acquaintance between the writer and Malaley was continued, and many times Malaley would stop at Pond Creek and see him. He loved to talk of the old days on the range, and he often stated that he wanted the writer to record his statement of the death of Hennessey. These matters were not considered so important at that time, and it was not attended to until it was too late.

W. E. Malaley, from photograph taken shortly before his death.

Finally Malaley went east with a Wild West show. He still maintained his reputation as a rider. During this trip, however, a horse fell on him, breaking his leg. The writer heard from him shortly afterward. He was confined to the Masonic Home or Hospital, which at that time was located at the old site of the Darlington Agency, where he had had many of his experiences on the frontier. Before the writer could get there to see him he had sufficiently recovered to travel, and had left the Home and gone to Kansas City. This Home is now removed to Guthrie, Oklahoma. The records of the office show that he was received in the Home at Darlington in July, 1918, and left at his own request November 18, 1918. The writer never saw him again. He lived only a short time thereafter. He died at Kansas City, Missouri, January 14, 1919. He was buried in Wisconsin. Malaley was married twice. His first marriage was in 1883. His last marriage was to Miss Addie C. Mitche at Fond du Lac, Wisconsin, March 22, 1913. His last wife survives him. She is now in the Masonic Home at Dousman, Wisconsin.

The writer knew Billy Malaley perhaps as well as any other man. For him he will say as to his opinion of him what can be said of few men; that, if his entire life and all the deeds of the same were bared to the world, he would need no other epitaph, no other monument or biography to cause his memory to be revered. Who can say more for any man?

Ben Williams, the Quaker United States Marshal at Darlington Agency.

CHAPTER IX.

BEN F. WILLIAMS

It is largely the purpose of the writer in this work to give attention and consideration to persons who are entitled to be remembered for their contributions of valuable services rendered in the civilization and settlement of the West. Many of those who are justly entitled to places in history have in the past failed to receive it. This lack of recognition is not due to any partiality or preference on the part of the historians, but rather to the lack of effort on the part of the individuals to bring themselves before the public eye; consequently, to the lack of knowledge on the part of the persons recording the history. Among every class or race of people there are persons of many different characteristics.

Among all of them are some who, on each occasion when they do or perform some act that they think is noteworthy, at once publish and broadcast the fact to the public. This process is continued until the party is familiar to people in general. These things are picked up and recorded by historians, and the party is then a historical character. This condition is largely brought about by the natural proclivities of the persons involved. Some persons are good advertisers, while others are totally unable, or do not have the inclination or self assurance, to bring themselves before the public. For this reason many persons, who have contributed largely to the history of the country, have been entirely forgotten, while others, who have contributed less, have had their names spread over pages of history. The writer is not condemning the activities of the persons who have brought about the placing of their names in history where they think they belong.

In fact there is an old saying which justifies such a course. As the writer now remembers, it was as follows: "Whosoever tooteth not his own horn, the same shall not be tooted." It is, therefore, largely the purpose of the writer to preserve the valuable history of this portion of the West, which would otherwise be lost, and give due consideration for merit to the persons who have not considered their own contributions of sufficient importance to have them preserved.

There is no better example of this class of unassuming frontier men, who saw nothing but their duty and never thought of having their deeds recorded, than the man who is made the subject of this sketch. Benjamin F. Williams was born at Salem, Ohio, in the year 1837. He was the son of Doctor Dearman Williams, a practising physician at that place. His mother was Mary Farmer Williams. These parents were members of the Society of Friends, generally known as Quakers. These parents lived and reared their eight children strictly in this faith. The mother, however, died when Benjamin was about eleven years of age. There was an extensive Quaker settlement in the portion of Ohio in which the Williams family lived. Their families intermarried and associated together on account of their religious faith. This was the case in the marriage of the parents of Ben F. Williams.

Although adhering strictly to their religious faith as members of the Society of Friends, yet the ancestors of Ben F. Williams were ever pioneers of the West. From the time they left the Quaker settlements of Pennsylvania they always pushed westward, until finally they reached the Pacific Ocean; and the earthly remains of Ben Williams rests on the shores of that ocean. Following this characteristic, Doctor Dearman Williams and his family turned their course to the West in 1855. This was after the death of the mother. Three of the sons accompanying the father in this move were destined to take a prominent part in the history of the then wild and unoccupied Indian Territory.

In making this move they sought another extensive Quaker settlement. This settlement was located at Muscatine, in the extreme eastern portion of Iowa. Many of the Quakers from eastern Ohio, in the vicinity of Salem, had preceded them to this location. Ben Williams at this time was about eighteen years of age. He received an ordinary education in Ohio and Iowa. He continued to live at Muscatine until the breaking out of the Civil War, when he enlisted in the Federal Army. There were four of the Williams boys and three of them joined this army, while John, the eldest, by agreement remained at home to look after their interests and families while the others were in the service. Ben Williams was captured and confined in Andersonville prison, where he remained until the close of the war. Upon the resumption of peace he returned to his home. His physical condition, owing to his army and prison life, was bad, and it took several years for him to recover his usual robust health.

Even before his service in the army Ben Williams had a tendency for the use of firearms. His service in the army before his capture had developed that art to a high degree, and he had become proficient as a handler of all kinds of weapons. Added to this ability he was large and strong; but regardless of his size he was very quick and active, being an expert in athletic activities. In 1869 Brinton Darlington was appointed by President Grant as agent of the Cheyenne and Arapaho Indians, who were being permanently located on a reservation in the Indian Territory. He had lived at Salem, Ohio, and had known the Williams family, and this family had come to him as their old friend and spiritual counselor when they removed to Muscatine.

At this time the Indian Territory was an unorganized country. There was no state or territorial government over the same. For that reason, it was imperative that the President appoint one or more United States Marshals for certain designated portions of this unorganized country. It became necessary that Brinton Darlington make this recommendation. In doing so he desired to keep the agency, as far as possible, under Quaker control. Such was also the wish of the President. The Williams family, while they always addressed Brinton Darlington as uncle, were not related to him. Their only affiliation was through the Quaker faith. Most persons who knew them on the frontier thought they were related by family ties.

Brinton Darlington, in looking about to procure a person to fill the position of Marshal, and knowing the dimensions of Ben Williams, both in physical and mental make-up, considered him a suitable person to subdue the lawless element of the frontier. He knew that he could deliver to the reckless violator of the law what was necessary to restrain him, even if it transgressed the strict Quaker principles; and even that when a man smote him on one cheek and he turned the other to be smitten, the smiter would look into the business end of frontier justice in the form of a .45 six-shooter. In any event, Ben Williams was recommended by Brinton Darlington, and appointed as United States Marshal, to act in conjunction with William E. Malaley. The country, over which they had jurisdiction, comprised all the portion of the Indian Territory west of the Five Civilized Tribes extending to the Panhandle of Texas. Williams entered upon the duties of this office in 1870.

The operations of Malaley were confined mostly to the eastern portion of the country, over which these two lone representatives of the law were to keep peace. Ben Williams' duties were in the western portion of this wild and lawless land. He spent most of his time in the Indian camps and in pursuit of

horse thieves and other desperadoes. He was a spectacular
person as he rode over the western prairies. He was six feet
tall, well proportioned, with a full beard, dark, and almost
black. A broad-brimmed Stetson hat, symbolical of both the
Quaker and the plainsman, sat upon his head. This was his
correct designation, and portrayed his exact tendencies. He
was a Quaker at heart, but it meant utter destruction to the
man who so aroused him until he was compelled to forget that
he was a Quaker, and it seems he forgot this many times during his tenure of office. When he forgot this faith he had no
other, and the range of his Henry rifle was the only limit of
safety for his adversary. So far as physical danger was concerned, he was utterly without fear. This was the reputation
he had and left on the frontier. He wanted peace and was going
to have it, even if he was compelled to fight for it.

The headquarters of this fearless peace officer was at Darlington Agency, where the old Chisholm Trail, the trader's
branch, crossed the North Canadian River. With two heavy
Colt six-shooters strapped around his waist, and carrying his
long Henry rifle in front of him, resting across his saddle, he
rode through herds of running buffalo, trailed law violators
across rivers, over hills and valleys, and brought them back
shackled to the horns of their saddles while he led their
horses by his side. It is also true that many of them, who refused to surrender and fought, did not have the privilege of
riding by his side, and the honor of having their horses led by
him. In any event, he never shot until it was necessary, but
with the characteristics of true sons of the West, who lived to
tell the tale, he always shot in time.

Many are the tales that the writer remembers, of the
prowess of this peace officer. The appearance of this firm-
faced, tall, imposing-looking officer was very impressive. A
number of outlaws in the Indian Territory, who had gained

prominence, named themselves "Wild Bill." Why they should do this is a question, as the original bearer of this name, Wild Bill Hickok, was not an outlaw, but an avowed and professional hunter of outlaws. This designation was, perhaps, applied on account of the high sounding quality of the name. In any event, it is said, that two western characters bearing this cognomen lost their lives by resisting arrest at the hands of Ben Williams and engaging in a battle with him.

For his service as United States Marshal, Williams received, what was then considered the high salary of one hundred dollars per month, out of which he paid his own expenses. He would shackle several outlaws at one time, put them into a stagecoach, seat himself in the other end, and remain there night and day during the trip of almost two hundred miles to Wichita, Kansas. On one of these occasions, the gang, to which these particular two outlaws whom he was conveying to jail belonged, tried to take them away from him. His audacity and fearlessness so struck his assailants with awe, that he was able to get his prisoners away without the loss of life or anyone being injured. On another occasion, while so traveling with two prisoners, he fell asleep in the stagecoach, and in the dark dropped his pistol, and had difficulty in finding it. Some time afterward someone asked him how much a certain gun was worth. He replied that it depended entirely on circumstances, and that on this occasion his gun was worth just as much as his life. Ben was always ready for a joke, and possessed much original wit.

The greatest service, however, that Ben Williams rendered, and which is, perhaps, the greatest service ever rendered by any peace officer of the West, was during the Indian War of 1874. Very little is known of this service, except by the persons who were present during this trouble. The writer's information came direct from them. Ben Williams never thought of advertising it, and took it just as a matter of duty on his part.

In 1874 the buffalo were disappearing from the plains; from general conditions the plains Indians were restless, and on the verge of rebellion. The situation was so tense that it was as impressive as the quiet condition just before a heavy storm broke. Stone Calf, one of the two leading chiefs of the Cheyenne Indians in the Indian Territory, heeding the appeal of the younger braves, had left the agency, and was upon the western plains. He was present at the battle of Adobe Walls, in June, 1874. These Indians were all wards of the officers at Darlington Agency, and they tried to protect them and their names as much as possible, but it was afterward a well known fact that it was some of Stone Calf's young braves who killed Pat Hennessey.

Agent Miles, who was then the Quaker Agent in charge at Darlington Agency (Brinton Darlington having died), went to Fort Leavenworth, Kansas, after soldiers for protection, for, unless the contingent of the Cheyenne Indians under Little Robe, as well as the Arapaho Indians, who constituted about one-third of the Indians on the reservation, could be held in check, it meant a bloody war and loss of life for many persons. These Indians, if unrestrained, could have destroyed the entire Indian Territory. In addition to the other outrages that Stone Calf and his followers had committed was the capture of and carrying off into captivity the four Germaine girls. This capture was made in southwestern Kansas. In this emergency an appeal was made to Ben Williams to help quiet the Indians.

In answer to this request he saddled his horse, strapped on his pistols, and, with his rifle in front of him, rode away. He first went to the camp of Little Robe, with its less troublesome portion of the Cheyenne tribe. After doing what good he could there and establishing communications with them, he rode on to the Arapaho camp and sought his old friend Jim Morrison, who was an intermarried white man, who had lived with the Arapaho many years, and had much influence with them. Ben Williams, Jim Morrison, and the Arapaho chiefs, who had friendly inclinations and opposed the war movement, started a campaign among the Indians to quiet the disturbance and tense feeling which existed.

Williams spent most of his time with the Indians, among whom he was known as Black Beard. He stayed with them all summer, or until the conditions were entirely settled. He also kept in touch with Little Robe. The difficulty that was encountered in holding these contingents of the tribes from making an outbreak was on the part of the younger men, and from the reports that were made on conditions it must have been bad. It is said that these young bucks, when they would meet Williams or any of the other peace inclined men, would scowl, hang their heads, and growl. A leader was all they needed to make a bloody outbreak.

Williams and his associates had so thoroughly organized the peaceable element of the Cheyennes under Little Robe and the Arapaho tribe that it was impossible for the disturbing element to get a leader capable of handling the affected element. After the battle of Adobe Walls the Cheyennes with Stone Calf went south, heading for the wild country in the Panhandle of Texas. The location of this old chief was learned by the parties in the Arapaho Camp. Williams had been with the Arapaho almost continuously since the preceding fall, and while with them, on all possible occasions, in order to keep them quiet, had taken them on hunting trips to the westward.

While on one of these expeditions, they came close to the camp of Stone Calf. Williams, Morrison, and some of the chiefs of the Arapaho went to Stone Calf's camp. These Indians gave them a very cool reception. They, however, knew Williams well, and knew him to be their friend, and he soon restored their confidence. They then permitted him, together with the parties accompanying him, to go to Stone Calf's teepee. Here they were surprised to find two of the Germaine girls. These girls were painted to represent Indians until it was difficult to discover that they were not members of the tribe. When they saw the white men, they began to cry, until the tears ran down their faces, leaving streaks in the paint. These were the two older girls.

Referring further to the capture and surrender of these girls, it appears that after the capture of the four girls the Cheyennes with Stone Calf divided. When this division took place, two of the girls were taken with the portion going with the leader, and the other two went with the other division. The part of the tribe having the two younger girls became alarmed and wanted to return them. They, therefore, spread a buffalo robe on the grass, and left the two girls seated on it in company with an old squaw. The Indians departed, and the two younger girls were thus found. The other two were found, as stated, with Stone Calf. These girls told Williams and his party that they had been made slaves of and compelled to perform all sorts of manual labor for the Indians.

Williams talked the matter over with Stone Calf; the old chief told Williams that he had about made up his mind to go into the Agency and surrender; and he finally agreed to do so. They all departed for the Darlington Agency, taking with them the two girls. They went in company with the Cheyenne contingent, which was remaining with Stone Calf. Some of his followers had returned before this time. Williams, Morrison, the Arapaho chiefs, and Stone Calf, taking the two girls with them, entered the office of Agent Miles before anyone at the Agency knew of their presence, or that the girls had been located. Much has been written of the return of these captives, and the writer understands that army officers have been given much credit for the same. All sorts of extravagant articles have been published about this matter. These are the facts as given to the writer by persons in position to know, and who did know, and the writer is satisfied as to the truthfulness of the same.

On many of his trips on the western plains country, Ben Williams was accompanied by George Bent, son of William Bent of Bent's Fort on the north side of the Arkansas River in eastern Colorado. His mother was a full blood Cheyenne, and George stayed with the Cheyennes in Oklahoma. George Bent recently died. He always spoke in admiration of the character of Ben Williams, and in wonder as to his fearlessness. Williams continued in his services to the Government through the years up to 1876. Many were the wanderers on the plains who had strayed there to seek refuge from the penalties of the law, whom he apprehended and brought to the bar of justice for their sins against the Government. When he started the trail was never too long nor the undertaking too difficult or dangerous for him to go forward to the end.

The expenses of the marshal increased as civilization crept in. Ben Williams in 1876 was nearing the forty mile mark in life. He had never been married, and it may have been with an eye to such an event that caused him to abandon his office. In any event, he resigned his position in 1876. Fort Reno had been established and was an aid to the peace officers after 1874. The Indian police had also been organized by Bill Darlington, and, under his command, rendered much service to the law enforcement.

When out on the plains at one time in 1873, the Indians had pointed out to Williams an ideal home site. This was a beautiful spot, with large trees along a creek, where a fine spring issued from the ground. Williams always said he was

William (Bill) Darlington, son of Brinton Darlington, the organizer of
the Indian Police at Fort Reno.

going to retire to this place and start a cattle ranch when he left the Marshal's office. He had been present and guided a troop of cavalry when Fort Elliott was established in 1874, and knowing this location was only a few miles east of Fort Elliott he selected and procured the same as a home. This location was later found to be west of the 100th Meridian, which marked the western boundary of the Cheyenne-Arapaho reservation, and he bought this site from the Government. It was located in Wheeler County, Texas.

After leaving the marshal's office Williams drove stage for some time, perhaps six months or one year. On one of these trips he brought down to the Caddo Indian school a young lady teacher. It is difficult to say, as bachelors do not always tell all they knew, whether he had known her before. In any event, he had not been out of the marshal's office more than a year until he and this lady teacher, whose name was Miss Affie Woodcock, were married. They retired to Kansas for the ceremony, and shortly after their marriage went to live at this location selected on the plains. Here, as soon as the buffalo were sufficiently crowded away, they established a ranch. They were accompanied in this enterprise by a brother of Williams' wife.

For a time in their new home their principal business was killing buffalo for their hides, and this they followed until the shaggy wanderers of the plains had disappeared. The first name given to this ranch was Hackberry Springs, but when the stage route passed and a postoffice was established there, this postoffice was named Affie, in honor of Mrs. Williams. About 1880 that portion of Texas was divided or redivided into counties. In any event Wheeler County was organized, and Ben Williams was one of the first County Commissioners of the County. Later, the exact date being unknown to the writer, Williams sold his ranch in Texas to a company known as the

S. R. E. Cattle Company. The place is now known as Williams' Springs.

It was, perhaps, in the middle eighties that he sold this Texas ranch. After traveling back over what had been the wide expanse of plains, over which he had roamed, and viewing the inroads that civilization was making on the same, even though it was still the frontier and Indian country, he headed his course for the extreme west, and located at San Jose, California. There congregated and settled at this point a number of the parties who had rendered service and associated together at Darlington Agency. Among this number was J. A. Covington, who moved there in about 1889. Both of these notable western characters died some years ago, and both of them lie buried in a Grand Army plot in Oak Hill Cemetery, San Jose, California. The earthly remains of these men rest far from where their activities began. On all the long trail, between the cradle and the grave, these men exerted all their efforts in the interest of good citizenship, and left the world better by their being. In his untiring and persistent efforts in the Indian outbreak of 1874 Ben Williams, by these efforts and continuous exposure to hardships and dangers, saved the lives of hundreds of white persons on the frontier, and a greater number of Indians. This he did without extra emoluments or hope of reward. Such men have not lived in vain, and their memories should be perpetuated and revered by future generations.

CHAPTER X.

BRINTON DARLINGTON AND HIS QUAKERS

When a small boy, one of the first things that the writer can recall reading was "Peter Parley's Tales of America." This was written in verse. One of the statements contained in the same, which made a great impression on his youthful mind, was as follows:

"Then William Penn, the grave peace-maker,
    Came over with many an honest Quaker."

Throughout the entire United States the minds of the young inhabitants were thus informed and impressed with the piety of the early Quaker settlers in Pennsylvania, the effect of their character on the civilization of the country, and especially their peaceful relations with the Indians with whom they came in contact. The entire country was advised that the kind treatment of the Quakers would even subdue the vicious characteristics of the wild Indians, and it did so in case of the early settlers of the East.

At the time General Grant became President of the United States the conditions of the country with reference to the Indian tribes were in a disastrous state. The plains Indians were roaming at will over the prairies of the West, seeking whom they might devour. Four years of war had torn the country, and the Government had not had the time and opportunity to properly look after the Indians. Hunters and adventurers were crowding upon the western plains, slaughtering the buffalo, imposing upon the Indians, and trespassing upon their lands. The agents and contractors of the West, who furnished the Indians' supplies, had been pilfering everything possible, and committing wholesale frauds upon these helpless wards of the Government. It was necessary that the Government not only gain the confidence of the Indians, but also fill the places of the Government representatives dealing with them with persons who could be trusted and whom the Indians would trust. This as a whole was no small undertaking. The President fully realized this fact, and sought to meet the situation. In doing so his mind reverted to the idea that had been fully drilled into every youth of the country; the quieting and beneficial effects that the friendship of the Quakers had had on the Indians of the East.

President Grant studied closely the Indian condition in the United States, and made a trip to the West, the main purpose of the same being to receive information first hand. He finally concluded, as far as possible, to place leading Quakers at the head of the different Indian agencies. The united tribes of the Cheyenne and Arapaho were to be placed under one charge. This included the Southern Cheyennes and the Arapahos. This was one of the most important, if not the most important, of the bodies of Indians to be held together in the United States. The President sought a particularly good and trustworthy man to fill the position of agent for them. The Cheyennes had been roaming at will for years, pillaging the other tribes and white settlers and terrorizing the frontier.

For this position the President selected Brinton Darlington. Darlington was a steadfast and leading Quaker of the virgin quality. He was born in Pennsylvania, the primary home of Quakerism in the United States. The exact location and date of his birth was at Harrisburg in December, 1804. He came from a long line of Quaker ancestry, and was reared in the strict Quaker faith. In early life he emigrated to Salem, Ohio, and while yet a young man, in 1838, moved to the then western frontier, settling in eastern Iowa. He organized the pioneer Quaker settlements at Salem, Ohio, Muscatine and

West Branch, Iowa. At Muscatine he gathered about him his Quaker brethren until it became the principal Quaker settlement of the West. He was always regarded as the leader of his church in the communities where he lived. Darlington was a merchant by business classification, and prospered as such. He was not wealthy, but had a comfortable income. He never held a public office prior to his selection by the President to take charge of the Indian assignment in the West. He had no political aspirations or even a passing consideration for politics. His selection was entirely unsolicited, and was not known until he was asked to take the place. With all this record behind him, the President considered Brinton Darlington the ideal man for the position he selected him to fill.

Darlington, at the time of his appointment to this position, was starting down the western slope of life. The appointment was made in 1869, and at this time he was sixty-five years of age. He had a comfortable home, was in good circumstances financially, had a profitable income from his established business, his family and brethren in the church surrounded him, and all honored him as a leader in his community. So far as worldly comforts were concerned, there was nothing to mar his prospects in his declining years. It was only his being prompted by a deep Christian spirit, unflinching devotion to his church, the cause of right and justice, and with a steadfast object to sacrifice his future happiness for the betterment of the world, that caused him to accept the charge. This he did, and from this sacrifice, instead of spending his declining years among his friends and associates and dying in their midst, surrounded with their blessings, he spent the last three years of his life among savage Western Indians, late from the bloody war paths and battle fields, and was buried with these same bronzed warriors surrounding his casket and mourning his loss.

When Brinton Darlington took charge of these Indians, they were quartered in the western portion of the Indian Territory, being in the neighborhood of Fort Supply. The first object was to select a site for the establishment of the agency. With this in view, they journeyed to the eastern portion of the reservation, and there at the very eastern side of the same, where the Chisholm Trail crossed the North Canadian River, in the level bottom land on the north bank of this river, they selected the site for the future capital of this Cheyenne and Arapaho Indian reservation. The Indians from the start respected this kind hearted old man, urged that the agency be named in his honor, and the place was always known as the Darlington Agency. Although the principal modern settlements have drifted away from this spot, what remains yet bears the name of "Darlington."

A circumstance that well illustrates the mental capacity and childlike simplicity of the Indians over whom Brinton Darlington was called to rule, and which shows the care that the agent must use in dealing with the ideas and opinions of his wards, happened in the early years of the Darlington Agency. Brinton Darlington had, before coming to the Indian Territory, lost his teeth, and wore a plate. The Indians, in sizing up and prying into every detail of affairs, discovered this fact, and looked with wonder on the agent who was able to remove and replace his teeth at will. That was not all; he would often do this for their amusement. After the death of Brinton Darlington, John D. Miles, another Quaker, who had served as agent for the Kickapoo Indians in Kansas, was appointed to take his place. By a queer coincidence, Miles also had lost his teeth and wore a plate. That condition was quite a problem for these simple minded people to fathom, but in doing so they arrived at the conclusion that the ability to remove and replace the teeth at will was a condition that must exist before a man could qualify as agent for them. They let the matter rest with that solution. From that time on, it was adopted as part of the sign language of these Indians that a motion as if something was being removed from the mouth indicated the agent removing his teeth, and in the sign language meant "agent."

Brinton Darlington was married twice. He had two children born of the first marriage. The oldest was William Darlington, who accompanied his father to the Darlington Agency, and who rendered valuable services in assisting him in his cares and duties there. Bill Darlington, as he was generally known, was never married. His service as organizer and commander of the Indian Police was well known throughout the Territory and the West. He organized and had charge of the Indian Police at Fort Reno, this being the first organization of that kind in the Indian Territory, and among the first in the United States. These Indian Police were well-trained and equipped, and rendered valuable services in future years to the policing, patroling, and keeping law and order in the country. Bill Darlington continued to live at the Agency and at Fort Reno until the country was opened for settlement. The other child born of his first marriage was a daughter by the name of Anna, who married a Quaker minister named Hoag.

Brinton Darlington and a man by the name of Peter Collins were associated together in the mercantile business at Muscatine, Iowa, and after the death of his first wife, Darlington married a sister of Peter Collins' wife. Of this marriage one child was born, a daughter, who was named Sallie. Sallie Darlington married J. A. Covington at the Darlington Agency in January, 1872. Covington was generally known as Amick Covington, but was better known throughout southern Kansas and the Indian Territory as Captain Covington. This name was applied to him for the reason that he accompanied and guided long strings of wagon trains from the Agency to the

Capt. J. A. Covington, from original photograph owned by the
author taken in 1882.

railway connection at Wichita and later to Caldwell, Kansas, after the line of the Atchison, Topeka, and Santa Fe Railway extended to that point in 1880.

Covington had been a soldier in the Federal Army during the Civil War, and had a great deal of ability in organizing and handling bodies of men. His success in conducting the Indians on these trips was truly remarkable. The writer can remember him well on these occasions. Amick Covington was the first agency clerk at Darlington Agency; he, together with all the other persons in charge at the agency, grew to be proficient in their dealings with the Indians, and in their ability to converse with them in the sign language and in the Indian dialect. It was Amick Covington, together with his wife, Sallie, baby daughter, Katie, and the remaining members of their party who found the burned and charred remains of Pat Hennessey on their journey out of the Indian country in July, 1874.

It has been observed in the prior article in reference to Ben F. Williams that his father, Dearman Williams, a Quaker doctor, left Salem, Ohio, and with his eight children, after the death of his wife, made his way to Muscatine, Iowa, and joined his Quaker brethren at that place. Dr. Dearman Williams had four boys, all strong, intelligent, able, ambitious, and trustworthy to the highest degree. The three brothers who had been during the Civil War engaged in the Federal Army had at the time that Brinton Darlington departed to take charge of the Cheyenne and Arapaho Indian Agency lately returned from that service. The eldest of these brothers, being the one who had remained at home, was a mechanic of high standing.

It was necessary that Brinton Darlington obtain a person of such capabilities to teach the Indians under his charge the art of caring for, repairing, and looking after generally the property with which they must deal in changing their mode of life to the white man's ways. In selecting such a person and all the other employees of the Agency, it was the purpose of the Agent to procure persons allied to him in the Quaker faith, and thus surround the Indians with their influence. In doing this Darlington selected for this position John F. Williams. In this, as well as all of the selections made by Brinton Darlington, he made no mistake. John F. Williams built a home at Darlington Agency, made himself as comfortable as possible among these wild children of the plains, and became one of the most proficient men in all the country in dealing with these savage associates. They trusted him; he could converse most fluently with them in the sign language, and grew to be entirely at home among these wild men of the prairies. He issued to them their beeves on foot, and sought to comply with their every wish as far as possible.

Brinton Darlington also sent for Ben F. Williams, and had him appointed as United States Marshal, with the result as heretofore seen. He sent for Edwin F. Williams, another brother, and had him bring, equip, and operate a saw mill. He cut and prepared lumber for the use of the Indians and the white persons in charge in building their homes. Edwin F. Williams was a mechanic of the highest ability, and made a great success of this work. He was the youngest of the Williams boys, and although he had served for a number of years in the Federal Army, was only about twenty-three years of age. After remaining for several years at the Darlington Agency, he entered school and went through college, gained a thorough education as a mechanical engineer, and invented the friction clutch for a safety device on mine hoists. This hoist was displayed at the Centennial Exposition at Philadelphia in 1876. He later gained much credit in the improvements made by him in compound engines of the vertical type.

Ralph P. Collins, former owner of the Red Fork Ranch.

There were other persons who came to the Indian Territory on account of the selection and installation of Brinton Darlington at the agency, some of whom were not Quakers. It has been seen that Brinton Darlington at the time of his appointment as agent was in partnership with his brother-in-law, Peter Collins. Peter Collins had a grandson, who was a bright, intelligent, trustworthy, and ambitious young man, and who was just out of school. This was Ralph P. Collins. He, seeking adventure in the West, accepted employment at the Darlington Agency. He first did general work there in helping care for the stock and like services. Four of the children of the Peter Collins family had married four of the children of the Williams family, which included John F. Williams. Thus, Ralph Collins was the nephew of John Williams. John F. Williams had two sons, Fred and Albion. These boys and Ralph Collins were double cousins. Ralph P. Collins and Fred Williams conceived the idea of buying, improving, and equipping the Red Fork Ranch, an important post on the Chisholm Trail, some thirty-five miles north of the Darlington Agency, it being located at the north side of the Cimarron River at the junction of the cattle trail and traders' trail, where the city of Dover now stands. This they did in 1881. They operated this ranch under the name of Williams and Company.

Shortly after the taking over of this ranch Fred Williams was stricken with typhoid fever, and removed to Darlington Agency, near Fort Reno, for medical care and treatment, but soon died, and was laid to rest by the side of Brinton Darlington in the cemetery north of Darlington Agency. In the death of Fred Williams a valuable asset for the betterment of the Indians was lost. Fred had spent a number of years with these Indians, and was loved and respected by them. They mourned his loss as much as they would the most loved member of their tribe. Ralph Collins continued to operate the Red Fork Ranch

Fred Williams, son of John F. Williams, one of the former owners of the Red Fork Ranch.

until 1885. He, at this time, had been many years with the Indians, and was far too valuable a man to spend his time in handling cattle and in the operation of a ranch along a cattle trail.

He had grown proficient in the dealings with these wards of the Government, and his services were sought to assist in handling the many Indian tribes under its care. The life of Ralph Collins has been spent in this work. He has held positions as agent of most of the important Indians tribes of the West, including the Osages of Oklahoma and the desert tribes of the West. The writer remembers Ralph Collins well while he operated the old Red Fork Ranch. The picture of him set out herein was taken during that time, and looks just as he did in those days. During the time that Ralph was at Red Fork Ranch in 1882 his younger brother Hubert visited him there.

Hubert, at that time, was a small lad, who afterward became a consulting engineer of outstanding ability, writing a number of books on building codes and kindred topics. He lived at Utica, New York, and the writer and Hubert wrote to each other at intervals for several years. Hubert and the writer were about the same age, and had met as boys at the old Red Fork Ranch. Hubert in 1928 wrote a book founded on his experience at Darlington Agency and the Red Fork Ranch in the early eighties. This book is entitled "Warpath and Cattle Trails." He died at Utica on October 31, 1932. The last letter received from him by the writer is dated May 3, 1932, and closes with the following statement:

"Good luck to you old pal, if we do not meet again on this earth, bear in mind, I am glad we got together when we did. Ralph P. (Collins) is up at Spanish Peaks building log-houses on his holdings for the purpose of ranging his grand-children."

Hubert Collins as a small boy, from photograph taken before he came to the Red Fork Ranch.

Hubert Collins, taken in later life.

Hubert had long contemplated writing a history of the Darlington Agency, including that of the Darlington, Williams, and Collins families, but he had been an invalid for some time before his death, and had not been able to write the same. Knowing that the writer was to some extent familiar with the facts, even though his knowledge was meager as compared with that of his own, he requested him to, at some time, record these facts as best he could. At the time the above letter was written Hubert was expecting to die at any time, hence the affectionate farewell extended to the writer. This farewell is characteristic of men who had met and been upon the frontier. It seems that among these men there grew up a friendship that can be formed in no other surroundings, and can only be severed by death.

In 1884 Ralph Collins was appointed as cattle commissioner for the Cheyenne and Arapaho Indians. This took him away from Red Fork Ranch a considerable part of the time. He purchased cattle along the trail wherever available, and had them driven to the Agency for the use of the Indians. There were two sisters teaching at the Cheyenne School at Caddo Springs by the name of Amelia and Elizabeth Kable. A romance sprang up between Ralph Collins and Amelia Kable, they were married, and soon left the Indian Territory and moved to Colorado. Here he located and established a ranch near Spanish Peaks in southern Colorado. While he made this his home, he continued to fill positions among the Indian tribes.

At one time he was school superintendent over the Hopi Indians of Arizona. He was also sent to the Sioux School at Rapid City, South Dakota. He established his home at Rocky Ford, Colorado, where he still lives. He has grown old in the service of his country, and in the service for the betterment of the Indians. The writer receives a letter from him occasionally.

He lives in the West, which he loves, in his declining years, surrounded by his grandchildren and those friends and relatives whose association he enjoys. Like all other men who once roamed the primitive West and old frontier, he loves to live those days over again in memory.

The life and surroundings in which he was thrown on the frontier were a departure from the former mode of living and association to which Brinton had been accustomed. He was too old to adapt himself to these conditions, and his health soon began to fail. He had taken and was holding his position for the advancement and benefit of the Indians, and considered and accepted the same as being delivered to him by the hand of Divine Providence for the delivery to the inhabitants of this earth the blessings that it was decreed he should help them receive. His purpose was an unselfish one, and was cherished by him until death. Even when the state of his health became critical he steadfastly refused to abandon the cause in which he had enlisted. He died, as heretofore stated, in 1872, less than three years after he had entered into the undertaking for which he finally gave up his life. The number of his days was evidently much shortened by his surroundings and habits of life on the frontier, and by the care and devotion he gave to his office.

Two of the old extensive and spacious store buildings where the supplies for the Cheyenne and Arapaho Indians were stored in the active days of the Old Darlington Agency are now used as storehouses for adjacent farmers. Aside from these and one old residence building none of the former structures or landmarks remain. The old general store is gone from the top of the bank on the east side of the Trader's Trail, where it turned to the south to cross the North Canadian River. The house of John Williams, with its fruit trees and picket fence around the same, on the west side and across the trail from the old store, no longer remains with its inquisitive Indians prowling around it at will. The old Trader's Trail no longer winds down in its southward course from Caddo Springs, no more over to the eastward from the Agency does the dust rise in clouds as it marks the course of the winding herds as they crowd up the old Chisholm Cattle Trail.

Instead of these surroundings, now the extensive buildings at Fort Reno are seen some two miles distant to the south, large trees now cover the ground on the site of the old Darlington Agency, and a large grove is found around the old Cheyenne School at Caddo Springs, where the smoke from the engine trails back as a long string of cars and engine pass. The old Arapaho school building at the Agency has disappeared, and the buildings of the prosperous city of El Reno rise in bold relief to the southeast, only a few miles away. From this city a long ribbon of cement extends out in each direction as far as can be seen, through it runs the paved surface of Government Highway 81, marking the general course of the old Chisholm Cattle Trail extending north and south, and over this route now rush extensive, handsome, and luxurious motor cars and busses, the cars traveling at the rate of sixty miles per hour. The Indians are now scattered over the surrounding country, and live on and cultivate their farms, using modern machinery and appliances the same as their white neighbors. The activities of the old Agency are buried beneath a half century of progress and time.

The writer recently visited the old Agency, and viewed the location familiar to him fifty years ago. He also visited the old cemetery on the hill, almost two miles away, toward Caddo Springs. Here, surrounded by graves of Indians, who were his wards, rest the mortal remains of Brinton Darlington. A modern granite monument tells the visitor that such is the last resting place of the old Quaker Agent. Only a few yards

Monument at the grave of Brinton Darlington in Darlington Cemetery, as it appears from photograph recently taken.

away is the broken and age worn marble stone marking the grave of Fred Williams. On this visit all the places associated with the old Agency appeared lonesome, desolate, and dreary. This was the contrast from the activity that the writer had known before. As he looked upon these scenes, he felt that he should attempt to reverse the hands of time and turn back through the many intervening years to look once more upon the activity and scenes of his boyhood around the old Agency.

As he stood in the old cemetery on the hill, he saw the path, plainly visible, where visitors had passed in solemn review by the grave of Brinton Darlington. Here doubtless pass Indians, many of whom are highly educated and genteel, none of whom ever saw the old Quaker Agent; but, as they pass the marker on his grave, they stop and gaze in awe and admiration. They all know the history, character, and life of the man whose remains lie there at rest. One thing can be said of Brinton Darlington that can be said of few men, and that is that no man of any race or nationality ever looked upon his grave with other than a feeling of pride, friendship, and admiration. He died without an enemy in the entire world.

CHAPTER XI.

THE DARLINGTON AGENCY

After the treaty of Medicine Lodge, made in 1867, two extensive Indian reservations in Oklahoma were laid out and established. One of these was the Kiowa and Comanche, lying west of the 98th Meridian and south of the Cheyenne and Arapaho. To this reservation was also subsequently brought some of the Apache tribe. The other was the Cheyenne and Arapaho, which was assigned by executive order to these tribes in 1869, and soon thereafter Brinton Darlington was appointed and sent as Agent for these Indians, as heretofore stated. This reservation embraced the following territory: All that country lying south of the Cherokee Outlet, west of the 98th Meridian, north of the Washita and South Canadian Rivers, and extended west to the Panhandle of Texas. This comprised 4,297,771 acres.

When the grass was growing green over the hills and valleys of this country, in the spring of 1870, there could be seen by persons traveling down the old Trader's portion of the Chisholm Trail an extensive outfit, consisting of Indians on horseback, a detachment of cavalry, and an army ambulance with a number of white occupants. These travelers approached the ford on the North Canadian River, where the Trader's Trail crossed the same, coming from the west on the south side of the river. They crossed the ford to the north side, where they halted. The river was a beautiful clear stream with a white sandy bottom. The Indians gazed and pointed to the north across a broad, level, fertile bottom, extending about two miles, with a background of hills skirted with scattering blackjack trees.

Residence of John F. Williams at the Darlington Agency. Note the Indians in the foreground.

The Chisholm Trail in approaching this river from the north, on nearing the same, turned westward up the river for a short distance until it reached a suitable location to cross. It was to the north of this crossing that these travelers halted. After some deliberation they dismounted and made camp. This was the body accompanying Brinton Darlington on his mission ordered by the Government to locate at some point near the eastern portion of the reservation a Cheyenne and Arapaho Agency. The point selected was almost at the extreme eastern boundary of the reservation. At this place the 98th Meridian is almost two miles west of the range line between ranges seven and eight, which marks the western boundary of the reserved lands to the east, now known as Old Oklahoma or the original Oklahoma lands. This was the point where the traders' portion of the Chisholm Trail always crossed the North Canadian River. This was also the future location of the Darlington Agency, which was to play so important a part in the history of the Indian Territory.

Brinton Darlington had been with these Indians only since the preceding fall, but they had learned to love him as much as these wild warriors of the plains could love anyone. At the solicitation of the Indians this agency was named Darlington, in honor of the Quaker agent. This spot would seem to be a beautiful and desirable location, but it appears the Commissioner of Indian affairs did not take kindly to it. In a report made by him a few years after the location we find the following:

"The agency is located on the east side of the Cheyenne and Arapaho Reservation within two and a half miles of Oklahoma, on the north side of the North Canadian River, and in the first bottom which reaches back to the high land, some two miles away. For miles from this point the banks of the stream are denuded of timber, and there are only such trees growing around the agency as have been planted in the last few years.

The situation is anything but good, especially when there are so many desirable spots so close at hand. During the rainy season pools of water stand all over this rich bottom land, and with the dirt about the camps it would be a stretch of imagination to call it healthy. The climate here is mild, so much so that any one coming from the extreme north would likely call it summer the year round. The nights are always cool and comfortable. In the early spring the prairies and canyons are covered with beds of gorgeous flowers, but the varieties are not so great as are seen in the eastern part of the Territory."

Store Houses at the Darlington Agency, west of the Trail. In these buildings were stored extensive supplies for the use of the Cheyenne and Arapaho Indians.

It was true that the land lying to the north of the agency was so level that the water did stand there in places, principally in buffalo wallows, after a rain, but this was no great inconvenience, and while there were no trees along the river at that point at that time, they soon grew around the agency. Down this river coursed an abundant supply of pure, clear water. Here grew to be the most important settlement on the Chisholm Trail in Oklahoma. Here large store buildings were erected. Houses were built and supplies freighted down the trail from the terminus of the railway. A saw mill was installed, logs cut and hauled from distant points to the same, and converted into lumber. The Indians looked on in wonder as a progressive settlement grew up at the agency.

To the travelers on the Chisholm Trail the agency, with its throngs of Indians around the same, presented a picturesque appearance. Long strings of freight wagons, drawn by many spans of mules attached to the same, brought in the freight and supplies. Here the store or commissary building was built on the south side of the trail. John Williams' house, surrounded with a picket fence and many fruit trees, stood across the trail to the northwest. Here was also built the Arapaho School, while the Cheyenne School was erected at Caddo Springs, some two and one-half miles to the north and east. To the south across the river, and about two miles distant, in 1875 Fort Reno was established. This fort was located just after the Indian outbreak in 1874, for the purpose of having available soldiers present in case of any future troubles with the Indians.

At the time of the location of the Darlington Agency, for many years prior thereto and many years thereafter, the Indian question was one of the greatest confronting the National Government. President Grant had been upon the frontier and had made a study of this question. He had concluded that the trouble with the Indians was largely due to the mistreatment of them by the agents in charge at the various points. As heretofore stated, he advanced and carried out the idea of placing Quakers as agents over these Indians, and they were in turn, as far as possible, to surround themselves by other Quakers, and thus place the Indians under complete Quaker control. This policy of the Natinal Administration was in a measure successful, but in 1874 the same fell sufficiently short that it would have produced a fatal result had not military assistance been procured in time.

Cheyenne Camp west of the store houses at Darlington Agency, as it appeared in the early days of the Agency.—Courtesy of the Oklahoma State Historical Society.

Brinton Darlington was a good man, and held the confidence of these Indians as long as he lived. When he died and was buried in the agency cemetery, in 1872, it was said that many of these hardened warriors of the plains, who had fought every step of the advance of the white man, stood by his casket, and many were the tears that coursed down their weather beaten cheeks.

While it was true, as has been stated, that the placing of the Quakers in charge of the Indians was a very wise thing as a whole, yet in doing so the administration did not realize the difference which existed as to the conditions at that time as compared with the conditions at the time of the settlement of the Quakers in Pennsylvania. At the time of the dealings of the Quakers of the East with the Indians, it was then only a question of good fellowship and association between them and the establishment of a feeling of brotherly love. At the time of the location of the Darlington Agency, however, it was the duty of the Quakers to so install this friendship as of old with the Indians, and thus hold them in check. The white intruders from the East were pouring in upon the Indian country, slaughtering their buffalo, and committing other depredations with impunity. Such was the Indian view of the matter in 1874, at the time of the outbreak and uprising at that time. These Indians were the fiery warriors of the plains, who had never known any master or any restraint. They boasted that they had never been whipped in battle and never would be.

At that time the buffalo were fast disappearing from the prairies. The Indians, not knowing any other available method of gaining subsistence, viewed a state of want and starvation ahead of them, and saw themselves being fast swallowed up by a superior race which was crowding in upon and crushing them. None of us, had we been in their place, would have viewed the matter any differently. Many of the old warriors among them, although their hearts were with the idea of rebellion and they felt like starting on the war path, were wise enough to see the futility of such a step, and refused to join in the movement. Little Robe and Stone Calf were the two leading chiefs of the Cheyennes. Little Robe was perhaps the greatest chief the Cheyennes ever had. While he deplored the position of the Indians and was desirous of taking the best course possible, yet it is questionable whether he really desired to enter into active resistance. In any event, he saw the impossibility of gaining anything by it, whether he really desired to avoid hostility or not. He advocated peace and opposed any active outbreak. This attitude he maintained throughout the entire trouble, and his people saw the wisdom of his position in after years.

On the other hand, Stone Calf yielded to the clamor of the less conservative element, and withdrew with a portion of the Cheyenne tribe onto the plains, engaged in the battle of Adobe Walls in June, 1874, and was compelled to return humiliated and deserted by the larger part of his followers. Thus, just prior to the time of the killing of Pat Hennessey, in July 1874, Major Miles, another Quaker, who had succeeded Brinton Darlington as agent, observing the situation and attitude of the Indians, and seeing that he was not able to any longer hold them in submission, realized that it was incumbent upon him to procure military assistance and protection. Agent Miles was a man of ability and sound judgment, and he saw the futility and inevitable fatality of longer attempting to restrain the Indians without assistance. On the fourth day of July, 1874, he took with him the persons he desired to remove to the settlements for safety, and with an escort started up the Chisholm Trail to Kansas; his ultimate destination being Fort Leavenworth, and his object being to obtain military

John D. Miles, Quaker Agent at Darlington Agency.

assistance and protection. On the second day of their journey they found the dead and charred body of Pat Hennessey.

Agent Miles passed through Wichita, Kansas, on the 7th day of July, 1874, and proceeded on to Fort Leavenworth. Hearing of the action of Agent Miles a body of Quakers at Lawrence, Kansas, were so shocked by the course he had taken that they called a mass meeting of Quakers, who passed a resolution of censure denouncing the agent and asking for his removal for incompetency. This resolution was forwarded by them to the President at Washington. The Wichita Eagle, then a weekly paper in its infancy at Wichita, published a severe denouncement of these Quakers and their resolution, using as caustic language toward them as they had used against the agent. The following is a portion of the article so published in the Eagle on July 16, 1874:

"These broad-brimmed, swallow-tailed worthies rolled their pious eyes and resoluted Friend Miles out of office because he asked for troops to save his hair. —Do these 'thee' and 'thou' dapper galoots imagine they can resolute a man out of office and into silence who is being made bald by a scalping knife? —Do these wall-eyed shad-bellies expect to sit upon their cushioned seats afar off in safety and by their pious twaddle about Indian schools and civil order silence the shrieks of the mother whose child has been ruthlessly torn from her arms by top-knotted painted red Devils, and its brains dashed out against the nearest stone? Or squelch Major Miles for asking for protection for himself and the defenseless?"

Darlington Agency was the center and seat of this Cheyenne uprising in 1874, so much so that the entire matter is a necessary part of the history of the agency. In order to fully understand the situation and place the blame for this trouble where it belongs, it is necessary to observe the situation in more detail.

The treaty of Medicine Lodge had been made in 1867, and one of the important provisions of that treaty was that the hunting grounds of the plains Indians should be protected by the Government from hunters on the frontier, and thus the buffalo saved from extermination. All the force that the agent at Darlington had was two marshals, both of whom had more than they could do without this work. These marshals spent all the time possible attempting to enforce this provision. They were the only ones who did. Here was the vast territory embraced in this reservation, with buffalo hunters crowding in upon it from all sides, killing buffalo for their hides and for the mere sake of killing. It was a pitiful sight to see two men trying to handle this situation. Apparently no assistance was rendered them by the soldiers. If so, it was very little. Thus this provision was not enforced at any time.

The buffalo were fast being exterminated. These beasts were just as much the food supply of these Indians as the extensive wheat fields and other crops are for the present inhabitants of the West. It was considered by the Indians just as much an intrusion to destroy their hunting grounds, as it would be for an invading force to lay waste our fields. The white hide hunters and sportsmen crowding into the West, coming even from the countries of Europe, were slaughtering the buffalo without restraint. The hide hunters killed them simply for their hides, leaving the carcasses on the prairies to decay, and after transporting the hides to the markets received only a small pittance for them, while the sportsmen coming from the eastern portion of the United States and from Europe slaughtered these animals by the thousands simply for the thrill of seeing them fall, and to observe the dying struggles of these monarchs of the plains. These Indians, being held in restraint, were compelled to witness all these things which were done in violation of their treaty, and done with impunity before their very eyes.

It is true, that they had a different mode of living than our own. This mode of life, which they had followed until it had become a part of their very existence, was being crowded out by force and by the intrusion of a superior race. Such has been the course of the world, both before and since we have had recorded history. This was evidently the course of the predominating races, as they crowded back and forth in this country in prehistoric times. Such was the history of the races in Europe, when Caesar led his tried legions through the hostile ranks of Gaul, laying waste their fields. Such was the case when Attila the Hun, known as the "Scourge of God," with the proud boast that the grass never grew where his horse's hoofs had trod, swept down from his home in the North, even to the gates of Rome. The history of all time tells us that in no such case was it the custom that the weaker race submit without resistance. Neither could it have been expected in this case. The writer does not mention this to justify any act of violence by the Indians, but to show that there were two sides to this controversy.

At the time that Major Miles went to Fort Leavenworth for assistance, the battle of Adobe Walls had been fought in the preceding month, and the dead and charred body of Pat Hennessey had been found by the side of the trail as he progressed on his journey. Stone Calf was then on the plains, on the war path, with white captives in his possession, was apt to return at any time with his bloodthirsty followers, and massacre the entire white population at the Agency. It is true that they bore the greatest respect for the Quaker agent and his assistants, and whether these people would have been molested by the Indians is problematical, but it was a matter on the determination of which depended their lives. They could not have been expected to have taken the chance.

The remaining portion of the Cheyennes had only been held in check by the influence of Little Robe, and the Arapaho by the diligence and efforts of Ben Williams and others. If they did break it might be a repetition of the massacre of Waililalpui at Fort Whitman, located two hundred and fifty miles up the river from Fort Vancouver, where on the 29th day of November, 1847, Dr. Marcus Whitman, the beloved missionary and teacher among the Indians of Oregon, was, together with his good wife and assistants, massacred at the instigation of the very Indians who adored all of them, the Cause Indians. It will be borne in mind that these Indians with all their barbarity could not work themselves up to a sufficient frenzy to kill these good people who had been their friends and done so much for them, but instead they induced a fanatical, ignorant, half-breed degenerate Canadian Indian to commit the act by inducing him to use what they termed the "charmed tomahawk."

During the existence of the Darlington Agency the following agents were in charge for the following period of time: Brinton Darlington, 1869-1872;   John D. Miles, 1872-1884; Daniel Dyer, April 1, 1884-Aug. 14, 1885; J. M. Lee, U. S. A., August 15, 1885-Sept. 15, 1886; Gilbert D. Williams, Sept. 16, 1886-April 30, 1889. The different agents of the Kiowa and Comanche reservation, which joined the Cheyenne and Arapaho on the south, and was also crossed by the Trader's Trail, and was just west of the Chisholm Cattle Trail, were as follows: Lawrie Tatum, July 1, 1869-1873; James M. Haworth, April 1, 1873-1878; P. B. Hunt, April 1, 1878-Sept. 1, 1878. The agency at this time was consolidated with the Wichita and moved from its former headquarters at Anadarko to Fort Sill.

After the establishment of the Darlington Agency it grew in importance year after year until it became a bustling little hamlet. All the travelers over the Chisholm Trail, including the heavy wagons of freight drawn by several spans of plodding oxen or powerful mules, together with all other conveyances journeying up or down the trail, passed on the main thoroughfare along the main street of this busy little village. After Fort Reno was established in 1875 the Agency still advanced in importance. Soldiers from the fort visited it in large numbers. They were only two miles or thereabouts apart. Throngs of the Indians of both tribes congregated around the store building and other places. Their inquisitiveness was without limit. Their familiarity was a nuisance around the homes of the employees. It was the custom of the Indians to eat whenever they were hungry and had anything to eat. They were always hungry, but did not always have all they desired to eat. If any of them were around one of the homes of the employees and saw the family start to eat it was the Indians' business to walk in and join them, whether invited or not. It was impossible for the employees to ask them constantly to eat with them, but a little point like that did not bother the Indians. They knew no better. This proposition was very annoying to the employees around the agency.

A little circumstance that happened at the Agency well illustrates the childlike ideas and simplicity of the Indians with whom the parties in charge dealt.

After Fort Reno was established the post had a guard house, where soldiers violating the rules of military discipline were incarcerated. The Indians looked upon the restraint in custody in this guard house as a great mark of degradation. Hogs had been distributed among the Indians, and they had raised a considerable number of them. They were also being taught to raise gardens and were doing well with them, but hogs, when permitted to roam at will, and gardens did not prosper well together. A pen was built near the store building, where those trespassing rooters were restrained. An Indian missed his hogs, and forthwith betook himself to the pound, where he found them. After sympathizing with his hogs in their disgrace the Indian, who could speak considerable English, proceeded to Amick Covington, the agency clerk, who had charge of the matter, stating: "What fer you put my hogs in the guard house, they done nothing." Covington informed the owner that it was necessary on account of the hogs destroying the gardens, to keep them penned. In answer the Indian informed him that it was the nature of these hogs to eat garden, they did not intend to do wrong, but, regardless of these innocent motives, his poor hogs had been locked up in the guard house, and thereby disgraced in such a manner that they could never outlive the humiliation.

There was for some time, the writer is unable to give the exact period, a paper published at the agency. The name of this paper was "The Cheyenne Transporter." It was edited by Lafe Merritt and George Maffet. George Maffet afterward married Elizabeth Kable, who was a teacher in the Cheyenne School, and a sister to Ralph Collins' wife.

Regardless of all the criticism of the Commissioner of Indian affairs, the writer knows that the old Darlington Agency was a beautiful spot and a beautiful place during most of the season of the year. It is true that the buffalo wallows in the level bottom to the north of the agency became full of water, but that really did not hurt anything; it soon soaked into the loose soil. The greatest difficulty considered by most persons was the mosquitoes during parts of the summer season. It is strange that the Commissioner did not mention that fact. He evidently was not there when these little pests were active, or he would have done so. During rainy portions of the season, when anyone would go through the grass to get his horses, these little winged songsters would rise up in swarms and clouds. One Irishman, a soldier from the fort, expressed it this way: he said if he had a stick he could write his name in them. They were not only numerous, but they were also large as mosquitos go, and vicious. At night one would be compelled, even though it was very warm, to cover his face with a tarpaulin, and they would even bite through this covering, and their singing was loud, monotonous, and unending.

To the person who knew Darlington Agency in the days of its activity and prosperity, it is now sad to visit the place. It reminds such a one of a deserted village or an ancient ruin. As those familiar with the old Agency stand on the bank of the river, it requires no great amount of imagination to see the blanketed inquisitive Indians strolling around investigating everything. The Cheyenne School at Caddo Springs, now Concho, some two miles north and east of the old Agency, still stands, the Indian children congregate on the bank near the railway, and watch the trains stop and take on or put off passengers. These passengers are principally children attending the school. The present frequenters of, and visitors to, the old Agency and its associated places see things as they appear today. The ones who knew it in the past can stand and meditate for hours and see the scenes of fifty years ago pass before their vision in a great and revived panorama, until they arouse themselves to realize that it is only a memory, a vision, that the parties they have been gazing upon, and reviewing memories of, have long since passed from the scenes of their earthly activity. Some of them rest in the cemetery on the hill, others of them have wandered far away, and lie buried in strange lands. But few of them still survive, and soon none will remain who saw this primitive western civilization, the central location of the taming of the Wild Cheyenne.

CHAPTER XII.

INDIAN TRIBES FAMILIAR TO THE TRAIL

The combined Cattle and Trader's Trail on the Chisholm Trail crossed squarely over the Cherokee Outlet from the point where it entered at Caldwell, Kansas, to where it passed into Old Oklahoma at Buffalo Springs. Yet the Cherokee Indians never used this Outlet or trail. In all the years that the writer traveled over this country he never saw a Cherokee Indian on either the outlet or trail, unless he belonged to the Indian Police. For that reason the travelers on the Chisholm Trail did not come in contact with the Cherokee Indians.

Going down the trail from Kansas the first Indians met were those at Darlington Agency. Here were found the Cheyenne and Arapaho. During the time that the writer knew the agency, there were in the combined tribes approximately 3,500 Indians on this reservation. Of this number about two-thirds were Cheyennes and one-third Arapahos. Around Cantonment, some forty miles up the North Canadian River from the agency, there was a large settlement of Arapaho. Thus, most of the Indians with whom the traveler came in contact were Cheyennes. They were what was known as the Southern Cheyennes.

The Cheyenne as a tribe were really northern Indians, belonging to the Algonquin or Dakota stock. At one time this entire band was settled in Wyoming. They were a nomadic race of people, fierce, resentful, impetuous, arrogant, and warlike. From 1861 to 1869, they were almost constantly at war with the United States Government and the settlers on the frontier. They stood with hostile ranks guarding the Western Plains against invasion and the extermination of the buffalo. In all of this they were compelled to give way before the relentless advance of the frontier settlements.

While this strife was progressing the Cheyenne tribe divided, the larger portion of them going onto the plains east of the Rocky Mountains. There, in western Kansas and Colorado, they took their last stand, and their depredations are a part of the history of this country up to 1869. At this time, they were driven south into the Indian Territory. There, in charge of the Quaker Agent, Brinton Darlington, together with the Arapahos, they were compelled to settle down on their reservation. From the report of the Commissioner of Indian Affairs some years later, it seems the Government was not very well impressed with this tribe. In his report we find the following:

"The Cheyennes are said to be the smarter race of the two, (referring to the Cheyennes and Arapaho). That they are at present further from civilization I am positive, and that they are insolent, headstrong, domineering, and hard to restrain cannot be questioned. They have never been whipped, and

Group of Cheyenne and Arapaho Indians, taken at Darlington Agency. Second from left in front row is Little Whirlwind, and third from left in front row is Little Big Jake, each sub-chiefs.

boast that they could wipe us out at any time, a matter that should be speedily called to the attention of the Government * * *."[1]

It is the opinion of the writer that the statement made in the foregoing report, and also the statements hereafter set out, do not apply to all the Cheyenne tribe, but it certainly does apply with the utmost aptitude to an element which existed among these Indians. Especially did it exist, in all its force and viciousness, during the time of the removal of the cattle from this country in 1884 and 1885. The remark has heretofore been made herein, and also the copy from the report set out, both showing the overbearing disposition and insolent demeanor of these Indians during that period. We will say here that it is impossible to describe it. A description is only words, and does not portray it. These Indians were trained in the sign language, which was largely expression and force of expression, and it is impossible to translate all this into words. It was well expressed by a party who came in contact with them. He said at first he was scared and was afraid they would kill him, but after they intimidated him for a time he was scared for fear they would not kill him and get him out of his misery. Continuing in this same report we find the following:

"Men that can fight as these have can work, and why a few score of young bucks should be allowed to interrupt public travel, levy tax on herds and freighters, intimidate, browbeat, and threaten the lives of people quietly passing through the country, compel the attendance of their own people upon the occasion of medicine making, whether they believe in it or not, under penalty of having their tents cut up, their dogs, horses, cattle, chickens, etc. killed, and create a disturbance at will, is more than a law-abiding citizen can understand. The relations of these Indians to the Government have never been cor-

---

[1] Report of Commissioner of Indian Affairs, 1884, Pages 72-74. Readings in Oklahoma History, Page 395.

dial. Nor is it strange at all when we consider that they have never been made to respect its authority. They are proud of their own tribe and despise the Arapahos. Part of their dislike comes no doubt from the fact that the Arapahos have stood by the Government when they were hostile. Cheyenne women sometimes marry Arapahos, but I am told the men never do so."[2]

The Kiowa and Comanche reservation lay just south of the Cheyenne and Arapaho, and both of these reservations were bounded on the east by the 98th Meridian. This meridian ran just east of Fort Reno. While the Trader's portion of the Chisholm Trail extended across both of these reservations, it will be observed that the Chisholm Cattle Trail passed a short distance to the east of the 98th Meridian. In the early drives it was much farther to the east. There was a reason for this, which may be understood from the portion of the report of the Commissioner of Indian Affairs above set out. That reason was to keep away from and avoid contact with the Indians of these reservations. They were continuously attempting to collect toll from persons crossing their country. This was the designation of their demands, but in plain English it was blackmail.

The members of the Cheyenne tribe were individually the finest specimens of physical manhood of any tribe in the Western country. They were tall and erect, their average height was about six feet, and they were as straight as the proverbial arrow. They were commanding in appearance, and all of their actions and demeanor displayed the confidence and exalted ideas they bore for themselves. They were also the finest horsemen of all the plains Indians.

The northern branch of these Indians was settled on the Tongue River Agency in Montana. They were given a tract of land there of 371,200 acres, and in 1899 these Northern Chey-

---

[2] Report of Commissioner of Indian Affairs, Ibid. Readings in Oklahoma History, Page 397.

ennes numbered, according to the Government report, 1,349. We will say here that it has been a very difficult matter for the Government to get an exact enumeration of most Indian tribes, but these numbers given are approximately correct.

In the active days on the Santa Fe Trail there had been a station established, fortified, and well equipped, which was used as a stopping place on the trail, and was operated by the Bent Brothers. This was located in eastern Colorado, on the north side of the Arkansas River, being a short distance east of the present City of Las Animas. This was known as Bent's Fort, and was the greatest stopping point on the trail between West Port and Santa Fe. George Bent, one of the brothers, married the daughter of a Cheyenne chief. One of the sons, George Bent Jr., chose the ways of his mother's people, and before they were settled on their reservation in the Indian Territory, roamed the plains of western Kansas with this tribe of wild Cheyennes. When they were brought to Oklahoma this son, George Bent Jr., was with them and remained with them. In the life of the Cheyennes in western Kansas young Bent was feared more than the full blood Indians. His wife was shot and killed in a battle with the soldiers who were seeking to restrain these wild wanderers of the Plains. When she was shot she held in her arms a young son, who was also named George Bent. This young Indian was brought to Oklahoma with the Cheyenne tribe, and was placed in the Cheyenne School at Caddo Springs.

Amelia Kable, who afterward became Ralph Collins' wife, was teaching at Caddo Springs at that time; she took an interest in this young Indian, and encouraged him in his work. He grew to fine manhood and gained an excellent education. He attended school at Carlisle, Pennsylvania, Haskell Institute, Lawrence, Kansas, and a Quaker College at Wabash, Indiana. He has spent most of his life educating and working for the

George Bent, mixed blood Cheyenne.

betterment of the Indians. He grew to be an athlete of considerable note, and has taught in most of the leading Indian schools of the country. He is truly an educated man. The writer has seen several letters written by him, and he has always given Mrs. Collins the credit of causing him to change his mode of living and forsake the wild ways of his Indian ancestors.

It has been seen that the Commissioner of Indian Affairs did not place a very high standard on the character and integrity of the Cheyenne in general, and as will hereafter be seen he placed a much higher standard on that of the Arapaho. In the judgment of the writer, there were very great exceptions to the rule, as stated by the agent, in both of these tribes. As to the Arapahos these exceptions will be noted later. As to the Cheyennes we will say that there were many exceptions, among which was that of Little Robe. The writer is obliged to confess that after a full study and understanding of Little Robe his opinion of this Indian has undergone a radical change. Little Robe was one of the two leading chiefs of the southern Cheyennes. He was blamed by some of the cattlemen for a portion of their trouble growing out of their leases, which blame may have been well founded. If it was he had a right to his opinions. He may have considered that the leasing of this land was only a further encroachment of the white man. He was, however, in favor of it in the beginning, and may not have been to blame for any of the trouble at any time. Little Robe had been one of the principal war chiefs on the western plains. He was ingenious and intelligent. He was reserved and did not appear to be interested in new acquaintances or care about familiarity with strangers. The writer shared in the prejudice maintained by some of the cattlemen against Little Robe. This opinion, however, underwent a change after a full understanding.

Little Robe, greatest of all the Cheyenne chiefs.

The Quakers completely won the heart of Little Robe. It has been observed that he held his portion of the tribe in the insurrection and trouble of 1874. He formed a great attachment for John Williams, the agency mechanic and blacksmith, who was a tall, spare, bewhiskered, good-natured Quaker. Little Robe took him into complete fellowship, and most of the Indians did the same. In 1872 or 1873 the Cheyennes had their last tribal buffalo hunt. In that fall they went into the Panhandle on this hunt, and remained for three months.

John Williams' youngest son, Albion, was then eleven years of age, and Little Robe persuaded Williams to let him accompany them on this trip. John had sufficient faith in Little Robe to do so. On the hunt this boy was the only white person with the Indians. Albion, when he left, was decked out in a buckskin suit, which he wore on the trip both night and day. He traveled in it, slept in it, bathed in it, and rode in the sunshine and in the rain in it. It shrank until it was as tight as the hide, but the lad continued to wear it. When the Indians returned to the agency Albion could not be distinguished from the Indian children. He was their equal in dirt, grease, and all. When with difficulty they removed the buckskin suit they were surprised to find a white lad within. Albion Williams afterward studied medicine, and upon his graduation from medical school settled at Seattle, Washington, where he died some years ago.

It remains as a part of the history of the Cheyennes and the Darlington Agency, that years after the establishment of the agency the Government had a great number of wagons, harness for the horses, and a consignment of flour in one hundred pound sacks all shipped together to Wichita, Kansas, which was then the nearest station to the agency. J. A. Covington was the agency clerk at that time, and his duties seemed to require him to do anything necessary to be done among the Indians. Therefore, Covington was sent, as usual, with a large aggregation of Indians to procure and bring to the agency these wagons, harness, and flour. The wagons when shipped were not assembled, but were in pieces, loaded on flat cars, or in box cars. These Indians did not know one piece of a wagon from another. All the wagons they had ever seen had been drawn on the trail principally by ox teams. It shows the stupidity of the Government officials to expect to ship these articles and have the Indians assemble the wagons, place the harness on their ponies, hitch these ponies, which had never been harnessed, to the wagons, and drive them off down to the agency, almost two hundred miles away.

It is readily seen that the task of getting the wagons, harness, and flour to the agency was a full man-sized job for the agency clerk. The flour was to be freighted to the agency in these wagons, and apparently the Government officials expected these warriors of the plains to hitch their unbroken ponies to the wagon loads of flour, seat their squaws and papooses on the top of the same, crack their whips over their ponies, and drive serenely off to the agency. If this was their idea of what would happen, it is difficult to understand how they could arrive at such a conclusion.

When the Indians started to assemble the wagons, it was like trying to work out a puzzle to them. They, in some cases, placed the large wheels on the front of the wagon. In some cases they had the large wheels both on one side and the small ones on the other, or they had one small wheel in front and one behind on opposite sides. When they tried to place the harness on their ponies, they had more trouble. When a Cheyenne was seated on a horse's back he was at home, but handling a horse otherwise was to him a different proposition. The harness, which was made for eastern draft horses, was too large. When, with the aid of the clerk, they finally put the wagons together and got the harness on their ponies, they had another trouble to get them hitched to the wagons. Neither the Indians or the ponies knew anything about this business.

It is a notable fact that even in later years, when they were traveling on the trail, the Indians did not use check lines on their teams of ponies. They fastened the two ponies working abreast together in some way, an Indian would ride at the side of the team, and lead the pony nearest to him. When they finally got these ponies fastened or hitched to the wagon loads of flour and attempted to start for the agency, it was, perhaps, one of the greatest sights that Wichita ever witnessed. The Indians had no control over these teams of frantic ponies; could not guide them. They went wherever they pleased, and where they pleased was no place in particular. So, inasmuch as the Arkansas River passed on two sides of the City of Wich-

Group of Cheyenne and Arapaho Indians, with John F. Williams. At extreme right in front is Powder Face, an Arapaho, and at extreme right in back row is the wife of Powder Face. Second from the right in front row is John F. Williams.

ita, most of them wound up in the sand in the bed of the river. Captain Covington stated that it took them about an hour after they started to get all the wagons into the river, and then it took a week to get them out. They finally, by the perseverance of the agency clerk, got started down the trail, and eventually arrived at the agency, traveling in state with these new wagons.

Around the Darlington Agency were many chiefs, both Cheyenne and Arapaho. The Cheyenne chiefs outnumbered the Arapaho in about the same proportion as the Indians. The writer is not sure as to which tribe many of them belonged. Little Robe and Stone Calf were the two principal chiefs of the Cheyenne. Powder Face was a fine robust specimen of Indian manhood, an Arapaho. The writer can remember him well. There was White Shield, Little Whirlwind, Little Big Jake, all of whom, as the writer remembers, were Cheyennes. There were many others now forgotten. The writer knows but very little about Stone Calf. There is very little record of him to be found, except that he led the contingent of the Cheyennes in their rebellion of 1874. Little Robe died in the spring of 1885, west of Clinton, Oklahoma, on Big Creek, which empties into the Washita, and was buried at that place. The eldest son of Little Robe, Sitting Medicine, was killed by unknown parties in the fall of 1884. His dead body was found some distance east of Fort Supply.

From the report of the Commissioner of Indian Affairs we quote the following as to the Arapaho Indians:

"The Arapahos are generally quite tractable, good-natured, and inclined to be progressive; but like all Indians they lack adhesion and zeal, and have aggressive habits, and in the tribe there are some who are as bad as the worst Cheyennes; and while I have laid little of our troubles at their door I have done so because they are generally more inclined to the right, and if separated from the Cheyennes would, I think, do much better. Still, some of the depredations reported are traceable directly to them, and while such reports are in some cases exaggerated, allowing a reasonable margin for enlargement, there is much that I know to be true that needs speedy correction. The ordinary police work of a great Government like ours ought to be sufficiently well done to render such scenes as are of weekly occurrence impossible." [3]

As to the statement of the Commissioner showing the departure of many of the Arapahos from the straight and narrow path, the writer fully agrees. In fact the rebellious contingent of the Arapahos in 1884-5 was just as active as that of the Cheyennes. It has been noted that many of the Arapahos settled and lived around Cantonement, up the river from the Darlington Agency. We desire to quote further from the report of the Commissioner of Indian Affairs as to the Arapahos:

"When the military abandoned Cantonement, Little Raven, an Arapaho chief, was given a hospital building, which cost the Government $12,000, for a residence. He sleeps in it occasionally, but has his tepee in the front yard, where his family lives. Raven has a farm of 40 acres in the river bottom; the land is most excellent. In the early spring he plowed it and planted corn, but at once abandoned it and left to lead the medicine making; the result is not an ear of corn, but a magnificent crop of weeds." [4]

The fact of Raven abandoning his house and sleeping out of doors seems peculiar to the Commissioner. The fact was, that while the Indians all wanted a white man's house, as soon as they procured it they refused to live in it, and lived out of doors. All of these tribes were very fond of green corn. When one would meet them and ask them about their corn, they would become very extravagant in their statements and declare that they had "heap-much-big-corn-white-man's corn." The fact

---

[3] Report of Commissioner of Indian Affairs—Ibid. Readings in Oklahoma History—Ibid.

[4] Report of Indian Affairs—Ibid. Reading in Oklahoma History, Page 398.

would be, that they would eat their entire crop in roasting ears. Most of the members of the Cheyenne tribe appeared to be as restless as caged eagles. The writer has seen them sit on their horses as imposing and immovable as statues; gaze off across the prairies as if dreaming of the free and wild life which was gone, and of which there was no prospect of return. As the teams and wagons, outfits of freighters, and persons crossing the country on the winding trails, would take their tedious way, these Indians would ride to the hilltops and gaze down on them, then ride to the next hill, and thus follow the travelers for miles.

While the settlement of Indians in and around Cantonement were in the main Arapahos, during the trouble in 1884-5 there were many of the infected Cheyennes remained around that place, the country adjacent, and to the southwest. All depredations possible were committed by these Indians. There were normally several hundred Indians living at Cantonement. They lived principally in stockade houses, with dirt floors and dirt coverings for the poles on the roofs. These buildings were usually one room affairs. At this time there was but one white man at Cantonement. He kept the commissary and looked after all the dealings with the Indians. There was a telegraph line running from this point to Fort Reno. This line was fastened to iron pipe or poles. These sort of posts were used for the reason that they would not be burned by the annual prairie fires. Full arrangements had been made at one time to equip this point at Cantonement as an important military post. Numerous buildings had been constructed there, built of native stone. The distance was so great, however, from the railways that dimension timber, boards, and shingles for roofing had not been obtained for many of these structures; when the idea of retaining this point as a fort was given up, these buildings had not been completed, and stood there roofless, doorless, and windowless. They resembled the ghost of what might have been.

It was at Cantonement, during these years, that the writer learned much of the character and habits of these Indians, and of their troubles with the Government and cattlemen. They were at that time possessed of an abundance of the best of firearms. They had good Colt .45 revolving pistols, 1873 model .44 Winchester rifles, both long and short, and also the late Sharpe's rifles, shooting the .45-70 Government cartridges. When fully equipped they bore a formidable and warlike appearance. The Government had much trouble at this time trying to take these arms away from them. Repeatedly detachments of cavalry from Fort Reno would appear at Cantonement. It was easy to foretell when the soldiers were coming. For hours before the soldiers would arrive, no Indian could be seen with any kind of a firearm. They would all be walking around looking as innocent, demure, and inoffensive as saints.

When the soldiers would arrive they would search diligently but in vain for weapons. The Indians would all be there, but minus any firearms. The soldiers would not be gone over one hour until every Indian would be in evidence again with all his equipment of war. It was a mystery what they did with these weapons. The soldiers could never find them. The writer has been told that they took them to a large sand-bar on the south side of the North Canadian river, northwest of Cantonement, up the river toward Sheridan's roost, there buried them in the sand, and then drove their ponies over the sand; thus obliterating all traces of the hiding place.

The Indians around Cantonement and all the way down the river to Darlington Agency had been furnished with farming implements for the purpose of engaging in farming and tilling the soil. Most of these implements rusted away in the shade under the trees along the river.

At one time, when the writer's party was camped on the river north of Cantonement, a body of Indians of one of the tribes, the writer cannot now recall which, camped near. It was cold, and the river was frozen over. One morning all in the vicinity heard a young Indian crying loudly, in fact he was bawling. On observation it was discovered that the lad was entirely naked, and a big stalwart Indian was leading him from a tepee down across the frozen water toward an open hole cut in the ice, where the water was a couple of feet deep. On reaching this open hole the larger Indian took the boy by the arm and thrust him entirely under the water two or three times, and then placed him on his feet on the ice. The lad ran for the tepee as fast as he could, sounding his distress as loudly as possible. Inquiry was made of the older Indian, who was the boy's father, and who could speak fair English, what the boy had done to have such punishment meted out to him. He replied that he had done nothing, but that he did it to make him "heap-much-big strong Indian."

The following article, copied from the Cheyenne Transporter, published at Darlington Agency, taken from the issue of May 10, 1884, speaks for itself:

"Trouble at Cantonment.

E. M. Horton, with a brother and two men, got into serious difficulty with the Indians at Cantonment, on Sunday morning last, which resulted in the killing of Running Buffalo, a Cheyenne. Horton was enroute from Texas, to Medicine Lodge, Kansas, with a herd of three hundred mares with colts, and, finding the river crossing on the western trail impassable, came down to the Cantonment trail and, after crossing, was met by Buffalo, who demanded some ponies. After being refused, he attempted to stampede the herd and, being interfered with, snapped his pistol at Horton, who shot him from his horse, and killed him as he rose to his feet. The Indians, watching the proceedings, then commenced to swarm, and Horton took his herd and went back into Cantonment, where the horses were turned into the old Government corral and the men took refuge from the angry Indians in the telegraph office, and sent word to Agent Dyer of the situation. Rev. Haury exerted himself among the Indians and kept secure their property until Agent Dyer could render help, which was telegraphed for. Agent Dyer immediately asked for troops from El Reno, and Lieut. Gibbon, with twenty-five men, started for Cantonment on Monday, while Wm. Darlington, with five Indian Police, went from the agency. In the meantime, Horton and his men, finding that the Indians were determined to have his life, moved from the telegraph office to the stone bakery building, on Sunday evening, and kept the excited Indians at bay until the Indian Police and troops arrived, late Monday afternoon. Horton and his men had neither food or water from Sunday morning until Monday evening, two days and one night. As soon as the troops arrived they took charge of the imprisoned men and escorted them to another building, followed on all sides by Indians with cocked guns, endeavoring to get a shot at Horton. Finding that they could not get their man they made known their intention of taking his entire herd and, finding the Indians becoming more furious each moment, the white men turned over half of the herd to the Indians and started to the Agency with the balance of the herd and their prisoners, arriving here on Thursday, at noon. This is the most serious affair that has occurred among the Indians for some time."

The Transporter of the issue of May 28 gives a further statement in reference to the matter, as follows:

"Orders from the Interior Department have been received by Agent Dyer instructing him to gather up the ponies seized by the Indians from E. M. Horton, at Cantonment, at the recent killing of Running Buffalo. Indian Police have been sent out in charge of Lieut. Wolf Robe to bring in the ponies."

Reference has been made in the foregoing articles as to the Indian Police. It has been stated heretofore that Bill Darlington organized the Indian Police at Fort Reno and from the foregoing articles it appears he was still in command of them.

These Indian Police made good and effective soldiers. As in this case, when sent out to serve against the members of their own tribe, they never faltered or flinched from their duty, and the writer does not recall any occasion when they were even accused of shirking any task thus imposed upon them.

Shortly after the killing of Running Buffalo the writer was at the TL Ranch, Dickey Brothers, which was some twenty-five miles northwest of Cantonment, and the boys at the ranch informed him of the killing at Cantonment, but stated that the Indian killed was Little Robe, which was a mistake.

Running Buffalo was taken to Cedar Springs, which was nine miles north of Cantonment, and an elaborate pow-wow was had for his funeral. He was sewed up in a raw-hide and stored away by hanging him high up in a large tree. His raw-hide hung there for a number of years, when it was cut down by some hunters from Chicago. Running Buffalo's horse and dogs were shot and left under the tree, so that they could accompany their master to the "Happy Hunting Ground."

A short time before the killing of Running Buffalo the writer and an outfit were passing Cantonment, and stopped at the store or commissary to make some purchases. An Indian, who from all accounts must have been Running Buffalo, rode up and tied his horse to a post, entered the store, and began talking in his native language to the man in charge. He became so earnest that a member of the party, who was doing the trading, inquired as to what the Indian wanted. He was informed by the interpreter that he wanted toll for the outfit traveling over his country. The spokesman then asked how much the Indian wanted, and after some palaver with the Indian the agent informed him that he wanted one hundred dollars. In answer the agent was told to inform that old Indian to go to a region the climate of which is extremely hot. When this remark was made, while the Indian had been speaking through an interpreter, he needed no intermediary to convey the meaning to him. He leaped into the air and strode across that room in long strides, swearing in English and Indian both at the same time. Finally he ran out and mounted his horse. Someone remarked that he would gather some of his associates and follow the outfit. The agent was informed that he should tell that Indian if he tried to carry out any such program that the Indian population of that region would be greatly reduced, rapidly, and without ceremony. We were a formidable appearing outfit to say the least, and no attempt was made by them to follow us.

It was the custom of these Indians to attempt to collect money from persons traveling over their reservation. They at all times resented the presence of these travelers and considered them as trespassers. This was more particularly applied to the Cheyenne and Arapaho Reservation. While reference is made to these Indians in general as to this matter, it is the opinion of the writer that there were only a minority of the members of the tribes that interested themselves in this regard. This proposition of charging toll for passing over this country, like the habit of taking up stock as strays, was evidently acquired by their association with white men.

CHAPTER XIII.

INDIAN TRIBES FAMILIAR TO THE TRAIL
—CONTINUED

In the early travels across the plains most of the wagons were drawn by ox teams. This was also true as to the earlier freighters on the Chisholm Trail and other western commercial routes of travel. These oxen were trained to heed the old commands as to the course they were to take. It will be recalled that check lines for driving were not used until less than one hundred years ago. Before that time the driver of a team of horses simply guided one horse while the other was fastened to it by a rope, strap, or often with what was called a jockey stick. This was a pole fastened to the bridle bit of one horse, while the other end was attached to the hames or collar of the horse guided. Thus the other horse would be controlled.

The most popular method of handling the horse to be guided was with a jerk-line. In using this jerk-line, which was a single line attached to the bridle bit of the guided horse, the driver jerked with a sharp quick jerk when he wanted the horse to go to the right, and gave the command "gee." When he wanted it to go to the left he would give a straight pull on the line, and give the command "haw." When he wanted to stop he would give the command "wo." The same commands were used in driving teams of oxen. Ox teams were usually driven entirely by this method, with the assistance of a long bull whip to punctuate the commands. The Indians hearing these commands given by all the drivers, called the oxen and all cattle "wo-haws." This designation was made by all the western Indians, especially the Plains Indians.

Capt. J. A. Covington and wife, Sarah, daughter of Brinton Darlington, taken a few years ago at San Jose, California.

There were many habits, characteristics and customs in the mode of living of these Indians which may seem peculiar to our race. When we stop to think the matter over, however, they are no more peculiar than some of our customs and habits were to the Indians. The writer can remember when these long strings of freight wagons, driven by the Cheyenne Indians, fresh from the war path and battle field, who under the command of Captain J. A. Covington, traveled over the old Chisholm Trail. These wagons were drawn by a number of ponies. They did not use check lines, but an Indian rode by the side of the ponies, leading and guiding them.

The squaws, perhaps many children (papooses), and other Indians would ride in the wagon, seldom on the seats, but more often sitting as near on the bottom of the box as possible. The driver usually progressed with that unending "who-ah", beginning and ending with an accent. He would suppose that he was singing, but there was very little to his efforts except noise. Often, as this string of wagons coursed slowly along, there would be extending at intervals of perhaps one hundred yards apart, and for a half mile on either side of the wagons, squaws wearing blankets. These squaws were gathering land terrapins.

The Indians usually wore blankets thrown around their shoulders and gathered over their arms. Their favorite method of carrying all articles which were not too large was to drop them into the folds of this blanket, which would thus serve as a sack or large pocket. The squaws would gather terrapins and drop them into the folds of their blankets. When the wagons stopped to make camp, they would come up and have, if their luck was good, perhaps a peck of terrapins each. These creeping inhabitants of the prairies would all be dropped into one bunch. A number of small Indians would be left to guard them. Each terrapin herder was equipped with a long stick,

Powder Face, a prominent Arapaho Chief, and his wife, taken at the Darlington Agency.

about the length and size of a walking cane; when a terrapin strayed too far away from the herd one of the herders would place this stick under the edge of the strayer, and flip it back into the bunch. These terrapins were used as food by the Indians. They would cook them by throwing them into the fire alive. When the terrapin crawled out the Indian threw it back again, until it was past crawling. They were roasted in this manner. This may seem peculiar to persons not accustomed to cooking in this way, but the Indians had no cook books or recipes for cooking terrapins. It will be borne in mind, however, that we cook smelt and other fish without dressing, and drop lobsters in boiling water alive.

Experienced persons in the Indian country could always ascertain whether vacated camps which were found had been occupied by Indians by the method the fires had been built. This was one of the marks examined by all frontier men in ascertaining this fact. Many white men who habitually lived on the frontier grew to build their fires similar to the Indians, and this would render uncertain this evidence. A white man generally built his fires by laying the sticks of wood down in a pile of uncertain order. An Indian always built his fire by laying the points of the sticks to a center. This last method was very much more economical in the use of fuel. It was a noticeable fact that the Indians had been so often compelled to economize in the use of so many things that it grew to be a habit with them.

There were many horses reared by the Indians belonging to the Kiowa and Comanche, Cheyenne and Arapaho, and Wichita tribes. The Kiowas and Wichitas in the vicinity of Anadarko raised many horses which were sold and driven to other parts. The Government had sent into this country many domestic horses. This made the breed much better than the mustangs found on the plains country. They were much more

White Shield, a Cheyenne Sub-Chief.

tractable, and easily broken to ride or work. Many of these horses were driven north, often as far as Dakota. The writer has driven and helped to handle many of these horses. They were usually raised around the Indian camps, and some were very gentle, but often very much spoiled. When a horse would be found that was really wild the Indians as usual used some ingenious method to "break it" or teach it to be ridden.

The writer recalls on one occasion the Indians near Anadarko had gotten several wild and obstreperous ponies. A large bunch of young bucks congregated and led these horses one at a time down into a large water hole on the Washita River, and dragged them, kicking and fighting, out to where the water was deep enough that the horses were compelled to swim. There they would hold the animals in the deep water while, not only one, but several Indians mounted and rode each of them as long as it could swim. They continued this process until each horse was thoroughly familiar with the riding process, but when he grew mean, back he went to the water. A few of these treatments were sufficient to educate the most ignorant horse.

Horse racing was one of the great sports indulged in by all these Indians. On the cattle ranges one of the favorite methods of running a horse race was to run one hundred or one hundred and fifty yards, turn a stake, and run back to the place of starting. This method was not usually adopted by the Indians, but they had another one which was used by all the tribes mentioned. This was to face the head of the horse, on starting, in the opposite direction from which it was intended to run. When the word was given or a pistol fired the horse would turn and run. The horses which became accustomed to this process became very expert in the same.

The writer at one time owned a Kiowa horse, which had been raised in an Indian camp. This horse had been ridden by Indian children ever since he was a few weeks old. It had been discovered that this horse could run, and he was trained in their method of starting. He could turn on one foot and jump at the same time. It was difficult for a man to keep his seat on his back when making this turn, and few persons could accomplish this feat without a saddle. This habit was a nuisance in using these horses. If they were being ridden quietly along and someone on a horse should gallop up to their sides they would whirl and be off, and could not be stopped for some distance. Hubert Collins in his book, "Warpath and Cattle Trails," tells of a circumstance in which a pony he was riding near Caddo Springs, and which had been used in this sort of racing, whirled with him and threw him, severely injuring him. The writer can appreciate what happened.

Horse race in cow-camp. Note the stake with flag which they are turning.

The Kickapoo Indian Reservation was far to the east of the Chisholm Trail, and east of the four tribes heretofore mentioned. During the time that the writer knew the Cheyenne and Arapaho Reservation, the Kickapoo would come west each fall and hunt the greater part of the winter as far west as they could find timber for shelter against the inclement weather. The Cheyennes regarded these Kickapoos with utter contempt. They were considered of such a lowly class as to be beneath the notice of a Cheyenne so far as recognition or association was concerned, and they very much resented the Kickapoos hunting within their country. A portion of these Kickapoos had been in Mexico, and spoke more Spanish than English. In trips to the west the travelers on the Chisholm Trader's Trail often came in contact with these Kickapoo Indians. They were much more friendly with white travelers than any of the four tribes who lived on the trail.

These Kickapoos were fine hunters, much better than either the Cheyenne or Arapaho. They used, at the time the writer knew them, the old Kentucky muzzle-loading rifles, of large caliber. The sights on these rifles were low, and the barrels long. For this reason they were not good to shoot at a moving target, but these Indians would drop down on one knee, take their accustomed rest over the hand grasping a long ramrod, and after taking deliberate aim, fire. Up to one hundred yards, which was about the extent of the accurate range of these guns, their aim was deadly. The Kickapoo when hunting always carried a long ram-rod, and when shooting they would drop down on one knee, grasp around this ram-rod with their left hand, just in front of their face, and rest the rifle over the hand grasping the ram-rod. The Cheyennes usually carried two of these ram-rods, would cross them in front of their face after dropping down on one knee, grasp the left hand around the ram-rods at the point where they crossed, and then rest their rifle in the fork above the hand. While the Cheyennes at that time used modern and very much up-to-date rifles, their accuracy in shooting would not compare with that of the Kickapoos.

The writer often met these Kickapoos in their travels to the west. During two seasons there was a young Kickapoo, about the same age of the writer, a son of a chief, with them. He was always referred to as "Kickapoo," and his name and that of his father are now forgotten by the writer. This young man had been educated at Carlisle Indian school, and spoke good English, but he dressed and lived just as the other Indians. The writer has hunted many days with this Kickapoo. In fact he lived in the same camp with the writer for some time. On the second year he hunted for the writer until he found him, and perhaps in subsequent years he hunted for him and did not find him, he not being there.

The writer was at this time the possessor of a new breech-loading, ten gauge, shotgun. In the times referred to, muzzle-loading guns were still used to a great extent. Kickapoo did not have much faith in the killing ability of a shotgun, but his muzzle-loading rifle was useless for hunting turkey on the roosts at night, and on these occasions he always wanted to exchange guns. Turkeys usually roost in the highest portion of the tallest trees, but in much of this western country there were no tall trees; the turkeys were compelled to roost on the blackjacks, and would not be more than ten feet or such a matter from the ground. Kickapoo in his moccasin feet would glide immediately under the turkeys, and in shooting tear them up badly. The writer protested in vain to get him to shoot at a greater distance. He did on one occasion get him to do so. He shot at a distance of about thirty yards, but the wing feathers of the turkey were thick, and he did not kill it. Always after that the closer he could get the better.

On one of these nightly excursions the writer and Kickapoo became separated. The writer, carrying a number of turkeys that Kickapoo had killed, and his long muzzle-loading rifle, started through several miles of timber and brush for camp. While fighting his way through dense thickets along a creek he came upon a fire, by which were seated two Indians, Kickapoos. One of the Indians was picking a turkey in his leisurely way. The writer did not know either of the Indians personally, neither did they him.

The predicament immediately occurred to the writer. There he was carrying an Indian's rifle and four turkeys; here were two of his companions who immediately recognized the rifle, and pointing at the old weapon they inquired earnestly as to the whereabouts of Kickapoo, and with all his best efforts the writer was unable to make them understand. With fear and trembling he finally continued on his journey, carrying this antiquated rifle, and reached his own camp in safety. The greater humiliation greeted him on meeting his companions. When they saw this old rifle, and that the new shotgun was gone, they discovered the best joke of the season. They assured the writer that he would never see Kickapoo or his shotgun again, but consoled him to the effect that he had a muzzle-loading rifle, which had been an excellent weapon fifty years ago. Their joking, however, was in vain. Kickapoo came in late in the night with a load of turkeys and the shotgun. A large portion of white men will steal from or rob a friend with as little hesitancy as an enemy, but it is unusual for an Indian to steal from or deceive a man whom he actually regards as his friend.

In hunting with the Kickapoos the writer discovered that these Indians had a code of unwritten laws governing their operations and rights with each other. Doubtless these laws or some laws existed among the Indians of all of the tribes as to all of their rights as well as hunting. In our hunting, when we were in a locality where no game could be expected, Kickapoo would walk along at such a pace that the writer would be compelled to run to keep up with him. As soon as a locality was reached where game would likely be found, this Indian would proceed very slowly and cautiously, searching every part of the timber. The parties would usually proceed about fifty yards apart. While passing through thick timber, on one occasion, the writer heard a shot to his right, in the locality where Kickapoo was presumed to be. The writer stopped and stepped behind a tree to listen. He could hear the brush cracking, and soon a young doe came along. Her left shoulder was broken. Her progress was slow. She was only a few feet away, and the writer easily placed a ball from his .44 Winchester rifle just behind her fore leg, killing her instantly.

Kickapoo soon appeared on the scene, and the first remark he made was, "Your hide." The writer did not make further inquiry at this time, but supposed from the statement that the Indian was going to give him the hide and he would keep the meat. He wondered at this, however, as he knew the Indians prized the hide more than the meat. The deer was dressed. It was almost grown and very fat. As soon as it was dressed Kickapoo took half of the meat, tied it up in the hide, and handed the same to the writer. Then he explained that under their hunting laws when one person crippled an animal and another killed it, the party finally killing was entitled to half of the meat and the hide, and the person crippling only half the meat.

It was a rather cold day, and they tramped along together. Kickapoo was carrying his meat, strung on his gun, both in front and behind him, so as to balance over his shoulder. In front of him he had hung the fat portion taken from the regions of the heart and liver. As he progressed he kept feeling of this tallow, and as soon as it grew sufficiently cool he began breaking it off and eating it.   The parties were extremely hungry, and he induced the writer to try it. He did so, and found it fine eating for a hungry person. It was not greasy as it looked, but had a dry taste, and he has often eaten like portions taken from beef since. Thus the habits of one race are acquired by another by association.

The writer became very much attached to this young Kickapoo as a companion. One winter we camped on Horse and Squirrel Creeks on the north side of the South Canadian River, above Little Robe Creek and below the present City of Taloga. Kickapoo would sleep in the front of the tent. There was much snow on the ground during this winter. He would wake up in the morning, raise himself on one elbow, and leap out into the snow in his bare feet. There was a pond formed from a spring below the camp. He would take the water bucket, walk down to this pond bare-footed, cut a hole where the ice had frozen over the opening during the night, dip the water bucket full of water, and bring it up to the camp before starting a fire. He would then take his moccasins, which had dried by the fire during the preceding evening and night, warm them, and put them on.

From here the outfit passed down the north side of the river, going to Little Robe Creek. Kickapoo went along. At this time there was a dim trail running southwest from Cantonment, crossing the Canadian River at the mouth of Little Robe Creek. Just before the outfit came to this trail it stopped, and Kickapoo said he was going back. Standing by the side of the writer on his horse he bade him good-bye, and this was the last time he ever saw him. Just before leaving he warned the party to look out for the Cheyennes. In this he referred to the renegade element of this tribe, of whom reference has heretofore been made. Had this warning been heeded, it would have saved trouble in the future.

It was late in the forenoon when Kickapoo left, and soon thereafter the outfit turned onto this dim trail going to the south, crossed the creek once or twice, and camped in a grove of small cottonwoods on the west side of the same. The noon meal was eaten, and as customary the first thing done was to stretch ropes from tree to tree, forming a corral to pen the horses during the night. There were then cut down some small cottonwood trees for the horses to feed upon, and they were left outside the enclosure eating them. Not knowing that there were any Indians near, all parties left camp. The writer crossed the creek, going east, and later in the day came back to the same, thence going down the creek south of camp toward the river.

At this point he was accosted by a bunch of seven marauding Cheyennes, all well armed, and was required to accompany them. All that took place for some one-half hour thereafter would take much space to detail. It would perhaps not be entertaining to the reader, and is not a pleasant memory to the writer, and will be omitted. The writer, however, immediately designed the purpose of these Indians. That purpose was to get him away while some of the other members of the band sought and found the horses of the outfit, and he realized that he must get away soon or they would accomplish their object.

The parties had gone about one mile on their journey, in which some of the Indians stayed as close as possible to make the march impressive. At this point a small draw came down to the creek on the east side, and the timber was heavy almost to the edge of the creek. The outfit was compelled to go down a cow-path at this point in order to cross the gully. The writer caught the left bridle rein of his horse, holding it down to the side of his saddle, and spurred his horse as if attempting to make him go down the cow-path, but in fact pulled him off to the left.

The distance, however, to the main timber was too far, and he was afraid to attempt the run for its shelter, but his horse was turned and several efforts were made to effect the crossing with the same results. The Indians would gather on the side of the path and "shoo" at the horse like an old woman driving turkeys, then would attempt to catch the horse by its bridle rein, but this horse, as most horses unfamiliar with Indians were, was much afraid of them and would not let them come near him. At every attempt to negotiate the crossing, however, the circle that the horse made grew larger until he was near the main timber, and finally instead of turning he continued in a run into the same. As he sped on his course, the writer could hear the Indians running and hollowing to each other in their search for him. These Indians never realized the ruse the writer worked in turning his horse.

As soon as the writer was out of sight of the Indians he turned back to the creek, and in order to keep a more direct course and remain out of sight crossed the same three times. It was cold; there was a thin ice frozen over most of the water, and his horse would slide down the banks into the same, which came up around his sides. When he arrived at camp his clothes were frozen. He immediately rushed the horses into the corral, and then started to revive the fire in order to dry his clothing. While doing this he had rested his rifle on one of the ropes of the tent. During this process he saw two Indians come over a small hill, making a direct line for the horses. These Indians carried ropes and had pistols on their belts but no rifles. He stepped out and hollowed at them several times. It was said in the plains country at that time that all men, whether Indians or whites, could be understood in one of three languages, to-wit: English, Spanish, or profane. He tried all three of these, but the Indians never wavered from their course toward the horses. In desperation the writer turned and grabbed his Winchester. As the business end of this gun dropped down to the proper position, this was a language they understood. They both turned and ran, and the last seen of them their heads were bobbing down behind the hill.

Soon other members of the writer's party dropped in, one at a time. They were compelled to watch the horses all night. Many times they could hear the Indians in the brush, but they did not get the horses. As soon as day broke the next morning, the outfit started on its journey from the Little Robe. When darkness fell that evening over the Cheyenne and Arapaho Reservation, the outfit was sufficiently far from the scenes of the preceding day that it was beyond a repetition of the same sort of trouble by the same Indians. The writer at this time was a lad of seventeen years of age, but had spent much of his life since he could take a comprehensive view of the same on the frontier, on the plains, and in the wild places.

The writer's party consisted of seven, all of whom were seasoned frontiersmen. There are, however, many more pleasant things to relate than the foregoing incident. Men who passed through these experiences do not like to recall them any more than they would care to revive in their minds the sensation of starting to fall over a cliff or the memory of a bad dream. This is why so many men seldom talk of facts and happenings in their lives, which people know they could tell. Men often say that they love to encounter danger, and this is perhaps true in some cases. The writer has felt that way himself, but after men have placed most of their span of life behind them, and they can see their days thinning in the future, they lose this ambitious feeling of youth.

It is easy to realize the dire result that would have followed had the rifle of the writer sent forth its messenger of death on the Little Robe that evening. The fate of his outfit would have been more disastrous than that of Horton at Cantonment on the killing of Running Buffalo. The parties were in one of the most remote and desolate portions of the Cheyenne and Arapaho country. The feeling that existed was smoldering and ready to burst into flame at any time, and, while they could perhaps have beaten off the immediate band of Indians, they would have had a larger contingent of the tribe to have fought before they could have gotten out of the country.

There were many similar occurrences in this country at that time. A freighter had reported just a few days before, that some of these Indians had taken his teams, and they required him to pay them fifty dollars for "taking them up." He had made arrangements to bring them the money at a certain time, but expected to bring a sufficient armed force to take his horses. He procured the assistance of several cowboys, went after the horses, but found a large bunch of Indians seated around with Winchester rifles guarding them, and he was compelled to pay the money.

Now all is changed in the country of the Cheyenne and Arapaho, and the Kiowa and Comanche Reservations. The Cheyenne and Arapaho Reservation of some four million acres was opened to settlement in 1892, and in 1901 the Kiowa and Comanche of near the same number of acres was thrown open and taken over by white settlers. The Indians retained allotments for homes. These allotments are scattered over the country. Much of the land of the Cheyenne and Arapaho just west of El Reno is taken in this manner and held by Indians.

All of these Indians have finally submitted themselves to the white man's ways. They no more bear the striking appearance of the slender, straight, erect warriors of the plains. Instead they are now, most of them, corpulent individuals, some of them stylishly dressed in frontier outfits, while others wear some sort of freak clothes representing some class of white men who have taken the wearer's fancies. Some of them still cling to their blankets of many colors. A few of them now possess large farms and are prosperous. As they pass, the men who have known them many years in the past, stop to wonder whether they are really happier than in the old days. They now have all they can eat and come into town and frequent soft drink stands, where they drink large quantities of sweet liquids, and grow still more corpulent. There are these things certain; that the grass has effectually grown over their warpaths, their battle trails, and battle fields have been plowed under, and the wild Cheyennes have been subdued. The old Chief Little Robe was long ago commemorated by the creek which empties into the South Canadian River, some twenty-five miles southwest of Cantonment being named for him. Also a post office in western Oklahoma bears his name.

CHAPTER XIV.

THE CHEROKEE INDIANS

The Cherokee Indians did not frequent the Chisholm Trail. The reservation on which they lived and had their homes was 125 miles to the east of the same. The Chisholm Trail, however, bisected the lands belonging to them, known as the Cherokee Outlet. Also the cattle industry with which the trail was allied was drawn into close contact with the Cherokees. From these associated relations the history of the trail is not complete without an observation of this tribe.

In setting forth what we do in connection with these Indians, as well as the other tribes, it is not the purpose nor will space permit going into the history of these Indians in detail. Such would require an independent volume for each. It is, nevertheless, highly important that the people in general should have a brief outline of the history, disposition, and character of these people with whom they are so nearly associated. This is especially true of the people of Oklahoma who are allied under the same state government with these different tribes of Indians.

When we mention the name "Indians," persons in general pass the matter with one sweeping observation, and let the matter rest with the understanding that the persons referred to belong to the general class of descendants of the original inhabitants of this country. No distinction is made as to the tribe, disposition, or classification. The citizens are not to blame for this attitude. They have not been taught to more accurately observe these things. Is it not unfair to place in the same class the Cherokee Indians, whose tribe has produced some of the leading intellectual men of our nation and who have never rebelled against the unfair laws and treatment of the representatives of our Government, with the fierce and savage Apaches, who tied their captives on ant hills to die the most horrible deaths, or with the Digger Indians, one of the lowest types?

Also, while there is a vast difference in the general characteristics of the different tribes, it will be borne in mind, that it is impossible to have all the members of the same tribe, the same community, or the same race, measure up to the same standard. We find those with superior dispositions and intellects in all races and parts of races; also in the same creed or associated with the same criminal and incorrigible class. Further, their contact with the white race has worked to the advantage of some of the Indians, while to others it has had the very opposite effect. The Indian who has embraced the opportunity to progress and rise on the same wave with his white brother, has been rewarded with the same results. The Indian who has only sought the association of the white race for the purpose of partaking of its "fire water," and ascertaining the greatest amount that he could consume, has made no improvement, and has simply retrograded to such an extent that he has combined the vices of the white race with the most brutal and inhuman disposition of the savage.

Our people have been taught the history of the atrocities and cruelties of the Indians, but very little has been said relative to the disposition and dishonest methods used by representatives of our Government in their dealings with the Indians. As time has progressed and the vindictiveness toward the Indians subsided to such an extent that we can take a reasonable view of the matter, people are informing themselves, considering the facts, and weighing the same. On being informed, when they do so investigate, they have ceased to blame one tribe of Indians for the acts of those of another, and have also ceased to lay the stigma on an entire tribe for some act of lawlessness done by some degenerate member of the same. They have also come to realize that the entire race of people cannot be blamed for the lawless acts of the criminal class among its members.

In the inception of their dealings with the white race, an Indian had the simplicity and mind of a child, and much more curiosity. They not only held the white race in reverence, but acknowledged its members as their superiors. In our dealings with them we have exercised all the domination and oppression that history reveals to us have always been asserted by the members of a superior race. Not only that, also the Indians during that time have been exposed to all the vicious and criminal influences that could be planted among them by the lawless element of a dominant race. With all the foregoing matters and things borne in mind, let us consider the case of the Cherokee Indians, and in doing so also consider the merits and demerits of the acts and attitude of our own Government in its dealings with this commendable people After doing this, we can ask ourselves whether our own race, acting under the adversities the Cherokees have faced, could have accomplished more than they.

When DeSoto and his intrepid followers, clad in their steel armor, traversed the continent of North America, and discovered the Mississippi River, in the waters of which this great leader after his death was, at the solemn hour of midnight, buried, they came upon and in their report mentioned the Cherokee Indians. While the home of these Indians was on the east side, some of their tribe at that time must have crossed to the west side of that river, and thus met the DeSoto expedition. The Cherokee were always looked upon as the most civilized of all the Indian tribes. From a report made of them in 1811 we quote the following:

"The Cherokee Nation has at length, in full council, adopted a Constitution which embraces a simple form of government. The legislative and judicial powers are vested in a General Council with less ones subordinate. In this Nation there are 12,395 Indians. The females exceed the males by 200. The whites are 341, and one-third of these have Indian wives. Of negro slaves there are 583. The number of their cattle is 19,600; of horses 6,100; of sheep 1,037. They have now in actual use 13 grist mills, 3 saw mills, 3 saltpetre works and 1 powder mill. They have also 30 wagons, between 480 and 500 plows, 1600 spinning wheels, 467 looms, and 49 silversmiths." [1]

The Cherokee is one of what is known as the Five Civilized Tribes. These Five Civilized Tribes, as heretofore stated, consist of the following: (1) Cherokee, (2) Creek, (3) Choctaw, (4) Chickasaw, and (5) Seminole. While the Seminole is given and recognized as an independent member of the Five Civilized Tribes, it is in fact a part of the Creek. This portion designated as the Seminole left the main Creek tribe and settled further south many years before the removal to the Indian Territory, eventually inhabiting the swamps and everglades of Florida, and were finally in their dealings with the Government designated as a separate tribe.

The authorities are not uniform as to the meaning of the name "Cherokee," or the derivation of the same. James Adair in his *History of the American Indians* states:

"Their national name is derived from *Chee-ra*, fire, which is their reputed lower heaven, and hence they call their magi, *Cheera-tahge*, 'men possessed of divine fire.'"

While Thomas Valentine Parker in his work, entitled, "The Cherokee Indians," claims:

"The word 'Cherokee' means 'upland fields,' and possibly refers to their country, which is thus described by Bancroft:—"

---

[1] Christian Observer, London, November issue, 1811. Chronicles of Oklahoma, Vol. XI, Number IV—Page 1062—December, 1933.

In any event, the Cherokee belong to the Iroquois branch, being so associated and traced by the similarity of their language. Such being the case, they are associated with the five nations of western New York. The other four of the Five Civilized Tribes are of the Muskogean line. At the time of the advent of the Europeans into this country the Cherokee occupied a large extent of territory east of the Mississippi River. They were first met by white explorers when DeSoto and his followers contacted them in their northward journey. The description given by Bancroft of the Cherokee country and the extent of the same is worthy of note, and follows:

"The mountaineers of aboriginal America were the Cherokees who occupied the valley of the Tennessee River as far west as the Muscle Shoals and the highlands of Carolina, Georgia and Alabama, the most picturesque and salubrious region east of the Mississippi. Their homes are encircled by blue hills rising beyond hills, of which the lofty peaks would kindle with the early light and the overshadowing night envelop the valley like a mass of clouds. There the rocky cliffs rising in naked grandeur defy the lightning and mock the loudest peals of the thunderstorm; there the gentle slopes are covered with magnolias and flowering forest trees, decorated with roving climbers, and ring with the perpetual notes of the whip-poor-will; there the wholesome water gushes profusely from the earth in transparent springs; snow-white cascades glitter on the hillsides; and the rivers, shallow, but pleasant to the eye, rush through the narrow vales which the abundant strawberry crimsons and the coppices of rhododendron and flaming azalea adorn ————. The fertile soil teems with luxuriant herbage on which the roebuck fattens; the vivifying breeze is laden with fragrance; and daybreak is ever welcomed by the shrill cries of the social night-hawk and the liquid carols of the mocking bird." [2]

Such is the historian's description of the ancient home of the Cherokee. Should we wonder that they were reluctant to

_____
[2] Bancroft's History of U. S. Vol. 2, p. 95.

turn their backs upon this country forever? The first actual relations of the Cherokee with the colonies was when a party of explorers from Virginia visited their country. The colonies then entered into treaties with them, there being a number of such treaties made. During the strife for supremacy among the English, Spanish, and French colonists, these Indians were at different times affiliated with first one and then the other. The fact is, that they associated with the one from whom they could get the best trade relations. During the Revolutionary War the Cherokees were allied with the mother country as against the colonies, but upon the resumption of peace, they made a treaty with the new Government and during the war of 1812 entered the same and fought against England.

As the settlements began to crowd westward, the settlers without regard to the rights of the Cherokees took possession of and occupied their lands. This naturally brought about a conflict of interest. After the close of the Revolutionary War, in 1785, the treaty of Hopewell was made with the Cherokees by the Federal Government. By the terms of this treaty the Indians were to have a deputy in Congress, and no white settlers were to be allowed to occupy any of their lands. In 1788 Congress caused a proclamation to be issued forbidding intrusion on these lands, and Secretary of War, Knox, stated that the acts of these settlers were a disgraceful violation of the treaty of Hopewell. The provisions of this treaty were not satisfactory to the states of Georgia and North Carolina, and they did not encourage the enforcement of the same. The citizens in contact with these states violated the provisions of this treaty with impunity. This was done regardless of the protests of the Indians.

On account of this constant turmoil in 1791, another treaty, termed the Treaty of Holston, was entered into by the National Government and the Cherokees. This treaty was slightly modi-

fied in 1794. The constant crowding on of the white settlements and their attempts to obtain the homes of the Indians
continued, and every possible effort was made to that end.
The following treaties were made by the Government with the
Cherokees: Tellico in 1798, another in 1804, another in 1805,
another signed October 27, 1805, and another in 1806. Each
of these treaties had but one purpose, and that was a further
encroachment on the Cherokees. They did not even go to the
trouble of naming these latter treaties. During all of this time,
the Cherokees wisely and sagaciously protected their interests
as far as they could.

Also, during this time, a continuous conflict was had with
the states of Georgia and North Carolina. In these states
laws had been enacted refusing to permit Indians to be sworn
and testify in any court, and denying them the privilege to institute a case in any court in the state to protect their rights.
Georgia passed a law forbidding any Indian to make a contract with any person, regardless of race, also forbidding the
Indians from entering into any counsel or legislative assembly.
It will be recalled that the Cherokees at that time had a well
organized government, which was conducted, in all probability,
with much more decorum that that of the State of Georgia.
Under these conditions the missionaries among the Indians
were arrested and thrown into prison, gamblers and liquor
peddlers were released among them, and armed men went into
their country and forced them out of their homes and took
possession of their houses, their crops, chickens, and stock.
A state of entire lawlessness reigned, the only object of which
was to compel the Indians to give up their lands.

The Cherokee nation east of the Mississippi was divided
into two portions, the upper and lower Cherokees. While both
branches of the tribe had been, as far back as the history of
the same revealed, as well as the colonies, engaged in domestic

pursuits, had lived in houses instead of wigwams or tepees, had farmed the land and raised crops, were settled on their homes instead of wandering from place to place, and had poultry and stock; yet the lower Cherokees were more inclined to the hunt and the pursuit of game. The upper Cherokee depended almost exclusively on their fields and stock for support.

As far back as the year 1800, on account of the oppression brought to bear on them by the white settlers, and the slowness of the Government to give them redress from the continued lawless condition brought about by the laws passed by Georgia, some of the members of the lower Cherokee were ready to move further to the west, while on the other hand the upper portion of the tribe, being exclusively an agricultural people, refused to consider or countenance such a proposition. As early as the year 1803, President Jefferson suggested that an arrangement might be made whereby the entire tribe could move further west.

In 1817, General Jackson was sent to confer with the tribe in that regard, but obtained no results. So far as the entire tribe was concerned, they refused to consider the proposition. A treaty was, however, made with the lower Cherokees, whereby about one-third of their number removed to Arkansas. A number of this part of the tribe had gone there some years before, and settled on the White River, where they were joined by these new members. It soon developed that the settlers had begun to crowd in upon their lands in Arkansas, and it was necessary for the Indians to make another move. This they did in 1828. This treaty dated May 28, 1828, provided that the Indians should have in exchange for their lands in the East title to seven million acres in the Indian Territory, and a perpetual outlet to the west as far as the limits of the United States extended, which at that time was the one hundredth meridian, the exact location of which had not been marked.

The oppression brought to bear on these Indians was such that it can hardly be realized it all took place within the bounds of an organized and civilized Government. Property was taken from them before their very eyes, they were arrested on trumped-up charges, and all possible indignities were forced upon them; while by provision of the state law they had no redress in court, could not institute or maintain a suit, and if arrested could not testify in their own behalf. If an Indian bought anything from a white man, the white man could charge any price he wanted, regardless of his contract, and the Indian could not resist it. The contract was void and the Indian could not testify. All of the Cherokees had been against removal, but, with pressure brought to bear on them, and they not seeing any hope for the future, some of the tribe had yielded, but the remaining portion were from that fact more set in favor of resistance.

With these conditions in view, in 1829 a meeting was held by the remaining portion of the tribe in the East. At this meeting Major Ridge, a leading member of the tribe and a very able man, with a national reputation, presented a resolution which was adopted and which provided that the Indians would give up no more of their lands, would yield no further to the demands of the states or Government, and further provided, that any member of the tribe who should thereafter attempt to cede away any portion of his tribal domain should be punished by death. It is a strange turn of Fate that this able man, Major Ridge, died as a result of a violation of this very resolution which he had prepared and presented.

The Supreme Court of the United States in a decision rendered by John Marshall, held the laws of the State of Georgia, heretofore referred to, unconstitutional and void. President Jackson was in favor of removal of the Indians, and it is claimed he not only refused to enforce the laws of the Government and have this decision carried out, but advised with the officials of Georgia in reference to their course. It is also claimed that the President stated that John Marshall had made his decision, and now he could enforce it. In any event, it was not enforced, and the Indians were defeated in the face of a decision of the Supreme Court of the United States in their favor.

While Major Ridge had been a staunch supporter of the opposition to removal, but had become satisfied of the futility of resistance availing them anything or of ever having any relief from this oppression, concluded the best course to pursue was to make the most favorable terms possible and submit to removal. He was supported in this course by Elias Boudinot, John Ridge, and other influential members of the tribe. At least three-fourths, and perhaps more, of the Cherokees were against him. John Ross, then principal chief of the tribe, was leader of the opposition. A bitter strife was waged in Congress for some time over this matter. The representatives of the Government resorted to every trick and device possible to find some excuse for claiming a treaty had been approved by the Indians, regardless of the legality of the same.

Finally a treaty was proposed and prepared by the faction in favor of the same, and it was ordered by the Government to be submitted to a vote of the Cherokees at an election to be held at Red Clay in October, 1835. A man by the name of Schermerhorn was sent by the Government with this treaty to be ratified. This representative of the Government, seeing the impossibility of having it approved, instead of submitting the same as directed, posted notices that another meeting would be held at New Echota, instead of Red Clay, in December following. Schermerhorn used the intervening time to try to devise some means and excuse for declaring the treaty as being approved by the tribe. John Ross was arrested and thrown into jail. His papers were all gone over and all possible means resorted to by the Goverment's representatives to keep him away from the meeting and to eliminate his influence. The Indians were poor. It was in the midst of winter, they had been dragged over the country from place to place to vote on this proposition with no result, and knowing that the agent had no authority to call it, they refused to attend this meeting at New Echota. There were some sixteen thousand Indians at that time in the tribe in the East. The testimony of McCoy, who was the interpreter acting at the meeting, was to the effect that only eighty-six votes were cast at the meeting. It was generally conceded that the meeting was illegally called. Schermerhorn had been sent but with one instruction, and that was to bear the treaty to Red Clay to be voted upon in October. He had no power to require these Indians to travel a hundred miles or more in the midst of winter at his behest to vote at a meeting which he had no authority to call.

This purported treaty, adopted by eighty-six members of the Cherokee Tribe, was borne triumphantly to Washington by this man Schermerhorn, and presented against the protests of the other members of the Commission, including Major Davis, who had been sent by the Government to try to induce the Indians to enter into the same. General indignation arose over the entire Cherokee country. A protest was signed and carried to Washington, bearing the names of some twelve thousand of the sixteen thousand Cherokees. Soldiers were sent to hold the tribe in check and prevent any outbreak. The treaty was submitted for approval and was approved by the Senate by a majority of one vote. The opposition presented to the same was that it was illegally adopted, or in fact was never adopted by the Cherokees. On May 23, 1836, the treaty of New Echota was proclaimed as being a law.

By the terms of this treaty, the entire Cherokee nation disposed of their lands, some ten million acres, for which they received five million dollars, and were to be removed to the seven million acres of land which had been assigned to them in the Indian Territory. An Indian might retain one hundred and sixty acres of land by purchasing it on the same terms as any other settler. The principal provision of the treaty was that they must remove from their homes and their lands in the East, which they had fought so long to retain. The soldiers were sent to remain and see that the terms of this treaty were carried out. When the tribe attempted to call a meeting for discussion of their affairs, they were arrested. They were informed that they could either remove or have war. The Georgia Militia was mobilized and sent to look after matters. This militia even refused to take orders from the officer in charge of the Government soldiers, and proceeded to inflict atrocities on the Indians according to its own notion.

John Ross returned to his elegant home to find that it had been sold, his wife and family summarily removed, and the purchaser installed therein. He was compelled to walk away and leave it. As he did so he beheld the grave of his little daughter, who had been buried under a tree near his home, trampled over and desecrated. This is not all the heart-rending result that he suffered. After he had traveled during the dead of winter in the perilous journey of removal, which will be hereinafter described, and had reached Little Rock, on the final lap of their journey to the West, his wife died, leaving him to complete the journey without her.

Before the final order on this treaty was enforced President Jackson had gone out of office, and President Van Buren had taken his place. Also there was a new Congress, and this matter was again presented for consideration. The battle was so heated over the same that the issues over the question of slavery were for the time forgotten. Webster and Clay espoused the cause of the Indians. Although Davy Crockett represented in Congress at that time a district which was affected by the removal, he boldly arose and stated that, regardless of the effect upon the security of his position, he was raising his voice in the interest of right and justice. He made a fiery and logical appeal in the interest of the Indians. A petition to Congress was sent to that body, signed by fifteen thousand six hundred and sixty-five Cherokees. This appeal, prepared and presented by these Indians, deserves a place in the pages of history. Representations had been made to the tribe that John Ross and his followers were misleading them, that no crime was committed, and that to resist was a delusion and a dangerous error. This appeal or a portion of the same reads as follows:

"*** 'duped and deluded by those we have placed implicit confidence in.' What the delusion? Delusion to be sensible of the wrong we suffer? Dangerous error to believe that the great nation, whose representatives we now approach, will never knowingly sanction a transaction originated in treachery and to be executed only by violence and oppression? Is it a crime to confide in our chiefs?——And now, in the presence of your august assemblies, and in the presence of the Supreme Judge of the Universe, most solemnly and most humbly do we ask: are we for these causes to be subjected to the indescribable evils which are designed to be inflicted upon us? Is our country to be the scene of the horror which your commissioner will not paint?

"For adhering to the principles on which your great empire is founded, and which have advanced it to its present elevation and glory, are we to be dispoiled of all we hold dear on earth? Are we to be hunted through the mountains like wild beasts, and our women, our children, our aged, our sick to be dragged from their homes like culprits, and to be packed on loathsome boats for transportation to sickly climes?

"Already we are thronged with armed men; forts, camps and military posts of every grade occupy our whole country.

With us it is a season of alarm and apprehension. We acknowledge the power of the United States. We acknowledge our own feebleness. Our only fortress is the justice of our cause. Our only appeal on earth is to your tribunal. To you then we look. Before your honorable bodies, in view of the appalling circumstances with which we are surrounded, relying on the righteousness of our cause and the justice and magnanimity of the tribunal to which we appeal, we do solemnly and earnestly protest against that spurious instrument (i. e., Treaty of New Echota).

"It is true we are a feeble people, and as regards physical power we are in the hands of the United States, but we have not forfeited our rights, and if we fail to transmit to our sons the freedom we have derived from our fathers, it must not be an act of suicide, it must not be with our consent.

"With trembling solicitude and anxiety we most humbly and respectfully ask, will you hear us? Will you shield us from the horrors of the threatened storm? Will you sustain the hopes we have rested on the public faith, the honor, the justice of your mighty empire? We commit our cause to your favor and protection. And your memorialists, as in duty bound, will ever pray." [3]

The prayers of the Indians being rejected by Congress, the pressure against the removal and the injustice of the same was so great that President Van Buren contemplated a suspension of the order for two years more. To this proposition the Governor of Georgia announced to the President that, if such action was taken, the militia of Georgia would take the law in their own hands and there would be open warfare between them and the Indians. This was in the early season of 1838. General Scott was in command of the soldiers of the Government. The misery of the Indians was so great that General Scott held the matter in abeyance until later in the year.

---

[3] Cong. Doc. 329, No. 316.

The Indians had been gathered and herded together like cattle. Some had fled to the mountains and could not be collected. Some had given up and gone west on their own account. Finally, on December 4, 1838, about fourteen thousand started on their perilous journey of about seven hundred miles to their new home in the Indian Territory. Their arms had been taken away from them, and they had been made prisoners. They were dragged from their homes, their fields of grain were left, and their homes turned over to the lawless element to plunder. Many of them had nothing left to take with them but the clothes they wore. The horrors of this journey in the midst of winter is beyond description. It is said that four thousand of their number died on this trip. Well has this migration been designated in history as the "Trail of Tears." Their tears moistened every foot of their pathway along this route of seven hundred miles. The graves of their dead marked every mile of the journey. The just people of the nation have well designated this act as "The Crime of the Ages," and as such it will go down in history. The tragedies of the journey are too numerous to attempt to mention. The reader must seek a publication exclusively devoted to this removal. [4]

They had no sooner settled in their new home than they attempted to organize a system of government for the entire tribe, including the ones who had previously made the journey westward and the later arrivals. In doing this the feeling which had arisen over differences in the policies of the Indians as to the removal broke out again. Their suffering had been so great that they could not forget it, and some of the members of the tribe were blamed for encouraging the acts of the representatives of the Government. The first meeting called was adjourned, and before another assembled Major

---

[4] See Indian Removal. A description of the emigration of the Five Civilized Tribes of Indians by Grant Foreman. University of Oklahoma Press, Norman, Oklahoma, 1932.

Ridge, Elias Boudinot, and John Ridge, son of Major Ridge, were killed. John Ross was President of the Constitutional Convention of the tribe in the East from 1828 to the time of the removal, and the choice of most of the tribe for Principal Chief after the final emigration. He was blamed by many for this killing, but full investigation has shown that he not only had nothing to do with it, but very much resented the act. The fact is, that he had nothing to gain by the elimination of these men, as he was the choice of perhaps three-fourths of the combined tribe for the position of Principal Chief. To this position he was elected and served until his death in 1866.

This killing of the treaty members of the tribe, as heretofore stated, was brought about on account of the passage of the resolution by the Indians in 1829, which resolution had been prepared and presented by Major Ridge himself. It will be understood, however, that Major Ridge was as much opposed to the removal as any of the Indians, but had advocated the treaty as being what he considered the best course out of the difficulty.

This killing, as John Ross plainly saw, only started a matter of reprisals and strife, which it took years to eradicate. A few years after this, Stand Watie, belonging to the treaty faction, killed James Foreman, one of the most prominent followers of the Ross party, and during the Civil War the beautiful home of John Ross was burned. The turmoil arising from this strife was followed by the misery and misfortune which overwhelmed the tribe during the Civil War.

John Ross was one of the ablest men that this country has produced. This statement is true without regard to race or color. He met, at a disadvantage on his part, the ablest statesmen the Government could pit against him, and emerged creditably. The representatives of the Government were unable to overcome him with diplomacy or skill, and were compelled to resort to force of numbers to subdue him. When the Civil War broke over the country Ross advocated neutrality and pursued this policy as long as possible. The emissaries of both the North and the South, however, invaded his tribe, and the feeling became so great that he could not longer hold them together. First one Army and then the other took charge of the Indians and levied recruits for its respective Army from their ranks. Part of the tribe sympathized with the North and part with the South. The tribe was torn asunder, and turmoil reigned supreme. When one Army took possession, the adherents to the other cause were compelled to flee, and the tribe was kept in constant agitation. A portion of the Northern sympathizers, consisting of a large number, were compelled to flee from the tribe, and took refuge in Southern Kansas, where they did not receive the support which they should have had from the cause they supported, and they suffered extreme hardships, privations, and misfortunes before the close of the war. They remained there, however, until the war did close, when they returned to their homes. It is said that Jesse Chisholm was with this portion of the tribe, and on account of his presence in Kansas at this time, afterward located his trading post on Chisholm Creek, now at the present site of Wichita.

At the close of the war representatives of the Government, following out their usual course of consideration of the Cherokees, in 1866 required the tribe to make a new treaty. The excuse for this treaty was that a portion of the tribe had cast its fortunes with the South, and it was necessary to make this new treaty in order for them to renew their allegiance to the Government. In this consideration, however, friend and foe were treated alike. No reward was given to the portion of the tribe which had suffered on account of its allegiance, and the new arrangement only had the effect of tightening the grasp of the Government on the lands of the Indians. The Government was given additional supervisory rights over their lands by this treaty. These rights were strongly asserted in the future when the question as to the title of the Indians to the land arose.

The treaty of 1835, being the treaty of New Echota, which the Indians had been compelled to accept, contained the following provision:

"The United States also agrees that the lands above ceded by the treaty of February 14, 1833, including the outlet, (referring to the Cherokee Outlet) and those ceded by this treaty shall be included in one patent executed to the Cherokee Nation of Indians by the President of the United States according to the provisions of the Act of May 28, 1830."

In the treaty of 1866 the Government reserved the right to settle other tribes of Indians on portions of the Cherokee Lands, for which the Indians so settling on the same should pay to the Cherokees a price that they might agree upon, and if they could not agree, the price was to be fixed by the President of the United States, after which the treaty contained the following provision:

"The Cherokee Nation to retain the right of possession of and jurisdiction over all of said country west of 96th degree of longitude until thus sold and occupied, after which their jurisdiction and right of possession to terminate forever as to each of said districts thus sold and occupied."

It is worthy of note, that the great complaint usually made by the people in general against the Indians was that they refused to submit to the teaching of the white man and to adopt his religious views, his ways of living, and methods of making a living. The Cherokees readily accepted and did all these things as suggested by the white race, and after so doing they were herded together in stockades, hunted, and forced from their country for no other reason than that white men should take the place of the Indians and acquire their valuable lands.

The Cherokees as far back as history has any record were not a nomadic people. They had settled on their fields and supported themselves as their white neighbors. Even while in their Eastern homes they had a well organized form of tribal government. They maintained a school system. Their country was as well supplied with churches as was any community on the frontier. They plowed and cultivated their fields, lived in houses as comfortable as their white neighbors, and their domestic stock of cattle and horses grazed over their pastures. They had an abundance of chickens, other poultry, and hogs. Upon their settlement in the West their first act was to arrange a well organized Government for their protection. This at first was not as successful as it would have been had the Indians been in their normal condition. Their wounds were still smarting from the wrongs that had been inflicted upon them, and resentment burned within them. This resentment they sought to heap upon anyone, who in their opinion could be blamed for contributing to their misfortunes.

Despite the domestic strife which continued in the tribe in their new home, they made rapid advancement. They had a good tribal government, modeled very much on the plan of our National Government. Their Principal Chief was the executive head of the same. The legislative department consisted of two branches, taking the place of the two branches of Congress. One branch, designated as the upper branch, was known as the National Committee, corresponding to the Senate of the United States. By amendment this body was subsequently known as the Senate of the Cherokee Nation. The lower branch was known as the Council, corresponding to our House of Representatives. There were originally just two-thirds as many members in the National Committee as there were in the Council. They also had a well organized judicial system. The nation was divided into portions similar to our counties, and there was a well organized system of government in these subdivisions. The officers in these divisions consisted of sheriffs and other necessary officers. On September 6, 1839, they adopted a constitution that was a credit to any civilized people.

The Cherokee Nation in the Indian Territory had a school system that was as well organized as any white community of its age. An alphabet had been invented by one of their own tribe which was better adapted to the sounds and words of the Cherokee language than the English alphabet. This consisted of eighty-five letters or characters. It is said that it was much easier to learn than the English, and it must have been, considering the ease with which it was mastered by the members of the tribe. They at all times had one or more well equipped printing presses, where papers were printed in their own language. Here these Indians lived a domestic and rural life until the Civil War tore them asunder. The suffering of the Cherokees during this turbulent period cannot be described here for want of space. [5]

As heretofore stated, the Cherokee Tribe has produced some of the brightest minds in the history of our Nation. John Ross was an example of this ability. Had he been able to exert his outstanding intelligence under better advantages and on a larger scale it would have had no limit.

Major Ridge was a man of high attainments and much ability. He had been a power among the Cherokees in the old home, and was in the West up to the time of his death. Among their number at the time of their removal were many men of high education, being college graduates. Among this

-----

[5] See Conditions in the Indian Territory and The Civil War in Oklahoma in READINGS IN OKLAHOMA HISTORY by Edward Everett Dale and Jesse Lee Rader.

number was Elias Boudinot, whose Indian name was Watie. He had been assisted in his efforts to gain an education by a man by the name of Elias Boudinot, whose name he adopted. Watie or Elias Boudinot was in the East the editor of the Cherokee Phoenix, a newspaper established by the Cherokee Council. He was a man of much ability, and the tribe suffered a severe loss after the removal by his untimely death. John Ridge, a cousin of Elias Boudinot, was also educated at Cornwall, Connecticut, and was a man of extensive ability. The number of outstanding characters of great importance produced by the Cherokee are so numerous that it would be an injustice not to name them all, but the number is so great that such would be impossible. Senators, representatives, judges, and many men of national prominence in the United States have belonged to this tribe. It may be claimed that most of these men had a large percent of Caucasian blood in their veins. Such is true in many cases. John Ross' father was a white man, and his mother had only a small percent of Indian blood, but such is not the controlling element in the case of many of the leading men of their tribe. It is true that most of them had some Caucasian blood, and were well educated. Jesse Chisholm, while a mixed blood, had no education whatever. Also, George Guess, better known as Sequoyah, while his father was a white man, was reared entirely by the Indians, and is often misstated as being a full blood Cherokee, never learned or spoke the English language. He knew nothing of the history of the same, nor did he know the sounds of the language. He did not have the efforts of past generations to guide him, and no one to teach or assist him, yet he retired to his study and worked, and in its solitude persevered for days, weeks, and years, and finally came forth and presented to his people a complete alphabet of eighty-five characters. This Indian, thrown upon his own resources, accomplished by himself as much as the combined efforts of the English educators and teachers had done in hundreds of years.

After the close of the Civil War, the Cherokees gained ground slowly, but finally became prosperous. Their government flourished. John Ross died in 1866 in Washington City, while there on a mission for his people, to whom his life was devoted. He had been Principal Chief of the Cherokee Nation in the West for almost 27 years. After his death other able men took charge of the government of the tribe. During the controversy over the leasing of the Cherokee Outlet to the cattle interests and the Cherokee Strip Live Stock Association, and during the negotiations for the purchase of the Cherokee Outlet from the Indians, no representative of the Government who dealt with or tried to deal with the leading men of the Cherokee Nation ever accused them of lacking in ability. Had the Indians had the power behind them that the party with whom they were dealing had, the Government would have had no advantage over them. Finally, in 1902, the United States Government passed an act abolishing all the power of the Cherokees to maintain a tribal government. At that time the Cherokee Tribe passed out of existence as a legal entity. It has, however, now been thrown among the mass of the citizens of the United States, and the members of the same will continue to make a creditable showing as citizens. But, for this tribe the grades have been steep and the trail has been rough.

CHAPTER XV.

THE WICHITA AND AFFILIATED BANDS

Another set of Indians who had communication with the Chisholm Trail was the Wichita and Affiliated Bands. These Indians comprised the remaining members of the once powerful Wichita tribe and the remnants of a number of other tribes, including Caddo, Wacoe, Towacanie, Keechie, Ionie, and a few Delawares.

Prior to the year 1828 the Government had by treaty procured from the Quapaw and Osage Indians, who claimed title to the same, the land afterward embraced in the State of Oklahoma. As has been heretofore observed, the Government had ceded to the Five Civilized Tribes the portions of the country occupied by them, and also to the Cherokees the Outlet. Subsequently the Kiowa, Comanche, and Wichita and Affiliated Bands claimed a portion of the western part of the Indian Territory. The Wichita claimed that they had inhabited this region for many generations. These Plains Indians did not recognize the right, given by the Government to the Five Civilized Tribes, to any lands which they claimed, and continuously threatened forays on these tribes. By the treaty of 1855, the Government had given to the Choctaw the land as far west as the one-hundredth meridian, and lying between Red River and the Canadian River.

A portion of the time up to 1855, the Wichita occupied parts of this country as far east as the ninety-eighth meridian. This occupancy was resented by the Choctaw. In 1856 a treaty was made between the Choctaw and Chickasaw and the Government, by the terms of which this land between the Red River and Canadian River and between the ninety-eighth and one-hundredth meridians was to belong to and be the common property of the Choctaw and Chickasaw Indians, and these tribes leased said land to the Government for the purpose of settling the Wichita and other bands of Indians on the same. The position of the Wichita had been somewhat precarious prior to this time. The fierce Comanche were threatening them from the west, and as they crowded east they trespassed upon the lands of the Choctaw and Chickasaw. This land embraced in the limits north of the Red River and between the ninety-eighth and one-hundredth meridians was known after this time as the Leased District. There were approximately 1,500 Indians removed from northern Texas and settled with the Wichita and Affiliated Bands. These Texas Indians were the remnants of various tribes.

On the breaking out of the Civil War, these affiliated tribes on the Leased District allied themselves with the Confederacy. The Wichita, however, soon had trouble with the Confederate Government, removed from the Leased District to southern Kansas, and remained there until after the close of the war. They lived, during this absence, on the site of Wichita, Kansas, and the town took its name from them. At the close of the Civil War the Choctaw and Chickasaw made another treaty with the Federal Government, as did all the other tribes, any portion of whom had affiliated themselves with the Confederacy. By the terms of this new treaty, the Choctaw and Chickasaw ceded the Leased District to the Government, leaving the western boundary of the Chickasaw Nation at the ninety-eighth meridian and the Choctaw Nation east of the Chickasaw.

There were at the close of the war about 1,500 Indians, consisting principally of remnants of the tribes, removed from Texas, still remaining on the Leased District. The balance had removed to Kansas; their number was approximately 1,500 more, and consisted of the Wichita and the original Affiliated Bands. These Indians who had removed to Kansas were returned to the Leased District in 1868, and settled on the Washita, west of the ninety-eighth meridian. During their stay in Kansas, the number of these Indians was depleted by the ravages of both the smallpox and cholera.

It is true that the Indian question on the part of the National Government was a very complex proposition to deal with. This has been true at all times. We have observed the injustice that was evidently done the Cherokees in the dealings had with the representatives of the Government. The complications that arose in these matters may to a great extent excuse these results. Whether for the same reason or not, there was also an injustice done in the dealings of the representatives of the Government with the Wichitas. These representatives could not make the excuse that the portion of the Cherokees, who had been loyal to the Federal Government, should be chastised for their conduct; neither could they make the excuse that the Wichita, who had been sufficiently loyal to the Federal Government that they left their homes and retired into Northern Territory to relieve them from affiliation with the Confederacy, should suffer for their conduct in that regard.

After the Wichita and Affiliated Bands returned to their former homes in 1868, the representatives of the Government persistently refused to enter into treaty relations with them and grant to them any permanent home, but simply let them remain on what had been the Leased District. Their occupancy of this land was precarious and only as a matter of sufferance. In vain these Indians begged for a permanent home. Disregarding these requests, the representatives of the Government in 1868 made a treaty with the Kiowa, Comanche, and Apache, whereby there was granted to these Indians the south half of the Leased District for their absolute use, but provided that such other friendly tribes of Indians as they and the Government might agree upon might be settled on these lands. The northern portion of the Leased District was by executive order in 1869 set over to the Cheyenne and Arapaho Indians.

Repeated recommendations were made to the departments of the Government by its agents, and representatives sent to make investigation as to these conditions. The complaints and appeals of the Wichita, that a treaty be made granting to them a permanent home were not heeded or granted. The ancestral home of the Wichita was on the Washita, and in the vicinity of the Wichita Mountains, which bear their name. From the report of Special Commissioner, Charles F. Garrett, we make the following quotation:

"Dispirited and despairing of ever regaining their beautiful homes in the Wichita Mountains, where the bones of their ancestry have reposed for ages, and obtaining compensation for their losses or reward for their loyalty, they appear unwilling to improve their homes unless first assured to them under solemn treaty stipulations, accompanied by reasonable indemnity for the magnificent domain of which they have been dispossessed, and which without consultation with them, and without regard to their prior territorial rights, has been again and again ceded by the United States to other parties." [1]

A continued effort was made to procure some permanent arrangement for the Wichita and their associates. The Secretary of the Interior in 1870 approved such a recommendation. These Indians agreed to accept a reservation in what was known as the Eureka Valley in this Leased District. Provision was contained in the Indian Appropriation Acts of 1872 and 1873 setting aside money to defray the expenses of establishing these Indians on this allotted reservation. In 1872 a representative of the Government sent to treat with these Indians

---

[1] Record Indian Affairs 1868, p. 288—Chronicles of Oklahoma, Vol. XI, No. IV, December, 1933—p. 1051.

concluded a treaty with them, whereby they were to have as a reservation the land lying between the Canadian and Washita Rivers, west of the ninety-eighth meridian and approximately forty miles wide east and west. In consideration of this grant these Indians were to release all claim to any other lands in the United States. This treaty was never ratified by the Government. Mr. Walker, the representative of the Government making this agreement, in his report recommended that this treaty be ratified, and that as soon as possible, and further stated that the Wichita had no treaty agreement with the Government, nor did they have any reservation, and that they desired some arrangement be made whereby they could have a home of their own.

Conditions continued the same. The representatives of the Government, seemingly, deliberately delayed giving attention to these tribes. So far as business affairs were concerned the old Indians had minds of childish simplicity. The first observation of a child is the justice or injustice of the acts and conduct of other persons in their dealings. These Indians were helpless, and the representatives of the Government knew their condition. Their requests, regardless of the justice of their cause, went unheeded. Had they been able to create terror throughout the country and devastate the frontier, they might have received attention. The wild Apaches of the plains had all of these things and many more. They had terrorized the country from western Oklahoma to Arizona. As a reward for this conduct, and, in disregard of the loyalty of the Wichita and their allies to the Government, the ancestral lands of the Wichita were taken away from them and given to the Apache. It seems the worst treatment was inflicted by the representatives of the Government on the most submissive Indian tribes. The writer is not attempting to lay the blame to any particular person, creed, or party organization, but is only relating the facts, and the reader is capable of placing the blame at the proper source.

The agitation for the settlement of these Indians on a reservation continued on during the eighties, but nothing was accomplished. The question of issuing allotments to the Indians came up in Congress, and an Act was passed in 1887 providing for the same. The Wichita and their friends were finally recognized in this act. It was considered that they had acquired title by prescription and occupancy on these lands as defined in the unratified treaty of 1872, and they were given recognition accordingly. It is, perhaps, the only instance in history where an unapproved treaty was given effect. The Wichita was one of the most submissive tribes that were domiciled within the United States. It, like many of the other Indian tribes, is fast losing its identity. While the tribe did not receive the proper consideration by the representatives of the Government, they are leaving behind their name, which will endure as long as the hills shall stand in the Wichita Mountains, and as long as the tall structures of cities shall rise in the West, in the name of the City of Wichita.

We have now taken a brief observation of several of the tribes of Indians with whom the traveler on the Chisholm Trail came in contact. While these observations have been brief, it is impossible to go into detail in a work not devoted to that particular subject. This observation is only intended to give a general idea to the public as to these tribes and their characteristics. This is deemed proper for the reason that so few people know much about these things; things which are so close to them, and which they in fact desire to know and should know. Before departing from this subject it is deemed advisable to also briefly refer to some of the acts of every day life of these Indian tribes generally, which are at variance with our own customs and mode of life.

The writer as a young man and boy had an opportunity to observe much as to the Indians. He associated with them, at times lived in close contact with them, hunted with the young men of the tribes, and grew to know their characteristics and many of the Indians well. The most detestable habits of the Indians were acquired from the white man. The Indians recognized and acknowledged the white race which was crowding in upon them as their superiors in intelligence. In matters of moral conduct they were easily misled by this association. The whiskey of the white degenerates, who peddled it among the Indians to steal and rob them of their money, did more to demoralize the tribes and the individual members of the same than any other one thing.

A white man creates an impression and attempts to gain an advantage by impressing people with his importance and knowledge. An Indian creates an impression, and gains his advantage by claiming to know nothing, and by impressing the person dealing with him, that he actually does not know anything. An Indian in his normal state was honest and had the greatest respect for friendship. His heart would be touched by an act of kindness when no other medium would have any effect upon him. All Indians were susceptible to strong prejudices, and from being so often imposed upon finally grew to be suspicious of all persons until their loyalty was assured. The acts of retribution for a wrong and vindictiveness accompanied by treachery were pronounced in all Indians, especially in the Western tribes. The fiery spirit of these Indians was aroused by wrongs and imagined wrongs on behalf of the white race and the Government until it became a raging torrent and consumed their entire mental makeup. No outrage was too atrocious for them to inflict; vengeance was reeked, and wrongs inflicted upon the first available individual for injuries received from other persons. They did not care whom they hurt, but they must hurt someone or their wrath would not be appeased nor their vengeance satisfied.

An Indian in his normal state was a student of nature. Persons who never came in contact with them would not realize the extent of their knowledge in this respect. Their lives for many generations had been spent in communion with nature, and they had become close students of natural history, although they knew nothing about history in its technical sense. Once an Indian boy surprised the writer by explaining to him the origin and evolution of a June bug from the common grub-worm.

The wild Indians of the plains, nor any other Indians, so far as the writer knows, had any regular meal time. They ate when they were hungry. If that happened in the middle of the night they would eat. An old trapper, who had lived long among the Indians and had become accustomed to their habits, was once stopping at an army post, and the writer has heard the officers say that many times he would arise in the middle of the night, stir up the fire, and cook himself something to eat. When traveling, the moving aggregation would start in the morning and travel until they would get sufficiently hungry that they thought they should stop, usually after the middle of the day. Unless they were in a great hurry, when they stopped there would be no attempt to proceed until the next morning. When hunting, an Indian arose at the break of day, and was on the hunting ground as soon as it was possible to see to shoot. When he started to get up there was no foolishness about the performance. He leaped from his bed as if he was going to war, and immediately threw himself into high without any ceremony. He was capable of enduring the most extreme hardships without complaint. In fact the writer never heard an Indian complain under the most severe punishment. They were the most stoical persons when suffering pain that the world ever knew.

It has always been asserted that Indian women were submissive, and drudges. It is true that they performed the greater part of the menial labor. This method was at variance with our customs, but the customs of the Indians grew up from the difference in their mode of living. Indians in their normal state were compelled to rely on the pursuit of game for their livelihood, and on their prowess as warriors for their existence. These were the necessary and fundamental problems of life for the Indians. In this pursuit the men became very efficient. If anyone thinks that Indian women can not be vicious, he or she should have seen them when they would get into a controversy with other women of their tribe. This usually occurred when they were either putting up or taking down tepees in the camp. Their ideas were always at variance, and before they got through it many times ended in a rough and tumble fight among them. The men of the tribe would enjoy this trouble, and never interfere, but would laugh and look upon it as a circus. The writer once knew a white man with an Indian wife. The husband on each available occasion would come home very much under the influence of fire-water. The boys at a nearby ranch often told the writer, that on these occasions the gentle Indian mother would procure a large black-snake whip, which they used to drive their cattle, and proceed to wield this gentle persuader around the limbs and more ample parts of the head of the household until he fully recovered and was entirely sober.

In the relations of the male members of the tribes with each other, they had but very little trouble. When in camp the men would usually associate or assemble together in groups and talk and joke. They always enjoyed a joke, especially if it was at the expense of one of their friends. They would engage in sports of many kinds. Horse racing was an important amusement among them. The systems of these races have

Little Joseph, Nez Perc, son of Chief Joseph.
He lived for some time at the Nez Perc Agency
in the eastern portion of the Cherokee Outlet,
and often traveled the Chisholm Trail to the
Darlington Agency.

been explained heretofore. They also played ball, using a system of their own, but enjoyed it very much. The women would go about their domestic duties, usually in a very agreeable manner. It seemed that the boys of the tribes were almost continuously engaged in practice with bow and arrows. They used blunt pointed arrows, and it is no wonder that by the time they became adults they were proficient in the use of this instrument. The boys of the Cheyenne, Arapaho, Kiowa, Comanche, Apache, and Wichita tribes, when not practicing with the bow and arrows, were riding their ponies or young horses. These Indians, and especially the Cheyenne, Comanche, and Apache, became famous riders. The Cheyennes were the superior horsemen of them all. It was said that an old Cheyenne warrior could drop to the side of his horse and shoot, literally sending forth a string of arrows, keeping the air full of them. They used a belt or circingle around their horse, with a contrivance especially constructed by them in which they would fasten a foot and drop down on their horses' side with ease.

The writer has read a great assortment of literature, charging the Indians with being the most filthy, and filth-loving creatures on earth. It must be admitted that, measured by the standard of our civilization and culture, they were dirty, and some even filthy; but would the condition of our best parlor-equipped and refined citizens have been any better if they and their ancestors had for generations lived and been surrounded by the same conditions as these Indians? In this regard, as in the white race, there was great variance. The conditions of life under which the Indian lived and was met with had much to do with his appearance. No general estimate or classification can be made in this regard any more than can be done among members of the white race. The fact, also, as to the condition of poverty or available means and supply of necessities of life had much to do with their appearance and habits. Many of the tribes or portions of tribes were so nearly starved and were so poor that existence with them was precarious. Under these conditions they had no opportunity to make a magnificent appearance as to cleanliness or anything else. When any person or animal, driven to desperation or starvation, finds anything to eat there will not be much etiquette used in devouring the same. It has been shown from the handling and dealings with the Indians that, when the opportunity presented itself, they were very susceptible to culture and refinement. As it would be with anyone trained and enured to the camp and plains, it took some little time to bring about this transformation, but they got it as quickly as a member of the white race would under the same circumstances, and they seemed to enjoy it just as much. In handling the situation the Indian showed as much adaptability and ability in meeting the situation as any other class of people.

The fact is that the agency Indian was the prey for every white parasite and renegade turned loose on the Western Plains. These men developed or retrograded, whichever term is appropriate, into tin-horn gamblers, and as such started out to fleece the unsuspecting Indians on pay-day, the date their annuities were paid. These parasites were not recognized by real gamblers, but were degenerates who would hang around the forts, swindling the soldiers out of a little money, and when these pay-days came, they would retire to the agencies and rob the Indians. The writer at one time in his life helped to drive north horses which were gathered in the vicinity of Anadarko. While gathering these horses, an associate of the writer related a circumstance which happened to one of these tin-horn gamblers who came out to fleece the Indians. This circumstance as hereinafter set out is very illustrative.

The Indians near Anadarko, where this circumstance took place, had, as practically all other Indians in this climate in the summer season, shades erected from brush tops with leaves on. This made a shady retreat, beneath which the breeze would circulate, and the cover would protect the portion beneath from the sun. The relator stated that he was riding along the road near one of these shades, when he saw a crowd congregated around the same. He dismounted and walked over to this assembled group. Here he saw a tall, well built imitation of dignified humanity, a white tin-horn gambler, who had come out from the fort to steal the Indians' money.

He had gathered around him a bunch of young men of the nearby Indian tribes. They had a blanket spread on the ground beneath this shade, and were seated around the same playing cards. This particular alleged gambler had the appearance of being quite prosperous. He was dressed in the latest style of the time. He wore a low cut vest with a wide expanse of white stiff shirt bosom extending out in front of him. The gambler had everything fixed and the cards well stacked. The Indians had all their money on the blanket. The gambler, knowing exactly what they all had and that he held the winning hand, said, "What you got, John?" They all laid their cards down, the gambler spread out his winning hand in front of them saying, "You lose, John," and prepared to reach for the pile of money on the blanket.

Across the blanket from him was a tall, young, robust, active Indian, who, before the gambler could drag the money in, reached out and grabbed all of the same and dropped it in the folds of his blanket. The gambler leaped to his feet, and the Indian started to run. Just to the north of this shade was a large bedding ground, where a herd of cattle was bedded each night. The Indian hopped across this bedding ground, keeping just in front of the gambler, but he could have run faster. As they crossed this expanse, the Indian reached down, gathered his hand full of the worst filth he could find, turned, and dashed it into the face of the gambler, completely covering him from the top of his face to the bottom of his starched shirt. This particular swindler of the Indians turned and slowly took his course back to his starting point, a much wiser and a very much worse looking bunco-man than he was when he started.

These Indians, suddenly removed from their wild, unrestrained life upon the plains and from their generations of training, were totally ignorant of the method of carrying on the life to which it was sought to transplant them. In these new ways they were in every particular simply children of the most tender years. The trials of the Indian agents were beyond comprehension. Even where these agents sought and honestly tried to do the very best they could, it was one of the most difficult positions imaginable. On the other hand, many of the agents, especially prior to or during the Civil War, were corrupt and did not care. After the war, corruption was a thing seldom found among these caretakers of the Indians. A very illustrative report, in which the agent was taking very much to heart the condition of his wards, but was a sort of a wag in expressing the situation, is shown in that of E. C. Osborne, agent of the several tribes at the Ponca Agency in 1885. A portion of his report reads as follows:

"The agency is composed of four sub-agencies and four distinct tribes of Indians, the Poncas, Pawnees, Confederate tribe of Otoe and Missourias, and the Tonkawa. Not because of the existence of any marked difference in the nature and customs of these Indians will I report them separately, but the promotion of system in the report renders it somewhat necessary. Whatever may be said of one of these tribes generally will apply alike to them all."

PONCAS

"The Poncas, numbering 546, hold in common 101,984 acres of as pretty land as the West can boast, by purchase from the Cherokees. Allotments of 160 acres have at some time past been made to considerable numbers of them, who have fenced small plats thereon, from 2 to 20 acres. As a whole, however, the Poncas recognize no special claim to their allotments, holding only that the land is the tribe's in common. This matter of allotments to them of their lands in severalty is quite a favored and hackneyed theory, and may be an unexceptionally good one, but the practical features connected with it are not unattended by difficulties of considerable moment: 1st., only a few want it thus; 2d, the balance will not permit these few to have it thus; and these conditions true, I think the third and other difficulties need not be enumerated.

"When I first took charge of this agency these Indians promised me great things, and, with only the idea of Indians which I had gathered from sundry romancing historians, I believed them. I was young then; I was enthusiastic then; but now I know better; even now, at the close of one brief year, I know better. In the early spring their clamor for horses with which to till the ground, enrich themselves, and make of themselves an independent and happy people, rang in my ears until I thought a denial of them or a relaxing of my efforts for one moment to get these horses for them at the earliest possible moment would not fall short of crime. With an enthusiastic energy, therefore, born of my aforementioned historical knowledge, I pulled steadily to the point of gratifying them. You remember, no doubt, sir, our several advertisements for bids to supply these horses, our failure to procure a bid within reason—so perfect did we want the horses, and our ultimate resort to open-market purchase. Well, some month or more ago we succeeded in getting them a lot of 124 as good and serviceable young horses as $90 per head could procure in this country. I issued them, first having branded them 'I. D.' and numbered them from 1 to 124, the pick horse to the pick Indians, 'and all was as merry as a marriage bell.'

"Not more than for three days thereafter was I permitted to enjoy the whisperings of my conscience, 'Well done, thou good and faithful servant,' when in they began to come, one by one, with the report of a horse being gone, strayed or stolen, or stabbed by a neighbor, or cut to pieces in a wire fence, or tangled or mangled with a lariat and stake-pin, and not much longer was it, in the midst of these distresses, before I had to summon the agency force and sally forth to disperse the whole tribe of them, which had met on the sunny side of a hill of mild declivity for the fall races! I have hounded them to the best of my fast failing mind, them and their treasures, with an eye single to the life, only the barren life, of their horses, until this morning I am appraised of the fact that some twenty of them last night, on their horses, stole out under the summer moon to their old home in Dakota.

"From the manner in which they treat horses one would imagine this to be the first lot ever issued them; but the records of this office show this to be purely imagination. If they will not fly the track, or, in the event they do, if I can have them brought back, I shall persist in attempting to make them care for their horses and other issues or to make their ownership quite doubtful.

"The general conditions and habits of these Indians are not at this time enviable; and I may be permitted to express a fear that they are retrograding sadly, as from a report of them in 1882 which I find in the Commissioner's Report of the year in this office I notice that they were very energetic and cleanly; that they were not infrequently found eating their meals in family circles around neatly spread tables; that comfortable homes were found on nearly every allotment; that the song of the husbandman was heard in the land, etc. I pledge you my most sacred word and honor that at this time all of them are lazy; that four-fifths of them are filthy; that they do not eat in family circles nor upon neatly spread tables, nor upon tables at all; that there are not exceeding a dozen of them who can shelter a horse, and no song save that of the dance is ever heard amongst them.

"May the good Lord have mercy upon these poor retrograding Indians, or upon the agent who reported them in 1882, whichever may most demand it, is my prayer. I hope and expect to improve their general condition and habits, but it will take more time to get them back to the glorious old 1882 than I can hope to be with them. They have from one to three wives; they eat dog and regard it a luxury; they choke ponies to death at the graves of their dead, and for weeks afterward carry provisions to the dead Indian and leave them at the grave. When the death of a favorite child occurs, the father, or the mother, if the father is dead, will give away all possessions, even leaving the family utterly destitute of food and raiment.

"We succeeded in persuading them to abstain from the annual sun dance this year. They had run pretty short on provisions, and the proffer you made them of a feast in lieu of the dance was too tempting to be rejected. Illustrating, however, the fixedness of their faith, there arose a quarrel between two of the men on the day of the feast, resulting in a blow which broke an arm. The forlorn recipient of this injury, while the arm was being set, looking over the crowd of us who were witnessing the operation, said in the most sorrow-stricken manner imaginable that the exchange of his sun dance for the feast had caused it all. The Indian who had caused his suffering and all animosity in the case was forgotten in this overwhelming conclusion." [2]

No one can read the foregoing without realizing the disappointment and regret of this agent, who was evidently a conscientious and trustworthy man. If he could see the change that has been wrought in these Indians at this time, see them as they stroll down the street wearing their ten gallon hats and fine boots, he would feel much gratified and surprised. Furthermore, a great many of the misfortunes met were brought about by the fact that the agent was as ignorant of what he

---

[2] Report of Commissioner of Indian Affairs, 1886—pp. 135-136. Readings in Oklahoma History, p. 400.

was attempting to do as the Indians themselves. If this agent had known and been experienced in handling horses of the class he was having turned over to these Indians, he would have known that the result of these inexperienced Indians handling such young horses would have been just what it was. This is largely the case with men who know nothing about handling horses. Indians, as the Cheyennes, who knew horses, would have been able to avoid much of this misfortune.

Indians did and still have a mania for racing horses, but that is no crime. If it was, many of the white race would be the worst criminals. Reference is made to these Indians eating dogs. Some tribes did eat dogs, but others were as averse to it as the white race, and they considered those who did engage in that practice as being degraded, and the worst denunciation they could make of them was that, "they ate dogs." In their primitive state Indians were often driven by hunger to eat most anything. The rites referred to in the above quoted article, which were held at the graves of departed members of their families, were only kind demonstrations exhibited by them in their sorrow. These were their customs and methods of expressing their feelings. They were ridiculous to us, but perhaps not any more ridiculous than many of our own are to races whose usages and customs differ from ours.

The general observation of the antecedents and history of the Indians, who came in contact with the portion of the now State of Oklahoma, which was traversed by the Chisholm Trail, will give the reader a better idea of the past life, character, and difficulties of these fellow citizens of the now great common· wealth which is shared by us all. Whatever this past has been, it is an undisputable fact that some, even of the full blood Indians today, and many of the ones sharing the blood of both the Indian and the white race, are superior in education, ability, and qualities which go to make good and effective citizens than many of the white race who have had the same or better opportunities. It is further apparent that the generations are not far distant when these people will be entirely swallowed up and absorbed by the dominant race.

CHAPTER XVI.

THE CATTLE INDUSTRY IN THE INDIAN TERRITORY

The cattle business in the Indian Territory was an industry developed from the establishment of the Chisholm Cattle Trail. Practically all the cattle that were held, reared, or fattened on the pastures of the Indian Territory traveled up this trail. Without any exception the grass that grew upon the fertile plains of what is now Oklahoma produced the finest pasture and made the country the finest grazing region in North America.

In connection with this chapter it is well to bear in mind the acquisition of the Outlet by the Cherokees and the progress of settlement adjacent thereto. The first recorded information we find as to the establishment of and granting the Cherokee Outlet to the Cherokee Nation is in the statement of the President of the United States communicated through the Secretary of War in March, 1818. This was followed by a second communication dated October 8, 1821. This was afterward embodied in the treaty with the Cherokees ratified May 28, 1828, and which is known as the treaty of 1828.

This grant was further affirmed by the Treaty of New Echota in 1835. It was also provided that a commission should be appointed to establish the lines of the tracts of land above described. By the terms of the treaty with Spain, 1819, the western boundary of the United States was fixed at the 100th Meridian west. The line between the Cherokee Outlet and Kansas was run in 1858, yet the survey of the Outlet was not made until 1872, when it was run from what was known as the Indian Meridian and a base line intersecting it near Fort Arbuckle. The first survey on either side of the Kansas and

Outlet line was in Kansas, when the Osage lands were surveyed. This survey was run from the Sixth Principal Meridian, which Meridian is located a few miles east of South Haven, Kansas. There was a discrepancy of about two and one-half miles in the surveys of the Osage lands in Southern Kansas, which was run from the 6th Principal Meridian, and the Oklahoma survey, which was run from the Indian Meridian. This strip of land was finally determined to belong to Kansas and was settled upon in the late seventies.

In any event, until the time of the Civil War, to all intents and purposes, so far as the citizens were concerned, these boundaries were simply imaginary lines, existing only on paper. The settlers crowded west after the close of the war. From 1870 to 1875 the lands lying to the north of the Cherokee Outlet and in the vicinity of the Chisholm Trail were settled upon as homesteads. These settlers were poor. A large part of them were young men who had served in the Federal Army. Most of them had married and moved to the West to procure homes for themselves and families. The worldly possessions of each of these settlers in most cases consisted of a wagon, team of horses, and such other equipment as he had hauled to his new home in his wagon. Southern Kansas was strictly a prairie country. The only timber that could be found there were the few trees, bordering upon and along the banks of the streams, which had escaped the ravages of the prairie fires that annually swept over the country.

Prior to the time of making the treaties above referred to, no attempt had been made by the Government of the United States to reduce this country, known as the Cherokee Outlet, to its possession. No tribe of Indians had any particular claim to any particular portion of the same, but all the tribes of Plains Indians roved over it at will. This condition existed until the settlements came into southern Kansas as above stated. Also the country prior to this time was covered by the apparently limitless herds of buffalo. These shaggy monarchs of the plains had for an unknown period of time in the past lived upon the rich pastures of these regions, had thrived, and multiplied. The higher land of this country was all covered by a beautiful coating of buffalo grass, while on the lower portions taller grasses, waist high, stretched for miles.

Old buffalo hunters have often stated that in the spring time, after the grass had grown to a good proportion, one could stand on an elevated point and look down over these valleys and see an unlimited number of circles some twenty feet in diameter. These were circles trampled in the grass where the male buffaloes had traveled in a circle around a mother buffalo and her helpless baby until it was strong enough to travel. This was done in order to protect them from wolves or any other harm which might befall her or her offspring. They also stated that further in the distance, as far as the eye could reach, could be seen the brown objects, members of the herd. In the harder or more solid ground, where the water was inclined to stand, were the deep and ragged holes torn out by the short stout horns of these monarchs of the plains. When it rained these depressions would fill with water and were used by the buffalo in which to stand or wallow. The dirt and sand thus accumulated in their long shaggy hair until it was so thick on the front part of the head that it would withstand the force of a heavy pistol bullet.

In the later years of the seventies, when this writer, then a small boy, first saw this country, these scenes had all passed. However, the holes left by the buffalo, universally known as "buffalo wallows," were still there; and while barren, the grass was crowding in at the sides, but the water still accumulated in them, as if, like the Indians, they were waiting for the buffalo to return. Also in the spring time, during this later period, when the prairie fires had swept across the country consuming the grass, as far as could be seen, stretched a limitless succession of white objects, each of which was the bones, the remnants of the carcass of a departed buffalo, which had probably fallen the victim of some hide hunter and been left on the plain to be devoured by vultures or predatory animals. One of the main sources of revenue among the early settlers was the money derived from the sale of these bones which they gathered and sold. Also, at this time extended across the prairies like long ribbons stretching out in the distance the buffalo paths or trails. These paths at places, especially where they crossed a depression, hollow, or stream, were cut deep into the soil, made by the long strings of buffalo, which, when traveling always trailed out in military fashion, following one another.

Cattle had the same inclination as buffalo in following one another when traveling, and thus establishing a path. The original ones found in this country were designated as "buffalo paths," and the later ones as "cow paths." There was one thing in which the buffalo and cattle differed. That was their idea as to the proper course to pursue in case of a storm or blizzard. As will be seen hereafter, cattle, when a blizzard struck them, would drift with the storm and crowd together. When buffalo would encounter a blizzard, they would turn their heads directly into it and facing the wind travel against it. The head and front part of a buffalo is covered with heavy thick hair and well protects the front portion of the animal. The hair on the rear portion of the body of these animals is extremely short, leaving this portion less protected. This being the case, the buffalo sent forward the most protected portion to meet the storm.

When the first settlers came into southern Kansas, there were scattering bands of migratory Plains Indians constantly traveling over and stopping upon the lands of the Cherokee Outlet. The description above given will show the conditions which surrounded these hardy pioneers. From the statement made, it will be readily seen that the worst difficulty which beset them was the lack of fuel. The old travelers on the plains had supplied this want by the use of "buffalo chips" left by the numerous buffalo, but the settlers could not avail themselves of this commodity. They could build their houses and stables of sod cut from the tough surface of the prairie. This they did, but they must have fuel to keep them warm and to cook their food. There was no coal in this region. The nearest railway, even after 1872, was at Wichita, Kansas, sixty miles away. Several streams of considerable size, including the Arkansas River, lay between these settlers and the railway. These streams must be forded, as there were no bridges at that time. During the winter season, the blizzards swept down from the north over this barren country, with the air filled with fine snow, shutting off the view. The outlaws from the plains stole the horses of the settlers, leaving them helpless and without resources, until they took the law into their own hands.

The timber on the streams in southern Kansas was appropriated with the homesteads on which it stood, and not being adequate for general use was held by the owners of the land. To the south, across the line of the Indian Territory, were a number of well wooded streams, much better than any found in southern Kansas. Bluff Creek was just over the line in the Indian Territory, Deer Creek was some ten miles beyond, while some twelve or fifteen miles further south was Pond Creek. The timber on these streams saved the day for the settlers in southern Kansas. Wood from them was hauled by them for forty miles north of the southern line of Kansas. The writer has seen strings of wagons one-half mile long all hauling wood from the Indian Territory. Also many houses were built from logs from the same source. The first house in which the family of the writer lived in southern Kansas was built of cottonwood logs taken from Bluff Creek.

According to the original survey of the Osage Trust lands, the home of the writer's family would have been on the extreme southern boundary of Kansas, but after the two and one-half mile strip was added, it was that distance from the state line. All of the settlers in this country soon acquired a number of cattle, which increased rapidly. As soon as the roving Indian bands ceased to frequent the borders of the Indian Territory, these settlers began to graze their small herds on the abundant supply of fine grasses across the line in that country. If not so grazed this grass would be burned in the fall and benefit no one.

Those were the days of the embryo cowboy. The herds coming up the trail were accompanied by sombrero-topped cowboys from the south, with their high-heeled boots, and Spanish spurs. It was only human nature that every boy who herded the family cows should want to imitate these professional cow hands. The country was not all settled and some of the farmers grazed their cattle on these unoccupied lands, but usually drove them across the line into the Indian country. It usually fell to the lot of the boys of the family to look after these cattle. This they did often, at first, riding one of the family work horses, perhaps without a saddle.

Proud were these lads when they could equip themselves with a broad-brimmed hat, were the proud possessors of a saddle, and, even more so, when they could afford a pony to ride. These boys were then ready to put themselves on exhibition. The writer heard of one boy who had advanced far enough to be the owner of a pair of chaps, a pair of boots, and spurs. He was not able yet, however, to own a pony, so when the family went to town in the farm wagon he would adorn himself in his cowboy attire, ride along until he reached the limits of the town, when he would get out, walk into town, and parade the streets, imagining himself the most observed by all observers. Many of these boys soon joined the ranks of the men on the range and spent most of their lives in the saddle. Others followed it for a time and returned to other positions in life.

As the country settled up more, obstacles were overcome, these herds along the state line increased, and pushed further down into the Indian country. Soon more capital came, partnerships and corporations were formed, cattle coming up the trail were bought and held in the Indian Territory. Some of the persons, seeking to be more secure in their possessions, procured permission and protection from the Cherokees. There were some thrifty mixed blood Cherokees who also held cattle in the Outlet. Among this number was Robert L. Owen, afterward United States Senator from Oklahoma. Then, as these lands became occupied, there came the conflict of interests. Those having holdings in the country had designated lines for their range. These lines were recognized, and payments were made for these rights to the Cherokees.

These were the days of the open range. There were no fences, but the borders of each range were ridden by line riders and the cattle kept in bounds the best that could be done under the circumstances. As the prairie grass would burn in late summer, the great menace to these cattlemen were prairie fires. Fires on the range early in the season would ruin the winter pasture, and the owners of the ranges would have nothing on which to winter their stock. The country at that time, except the lowlands, was covered with buffalo grass. This is a short curly grass running on the ground instead of growing upright. When growing prolific it forms a mat over the ground. Late in the season, when it becomes dry, this grass dies at the root first, retaining all the nourishment in the stem, and cattle grazing on the same will fatten even when the grass has dried. Thus the cattle would live on these ranges the year round.

This buffalo grass during the winter season, when it had not been pastured heavily during the summer, would fatten cattle like corn. When not heavily grazed, it often grew in some localities so abundant that it would appear to spring under foot when walked upon. In portions of the country, it was mixed with a very small pea-vine with small pods on it, which added to its nutritious qualities for pasture. In later years it seemed that the tall blue-stem and cotton-top prairie grass, which grew much taller, crept in and killed out much of the buffalo grass. After the buffalo ceased to tramp over the country these heavier grasses generally grew much more abundant. This larger grass was not good winter pasture. To this condition, and lack of the old supply of buffalo grass, was doubtless due in later years, during the winter season, much of the mortality among the cattle.

In order to eliminate the dangers from fire, around each range, and also crossing the same when it was large, were plowed and burned fire guards. These were usually constructed by contract by persons engaged in the business. These were constructed in the following manner: The prairie was covered by a heavy sod, rendered tough by the strong roots of the prairie grass holding it firmly together. In breaking these fire guards men with sod plows, such as were generally used in plowing or breaking prairie, and which were drawn by several yokes of oxen or teams of mules, would plow a furrow where the fire guard was desired, then another was run with the plow parallel to the first, and about twenty or thirty yards distant. A second furrow would then be plowed by following the first one all the way around. Thus there was left a space of grass about twenty or thirty yards wide with two furrows on each side.

A time would be selected when the wind was not blowing. A piece of cloth, gunny-sack, or other similar material, would be saturated with kerosene. To this would be attached a wire several feet in length, and this wire in turn would be fastened to a rope. This rope would be fastened to the saddle-horn of the saddle of a cowboy on a horse. This saturated material would then be lighted and dragged along perhaps thirty feet behind the rider. This burning process was begun on the leeward side of this strip of grass, so that the fire must run against the wind, if any. Other cowboys followed with sacks or pieces of blankets soaked with water, and if the fire broke over the furrows at any point, they extinguished the same with these water-soaked materials. They would also be followed by a wagon containing barrels of water to wet again the sacks or blankets when needed. These fire guards could be burned as fast as the horseman dragging the fire-brand could travel with his horse walking along the edge of this grass. Many miles would be burned in one evening. This would leave a burned strip twenty or thirty yards wide, which would stop most any prairie fire. These fire guards were established at certain intervals, depending largely on the character of the grass, the presence of creeks or rivers, or other natural fire obstructions.

In 1883, the entire Cherokee Outlet was leased by the Cherokee Strip Live Stock Association, and permission was inferred to fence the ranges. They were soon all fenced and most of them cross-fenced. During the period of the open range, it had been very difficult to hold the cattle where they belonged. This was especially true during the winter season. When the blizzards blew across the country, driving sleet and snow through the air, the cattle would drift from their range and travel many miles seeking shelter or going, they knew not where, just traveling with the storm. After the fences were built it eliminated this trouble to a certain extent, but at times during very severe storms, especially late in the season, these fences caused a heavy loss of life among the cattle by holding them back. On other occasions, the cattle would crowd against these fences, when drifting before the storm, until there would be such a congested mass they would break the wires of the fences, and as these storms invariably came from the north, drift on south. In the latter instance, many of them would not be retrieved until the spring round-up.

These fences were constructed of barbed wire. They were almost all built in the same manner, being of three wires with posts set about two rods apart with a stay between them. Each range was surveyed by a surveyor and the exact amount of land received by each person or company was recorded. The posts and material for these fences, other than the wire and staples, were cut and procured from the adjacent land when the same was possible or available. In the northern part of the Outlet, however, the streams had been so denuded of timber by the settlers in southern Kansas that the ranchmen in this portion were compelled to buy posts to fence their ranges.

Under the best of care and management, even after the ranges were fenced, many cattle, principally during the winter season, escaped and drifted into foreign pastures. This necessitated sorting them and returning the strays to their home pasture. This process was carried on in a very systematic manner, and was called the "round-up." These round-ups were always held in the spring time, just after the grass started and had grown to such an extent that cattle were in a thrifty condition. They were curried on by the representatives from all the ranches or ranges that would likely have cattle in the pasture that was being rounded up.

For instance the round-up would begin at the ranch or range on the northwest corner of the Cherokee Outlet, and all the ranchmen whose cattle could possibly have strayed to this pasture would be represented. The representation of each ranch or range consisted of a chuck wagon, a bunch of cowboys consistent with the number of cattle bearing their brand that would likely be found in that portion of the country, and to the end that the cattle found could be taken care of. These men also had a sufficient number of saddle horses, including "cutting horses." Each cowboy usually had seven head. These horses and men were used to cut out, care for, and return to their respective ranch all the cattle found bearing the particular brand they represented.

Some little explanation might be made here as to what is meant by a "chuck wagon" and a "cutting horse." The "chuck wagon" consisted of an ordinary wagon equipped with wagon bows and wagon cover, very similar to the wagons used by the pioneers of the West. In the rear end of this wagon was what was known as the "chuck-box." This was a box arranged similar to a cupboard and raised up higher than the top box of the wagon. It had a door with hinges at the bottom. This door dropped back, and when opened left a level board surface, which served as a sort of a table on which the plates and food could be set. A cowboy usually ate, however, by taking such food as was desired on his plate in one hand, a tin cup filled with hot coffee in the other, and seating himself on the ground "tailor fashion." If the ground was wet he would place his cup on something and remain standing while he ate. Fires were built on the ground with either wood or cow-chips. The writer does not now recall that he ever saw a stove on the range, except occasionally a small sheet-iron affair. These "chuck wagons" carried all the necessaries and equipment of the outfit, including the tarpaulins and blankets of all the cowboys, and the groceries and supplies, usually including several musical instruments, classed as necessaries.

A "cutting horse," as the term was used, meant the horse ridden by a cowboy in cutting out the cattle from the rest of the herd and removing them to the bunch of the brand to which they belonged. This might seem a simple process to one who never tried it, but it was anything but simple. A trained cutting horse knew more about cattle than most men. When a round-up was to be made of a pasture, all the cattle in the pasture were gathered together. Then the different brands were sorted out. One animal which bore a certain brand would be removed from the common bunch and placed by itself. Then another one would be taken out, and if it was of a different brand it would be removed to a different place. All cattle of the same brand were held together in a separate bunch and guarded by cowboys belonging to that outfit. This process would continue until the common herd was exhausted, when each outfit would remove the cattle bearing its brand and which had been turned over to it. If the outfit had a sufficient number they would be sent under the care of cowboys to the home pasture.

This cutting process was done by riding the horse to the edge of or into the common herd, driving, and removing these wild, vicious, and active animals from their associates. This process was the last thing that one of these animals wanted done, and the person who tried to drive one of them from the herd soon discovered this fact. Leaving the common herd and associates, with these cattle was like parting with life itself, and was resisted to the same extent. To accomplish this result an experienced horse and man were required. It was an impossibility for a man who was not a trained rider to remain seated on one of these horses in driving an animal from the herd in which it was found. If the horse was let alone, when it discovered the animal wanted, it would take it out and drive it away; but, if the man did not know how to ride a horse experienced in this work, it would not be long until the horse turned and the rider went straight on. When this happened, the horse lost its moral support and confidence, and the process ended in disaster.

When the round-up was completed on one ranch the aggregation would go on to the next. There the process would be repeated. These round-ups involved very hard work for both horses and men. A good cutting horse, from the nature of the work in which it was engaged, being compelled to stop and turn so suddenly, was soon "stove-up," or in other words, its feet and legs were so jammed from the constant shock that there would be large knots or lumps on its joints and the animal would be very stiff and lame, especially when first ridden in the morning. A cutting horse five or six years old was considered an old horse. Their usefulness was very short lived.

These round-ups threw together cowboys from all the ranges within a large radius. At these times old acquaintances were renewed; boys would meet others with whom they had worked at different times in the past, and it was much enjoyed in this respect. It might be further mentioned that each of these wagons on the round-up was accompanied by a cook, whose duty it was to drive the team and also do the cooking. When wood was used it was either carried in the wagon or procured at camping time from nearby timber. The riders usually assisted the cook in procuring this wood. In bringing it in, a cowboy used what to a stranger would be a novel process. He would fasten his rope around a bunch of limbs or a small log, attach the other end to his saddle-horn, and drag it on the ground. A cow-pony would drag its weight and more by this method. Dragging by the saddle-horn was the cowboy's method of moving any object which he could not conveniently carry.

In the early eighties, there was a craze among the cattlemen of introducing on their ranges the muley Poland-Angus cattle. These cattle came from the far North in Europe, and were enured to the rigorous winters in that climate, and for this reason it was presumed they could and would stand the cold blizzards to which they were exposed on the ranges. The Panhandle of Texas, at that time, was the breeding ground for the ranges in the Cherokee Outlet. The cattle were sent from there to be reared or prepared for market in the Outlet. Many of the bulls of this breed were shipped from Europe and placed on the ranges of the West and Southwest. Prices in excess of $3,000.00 each were paid for many of these high-bred animals. This experiment proved an utter failure. On the ranges the old southern long-horned cattle would dig the grass from the snow and could subsist on a very small amount of food. These big-boned, broad Poland-Angus cattle had an appetite in accordance with their size, and did not know how to procure their food under difficulties. Consequently, even though they could stand a great amount of cold, when the blizzards came on they sought the nearest protection from the storm, backed up against a bank, waited for someone to bring their food, and, when they did not get it, just stood there and starved. Further, they had too much bone to make good beef cattle.

After the leases made with the Cherokees were declared void, the ranges were broken up, and the cattle ordered out of the Cherokee Outlet, and there was no recognized right for anyone to pasture this land. The luxuriant grass over this entire country simply grew, was burned in the fall, and did no one any good. At this time cattle were so cheap that no one cared much what happened to them. Persons in Kansas, near the

Kansas-Indian Territory line, drove their cattle into the Outlet and pastured them until the time the country was ordered opened for settlement. They would drive them across the line as far as desired, and a trip would be made every few days to look after them. When fall came, they would remove them to Kansas, where food was prepared to winter them. This food would consist of cornstalks, from which the corn had been gathered, cane, hay, and straw.

From the time of the agitation by the Boomers for the opening of the Indian Territory lands for settlement, soldiers were kept at several points on the principal trails entering the Outlet. One of these camps was on the south side of Pond Creek, at the old crossing, about one mile southeast of the present town of Jefferson. A body of soldiers was kept at this point almost continuously for several years. They were under the command of Captain George Dodd, who made his headquarters at Caldwell, Kansas. Captain Dodd was afterward killed in Cuba during the Spanish-American war. He was at the old ranch and station of Pond Creek on the day of the opening. The writer knew Captain Dodd well, often carried messages from him to his soldiers at Pond Creek, and spent many pleasant days and nights with these soldiers. They were jolly, good-natured fellows, and always glad to have company. We spent many days shooting prairie chickens in the adjacent sandhills, and pleasant evenings in their camp. These soldiers patrolled the Salt Fork River east and west. The patrol went west as far as the mouth of Wagon Creek, a distance of about twenty miles, and east to the mouth of Pond Creek, which was about the same distance from their camp.

Captain Dodd and his soldiers stood on the box-cars at the Pond Creek station, watching the race as it came down from the north on the day of the opening. On this day, September 16, 1893, this land over which once had roamed the buffalo for ages untold in the past, and which had been taken charge of and occupied by the broad and extensive cattle ranges, was appropriated by the homesteader, the husbandman with the plow. These men were from all parts of this broad land. They divided this country up into farms of one hundred and sixty acres each. So, where once the buffalo roamed and where the cowboy rode, now extend broad fields of grain, while the water tanks and tall buildings of the cities raise their heads as if looking and inquiring as to what has become of these old possessors who have disappeared from the land forever.

CHAPTER XVII.

THE CHEROKEE STRIP LIVE STOCK ASSOCIATION

It has been seen that the initial right to the Cherokee Outlet was given by the Government to the Cherokee Indians some thirty years before the advent of the Civil War. At this time practically nothing was known of the character of the land or fertility of the soil of this vast region. By most persons this country was considered as the border land to, if not a part of, the Great American Desert. For this reason, the Government was generous with the Cherokees; especially so from the fact that it was more than anxious to get them to give up their title to the valuable lands held by them in their ancestral home. The proffer of this extensive country, fifty-eight miles wide and extending from the Cherokee Nation on the east to as far west as the Sovereignty of the United States extended, must have been quite an inducement. This land was given to the Cherokees in fee simple, as shown by the provisions of the treaty heretofore set out, and the construction placed on the same by the United States Supreme Court in the case of Holden vs. Joy, 17 Wall. 211.

It has, also, been observed that in the treaty of 1866 the Government had obtained the right of the Cherokees to settle friendly tribes of Indians on the Outlet. By an examination of a map of this country, it will be observed that the lands set apart for the Cherokees as their home was and is in the extreme eastern portion of the Indian Territory, now the State of Oklahoma.

This land is entirely different from that in the western portion. The eastern lands are mostly wooded, some hilly and rough, and still other portions mountainous and rocky. An examination of the map will also disclose that after 1870 immediately to the west of the Cherokee Nation lay the lands of the Osages, reaching westward to the Arkansas River, the new eastern boundary of the Cherokee Outlet. This reservation was given to the Osages in 1870 by virtue of the Cherokee Treaty of 1866. This Osage land was from twelve miles wide at the narrowest point to sixty miles in the widest portion. This discrepancy in the width was caused by the bends of the Arkansas River.

Also, after the treaty of 1866, the Government, further availing itself of the provisions of the same, caused friendly Indians to be settled on the Cherokee Outlet. In this process the Pawnee Indians were settled on the west side of the Arkansas River immediately west of the Osage Nation, while the Otoe and Missouri, the Ponca, the Nezperc, and the Kaw were all given reservations in this locality. These reservations all joined the Arkansas River on the west, except the Nezperc, which joined the Ponca on the northwest. It will thus be seen that a complete wall of reservations was constructed between the home of the Cherokees and the Cherokee Outlet.

By the time the buffalo disappeared from the plains, it was discovered that this Cherokee Outlet comprised the best and most valuable lands in all the plains country. In later years, when the legal question arose as to the title of the Cherokees to the Outlet, and the Government and persons disputing the title of that tribe to this land, were faced by the decision of Wall vs. Joy *supra,* they answered it by saying, that, by the terms of the treaty of 1866, the Government had reserved the right to locate other tribes of Indians on the Outlet, it still had that right, and that such was a restriction on the ownership and title of the Cherokees. They further asserted that the Cherokees, on account of this provision, could not dispose of any portion of this Outlet or any interest in it, even by a short term lease, because the same would interfere with the right of the Government in case it wanted to locate other Indians on the same. It is readily seen that the treaty of 1866 placed a restriction on the Cherokees which they did not contemplate at the time it was made. From the foregoing, it is not difficult to observe, that, so far as actual use to the Cherokees was concerned, the Outlet was useless, and they could only hold it in readiness to be turned over to the Government when it found friendly Indians to place on the same.

It has been heretofore observed as to the manner in which the cattle from the north crept further into the Cherokee Outlet as the dangers from the wild Indians receded. These grazing sections were handled by common understanding among the owners of the cattle for some time. Then grazing permits were given by the Cherokees, and receipts were issued by their treasurer. Charges were made and privileges paid for at first at so much per head. This was a very unsatisfactory method, for the reason that it was almost impossible to keep track, with any degree of certainty, of the number of head of cattle held by any particular owner. It could not be supposed that any person would pay for the pasture of more cattle than he grazed, and in most cases it is very probable that there were many more grazed than were paid for.

In 1880, the year that the railway extended south to Caldwell, Kansas, there was a general meeting called and held at that place, which was participated in by all the grazers of cattle in the Outlet. At this meeting an organization was formed by these cattlemen. Committees were appointed and rules established to govern the affairs of the cattlemen among themselves. These rules provided for the round-ups and other matters in common among them, including the protection and preservation of the rights of the individual owners or ranchmen. It will be well remembered, by men who knew the conditions at that time, that few controversies can be recalled occurring after that time among the cattlemen of the Outlet. The law of right and justice was recognized by all. There was in fact no effective law of any organized government extending over this country. It is true, that so far as any transgressions against the Government were concerned, the laws of the United States generally covered the same, but it was most impossible to use these laws in controversies between individuals.

Rules of conduct are not difficult to regulate, when the persons governed by them desire their enforcement. On the other hand, laws, regardless of the stringency of their provisions, are more than useless and only lead to a general disregard when the persons governed do not desire their enforcement. Everyone knew that the transgression of the law of right would bring an avalanche down upon the head of the transgressor, and for that reason this law was seldom infringed. Whenever a bunch of stern-faced cowboys or cow-men sat as the judge and jury no arguments were heard, but justice was administered without favor or partiality. Seldom was it necessary to adjust any controversy, but when it was, Frontier Justice settled the same.

Conditions continued in this manner, and the cattlemen thrived and were happy. In order to further protect their interest, another meeting of these ranchers was called at Caldwell in 1883, at which time it was arranged to perfect a corporation among them to more accurately arrange their affairs and to deal with the Cherokees. Pursuant to these arrangements a charter was issued to THE CHEROKEE STRIP LIVE STOCK ASSOCIATION. The writer has in his possession a certified copy of this instrument. The names of the persons perfecting this organization are familiar to all persons who can recall the cattle industry of the Outlet at that time. For the purpose of showing these names, and also to show the purpose of the organization, a copy of this charter is set out and reads as follows:

"CHARTER OF THE CHEROKEE STRIP LIVE STOCK ASSOCIATION

We, the undersigned persons of competent age do hereby associate ourselves together for the purpose of forming a private corporation under and by virtue of the laws of the State of Kansas, the purpose and object of which said corporation is and shall be 'The improvement of the breed of domestic animals' by the importation, grazing, breeding, sale, barter and exchange thereof.

The name of such corporation shall be 'THE CHEROKEE STRIP LIVE STOCK ASSOCIATION.'

SECOND. The purpose for which the corporation is formed is the improvement of the breed of domestic animals by the importation, grazing, breeding, sale, barter, and exchange thereof.

THIRD. The principal office and place of business of the corporation shall be at the City of Caldwell in Sumner County, Kansas, but its place or places of and for holding, breeding, grazing, selling, bartering and exchanging the domestic animals, for the improvement of the breed of which the corporation is, as aforesaid, organized, shall be wherever the same can be, in the opinion of the directors, or such other body of the stock holders, or members of this corporation as may be authorized to act for the corporation, most advantageously located.

FOURTH. The term for which the corporation is to exist shall be forty years.

FIFTH. The number of the directors of the corporation shall be nine, and the following named persons are appointed directors for the first year viz:

E. M. Hewins, whose residence is Cedarvale, Kansas.
J. W. Hamilton, "   "   " Wellington, Kansas.
A. J. Day,   "   "   " Caldwell, Kansas.
S. Tuttle,   "   "   "   "   "

M. H. Bennett,   "   "   "   "   "
Andrew Drumm,   "   "   "   "   "
Ben S. Miller,   "   "   "   "   "
Chas. H. Eldred, "   "   " Carrollton, Ill.
E. W. Payne,   "   "   " Medicine Lodge, Kansas.

In Testimony Whereof we have hereto set our respective hands this 7th day of March, A. D. 1883.

E. M. Hewins	Andrew Drumm
J. W. Hamilton	Ben S. Miller
A. J. Day	Chas. H. Eldred
S. Tuttle	E. W. Payne.
M. H. Bennett	

State of Kansas, Sumner County, SS.

Be it remembered that on this 7th day of March, A. D. 1883, before me the undersigned a notary public within and for the county and State aforesaid, personally came and appeared

E. M. Hewins, of Cedarvale, Kansas
J. W. Hamilton, of Wellington, Kansas
A. J. Day, of Caldwell, Kansas
S. Tuttle, of Caldwell, Kansas
M. H. Bennett, of Caldwell, Kansas
Andrew Drumm, of Caldwell, Kansas
Ben S. Miller, of Caldwell, Kansas
Chas. H. Eldred, Carrollton, Ill.
and E. W. Payne, of Medicine Lodge, Kansas

who are each and all to me personally known to be the same persons who executed the within and above and foregoing instrument of writing and such persons each and all before me acknowledged the execution thereof.

In testimony whereof, I have hereunto set my hand and affixed my notarial seal the day and year first above written.

(Seal)   S. S. Richmond,
          Notary Public in and for Sumner County, Kansas.
My commission expires March 16/86.

Filed for Record Mar. 8, 1883, James Smith, Sec'y. of State."

Prior to the organization of this corporation, many of the ranches in the Outlet had been fenced and others partly fenced. There had been no agreement made with the Cherokees to build fences. They, however, had made no objection to the building of the same. This matter was reported to Congress, and action was taken ordering an investigation.

In the spring following the organization of the corporation, a lease was entered into between the Cherokee Strip Live Stock Association and the Cherokee Government for the leasing of the Outlet for a period of five years on payment of the sum of $100,000 per year. This sum was to be made in two semi-annual payments. A board of arbitration was appointed to settle all controversies arising between members of the corporation. All these matters, however, were finally or could be settled by the association acting through its directors, and the board of arbitration as an intermediary body to manage the affairs in the first instance.

After the incorporation of the Association and the leasing of the Outlet, the same ranges were held by the individual members or companies as before. Surveyors were employed and sent into the Outlet, and all ranges were surveyed and the number of acres included in each definitely ascertained. Each and all of these ranges were then fenced, most of them cross-fenced, and many of them divided by fences into a number of different pastures.

In order to raise the money to pay the Cherokees for the lease, there was set over by the Association to each ranchman the range which he occupied, and for which he agreed to a rental of two and one-half cents per acre for each year. These sub-leases were signed by the ranchman and by the Association, and were to extend for the period of the original lease. The rental money was to be paid by the ranchmen semi-annually, in time to make the semi-annual payment to the Cherokees.

There were estimated to be approximately 6,000,000 acres of land in the Outlet. As a business proposition, it will be observed that the Association could pay the Indians and then have $50,000 annually left to defray general expenses.

At that time, so far as the cattle business in the Outlet was concerned, all difficulties had been overcome, every cloud had disappeared from the sky, and the pathway of the cattlemen to success appeared to be straight and unobstructed. All connected with the business, from Major Drumm, the President of the Association, down to the horse wranglers in the cow camps, were happy. Each ranch had its own brand, which was burned on the animals belonging to it.

The only newspaper at Caldwell, Kansas, at that time, was "The Caldwell Post," a weekly paper. Well can all persons living there at that time remember when one or more pages of this paper were covered with the brands of the different ranchers. These brands were inserted in the paper, together with the name of the man or company owning the same. This would advertise the brand, and in case any cattle strayed the brand would be recognized and the owner known. To persons who are not familiar with the branding of stock the following explanation will suffice:

A brand is an arrangement of one or more letters, figures, or characters, usually a joint combination of letters, figures, or characters. These were so arranged, that an iron could be prepared forming the characters, letters, or figures selected, and could be made as compact and stout as possible. One great object was to make a selection so that when the brand was burned on the animal it would not blur and would stand out plain. These brands were placed on the animals when young. The unbranded animals were termed "Mavericks," for the reason as hereinbefore explained. It is estimated that there were over one hundred separate brands used in the Outlet.

Caldwell, Kansas, in those days, was the cowboy capital of the world. The herds from the Panhandle of Texas were crowding over the Western Plains to the Chisholm Trail, and thence on to the loading pens up the trail. It has been the history of the frontier, that the cattle industry has always been the connecting link between the unrestrained wilderness and the civilization that lay on the other side or behind it. When the progress of agriculture becomes too strong upon it, this link breaks and the industry disappears. The agitation of the "Oklahoma Boomer" arose in the land. This was the first cloud to appear on the horizon for the cattlemen. In the beginning it was regarded as visionary and a forlorn hope. It soon gained so much momentum, that the rights of the Cherokees were but a feeble barrier in its course. The portion known as "Old Oklahoma," located in the central portion of the Indian Territory, was opened to settlement in 1889. A Congressional investigation was had in 1884. The cattle were removed from the Cheyenne and Arapaho Reservation in 1885. Troubles gathered thick and fast for the Association.

The winter of 1885-6, which followed the removal of the cattle from the Cheyenne and Arapaho country, was one of the hardest blows that struck the members of the Cherokee Strip Live Stock Association. On the evening of January 6, 1886, there came down from the north the worst blizzard ever known to the plains country. The writer on this evening came from the southwest over the Cantonment Trail to the Chisholm Trail, arriving at the Pond Creek Ranch, just south of the present town of Jefferson, at about four o'clock in the evening. It had been a beautiful day, with a few small patches of snow on the ground, which were fast disappearing. The writer intended to travel on to Caldwell that evening, a distance of twenty-six miles, and actually made the start, but a heavy dark cloud appeared in the north, which caused him to turn back. Had he not done so, these lines would have been written by someone else, if at all. The ranch house was crowded before the writer's return, and he and many others protected themselves as best they could by camping in the adjacent timber on Pond Creek. There they remained huddled up for over three days. Many men froze and died all over the country.

The effect of this storm on the range cattle can hardly be realized. They drifted with the storm. When the leaders came to a fence they stopped, but the cattle following crowded them on until the pressure became so great that the fences gave way. They then drifted in the blinding storm. The leaders often walked over steep banks or precipices. The ones behind in turn fell onto them, and they remained a helpless struggling mass, all to die together. On the Quinlan Range, located on the north side of the Cimarron River at the mouth of Indian Creek, there were large ponds, in which the water settled during rainy portions of the season, but were dry during the remainder. Large cottonwood trees grew in these ponds. Water was standing in them at the time of this storm. The cattle came down from the north. The leaders walked out onto the ice and fell. The ones behind them walked over their prostrate leaders, and would, as soon as striking the ice, in turn fall. This process was continued until the line of these ponds and ice could be determined by the string of dead cattle. This condition existed for miles at this place.

When spring opened and the thaws came, men with wagons came by hundreds into the country for the sole purpose of skinning these dead animals. In performing this operation one man would take a sharp knife, cut down the legs, around the hoofs, and the hide, as is ordinarly done in the skinning; then the dead animal would be securely fastened to a stout stake or tree, and a team of horses hitched to one end of the hide, when it would be literally pulled from the carcass. Men in great numbers made good wages in this business. They continued until the spring was so far advanced that decomposition compelled them to stop, and thousands of these dead cattle never were skinned.

To make matters worse, this storm was followed by cold weather, and in February, when the cattle were almost exhausted and suffering from lack of food, another blizzard came, and the process as stated above was repeated. Although this last storm was not as severe as its predecessor, on account of the emaciated condition of the cattle its results were worse. The ranchmen were helpless. They were compelled to stand as silent observers, while their fortunes were swept away as if borne by an avalanche. Men who but a few months before had dreams of soon becoming millionaires, when spring broke, were financially ruined. It is a sad fact, that but few of them ever regained their lost fortunes.

As early as 1886, the Cherokee Strip Live Stock Association started negotiations to have their lease with the Cherokees renewed for an additional period. It will be recalled that the five-year lease made in 1883 would expire in 1888. At this time, the Cherokees agreed to lease the Outlet for an additional period of five years for an annual rental of $200,000. In 1889 negotiations were started with the Government and the Cherokees for the purchase of the Outlet. Secretary of the Interior Noble held that the title of the Cherokees to the Outlet was only an easement. The Attorney General held that the Cherokees did not own the Outlet. President Harrison was more lenient with the cattlemen, but, in the early part of the year 1890, issued a proclamation holding the lease of the Association void, and ordering the cattle removed from the Outlet. The time for such removal was delayed until the latter part of the year 1890.

In this matter the ranchmen were again helpless. They could not even have the benefit of any court to pass on their rights. Any resistance to the order of the officers of the Government was enforced by the United States Army. Neither the orders of the executive officers of the Government nor the operations of the Army could be governed by court orders. The serious question was as to the method to be followed to obtain the judgment of a court to construe the meaning of the treaties and determine the rights of the Cherokees, and hence the rights of the Association and ranchmen under their lease.

The lease holders were compelled to obey the order for removal. At this time, the writer was a law student in the office of Jno. L. McAtee at Caldwell, Kansas. McAtee had formerly been engaged in the practice of law at Hagerstown, Maryland, but had removed to the West and engaged in the cattle business with A. M. Colson. They had a range about ten miles west of the present town of Jefferson. McAtee had removed his law office to Caldwell, and was General Attorney for the Cherokee Strip Live Stock Association. After the opening of the Outlet to settlement he was one of the Federal Judges constituting the District and Supreme Courts of the Territory.

The notes given by the ranchmen to the Association for the rental on their leases were delivered to McAtee for collection. Through these notes a method was devised for procuring a judicial determination as to the rights of the Cherokees to the Outlet, under the treaties made with the Government. Suits were first brought on some of these notes in the United States Circuit Court at Kansas City, Missouri. The theory on which these suits were prosecuted was, that the Cherokees were the owners of the Outlet and had a right to lease the same; that the Cherokee Strip Live Stock Association had procured a legal lease to the land, that in exercising its right under this lease had sub-leased to the individual ranchmen, and the notes were given as rental for these sub-leases. If the Cherokees had a legal right to make the lease, this contention was absolutely good.

The only defense that could be made to the collection of the notes under the theory stated, was that the holders of the sub-leases had been ejected from the land. If the Cherokees had a right to lease the Outlet, this ejectment was illegal. The reply to this contention by the Association, therefore, was, that while the sub-leases guaranteed that the Association had a right to make them, it did not guarantee that the party taking the lease would not be illegally ejected, and if the sub-lease holders permitted themselves to be illegally removed from the land, such was a risk of their own, and one for which the Association was not responsible. In other words, the contention of the Association was that the illegal ejection was not such a defense as would render the notes void. It will readily be seen that this contention drew into the courts the direct determination as to the title of the Cherokees to the Outlet and their right to make the lease to the Association.

The first cases were decided in the trial courts in favor of the validity of the lease. Following the decisions of Wall vs. Joy, *Supra*, the court decided that the Cherokees held title to the Outlet and could lease the same. These cases were appealed to the United States Circuit Court of Appeals. The writer assisted in preparing the briefs to be used on these appeals. The question involved was of far-reaching effect, and was a matter of great importance. Large boxes of these printed briefs were received from Kansas City. Despite our efforts, the United States Circuit Court of Appeals reversed the lower court, and in so doing held that the Cherokees did not hold a fee simple title to the Outlet. One of the principal contentions made in opposing the title of the Cherokees was the provision of the treaty of 1866, permitting the Government to settle other Indians on such portions of the Outlet as it desired.

The Cherokees and the cattlemen had sought the judicial determination by the courts. Such was their last resort, and by this decision the last fortification the contenders for the title of the Cherokees had was levelled to the ground, and their defeat was not only inevitable, but was at hand.

There could not possibly have been any objections to the Cherokees leasing this Outlet and receiving the rental money therefor, as the money received from it would have relieved the Government to that extent from caring for these Indians as the wards of the Government. There was, however, a reason for desiring these leases terminated. As has been seen, the representatives of the Government were carrying on negotiations with the Cherokees for the purchase of their right in the Outlet, and as long as the Indians were receiving large sums of money for their lease on this land they would not sell; also the ranchmen had entered into competition with the Government as a purchaser of the Outlet, and had offered the Indians more than twice as much for the same as the Government. It was under these conditions that the executive order was issued to remove the cattle and the ranchmen from the Outlet.

This removal was accomplished, as has been observed, in the latter part of the year 1890, but cattle were actually grazed on the lands of the Outlet to within a few months of the time of the opening of the country for settlement on September 16, 1893. This grazing was not done by any concerted action on the part of the cattle interests, but was done by independent persons who let their herds graze at such points as they selected, holding themselves in readiness to remove at any time. As soon as the ranchmen were removed their fences were also torn down and taken away. There was enough barbed wire taken out of the Cherokee Outlet to construct barbed wire entanglements in four World Wars.

When these notes given by the individual ranchmen were turned over to the Attorney for the Association for collection, as stated, the writer was in the office of the attorney. Shortly after the receipt of the same a receiver was appointed for the Cherokee Strip Live Stock Association. The receiver accompanied by the marshal came to the office. McAtee was absent, and the writer was in charge of the office. They exhibited their order of the court for the delivery of the notes. The writer at that time had not seen as much of the world as he has since; it placed him in a difficult position, and it was quite a proposition for him to handle.

There was only one thing certain, and that was, order or no order, these parties were not going to get possession of these notes, and they did not. It was a contest of strategy, wits, and diplomacy between the officers of the law and an inexperienced boy, and lasted for several hours. If they could have found the notes they would have taken them, whether delivered voluntarily or otherwise. The writer grew to know these men well in after years, and they often joked with him about this matter. They were positive that the writer knew the whereabouts of the notes, and it was only a qeustion of them finding them. The writer always told them afterward that the most settled and determined matter in his mind, at that time, was that they could have taken him, as they threatened to do, but the notes, never. After McAtee returned, an arrangement was made with the receiver, whereby he kept the notes and brought suit on them, with the result as above stated.

The sympathies of the writer, together with his interests, have always been with the Indians and the ranchmen. He has spent much time briefing the subject to sustain the contention of these claimants, and he is willing to concede the prejudice that may accompany an opinion in the situation, and under such circumstances he will refrain from expressing the usual assertion of the vanquished in a legal controversy. All he will say is that he was and is firmly convinced of the justice of his contention, and also of the legal aspect of the same, based on the intention of the contracting parties.   The question is settled, and he with his associates have abandoned the field to the victors, with the ever present fact that:

> "Westward the course of empire takes its way,
>   The first four acts already past,
>   Time's noblest offspring is the last."

With this assurance, the broad fields of wheat rear their millions of heads over the land for which the Cherokees and cattle interests contended. On some of this soil, wide areas of oil derricks stand like monarchs in a forest, from which flow a steady stream of golden liquid, the value of which would put to shame the price of all the herds for the pasture of which contention was made.

Charles A. Siringo, cowboy, author, and detective of note. He helped to take the wild, long-horned cattle out of the chaparral thickets of southern Texas. He was a boss on the trail for years, and one of the most effective cowmen who ever traveled the same.

CHAPTER XVIII.

THE COWBOY

Having gone over and observed the associated conditions connected with the Chisholm Trail, we will now turn our attention to a brief observation of the actual travelers over this lonely highway, extending far from the threshold of civilization. Let us remember, as we do, that the men with whom we are dealing belonged to another age, and are not to be measured by the standards of either the iniquities or the refinements of today. In some particulars they may have been worse, but in many others better.

Not long ago the writer had occasion to read a letter written by an old man who as a boy rode the cattle ranges of the West. The letter was written to a companion of many years ago; now by one old man to another. In commenting on the remnants of the once numerous members of their clan, the writer lapsed into a little poetical parody in which he wrote:

"Few are left to greet us now,
And few are left to know,
Who rode with us upon the plains,
Some fifty years ago."

These old men once were boys, and, as they now travel down the declining slope of life, they love to revel in the scenes of their youth, when dangers and hardships were many and life lay before them.

The old cowboys of the plains and open ranges have disappeared from the face of the earth. People in general now only know them from extravagant and colored stories, many of which are written by persons who never saw one of their kind.

Most of the readers of these articles, should they have occasion to meet face to face one of the kind-hearted boys of the ranges of fifty years ago, would not know him.

It is not the purpose of the writer to attempt to convey to his readers the impression that he has spent his life, or any great portion of the same, on the range, engaged in the actual business of a cowboy. All persons familiar with him know that such is not correct; that he could not have done so, and, also, done the many other things that he has. It is the purpose of the writer, however, to inform his readers that he has had an abundance of actual experience in the matters of which he writes, amply sufficient to know whereof he speaks, and that without assumption or extravagance. He also desires to state that there have been few men of the West or range country who knew more men on the frontier, and knew and associated intimately with more persons engaged in the cattle business, from the owners of the herds to the lowliest cow hands, than the writer. This information is only given to show the attitude of the writer in dealing with the matters included in this entire volume. The writer will attempt to portray a picture of these young men, which has been gained by actual association, so that they will be presented as they were, as he actually considers them, and from which they can be recognized.

The cowboy of the present day, while bearing some resemblance and having inherited some of the characteristics of his predecessor, is surrounded by different conditions. The present civilization has crowded in upon him, his associations and environments are entirely changed, and he has been molded and recast into an almost different character. The cowboys, as they were, were simply men, and, being men, there existed among them as much variation as to temperament, disposition, and personal characteristics, within certain bounds, as is generally found among men. These variations were, however, surrounded by unsurmountable barriers, which enclosed them within certain restricted areas, the bounds of which were never transgressed.

Many of these men came from the best homes to be found in various parts of the country, and some of them were well educated, but, being thrown into the surroundings which they were, they soon became a part of them, and were molded into that peculiar class of people of which there was no other like it in the entire world, never was before, and, perhaps, never will be again. Some of them sought the West and the life they engaged in to gain their fortunes, others desired excitement and adventure, while others embraced this life as a matter of necessity to earn a livelihood. Some of them remained and spent their lives upon the range, while others returned to civilization and engaged in other pursuits. It is a well known fact that some of these in later years developed into as able men as were found in the intellectual life of our country.

The cowboys of the plains, the open ranges, and the trails, as a whole, had certain fixed and definite ideals, as to their dress, personal appearance, ways of thinking, and ideas as to things which were commendable, and of things that were absolutely below their dignity. These matters were firmly established in their minds, and were as permanent and immutable as the laws of the Medes and Persians. These matters and ideas became a part of them, as much as the broad-brimmed Stetson sombreros which they wore upon their heads, the "Fish Brand" slickers which they always carried tied behind their saddles, or the high-heeled boots which they wore.

There were no laws to adjust the differences between himself and the persons with whom he dealt in the land where the cowboy lived. From this condition grew the fact, that the word of a cowboy given to a companion was the most binding obligation that could exist between men. It was always better than a mortgage or a bond. This was true from the fact that it needed no court to enforce it. The man who would violate this obligation was ostracized from companionship with his fellow men, discountenanced, and conditions were made such that he shared the lowest rank in society. There were no laws among them to protect the weaker from the stronger, but the ideas of justice among this mass of men, their companionship, and association rendered every man as safe, and he was as much protected, as if the most stringent laws were called to his assistance.

The cowboy was generous to a fault. There were few among the men of the plains but were free with their money. If a man had but ten dollars, he would, without a thought as to generosity, divide it with a friend or any person in distress, or, if he thought the donee needed it worse than he did, he would give it all to him. In such a case or at any time when he found himself without funds, he would saddle his horse, turn its head to the open cow-country, and start back to work, with his horse taking that jog trot so familiar to all travelers on horseback in the old West. He would return to his ranch, and work for one dollar per day until he had another stake.

The majority of the men on the ranges and Western Plains carried firearms of some kind on their person, or kept them in their immediate vicinity, ready for instant use. This grew to be a practice, and was quite natural from the conditions which surrounded them. They were in a land where at all times dangers of many kinds, either from wild animals or wilder men, beset them, and their preparedness was a caution born of necessity and long experience. There were exceptions to this habit of carrying firearms. Some as good and as courageous men as there were on the cattle ranges never carried weapons of any kind, and looked with contempt on those who did.

Charles F. Sprague. A native of Massachusetts, he spent twenty-five years on the trails and cattle ranges of the Southwest, during a portion of which time he managed a trail herd or outfit. He traveled the Chisholm Trail for years. He has been for over fifty years a close friend of the author. He now lives at Medford, Oklahoma, is over eighty years of age, and still going good.

The writer now recalls a prominent man among the cow-boys, who was born and grew to young manhood in the East. Upon entering the ranks of cowboys he soon rose to a position of importance and responsibility, and managed many men. He was a man absolutely devoid of fear. He never carried a gun. This man has many times told the writer, that he knew his own temper; he knew if he kept a weapon within his reach, and suddenly became aroused, he would do something that he would regret all the remaining portion of his life, and for that reason he was willing to be without one when he might need it, rather than to run the chances of doing something that, in more de-liberate moments, could not be undone. This party who is mentioned was a man known and respected in the cow-camps. He was a man of much force and ability, and was always treated with consideration. The men of the plains in general had the utmost contempt for a braggart, a bully, or any one who as-sumed superiority or attempted to impress others with his im-portance. On the other hand, they had no time for a weakling, a coward, a man who was merely passive, or had no force of character.

Many of the men of the range, who did carry firearms, through years of constant use, became very efficient with them. The two weapons in universal use in early days on the frontier were the Colt .45 caliber, single action, Frontier Model revol-ving pistol, with 7½ inch barrel, and the .44 caliber Winchester rifle of two types, one with short barrel, carrying nine cart-ridges, and the longer barrel, carrying sixteen. It is said that these two weapons did more to open the pathway for civiliza-tion than the United States Army or any other power. The question is often asked the writer by persons of the present day as to the methods or styles used in carrying these weapons. The men who carried them had as distinct a method and style of doing so, as the men and women of today have of wearing their clothes of latest pattern or exhibiting their etiquette at a fashionable dinner party.

The manner of carrying firearms was only selected as being the most convenient method. In the days of the long-barreled pistols, if the carrier was what was known as a one-gun-man, the pistol was usually carried on the left side, with the handle pointing to the front. The barrel was long, and the gun liable to stick in the scabbard when withdrawing the same. When carried on the left side, and it was to be withdrawn, the scabbard was seized by the left hand while the gun was withdrawn with the right. This was the process used by a right-handed man. By a left-handed man it would be reversed. If the carrier was a two-gun-man, the pistols were carried one on each side of the body, with the handles or stock pointed to the rear. In that case the guns were withdrawn by seizing in the hands and pulling straight up, and the points of the scabbards or holsters were usually fastened to the body to prevent the pistols from sticking. In later years, according to the style, the barrels on these pistols were made shorter. For that reason, it grew to be the custom for a one-gun-man to carry his pistol on the right side, with the handle pointing to the rear. This custom was adopted for the reason that the gun with the short barrel was not so difficult to draw from the scabbard, and could be easily pulled straight up.

Few double-action or self-cocking pistols were found on the range, and few cowboys used them. One of the notable exceptions to this rule was William H. Bonney, better known as "Billy the Kid," who was a typical young cowboy. His favorite weapon was the Colt .41 double-action pistol. He came to be an expert in the use of this weapon. Many of the men using these .45 Colt single-action pistols became experts in the use of them. Some of these men would have the triggers removed from their pistols, and would fire them by the simple process of raising the hammer and letting it fall on the cartridge. It was really remarkable how accurately they could shoot in this manner, especially at a moving target. Their expertness was brought about by constant use and practice, and their shots were snap shots.

The two styles of Winchester rifles, which composed the 1873 model, were the first well established repeating rifles. The old Henry rifle, which shot a short .44 caliber rim fire cartridge, was built much on the same plan, but was not so effective as its successor, the Winchester. When this weapon was carried on the saddle, the best adopted method was to have the same placed in a scabbard of heavy leather, and a light strap passed around the rear end of the scabbard. This strap was held in place by passing through loops on either side of the scabbard, it was then buckled and hung over the horn or pommel of the saddle, the scabbard then was passed back under the stirrup leather and skirt, another light strap in loops passing around the scabbard was buckled into the ring of the rear cinch. This left the stock of the gun pointing to the front. There were a few who carried their rifles with the stocks of the guns pointing up at the rear of the saddle.

Of the rifles above described, the short ones were much more convenient to carry on the saddles on account of their abbreviated length, but the long ones were more accurate when used. When the carrier desired to remove one of these guns from his saddle, together with the scabbard, he simply unbuckled the strap attached to the ring of the cinch and lifted the strap from around the saddle horn. These weapons heretofore described all used black powder, as that was the only known powder in use at that time. The writer still owns and has in his possession one of these old pistols, and a sixteen shot 1873 model Winchester, which was purchased by him in 1885.

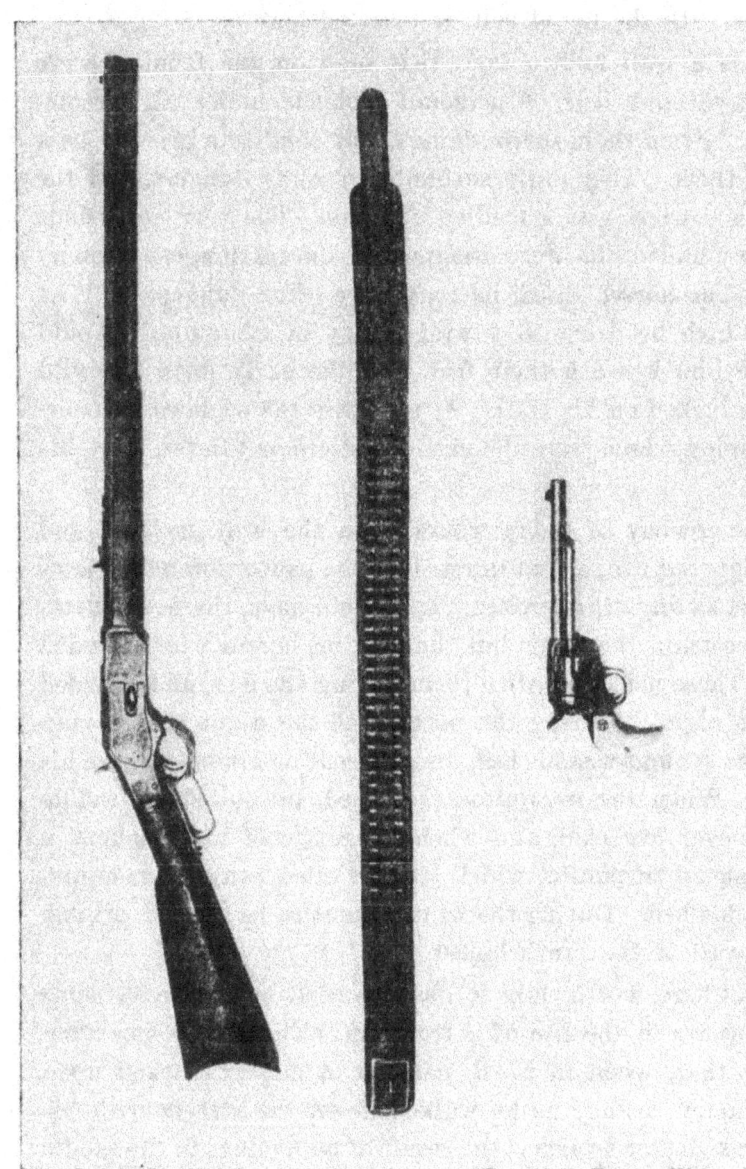

Forty-four Caliber, 16 shot, 1873 Model Winchester rifle, and Forty-five Frontier Model Colt six-shooter, with 7½ inch barrel, together with cartridge belt, both having been owned by the author for over fifty years, and both of which are in good, serviceable condition yet.

Both are in good shooting condition yet. A picture of them, together with the pistol belt, is inserted herein.

It is a well known fact, that men on the frontier were usually without fear of personal violence under all circumstances. From their surroundings, this condition grew to be a part of them. They daily encountered many dangers, and the life of a cowboy was a medley of them. The very conditions that surrounded him were designed to conceal dangers of many kinds. The horses which he rode were often dangerous. The herds which he drove in a wild frenzy of a stampede would trample him beneath their feet. In the early days the wild Indians lurked on his trail. At all times the outlaws, conspicuous among whom were the cattle rustlers or thieves, were his foes.

The cowboy of today works upon the well enclosed and well improved range, and in reach of the protection of the laws the same as any other citizen. In the old days, there was nothing to restrain the herds but the men on horses who attended them. These men rode with them during the day, and guarded them at night. During the portion of the night that a man slept, the ground was his bed, and his coat or his saddle was his pillow. When the mosquitoes bothered, he pulled his saddle blanket over his head, and when it grew cold his blankets, a wagon sheet, tarpaulin, which was an oiled canvas, made and covered his bed. During the winter months, he slept in a bunk on the wall of the ranch house.

It is here worthwhile to observe with particularity some of the events in the life of a trailman. The writer has often thought that, when in town, persons in general looked upon the ordinary cowboy as he walked down the streets with his peculiar swing or swagger, the result of many days in the saddle and following the stride of his horse; they did not fully appreciate him or the life he lived. That if they could have looked upon and fully known the everyday events in the active life of this peculiar being, they would have immediately changed their opinion of the person on whom they gazed. The fortunes or misfortunes of this everyday existence he accepted without a murmur, regardless of their severity. At night he made his bed in the open, exposed to all the elements, marauding beasts or men. If the stars shone or the rain poured before the dawn of another day, he accepted it as a part of the day's work, and in the latter case he sought the best protection he could. Solitude and isolation from his fellow man was the accepted lot of the cowboy.

All day, far from civilized men, he rode behind or by a vast herd of cattle, crowding them on and on. When dry weather came, if he was on the range, he sought for and suffered for lack of water, and when driving his herd on the trail the dust rose to the heavens in a swirling, blinding cloud, and settled over and upon him, his horse, and his cattle until the color of none could be determined. When the clouds gathered, the lightning flashed and played around the feet of his horse and cattle, he remained firm at his post. At night, and while the elements surged, he rode around and sang to his cattle to relieve their fears, or followed them in a mad stampede.

After riding all day with his herd on the trail, the cowboy stood his alloted portion of guard on night-herd, known as his shift. If a storm arose and the cattle stampeded, every man in the camp must be in his saddle and with the stampeding herd. On these stampedes he rode through pitch darkness, with only Divine Providence to guide and protect him. He did not know at what minute his horse would plunge over an embankment, falling upon him, or step into a hole and hurl him head long beneath the rushing feet of the charging herd. Looking back now one can only wonder how a single man escaped death.

When the rivers were swollen, without hesitation he plunged into the flood of cold water. There he kept his assigned place, as true as a soldier in line of battle. His horse lunged through the quicksand, swam, and was tossed upon the waves of the whirling flood, where sticks, brush, logs, and foam alike swept down, crowding his herd from its course in crossing. This he did in attempting to guide and land an aggregation of wild, frightened, stubborn, and unmanageable cattle. When he landed he must return and help bring the wagon across, and then ride shivering until his clothes would dry on him. These are but a few of the many trials that were a part of the daily life of the cowboy.

The personal appearance of the cowboy was characteristic. He had a style of his own, copied from no man or set of men. These styles and habits in his daily life were the outgrowth of necessity or convenience. He invariably wore upon his head the broad-brimmed Stetson *sombrero*.[1] In later years the brims of these hats were made very stiff, so that when the wind blew, they would not bend or flap into the face of the wearer. Their colors varied, but were usually white, brown, gray, or some other light color. His shirts were usually of a good quality of wool of various designs, and always with attached collars. His trousers were of very durable material, usually of a good quality of wool that would wear well. He seldom walked, and his trousers buttoned tight around the waist. One of the designations of degradation, which he applied to anyone he did not like, was that he suspected that he "wore gallusses." The dress of his head and feet were his pride.

The early cowboy wore a leather belt or band around his hat. Some of these were as much as one and one-half inches

---

[1] *Sombrero* is Spanish. Its literal meaning is "sun-shade," but in Spanish the name is used to designate a hat and is translated as "hat." It is so designated for the reason that a hat is used as a shade from the sun.

wide, and were fastened with two small straps and buckles. During the eighties, a practice developed of wearing around the hat what was known as a "roll." These were called "silver rolls" or "gold rolls," according to their color. These rolls were made to represent a braid of three strands with tinsel or a bright material worked into them. They were often as much as one inch in diameter on the front and back of the hat, but running down to one-half inch at the sides. They served as a band around the hat.

The boots of the cowboy were made exactly to his liking. These had quilted tops, artistically flowered, with the seams of colored thread with which they were sewed. These tops were cut straight across, and extended as high as they could go without interfering with the bending of the knee. When riding and at most other times the bottoms of the trousers were enclosed in these boot tops. This arrangement kept them from slipping up when riding. The heels of these boots were high, in many cases over three inches. They slanted forward, and the bottoms of the same were very small, usually not larger than a twenty-five cent piece, and many of them smaller. In fact at one time the writer saw a cowboy who had the heels of his boots rounded at the bottom. This was a freak case, however.

These boots were all made to measure, to order, and of the very best calfskin. They were usually made to fit close on the feet, and it is a well remembered fact by the men who wore them that they were very hard to "break in" and difficult to remove when wet, but it was almost impossible to wear them out. These boots, even in those days, usually cost from twelve to twenty-five dollars per pair. The high heels were constructed as they were for convenience in riding. The stirrups used on the saddles were usually made of iron and were always narrow, and some of them were covered with leather.

These stirrups would fit beneath the foot in front of these high heels, holding the foot securely in place. It was said in riding that half of the weight should be thrown on the feet, and this weight rested in the center of the foot, so it was not so tiresome to the rider.

The saddle was an important part of the equipment of the men on the range. They lived in these saddles, and from constant use selected the most convenient and comfortable ones possible. In later years, there was but small variation in the class of saddles used. These were what was known as the California tree. It is understood that the shape of this saddle was first designed in California, and was so named. These saddles were made with a small and high pommel or horn. The fork was made of cast iron or steel. The cantle or seat was long, upright, and straight. This saddle fitted down well over the weathers of the horse, and held its place better than any other one in use.

During the early years of the cattle industry in the Southwest, the saddles used were very primitive. They had large flat horns, while the cantles were flat, low, and straight. They would not hold their place on a horse's back, were hard on the horses, and on the men who rode them. There were later, also, very good saddles used by some which were low both in cantle and pommel, but were square built and fitted well on the horse's back. These were known as "half-breed" saddles. There were also used to some extent what were known as the apple horn saddles. These were on the plan of the California trees, but had skirts of solid leather, and the tops of the horns or pommels were round, and for such reason were called "apple-horns."

On the ranges in the Middle-West, saddles with double cinches were universally used. In portions of California the single cinch saddles were in use to some extent. Among the cowboys of the Middle-West these were known as "center-fire" saddles, and some attempt was made to introduce them into this country, but without success. It seemed that the cowboys of this locality could not fasten them onto their horses so they would not turn in heavy work. All these saddles were manufactured by well known saddle makers, whose brands were guarantees of satisfaction. The same was true of the cowboy boots, and large establishments were built up in these industries during the cattle days. The one-piece saddle covers or skirts were early discarded for the lighter ones made in small pieces. The cowboy's saddle cost from forty-five dollars, or thereabouts, up.

A cowboy always mounted his horse from the left side. If a man wanted to court instant death, one of the best ways of doing so was to approach an old-time cow-horse from the right side. From this fact it was often stated that a cow-horse was never more than half broken, as he could never be approached or mounted except from one side. Dealing with these horses was a matter of custom, and when the customary routine was departed from, the horses were as wild as if never broken.

The Eastern cattle drovers used a long cattle whip in their driving. The cattle drovers and cowboys of the West never used a whip. Many pictures of cowboys driving cattle have been produced showing them with long, short-handled whips. When the reader sees one of these pictures, he can readily and safely make up his mind that the maker, or person responsible for the making of the same, never saw cowboys, and knew nothing about them. The only whip used by the cowboy was his quirt. He often trailed several yards of rope at his horse's side. This rope had a knot in the end, and he could deal an animal an unerring blow with this knot.

This quirt was never absent from a cowboy's equipment. It was a small whip, about fourteen or sixteen inches in length.

It was braided, and the butt end of the same enclosed an iron or steel rod about three-eighths of an inch in diameter. A sufficient portion of this iron, used to grasp the hand around, was covered with leather, while the bottom portion was constructed of braided leather, which at the thickest point was about one inch in diameter, extending on from this iron or steel rod. The bottom portion had a loop in the end, through which was run the lash, some eighteen inches long, which consisted of a piece of heavy raw-hide or sole-leather doubled. The top end of the quirt had a Spanish knot braided on it, with a string in the same which fastened around the wrist of the user. Instead of the iron or steel rod, some were made with a buckskin pouch filled with fine lead shot, securely sewed and leather strings braided over it. These quirts were effective weapons in the hands of men accustomed to use them. A man could with ease knock a horse down with one of them, while a stroke with the lash would readily raise a welt.

Many cowboys were experienced in the braiding of these quirts and other leather work. The Mexicans were experts in this art. They were also skilled in working with horse-hair, and could weave most artistically with it. The writer acquired the art of this leather braiding, including the tying of Spanish knots, early in life, and once acquired, it is never forgotten.

On the right side of the front of the saddle of the cowboy, hung a coil of rope. This rope served as his lasso, and also for lariating his horse. It was attached to his saddle-horn by a string of sufficient length, with the ends tied together and passed over the saddle-horn, then several times around the coils of rope, and back over the saddle-horn. Thus the rope was held securely in place, but could be released with little effort.

The saddle of the cowboy was not buckled on his horse, as might be anticipated and as was done with Eastern saddles, but was fastened on the horse by cinch straps. The tying of these straps, to a person not accustomed to the process, was more difficult than the diamond half-hitch. These cinch straps were each five or six feet long, and were fastened into the rings on the side of the saddle. In tying this knot when fastening the saddle on the horse, the strap was run from the ring on the saddle to the ring on the cinch, then back up and through the cinch ring on the saddle from the front, out at the left side, then under the top strap running between the two rings, then under the cinch ring on the saddle at the right side, and then back and under the strap at the right side just before it passed under the cinch ring the last time. The cinch strap would then be pulled as tight as possible and the knot tightened. A knot so tied can never slip or give. In saddling cow horses, after they had been used for some time, they would acquire the habit of swelling themselves by expanding their bodies when the rider tightened the cinch. In this case, after riding a few miles the rider must dismount and tighten the cinch again. Saddles were always cinched on the left side.

The bridles used upon the range were as simple in construction as possible. They consisted of a head stall with a throat latch that could be buckled up sufficiently tight that the bridle could not be slipped off, and a brow band to keep it from slipping back. The bit used was known as a curb bit. By a curb bit is understood as being one with a solid bar running through the mouth with a curb extending from the center of the bit up in the mouth. These curbs were some of them two inches long, and had a roller in the center of the same, which the horse would roll with his tongue, making a rattling noise. These bits had a chin strap extending from the ring on the top of the bit on one side to the ring in the top on the other side. The bars or shanks on the side of these bits were several inches long, extending down below the horse's mouth. The bridle reins were attached to the lower end of these bars, and when this chin strap was buckled tight and the reins tightened, the lower jaw of the horse was clamped tightly, as by a lever. There were bits made with large rings which would run around the entire under jaws of the horses, and were attached to the top of the curb in the mouths, but these were so severe that most men would not permit them to be used on their horses.

The horses of the cowboy were a principal part of his equipment. He usually had some seven head allotted to him for use. A description of these horses is reserved for another chapter.

The most pronounced characteristic of the old cowboys, as well as other men of the frontier, was their fidelity to their comrades. These comrades shared their dangers, their sorrows, their cares, their pleasures, and their joys. This fidelity was never ending. In prosperity, in poverty, in honor, or in dis- grace, it was always the same. When these isolated men of the West met, there were many songs sung in the cow-camps, around the camp-fires, or on the sides of moonlit hills at night. Often these singers had excellent voices, and, if they had been so situated as to have had the proper training, they might have acquitted themselves with credit in any contest. Men's songs, to a certain extent, reflect the thoughts, minds, and inclina- tions of the persons among whom they are current. Napoleon once said: "Let me make the people's songs and I care not who make their laws."

Many of these songs refer to the loyalty that existed among these men of the plains. The writer recalls a portion of a song, often sung among them, which was known as "Tom Shurman's Bar-room," [2] also as "The Dying Cowboy." There

---

[2] Tom Shurman's Bar-room was a saloon and dance hall located in Dodge City, Kansas, during the days when Dodge City was the "Cowboy Capital." It was well known throughout the cattle country.

were, however, a number of different renditions of the "Dying Cowboy." Without vouching for the rhythm or meter this portion is set out as follows:

> "We beat our drums lowly,
> We played our fifes slowly;
> We played the dead march
> As we bore him along.
> We all loved our comrade,
> So gay and so handsome;
> We all loved a comrade,
> Although he did do wrong;
> For we know in his saddle
> He used to be dashing,
> That once in his saddle
> He used to dress gay;
> He first took to drinking,
> Then took to gambling;
> Was shot last night,
> Now we have borne him away."

Another of these songs which referred to the fidelity of companions of the frontier is the song known as "Sam Bass," which was extensively sung, and a portion of which runs as follows:

> "Sam had four companions,
> Four bold and daring lads,
> They were Richardson,
> Jackson, Collins, and Old Dad."

The latter and closing portion of this song is thus:

> "Jim Murphy borrowed Sam's good gold
> And then refused to pay,
> His only plan it was
> To give poor Sam away;
> He sold out Sam and Barnes
> And left their friends to mourn,
> So won't Jim Murphy's eyes bug out
> When Gabriel blows his horn?"

These songs were seldom reduced to writing, but were committed by having been heard so often. For that reason considerable discrepancies are found in the different renditions of them, and often some of the song is left out.

A portion of these men could not remember of any homes or family ties. Their lot had been cast so they really had none, but most of them had been reared in respectable homes, in kind and affectionate families. These men during their hardships often referred to the homes that they had left behind, and especially to their mothers and sisters. This was done in the most endearing terms. Again the writer will refer to a portion of the words of "Tom Shurman's Bar-room" to prove his statement, as follows:

> "Go break the news to my old gray-headed mother,
> Go bliff the news to my sister so dear,
> And not one word of misplace do you tell them
> As they gather around you, my sad story to hear.
> There is another as dear as my sister,
> I know she will weep when she hears I am gone;
> Tell her some other will win her affection,
> For I'm a wild ranger, I know I have done wrong."

The writer also recalls a short portion of another song, which he has heard on the range many times, and which would never fail to bring tears to the eyes of boys fresh from home, and to some who had been gone from there long. This song was entitled, "Two Thousand Miles Away," and a portion of the same follows:

> "Blame me not for weeping, blame me not I pray,
> As I think of a mountain-side home, two thousand miles
> away.
> Blame me not for weeping, blame me not I pray,
> As I think of a lonely mother, two thousand miles away."

Another song reflecting the sentiment of the boys in the cow-camps, and which is the true rendition of the "Dying Cowboy," is as follows:

> "Oh bury me not on the lone prairie,
> Where the wild coyote howls over me,
> In a narrow grave, just six by three;
> Oh bury me not on the lone prairie.
>
> It matters not, I've oft been told,
> Where the body lies if the heart is cold.
> Yet grant, oh grant, this wish to me
> Oh, bury me not on the lone prairie.
>
> I've always wished to be laid when I died,
> In the little churchyard on the green hillside,
> By my father's grave there let mine be,
> And bury me not on the lone prairie.
>
> Let my death-slumbers be where my mother's prayer
> And my sister's tears will mingle there;
> Where my friends can come and weep o'er me;
> Oh, bury me not on the lone prairie.
>
> 'Oh, bury me not,' and his voice failed there,
> But they took no heed of his dying prayer.
> In a narrow little grave just six by three
> They laid him away on the lone prairie."

Women of good character were held in the highest esteem in the cow-camps, and should such a woman have happened to be stranded or left there without a companion, she would have been in the safest place in this entire world. She would have been protected better than all the officers of the Government could have protected her. No man could court trouble, and serious trouble, quicker among a set of cowboys, than to cast some aspersion upon a woman whom they knew to be of good character, even if she did not have a relative or associate present. These men, in the presence of ladies, were always courteous and polite to the best of their ability. Their manners might be poor, but they would be the best they knew. They lived away from civilization, seldom saw ladies, and they naturally grew uncouth and careless in their manners and habits, but when they did meet ladies, they pulled themselves together the best they could.

Most men on the range smoked cigarettes. These they would roll themselves. The "makings" of these were universally Durham tobacco and rice straw paper, usually brown. The round tags from their packages of Bull Durham hung from their shirts or vest pockets. Some of these men or boys became very proficient and artistic in the making of these cigarettes. They would roll and light them while their horses loped across the prairie. Some could roll them with one hand, either from or toward them.

Cowboys are often looked upon as a class of persons whose principal business was drinking bad liquor and causing all the trouble in circulation. As a class they used as little liquor as any other men. These men spent their lives far away from civilization and cultured society. They did not see towns or settled communities for months at a time. When they did visit towns or cities, there were few of them who did not take a drink, but there were not a great many of them who habitually drank to excess. Some of those who did, after days of protracted drinking, became hard to manage. The effects of the open, free, and fearless life which they had lived, when stimulated by strong drink and their mind befuddled by days of the use of the same, often resulted in an imaginary grievance toward someone, perhaps the authorities who had been compelled to restrain them. Such men were occasionally hard to deal with. When one of these cases did happen, it was always charged to the body of cowboys in general. Often submissive, honest, and trustworthy boys or men under the circumstances above stated became roaring, raging, charging maniacs.

If a crime was committed by anyone who had ever been in a cow-camp, it seemed that it was advertised that the culprit was a cowboy, and the entire business would be charged up to the cowboys as a class. This is not just to the thousands of law-abiding boys who spent years of their lives in the cow-camps and on the range. It would be equally as just, whenever a minister of the gospel or an ex-minister of the gospel, committed a heinous crime to charge his offense up to the good, God-fearing men who are loyal to their calling. Colonel Pierce, a cattleman from southern Texas, better known as "Shanghai Pierce," once engaged a missionary in a game of monte and relieved him of all his earthly possessions. Pierce then offered the State of Nebraska $10,000 annually for the exclusive privilege of dealing monte on their railway trains crossing the State, and, further agreed to stipulate that he would allow no one but missionaries and ministers to play at his game. This did not imply that all these men were gamblers.

There were many wild and desperate men released who preyed upon the plains country. Some of these drifted into the cow-camps. These men were not liked by the cattle owners, nor by the cowboys, but unless they committed some offense there, they had no excuse to compel them to leave. It was a custom as old as the range itself, that the doors of every ranch house were open to the traveler, and he was free to remain for days. This desperate class of men took advantage of this generosity.

In many of the old cow towns there were established what they termed "boot hill" cemeteries, where only the men who died violent deaths in conflicts in these towns were laid to rest. The men who slept in these cemeteries were designated as cow-

boys. They might be outlaws or the worst enemies the cowboys had, some of them might be good, honest boys who went
wild; again, others of them resting in these cemeteries might
be better than the ones who killed them, or they might be the
victims of some over zealous officers who were more anxious
to make a reputation and mark up notches on their guns than
to preserve life in their towns. While this last stated condition
did not often happen, yet all classes of men were found in the
West, even among the officers of the law.

The writer recently read an article printed in a reputable
periodical and by a reputable author, stating that the old cowboys coming up the Chisholm Trail, the old trail drivers from
the South in its early years, were men principally from the
Confederate Army, who, in their travels north, sought the
opportunity to even up with the officers in the towns at the
northern terminus of the trail. From the observation, experience, and information of the writer, it does not seem possible
that this condition existed. Among these men, the writer never
heard of trouble growing out of the Civil War or politics. Ex-
soldiers of both armies worked side by side on the range, and
were as companionable as the veterans who served together.
The fact is that the cattle dealers and ranchmen of Texas had
among them many men from the North, many of whom had
belonged to the Northern Army. These men went west after
the war, seeking their fortunes, and many of them acquired
the same in the cattle business of Texas. Pierce Brothers, one
of the brothers of whom was Colonel Shanghai Pierce[3] above
referred to, were dyed in the wool Yankees from New England.

---

[3] A. H. Pierce, known in the cattle country as Colonel Shanghai Pierce, was a
native of Connecticut who came to Texas after the Civil War, engaged in the cattle
business, and grew to be one of the largest cattle dealers of the West. He wore
a full beard, stood six feet, four inches in his cowboy boots, and weighed two hundred and twenty pounds. He worked and rode side by side with his cowboys, drove
up the trail each year, and was a well known and familiar figure at the northern
terminus of the same.

Col. A. H. (Shanghai) Pierce. A Yankee who made a fortune in the cattle industry in Texas.

These men were loved and respected by the men who worked for them, many of whom were men who had served in the Confederate Army.

If anyone desires to go further and investigate to any greater extent the character, standing, and reputation of the men who rode the ranges of Texas and Indian Territory, they can take the roster of the Old Trail Drivers Association of Texas and that of the Old Cherokee Strip Cowpunchers Association of Oklahoma, run over them, and see how many desperadoes, disreputable men, or killers are found in these lists. In doing so, they can also compare the number they find with those among them who have risen high in life as financiers, professional men, and those who have risen to postions of honor and trust in their Government. This comparison would not make as much excitement and would not bring as great returns for the effort as would exaggerated and colored articles of bloody deeds of Western gunmen, but it would make a better showing for the cowboys.

We desire to here set out a poetical description of the cowboy. This commendable article, entitled "A Cowboy's Toast," was written by James Barton Adams, and we quote it in full as follows:

"Here's to the passing cowboy, the plowman's pioneer;
His home the boundless mesa, he of any man the peer;
Around his wide sombrero was stretched the rattler's hide,
His bridle sporting conchos, his lasso at his side.
All day he roamed the prairies, at night he, with the stars,
Kept vigil o'er thousands held by neither post nor bars;
With never a diversion in all the lonesome land,
But cattle, cattle, cattle, and sun and sage and sand.

Sometimes the hoot-owl hailed him, when scudding through
　　the flat;
And prairie dogs would sauce him, as at their doors they sat;
Some Texas steer pursuing o'er the pathless waste of sod.
The rattler hissed its warning when near its haunts he trod,
With lasso, quirt, and colter, the cowboy knew his skill;
They pass with him to history and naught their place can fill;
While he, bold broncho rider, ne'er conned a lesson page,
But cattle, cattle, cattle, and sun and sand and sage.

And oh! the long night-watches, with terror in the skies!
When lightning played and mocked him till blinded were his
　　eyes;
When raged the storm around him, and fear was in his heart,
Lest panic-stricken leaders might make the whole herd start.
That meant a death for many, perhaps a wild stampede,
When none could stem the fury of the cattle in the lead;
Ah, then life seemed so very little and death so very near,
With cattle, cattle, cattle, and darkness everywhere.

Then quaff with me a bumper of water, clear and pure,
To the memory of the cowboy whose fame must e'er endure
From the Llano Estacado to Dakota's distant sands,
Where were herded countless thousands in the days of fence-
　　less lands.
Let us rear for him an altar in the Temple of the Brave,
And weave of Texas grasses a garland for his grave;
And offer him a guerdon for the work that he has done
With cattle, cattle, cattle, and sage and sand and sun."

In *Chronicles of Oklahoma,* issued by the Historical Society
of the State, in the June number, 1931, is an article entitled
"The Cowboy 1880—The Statue 1931," by Frank C. Orner,
in which we find the following apt statement as to the achieve-
ments of many of the old cowboys:

"The Cowboy became a plow boy achieving on from the
campfire's glow and trail dust to the zenith of all vocations."

Whatever the faults and frailties of the old cowboys were, and being merely men, they must have had many, their commendable customs, habits, and everyday life will measure up and stand a favorable test with any other class of men. This statement is made after years of knowledge and association with these men and a wide and extensive experience with men in other walks of life. Whatever the judgment may be of these men of the range and of the prairies, who did more than any other class to prepare the West for the civilization that followed, the writer desires to say, in the words of the greatest poet of all time:

> "The evils that men do live after them,
> The good is oft interred with their bones."

CHAPTER XIX.

TALES OF A COW-CAMP AND BREAKING IN A COWBOY

It was in the springtime of a year in the early eighties that an outfit of cowboys had been assembled for the trip down the Chisholm Trail. Their route of travel was to be down this trail, then west, traveling in that direction until they passed into the State of Texas, past Mobeetie and over the broad plains of the Panhandle. This was the regular procedure at that time for cowboys who had wintered in the North. They would go to the Panhandle of Texas in the springtime, driving their horse *remudas,* and when grass was good would return with a bunch of Texas cattle for the pastures of the Cherokee Outlet or for shipment at the railway terminus.

This outfit consisted of the boss, six other riders, and the cook. The camp where they were assembled was twenty-six miles from the end of the railway at Caldwell, Kansas, and the boss had gone to that town to make final arrangements for their departure. The chuck-wagon, the saddle-horses, and the seven men were left at the camp. This camp was at a well known point along the trail, near a grove of timber along Pond Creek, and a short distance from the ranch on the trail of the same name. A couple of saddle-horses were tied near the camp, and the rest of the saddle animals were grazing in the bottom between Pond Creek and the Salt Fork River. The chuck-wagon, with its cover partly drawn, and the large door to the cupboard dropped back forming a table, with cooking utensils piled on the same, was standing to the northward, and about twenty feet distant from the tent. This tent was a square affair, with guy ropes, known as a wall-tent, about fourteen by sixteen feet in size. The flap of the tent was thrown back, revealing the blankets and beds of the men.

The noon meal was over, the sun was slipping down in the western sky, and all the men were in camp waiting for the return of the boss. They expected him the next day, after which they would start on their long journey. This bunch of men had not been together long. They had been assembled from the country along or near the Kansas line. Cowboys often delighted in spending a winter in civilization, dancing and associating with people in a settled community. Others would work on ranches along the state line during the winter. These men were procured from the classes just referred to, and were entire strangers to one another before their meeting in this outfit. They were now, however, to be companions and associates for weeks to follow, and were getting acquainted as fast as possible. In the few days of their association nick-names had been applied to most of them. These names would follow them, and they would be known only by such as long as they remained together.

They were congregated in camp and lounging around the campfire, between the rear of the wagon and the front of the tent. The individual description of these men, together with the appearance and disposition of each is worthy of note, and should be observed in order to appreciate all that followed.

Gene Marsh was a man whose age might be placed in the middle thirties. He was of medium height, inclined to be cor-pulent, with a short, thick neck and red face. His extraordi-nary strength was plainly apparent. His countenance was pleasing, but his face showed the strength of character that was housed within him. He was well educated and displayed much ability. He was not verbose and his past was unknown, but he was easily the natural leader of the men thus assembled.

He was one of a remarkable class of men who say much without speaking a word.

Another of the outfit was a well dressed young man, who at this early date had been designated as "Billings." He was so named for the reason that a couple of years prior to this time he had come out from his home in the East; had traveled to his uncle's ranch near Billings, Montana, where he expected to be instantly installed in the romantic occupation of a full-fledged cowboy. After helping to cut and put up hay on this ranch for two summers, put in the balance of the two years feeding the same to the cattle, and having accumulated a few dollars extra cash as compensation for this work, he concluded to drift further south, where he considered the cowboy business had more thrills and less manual labor. He was continuously telling of his experiences and deeds of valor performed at Billings. As a natural result he was named "Billings," and to all of the men thus assembled he would never be anything else. During the scene that followed he was leaning upon a roll of bedding at the rear end of the wagon, and the ivory handle of a six-shooter extended from the scabbard swinging from a belt, well filled with cartridges and encircling his waist.

Pecos was the name of another member of this outfit. He had been an old buffalo hunter, and had traveled the plains in all directions. He had been known by this particular designation for years throughout the cattle country, having been so named on account of his association with the historical river of New Mexico of that name.

Asa Wilde was another old westerner belonging to the outfit. He was but little younger than Pecos, and was also an experienced man of the plains.

Another of this body of men was Texas Mike, generally known as "Tex." He was originally from eastern Texas, but had spent most of his life in the western cow-camps. He was a tall, angular Texan, and every move that he made denoted that he was as free and easy as he was fearless. His trips up and down the trail had been so numerous that in all probability he could not remember them all.

Archey was the cook of the outfit. His home was in the town at the end of the railway. Here he had a wife and children. He made these trips down the trail each year for his summer's work. He was a quiet, unassuming, honest fellow, whose services were always satisfactory to his employers. He made these trips for the money he would bring back at the end of the season.

The last man of the outfit was Pedro, the horse wrangler. Pedro was a Mexican, who had spent his first winter in the North, and was now anxious to return to his native country. He was black, short, stout, and his hair grew down well over his forehead. He was always known by the abbreviated name of "Mex." He usually listened, but said little. He was seated on the ground, his knife open in his hand, his feet crossed in front of him, engaged in his customary pastime of playing "mumble-peg," so called in the cow-camps, the correct name of which is mumble the peg. This, played by throwing and sticking a knife in the ground, was a very common game on the range, as it could be played by but one man.

All the outfit left by the boss had congregated in camp for the first time since the midday meal. Tex had just returned across the bottom from a trip down to look at the river. As he seated himself on the blankets in front of the tent he said:

"I have camped in this bottom many years, and at all times of the year, and I never did like the old population around here; that is the ones that were found here by Jesse Chisholm or whoever discovered this part of the world after it was made. In the summer time this pond here raises skeeters as big as butterflies, with bills as long and sharp as a woman's tongue after she has been married ten years. And this bottom twixed here and the river is full of rattlers as big as sea sarpants and as mean and quarrelsome as old Belzebub himself. As I come across this bottom this afternoon I run onto one of these old nesters, as big round as a full grown stove-pipe. He coiled up ready to deal death and destruction, then stuck his nose up from the middle of a bunch of snake and stuck his tongue out and tried to flirt with me. I never cud figger out what a snake wanted to always stick his tongue out that way fer, unless he jist wanted to show you how forked it wuz."

Then Asa spoke up:

"You know I have reckoned on that a heap myself, and I finely thought when a snake done that he was making a face at me and darin' me to battle. Marsh here is a man of larnin, and if he ever studied about snakes or other varmints he might tell us what the truth is about this."

Gene Marsh was surprised to be called to solve this sort of a problem, but answered thus:

"I never studied snakes in particular, but I have studied natural history. All of you would perhaps be surprised if I told you why a snake sticks out its tongue when molested or anything approaches it. You have perhaps noticed that a snake has no ears. That being true, its tongue serves the purpose of ears, sticking out its tongue it catches the vibrations of sound on the same, and by that means hears all the sounds in the vicinity."

Pecos then said:

"That explanation is probably right, but I never did know before that a rattle-snake, in addition to carryin a bell on his tail, also carried ears on his tongue. But a man never gets too old to larn. Now Asa you have enlitened us on that mystery, now can you tell us why when a blasted little skeeter bites you it raises a big welt and hurts bout as bad as if you was shot with a forty-five?"

Marsh then answered:

"Well, that is another matter that is not generally known. We all know that these bites cause just what was stated, but we do not generally know why. In the first place, the purpose of a mosquito in what is called "biting" is to suck blood from the person or animal bitten. Blood is composed of white and red corpuscles, or small sacs, which carry the different constituents of the blood. The opening is so small in the long bill that the mosquito uses to bite or suck the blood with that these corpuscles will not pass up through the same. The mosquito has connected with this bill a small container full of a certain fluid which will break up and dissolve these corpuscles, so that it can draw the blood up as food. Thus, before sucking the blood, the mosquito injects some of this fluid into its victim to dissolve the corpuscles. This fluid poisons the flesh, causing the painful sensation, and result we experience."

Then Tex again entered into the conversation, saying:

"Acceptin that explanation as true, which we must, bein it come from a man as well edecated as Marsh, all I have to say is: that as thick as these little pesterin varmints are around here in the summertime there must be a heap of this pizen hereabout for these little cusses to load themselves up on to do all the biten and pizenen they do."

For some time nothing was said, but all of Marsh's listeners revolved in their minds the lesson that they had just learned.

All hands appeared well contented, and comment passed around as to what they would do when the boss returned. When a cow-camp is in perfect peace and quiet it means that the universal inclination is at hand to engage in story-telling or reminiscenses.

Young Billings was the first to have the spirit move him, and launched forth with a tale which represented his disposition. He told of a hair-raising and bloody encounter in a dance hall in Billings, in which he was easily the hero of the hour, relieved one of the wild boisterous characters of the Northwest of his lady friend, and, like unto Lochinvar of old, bore her away in triumph. In all of this controversy, as he explained it, his trusty and ever ready .45 Colt, with the ivory stock, played a prominent part, and in this encounter he sent his adversary skulking away in humiliation and disgrace, shorn of all his prowess, and completely ruined forever.

After this story was completed, quiet reigned, and not one word was spoken for a full minute. Then Tex spoke up and said: "Young man, that air conflab was a good one. You could not have told a bigger tale of day-dremin and one that every one would recognize as a full fledged fairy story if you had studied for a month. How many buryin grounds did you patronize with your dead while you was up thar?"

Billings replied that in this affair he meant business, as he always did, and if anyone present did not take it that way he had better arise, step in, help himself, and he would give him a free demonstration first hand.

To this Tex replied: "Great man of the North Country, I am a mighty sight older than you are, and have spent most of my life on these ere plains and trails where no man's law rules the land. Durin this time I have had the pleasure to survey some of the worst men that ever stood in shoe leather. From all this sightseein I have come to the conclusion that there never wuz a man so bad but what some time he found one just a little worse. So if you have an idea you are a bad man from Bitter Crick, and if you think the further up the crick you go the worse they git, and that you live in the last house, you are goin to find out when it's too late that there is a man campt with a tent a mile further up the crick than you ever been or have any knowledge uv."

This matter was then terminated by Pecos when he said:

"Speakin of bad men reminds me that I spent the last years of the seventies in New Mexico. I navigated the country from South Springs ranch to the Capitans, and was up and down the Pecos north past *Bosque Grande* to Fort Sumner. I knowed Major Murphy, John Chisum, and Pat Garrett well, and have taken many drinks with them. I knew Billy the Kid as well as any of them. When this boy appeared on the range there was no signs of bad man sticken out of him. He didn't have his battle flag up. He never did brag about anything or exaggerate anything he had done. When the drunken hirelins, sent out by Murphy to kill anyone who did not agree with them, found and killed his friend Tunstall, an innocent old Englishman, who the Kid was working for, this little insignificant runt of a boy kneeled down by the side of his dead boss, and with tears runnin' down his cheeks he raised his little hand, swore an oath that was sincere that he would kill every man who helped to do that dirty trick. When he loaded Bob Olenger down with buck-shot at Lincoln he had just about made this promise good.

"It has always been my experience that the feller that comes among us with tales of blood and battle are not really dangerous, and I never pay any attention to their dangerous talk, but when some kid comes along who is too timid to answer when you ask him to take a drink, and is so tender-hearted that tears will come to his eyes when you sing a song about his home and his mother, then look out for that lad and do not stir him up. If you do, he will kill you."

After relating this portion of Western history, which Pecos was capable of doing, silence reigned again, during which time Mex with skillful curves whirled his knife with regularity. Then Asie Wilde spoke up and said:

"This weather reminds me of a day when I was hunten buffalo down on the Paloduro about ten years ago. I was wantin' to git some bull buffalo hide for heavy raw-hide that I needed. This kind of a buffalo was usually easy to find and kill. I went out and hid in a buffalo-waller to get in range of several that was comin that way. One big, old bull stopped broad-side, about one hundred yards from me, and I drew a bead on him with my Sharp's rifle. I wasn't very careful in taking aim, as it appeared to be such an easy shot. When I fired, the old fellow toppled over, and I started up to him very much unconcerned as to the state of his health, but when I got right up thar, and had commenced to figure out the skinin' operation, the old cuss jumped up, swung around to-ward me, shook his head, and took after me. I run as I had never run before. I saw a valley ahead of me, and as I neared it I come to a bluff about ten feet high. As good luck would have it, there was a piece of the bank caved over, and I slipped down as far as I could into this opnen. I sure wished I was smaller so that I could go down further. Just as this old bull was reachen fer me with his horns I had dropped out of sight. He was looken at me, and not the bank, and he went on over in the most ungraceful manner that a buffalo could go."

After this tale was completed, for fear someone would get in first, Pecos immediately resumed the conversation and said:

"Say, you know that sure reminds me of a little experience I had about the same time, except that mine happened up on the Brazos. I was the proud possessor at that time of the derndest, biggest buffalo gun that ever come onto the plains. I had bought it off from a feller who had come out from the East. This feller sold it because he couldn't pack powder and lead nuff to keep it loaded. I don't know what caliber it was. I don't think it had any. If it had been a shotgun I don't think it would have had any gauge. Well, there was an old wooly varmint of a buffalo bull out a ways from camp one day, pawen up the ground and cussen a streak at our oxen. I thought he might put his threats into execution, so I took this big piece of artillery and strolled out to see what I could do for him. He did not fear man or beast, and stood right thar and told me so to my face. I got up in about sixty yards of his side. I dropped down on one knee and rested my gun over my hand, which gripped around a ram rod for a rest. I pulled a bead on him with old Betsy and shot. He very accomodatin like rolled over as if to say he was dead and ready to be carted off.

"Carryin my gun in one hand I started up to him, for I was sure that he had a hole bored through him that I could mighty near crawl through. When I got right onto him, this old wooly, self-conceited brute did exactly like yourn did. In spite of his bein dead he hopped right up, wound himself up, and took after me. There was open and level prairie as fer as I could see in every direction. I did not have a chance from the very start. I would have been prouder than Columbus was when he found America if I could have discovered a hole half as big as the one you found. I did my very best though, and put in my best licks to make a record. It did no good, and I hadn't run a hundred yards until I knowed I was a gonner. I didn't have time to look around, and I expected every second to feel the prod of this brute's short, black, ugly horns as he lifted me into the Kingdom come with his stout neck. The only hope that I could figger out was that he would throw me so high that I wouldn't come down until he had give me up and gone away.

"Anyway he got so close that I could feel his breath on my feet, and his shaggy forehead tickle the seat of my pants, as he rushed on with head down. At this time I was so near all in anyway, and knowin what was comin, I was gettin some impatient on account of the delay. I had give up, and to add to my misfortune I stubbed my toe, old Betsy flew out of my hand and rolled out in front of me with the muzzle pintin right at me. Then I thought I discovered a ray of hope. Can any of you philosophers guess what it wuz?" Then Tex spoke up saying: "I'll swear I don't believe you ever got away, knowin them critters as I do. If you didn't, we're all on the same side. I wish somebody would pinch me and see if I'm alive. If I ain't, this is a cow-camp full of ghosts."

Then Pecos replied: "Well sirs, I took the only chance of gittin away that I ever had in that race." Then Archie remarked anxiously: "For heaven's sake, tell it. What was it? I can't see no chance. It sure looks bad to me." To which Pecos answered: "Well it was easy. I just run plumb up inside that gun barl, and that wooly brute went right on over me, same as did the one that was after Tex. These animals had a habit of doin that very thing in such cases made and provided. I never would have thought about this episode if it hadn't been for Tex telling that story of hisn."

Asa Wilde then said: "Well, it is about my time to speak my piece, and the first thing I am going to do is to take the responsibility of nominating Pecos as the champion liar of the whole Cherokee Outlet or any other outlet. After which I am going to tell of a little experience I had. It wasn't the same kind as that of Tex or Pecos, and I won't try to compete in the contest with Pecos. You know a few years ago I took a trip up the west cattle trail, and went on to deliver some horns and hides for Uncle Sam to some starven Injuns. We got up in western Kansas, where we passed the abode of a homesteader or a hoe man, who had crowded out onto the plains where he could build a happy home and worship acorden to the dictates of his conscience, with no one to bother him. His neighbors was mighty scarce. A few miles after we passed this home on the prairie, the cook run off a bank and had a crack-up. We worked for a long time to repair the damage, but finally discovered we had lost our monkey wrench, and that we had to have one or leave a good chuck wagon on the prairie. I was elected by a large majority to go back and see if I could borrow one at the house of this granger. When I rode up, the lady of the house planted herself in the door with some five or six promisin offsprings huddled about her. She wasn't a bit scared, but was brim full of importance.

"In a very polite like manner I asked her if she lived there. To which she replied: 'Well you don't suppose I am visitin here with all my children when there is no body to home.' I apologized for my ignorance, and in order to arrive at the pint involved, I asked her if they had a monkey wrench, to which she replied: 'Oh, Lord no. Smith over east here has a sheep ranch, that causes us a lot of trouble, Williams further south has a horse ranch, up north you will find several cattle ranches. This is a plain farm, and no one around here yit has been fool enough to start a monkey ranch, and I hope you got no such a pesterin notion, cause they will be a mighty sight worse on us farmers than the sheep.' It took me all evenin to figger out whether I had made the mistake or whether it was her. I went back without the monkey wrench, told the boys that another trip like that and I would go coo-coo, and that I wasn't sure now that I was just right in the head. I wish you fellers would figger out how I could have done any better. Gene, you tell us something and I will quit."

Gene Marsh then said: "The first important thing that I want to impress on this body assembled is that I never tell anything but the truth. I can't tell a story, but will tell you a little circumstance that is the truth.

"A year ago last summer I took a little jaunt west to see my cousin who lives out near Santa Fe, New Mexico. This cousin is a shepherd. Not the kind you read about in the Scriptures, but just an ordinary sheep man of New Mexico. This circumstance that I am about to relate happened to him just before I came out, and the prime factor in the drama was still there. The facts were as follows: My cousin was preparing to make a trip back to his eastern home to see his father, who had been ailing for some time, and he wanted to get someone to look after his sheep while he was gone. Some of the neighbors knowing this fact had sent a young fellow, who was inquiring for work, over to see him.

"When the young man came up, my cousin naturally inquired as to his antecedents and qualification. He stated that he had been going to school in the East, his health had failed him, and he wanted to get a job in that climate to recuperate. He stated that he was not much of a rider if there was any riding to be done. My cousin informed the young man that they did not use horses in their sheep herding, but walked, and often it was much trouble to keep the sheep together. The ex-student told him that there would be no trouble about that, as he was a foot racer, having gained some distinction as such in school. My cousin was favorably impressed with the young man and hired him, but charged him to keep the sheep in bounds.

My cousin departed for the East, and was gone some six weeks. When he returned, he found his hired hand well, happy, and looking much more robust than when he left. He inquired about the sheep and how he had gotten along with them. The young man assured him that he had had no trouble with the old sheep, but said the lambs were mighty bad, and that they had finally grown so unruly and bad about straying off until he had been compelled to catch several of them and tie them. My cousin was much interested about this condition, and accompanied the young man around back of the sheep corral to see the wayward lambs. There he beheld a sight which staggered him. The young fellow had a bunch of jack rabbits securely tethered out. Now if you don't believe that, you can take a trip to New Mexico and verify it."

After silence for some time, during which several cigarettes were rolled and lighted, Acey Wilde rose up in full length, as if reviving himself for the occasion, and said:

"Ever since Pecos got off that dod gasted tale about that mountain howser of hisen I have been studyen the situation over, and I come to find out I once had some gun of my own. This gun shot so hard and far that it would have been agin the statutes in a civilized country to shoot it off. I had that gun on a buffalo hunt about five years ago, when we drifted back to the cross timbers, and there in a grove of heavy trees we had made a camp and stopped for some time. I was settin there in that camp one day with that instrument of death and destruction across my knees, cleaning it and working with it, when it accidently went off. Knowing that gun as I did, I deemed it my duty in the interest of humanity and the world at large to follow that bullet, and see what destruction it had left in its path, and see what all it had killed, maimed, and mangled.

"You know I had not gone fur until I come to a tree where that ball had struck a limb and split it in passing through. It happened that at that particular time a bunch of big turkey gobblers were settin on that limb, and when the limb closed up where it had been split, it caught the toes on both feet of nine of these big fellers, and when I got on the scene there they were all hanging by the toes, done give up and quit floppin. The bullet had gone on and I still followed. Quite a ways on I found where it had struck a deer and killed it dead as a mackerel. It had been real lucky that the bullet had not struck anything more than it did, as it might have done lots of harm. The last thing it did though was to hit a bee tree and split it open. I found the honey running out, and we got over a hundred pounds from that one tree. That was lucky, as you never could have told that it was a bee tree from looking at it.

"I went back to the camp to get a conveyance to haul all this stuff in, and all that we had was a sled that one of the boys had rigged up to tantalize antelope with until they would come close enuf to kill them. All the harness we could use with this was made of raw-hide. I hitched up a horse with this outfit and loaded all this stuff on the sled. Before I got back to the camp there come up a rainstorm for a few minutes, and when I led my horse up into camp and looked for my sled, these tugs had got wet and stretched until the sled was a quarter of a mile behind. That worried me some, but my head was in good working order, and I just led the horse round a tree and fastened the tugs, and waited until the raw-hide dried, and it pulled the sled right up to the tent."

Nothing was said for some little time. Then Pecos remarked: "Say, Asa, what do you suppose would happen to all of us if you had lied about part of that business?" To which Asa replied: "You fellers after tellen about runnen up gun barls, runnen down jack-rabbits, and startin monkey ranches are nice specimens to accuse me of lying when I tell a nice little circumstance true to life. If I would hang around with you fellers awhile and did not lie occasionally I would feel so small that I could crawl up a gun barl that wasn't any bigger than a twenty-two."

After a brief silence, Texas Mike spoke up saying:

"As years roll by and I feel old age creepin over me, I often meditate long and earnestly as to my past life and go back to my boyhood days down in eastern Texas. When I was a small lad my trustin parents once tried to make a fashion plate out of me; that is, a dressed up urchin. It turned out to be a total failure, and in fact ruined my whole life and prospects for a brilliant future, and it all come about because I was a poor boy and had to work, and in the course of my daily labors I was compelled to feed a blasted calf.

"I can't tell this story, I mean true incident, without illustratin every part of it. I don't spose our friend Billings would object to assistin me in that illustration in order to rehearse one of the interestin scenes of my boyhood days, so that he can get the full effects of the affair."

There being no protests, Tex continued:

"The fact is that I was a very promisen youngster accordin to the idees of my dotin father and mother. We lived way down on the waters of the Attoac River, that is when the river had any water in it. That was away over among the pine trees in Rusk County, Texas. We would go to Henderson, the nearest town, every Saturday afternoon. My kind parents had equipped me with a new suit of cloths, including a nice pair of boots, a white shirt with a ruffled front on it, a little hat that turned up all around the brim, and with a crown that fitted tight on my belfry. I had got all dressed up, and we

was all ready to start for town, when somebody remembered
that I had got so excited over wearin my new clothes that I
had forgot to perform one of my important duties in feeden
the calf, which was tied on a rope down by the barn. I knowed
that I had to do this before I could go. I got the bucket of
milk and started down the crooked path, through the stumps
of the clearin, to the barn. The tears was not only runnin
down my cheeks, but I was bawlin worse than the calf would
if it hadn't been fed. I got down to where that calf was with
my feelins all hurt and some riled up, and set the bucket down
for it to drink. If you ever fed a calf, you know they have a
fool habit of sticken their nose down to the bottom of the
bucket and then try to drink through their nose. I was holdin
to the sides of this bucket to keep it from upsettin it, and the
actions of this calf at that time was no exceptions to the rule,
and when it got its nose and all connections thereto full of
milk it raised its nose right square up in front of my nice, white,
ruffled shirt and shot forth a stream of milk that would have
done credit to a four-inch hose, drenchin me from my nose
down. I think that was the maddest I ever wuz in my whole
life.

"I could see my whole future life ruint by this one act
of pure cussedness of this insignificant brute. The cry for
vengeance went through my whole sistem, and (reaching out
and grasping Billings firmly by the ears) I got that calf right
square by the ears, so it couldn't git away, and I yanked it
up to the bucket just like this, and I stuck its nose down into
the bucket this way, and while it kickt and cavorted around
I held it there until it mighty near croaked, and pulled it over
that barnyard and jerked it up and down just like this, and
the longer I pulled the madder I got, until I threw that blasted
calf away from me just this way, and went back to the house

all soaked with milk and all tore up and ruint, and I have remained ruint to this very day."

While all this was going on, Tex was dragging Billings around over the ground, jerking his head up, then rubbing his nose in the dirt, and finally threw him away from him in illustration. The crowd present watching the performance was yelling with laughter. All of the persons assembled knew that this was an old trick in the cow-camps. As soon as Billings was released and gained his equilibrium he reached for the white handle of his Colt pistol. Tex paid no attention to this performance or his threatening attitude, but Gene struck his wrist, causing the gun to fly out of his hand. Then he picked up the gun, raised the hammer to the middle notch, throwing open the gate on the side with the muzzle up, and turning the cylinder, let the cartridges drop into his hand one by one. Then he grasped Billings by the wrist with one hand, holding him with a grip that would convince any one that resistance was useless. Grasping him thus and holding out the gun in the other hand he addressed this man from the North as follows:

"Young man, it is dangerous for you to be carrying weapons like this. You will take notice of the front sight on this piece of artillery, will observe that it is almost one-half inch long, and reasonably sharp on top, further it is quite firm and substantial, in case anyone should take it away from you, as has just been done, they might disfigure your countenance or otherwise operate on you with the sharp sight in a manner that might not only be dangerous, but very painful, and might inflict bodily and lasting injuries upon you, so if you tote this gun around anymore you had better take it to town the first opportunity you have and have this sight taken off. You could shoot just as well without it."

Gene then tossed the gun into the wagon and continued:

"Further, there are well established rules and precedents on this trail, and for those who do not understand them and know enough to follow them we have ways of impressing those things upon their memory in such a manner that they will remember them as long as they live. One of these things is that you shall not blow your own horn about your ability so loud that it is ridiculous. This you should realize as you stand here helpless and alone. You should let people find out your merits from other sources; they will better consider them and remember them longer. The next and most important thing for you to remember is to learn to take a joke, treat your associates with respect, and get this 'bad-man' notion out of your system.

"It is through an act of kindness to you that we are about to administer unto you the old and established degree installing you into the body of cowboys who ride this trail, and we will do so with a painful but well meant and impressive ceremony. You may object, but I would advise you not to make too much trouble, as it will avail you nothing, and will make matters worse."

With this, and while still holding Billings by the wrist with a firm grip, Gene turned to Pedro, saying "Mex, get into the wagon, bring those heavy cow-hide leggins of mine, and also bring the rope lying by the side of the wagon."

At this time Tex spoke up saying: "Oh, let him go, he is harmless. He don't know any better, but may learn something in course of time."

To this Gene replied:

"It is for his own good. The next man may not be as gentle with him as we have been. In that case he may be planted along the side of the trail, and then chastisement will do him no good. We must teach him to live among us in peace and harmony before he will be a respected rider of this trail."

With this Gene Marsh led his victim along, he going with much reluctance. Thus he conducted him until they reached the edge of the timber. There a large tree had been cut down, and a portion of the trunk still lay upon the ground. The rest of the outfit followed close behind, except Tex, who remained in camp. Pedro brought along the leggins and rope. All of the men knew what was going to take place, and all knew their duty well under the circumstances. Tex did not think it diplomatic that he should take part in the exercise which was about to take place, and remained away.

One of the men wound the rope around the legs of the unfortunate young man, just above the feet. Two of them grabbed the hands of the victim, and passing around the log placed him squarely across and over the same. Thus he was held by parties on both sides, held helpless. Thus lay this young man Billings, who by his own acknowledgment was the terror of the Northwest, and who had come to the Cherokee Outlet expecting to be feared and dreaded. Thus he was drawn across a log by common cowboys in an ignominious and disrespectful manner. One man holding the rope behind drew his feet back and held them fast, while two in front pressed his stomach against the log with his body drawn tightly over the same. Thereupon, Gene Marsh addressed the subject in the following language:

"Young man from the Northern Country, before you can serve successfully as a cowboy on this trail, you must learn to wear these leggins or chaparajos in a manner becoming to one of your proud profession. They are the emblem of our calling, protect us from the driving rain, ill winds, and many other pains and discomforts which we encounter on the trail. You cannot so wear them until they have been placed upon you in proper form, with due ceremony and reverence. I am now about to perform that official duty and mete out to you the painful process of so doing. When it dawns upon you that you are willing to promise us to wear these leggins with dignity, respect, and kindness to all, and as one of us, you will so manifest by asking me to forbear, but you must be sure to begin in time, because in order to be assured that you are in earnest, we are to give you six strokes after you have so manifested."

At this Gene took the heavy cow-hide leggins in both hands, grasped them near the top, and raising on his tip-toes brought them down upon the rear side of the ampler portion of this would-be bad man until the report echoed through the timber like a pistol shot. This process was repeated ten times in quick succession, when the victim yelled for him to stop, that he was killing him, and he would promise anything. Six additional blows followed with undiminishing force, while the victim yelled for mercy, and begged to be spared, saying that it would kill him if he received another blow.

When the echo of the sixteenth stroke had died away in the timber, Gene commanded them to release the victim. Billings rose unsteadily to his feet, and Gene steadied him with an iron grip on his arm, saying:

"Well, young companion of the trail, it is for your own good, in keeping with a long established custom, that we have been compelled to administer this punishment upon you, and it will avail you nothing hereafter if you do not remember the lesson. Bear in mind that your threats, your attempt at intimidation, and your proffered use of violence and firearms do not bother us in the least, and none of us are afraid of you or your talk or guns. If you will heed the lesson that we have today given you, you can wear these leggins, go among us, stand as a useful and upright rider of this trail, be a man among us, and we in turn will stand your firm protectors and defenders in trouble, in danger, in sorrow, or in dishonor and disgrace. No man can do more for a companion, and this we will do so long as you comply with the unwritten law of this land, and that protection will be extended to you regard-less of whether you are right or wrong."

With this, all parties returned to camp; Billings shook hands with Tex, and apologizd to him for what had happened. From this time on, Billings was a changed man. The next day the boss returned, and the wagon and horse *remuda* was pointed to the southward, and traveled down the trail. Billings accompanied his outfit, wearing his leggins honorably and true to his trust. This he did until the railway built into the coun-try, the trail was no more, and until the ranges were broken up. Then he turned his course to New Mexico, following the fast disappearing old West. [1]

---

[1] The ceremony detailed here was termed "putting the leggins" on a cowboy, and was a system of hazing similar to what is followed in schools. Even men who have been victims of hazing in schools will admit that it bears the best results of any lessons that are taught. It brings the subject to a realization of his proper po-sition, and removes the obnoxious feature of his egotism, when no other power can do so. This was particularly applicable in the cow-camps, as some of the subjects were hard to handle, but there were always men available who were able and willing to take care of the propositions, and these obnoxious characters were reduced to the level to which they belonged. It was not often that it was necessary to resort to this performance.

THE ROUND-UP

From original painting by Frances (Cheney) Ball. Painted after observing and studying the operation of a round-up. Owned by and kept in the Stock Exchange Bank of Caldwell, Kansas.

CHAPTER XX.

A DAY ON THE ROUND-UP

During the old cattle days in the Southwest the happenings hereinafter set out were usual occurrences in a day's work on the round-up, and for those who do not know of the process used in the same the following will be of interest.

During the winter season, and especially during driving storms, even at the times when the cattle ranges in the Outlet were securely fenced, many cattle escaped from their home range and became mixed with other brands. It was actually remarkable the number of these strays that would be found and the distance that some of them would travel. In all countries where cattle were kept in such numbers that the owners could not know each individual animal and would not know when one was missing, it was necessary to have a round-up each spring in order to gather in the strays. This work was done in the early summer, before the calves born in the spring were weaned and separated from their mothers. The round-ups in the Cherokee Outlet were held in the springtime, as soon as the grass was advanced far enough so that the cattle would be in good condition, usually in May or early June.

The round-up would eventually cover the entire Outlet. It would not, during the entire progress of the same, include the same outfits, as some would drop out, for the reason that the round-up had gotten so far from their range that no strays had gone that far from their home pastures. Others from ranges in the new district would then take their place, and thus it would continue over the entire cattle country.

The time referred to in this article is the latter part of May in the middle eighties. The location of the camp of the

Cow and Calf Round-up.

preceding evening was on a branch of the Eagle Chief Creek, north of the Cimarron River, on the T5 range. On the following day the round-up was scheduled to move eastward onto the —BQ (barBQ) range. The scene opens just before daylight, and before the world in that vicinity awoke to activity.

The full moon of the early part of the night had dropped some hours before beneath the western horizon. The morning stars, which the night herders had grown to know so well, still twinkled in the heavens, and on account of the clearness of the sky a fair light spread over the surrounding country. With the exception of the few trees skirting the immediate creek, the open prairies stretched away in each direction, but to the south could be seen in the early morning the dim outlines of the distant black-jack timber, extending away toward the Cimarron River. The increasing light in the east gave notice that the daylight was not far distant. A herd of cattle was bedded on the prairie to the north, while the night herder on the morning shift kept a silent vigil over them. As the light increased, a number of wagons in camp along the bank of the creek were soon plainly visible. The tinkle of a bell on some leader of a horse herd was the only sound breaking the stillness. A coyote skulked away to the west, departing from its inspection of the wagons. The camp soon broke into activity, the first sign of which was the ascending smoke from the camp-fires.

The day on the round-up had begun. Silent riders, fresh from their warm blankets, guided their horses from the camp. One headed to the cattle to relieve the last night herder. Others started for the horses belonging to the various outfits. Soon a bunch of saddle horses galloped across the prairie to the camp. As these animals approached the wagons a cowboy raised a rope, one end of which was attached to a wagon wheel. Other cowboys held the farther reaches of the rope, and soon the horses were almost encircled by a rope corral held in the hands of the cowboys. The horses that were gentle enough were approached by the cowboys, to whose allotted strings they belonged. The ones which could not be approached had ropes tossed over their heads, and each rider soon had his mount saddled and ready for the day's work. The cry of breakfast was then sounded from each wagon, and the men approached, took their pint tin cups of coffee from the lid of the chuck box, the door of which had been dropped and served as a table, on which were placed the various articles of food. Each man took his plate and helped himself to the bacon and other articles, and seated himself on the ground in tailor fashion, and breakfast was soon over.

With one of these outfits was a young cowboy, who had recently joined the same. He had soon made it known according to his own admissions and statements that he was an unusually effective rider of bad horses. He had also made it known that in riding these horses he used what was known as a "pitching or bucking strap." This was a long strap securely fastened to the saddle, to which the rider would hold and brace himself while his mount went through all the contortions known to it in trying to dislodge him. The use of this strap was considered to be below the dignity of a broncho rider, and was a violation of the legitimate rules of broncho busting and bad horse riding. Even holding to the saddle, which was termed "grabbing leather," was designated as a weakness. However, men on the range have often seen this strap used, as well as hobbled stirrups. [1]

On account of the self-advertised ability of this young man to ride, he was quietly slipped the worst horse in the outfit. He had not ridden this horse before, but on this particular

---

[1] Stirrups were hobbled by some in riding bad horses. The process consisted of tying the stirrups together with a small rope or strap beneath the horse. The rider could then brace himself securely in the saddle by pressing out on the stirrups.

morning it was caught and tied for his use. As he approached with his saddle, it rolled its eyes until the white portions were the most conspicuous part of the animal.   It looked at the rider with apparent contempt, as if to say, "If you think you are going to ride me, you are just fooled." The horse gave a gigantic snort, jumped sideways, and pulled further away. Another cowboy, as was customary under the circumstances, came to the assistance of the rider. The horse was securely tied, the bridle placed on him, and he was blindfolded. The saddle was placed on his back and was cinched tightly with both cinches. The rope was taken up, the young man landed in the saddle, and anchored himself to his trusty strap. The blindfold was removed, and the rider's quirt cracked in the horse's flank. This outlaw-horse, for he was an outlaw, from the very tracks in which he stood sailed through the air. These horses, being well experienced in separating their riders from their saddles, became absolutely proficient in the various tricks adopted to bring about that result, and the longer they practiced the more proficient they grew. This animal was large and strong, and certainly had had experience.

Many of these horses had tricks of their own, and it was very seldom that two horses were found which had the same routine or went through the same performance. A man unfamiliar with the plan followed by a particular horse labors under a disadvantage in riding the animal the first time. Most horses drop their heads and raise their rumps high, and then twist and sun-fish. This horse, with all his independence, disdained this method. He reared his head high and sailed through the air as if he intended to quit the earth. When he came down his rear portion was at such an elevation that he was almost standing on his head. The shock of the landing was almost beyond endurance. The sudden change of his course and the landing was sufficient to break a man in twain.

This rider stayed on the horse's back during all his contortions and efforts that would have apparently dislodged anything. During all this time, however, he was hanging tenaciously to his strap, to which he was as much attached as a drowning man would be to a life-preserver. Finally the horse made a terrific plunge, and as he suddenly changed his course the strain on this strap became too great and it broke. The rider literally drew a semi-circle in the air as complete as a rainbow and landed squarely on the top of his head. He did not move for some time, but by the time the other boys reached him he had begun to stir. He soon raised up, rubbed his face, shook his head, as if to determine whether it would fall off, and presently stood on his feet rather unsteadily.

By the time the dismounted man could walk well, the horse had been caught and brought back. The rider procured another strap and prepared to mount again. From this determination he gained the respect of his fellow riders, and they expressed themselves to the effect that he was not so bad after all. These boys who had been so intent on teaching him a lesson, after observing his grit and determination, and knowing the reputation of this horse, tried to persuade him not to try to mount the animal again. He was, however, determined and assured them that his bucking strap would hold this time, and that he had ridden worse horses. He mounted the animal again, in spite of their protests, and by so doing won the respect of his associates. He rode this horse, and not only subdued it, but convinced the entire outfit that he really could ride, even though he did use a strap to anchor him.

The riders who had congregated to see the fun now dispersed. The wagons of the different outfits were soon loaded and on the move. The different bunches of cattle held by the various brands, which had been gathered and sorted out to them, together with their horses, moved off to the eastward.

The teams drawing the chuck wagons exhibited the same spirit of reluctance on being pushed into the collars as did the ones placed under the saddles. These horses hitched to the wagons plunged and reared for a time, jerking the wagons along with uneven movements.

The entire round-up moved to the east across the divide between Eagle Chief and Turkey Creeks. It crossed the Dodge City and Red Fork Trails, and entered upon the — BQ range. Here it crossed the brakes on the head of Turkey Creek, where the first mishap of the day occurred. The chuck wagon belonging to the triangle brand was drawn by a pair of rather spirited ponies, which were not well broken, and while crossing a tributary on the head waters of Turkey Creek, they rushed a steep hill, overturning the wagon, wrecking the chuck box, turning all the contents onto the ground, and releasing themselves from the wagon. Some of the riders soon captured the run-aways and returned them. The wagon was soon righted, the broken parts patched up, the contents placed in the wagon, and all were on the move again. An accident of this sort was an ordinary occurrence on the round-up. The routes over which these wagons traveled were usually across country with no trails. The wagons were often bogged in quick-sand in crossing streams, or turned over in crossing rough places. In case of a bog in quick-sand several of the riders would appear and attach one end of their ropes carried on their saddles to the front end of the wagon tongues, fasten the other end to their saddle horns, and the wagon would soon be drawn clear of the river.

On entering the — BQ range the outriders took their courses, encircling the range to gather the cattle for sorting. The point of round-up was to be lower down Turkey Creek at a favorable location, a short distance above where the Cantonement trail crossed the same. To this point the wagons jour-

neyed and made their camp for noon. This was also to be
their camp for the next night. By noon time the cattle were
gathered and ready to be cut out for their owners. Dinner
was served with an abundance of good, substantial food, which
was always supplied in cow-camps. The process of eating the
same was a repetition of the morning meal. The horses of
the riders were changed and the cutting process began.

It has been explained that during this procedure all the
foreign cattle were cut out and held in separate herds, each
belonging to the owner of a particular brand. The process of
this separating has also been somewhat explained. To this may
be added that a proficient cutting-horse was well trained; he
knew his own business, and it was impossible for an animal to
dodge one of these horses. It was often remarked in the way
of a metaphor that one of these horses could turn entirely
around on a silver dime. This laborious cutting process continued during the entire afternoon. A portion of the cowboys
held the main bunch, others held the bunches cut out belonging
to the different brands, and still another portion did the cutting or separating of the strays. The day was warm, and the
horses engaged in the cutting were soon exhausted. Others
were procured, the saddles removed from the tired mounts and
placed on the fresh horses. Some of these horses were so
exhausted that they would stagger when the saddles were removed. Each cowboy engaged in the cutting process was compelled to use a number of horses during the day.

The sun gradually sank down in the western sky. The
herd from which the cattle were being taken grew smaller until
all were separated. The cowboys not engaged in holding the
strays returned to the camp. A fire was soon burning near
each wagon, the boys who had ridden during the day visited
from wagon to wagon, and pleasant jests and conversation
passed back and forth. The evening meal was then completed

and the horse *remudas* turned loose for the night. A beautiful moon swung up in the southeastern sky, and the camp on this hillside sloping to the south was almost as light as day. The round-up, while hard work, was the carnival time for the cowboy. Here he told his jokes, sang his songs, and engaged in reminiscences and gossip. The sight of this camp was sufficient to arouse the sentimental spirit of any man, and also a feeling of life and vigor.

It was a poor cow outfit that did not have in its equipment at least one violin or banjo, and a man who could play the same. Some played well, and others not so good. The sound of one of these instruments always attracted the attention of a cowboy. The evening meal was no more than over, when from down the line of wagons the ping of a banjo was wafted forth on the clear night air. The operator of this instrument was seated on a spring-seat removed from the wagon and placed on the ground by the camp-fire. He was a man well along in years and the cook of his outfit. This man had spent his active life on the frontier, a large portion of which had been in the mining camps of the West. Somewhat oblivious of the gathering crowd he soon broke forth into song. This song came forth as if gushing from his heart, revealing his identity and his life's experience as the following was borne, in accompaniment to his banjo, on the atmosphere of the evening:

> "You are grazing now on Old Tom Moore,
> A relic of by-gone days;
> A bummer sure they call me now,
> But what care I for praise;
> As I sigh for days of old,
> And thus I do repine,
> For the days of old,
> The days of gold,
> The days of forty-nine.

There was Lone Star Jake,
Who in a game of draw,
Would go you a handful blind,
But in a game of death,
He lost his breath,
In the days of forty-nine,
In the days of old,
In the days of gold,
In the days of forty-nine.

He ran against a knife,
In the hands of one Bob Cline;
It was his last lay-out in fine,
So over Jake we held a wake,
In the days of forty-nine,
In the days of old,
In the days of gold,
In the days of forty-nine." [2]

After this old miner had entertained the crowd for some time, a cowboy, recalling the happenings of the morning when the young cowboy was thrown from his horse, called for the boy with the bucking strap. This was the name given him for want of a better designation. It was the custom when a man's name was not well known to designate him in any way from which he would be recognized. He was soon found and presented to the assembled cowboys. He was informed that they had a song they wanted to sing for him. A Texas cowboy, named Jim, was produced as the singer. Jim was a well known character on the round-ups. His home had been at Denton, Texas. He was a chunky built, square-shouldered, square-faced cowboy, of about thirty years of age. He wore a gray, flannel shirt, throw open at the throat. Among other things he was

---

[2] This is not all of this song. It was known as "The Days of Forty-nine," or as "Old Tom Moore." The writer has been unable to procure a copy of it, and these words are given after hearing them sung almost fifty years ago. The failure to correctly reproduce the same may thus be excused. What is recalled, however, will give an idea of the spirit and sentiment of the song.

known as the swiftest runner in a hundred yard dash there
was in the cattle country. His greatest accomplishment was
as a singer. He had an excellent voice, and it was said he
could sing all night and never repeat the same song. Jim
proceeded to sing for the benefit of the assembled cowboys,
the following:

> "If a feller's been a straddle
> Since he's big enough to ride
> And has had to sling his saddle
> On most any colored hide,
> Though it's nothin they take pride in,
> Still most fellers I have knowed,
> If they ever done much ridin,
> Has at different times got throwed.
>
> All the boys start out together
> For the round-up some fine day
> When you're due to throw your leather
> On a little, wall-eyed bay,
> An' he swells to beat the nation
> When you're cinchin up the slack,
> An' he keeps an elevation
> Of your saddle at the back.
>
> He stands still with feet a-sprawlin,
> An' his eyes show lots of white,
> An' he kinks his spinal column,
> An' his hide is puckered tight,
> He starts risin an' a-jumpin,
> An' he strikes when you get near,
> An' you cuss him an' you thump him
> Till you get him by the ear—.
>
> Then your right hand grabs the saddle
> An' you ketch your stirrup too,
> An' you try to light a-straddle
> Like a wooly buckaroo;
> But he drops his head an' switches
> Then he makes a backward jump,

Out of reach your stirrup twitches
But your right spur grabs his hump.

An' 'stay with him!' shouts some feller;
Though you know it's hope forlorn,
Yet you'll show that you ain't yeller
An' you choke the saddle horn,
Then you feel one rein a-droppin
An' you know he's got his head;
An' your shirt tail's out an' floppin;
An' the saddle pulls like lead.

Then the boys all yell together
Fit to make a feller sick;
'Hey, you short horn, drop the leather;
Fan his fat an' ride him slick!'
Seems you're up-side-down an' flyin;
Then your spurs begin to slip.
There's no further use in tryin,
For the horn flies from your grip.

Then you feel a vague sensation
And upon the ground you roll,
Like a violent separation
Of your body and your soul.
Then you roll agin a hummock
Where you lay and gasp for breath,
There is somethin' grips your stomach
Like the finger-grip of death.

They all offer you prescriptions
For the grip an' for the croup,
An' they give you plain descriptions
How you looped the spiral-loop;
They all swear you beat a circus
Or a hoochy-koochy dance,
Moppin up the canyon's surface
With the bosom of your pants.

> Then you get up on your trotters,
> But you have a job to stand;
> For the landscape round you totters
> An' your collar's full of sand.
> Lots of fellers give you prescriptions
> How a broncho should be rode,
> But there's few that give descriptions
> Of the time when they got throwed."

By mutual request Jim continued to sing. He was in his element and all were entertained. The night and moonlight were beautiful, and each song kindled memories in the minds of the listeners. Three different renditions of the "Dying Cowboy" were sung, but the words of the same are buried in the past by fifty years of history, and cannot be recorded. Then a tall Texas cowboy rose during a brief pause and said: "There was never a meeting of this many well developed cowboys on the round-up, trail or camp that the song of "Sam Bass" was not sung. We can't go back on Old Sam. He was once a boy of the wide range the same as us. It is true, he went wrong, but our fraternity is noted for never deserting a companion of the range, whether right or wrong. He retained our motto of bravery, companionship, and generosity to the last, and he should still live in song. Jim, give us Sam Bass."

The singer continued without further comment. The following in a bold strong voice sounded over the camp:

"Sam Bass was born in Indiana, it was his native home,
And at the age of seventeen, young Sam began to roam.
Sam first came out to Texas, a cowboy for to be,
A kinder-hearted fellow you seldom ever see.

Sam used to deal in race-stock, one called the Denton mare,
He matched her at scrub races, and took her to the fair.
Sam used to coin the money and spend it just as free,
He always drank good whiskey wherever he might be.

Sam left the Collins ranch in the merry month of May,
With a herd of Texas cattle the Black Hills for to see,
Sold out in Custer City and then got on a spree,
A harder set of cowboys you seldom ever see.

On their way back to Texas they robbed the U. P. train,
And then split up in couples and started out again.
Joe Collins and his partner were overtaken soon,
With all their hard money were forced to meet their doom.

Sam made it back to Texas all right side up with care;
Rode into the town of Denton with all his friends to share.
Sam's life was short in Texas; three robberies he did do,
He robbed all the passenger, mail and express cars too.

Sam had four companions, four bold and daring lads,
They were Richardson, Jackson, Joe Collins and Old Dad;
Four more bold and daring cowboys the Rangers never knew,
They whipped the Texas Rangers and ran the boys in blue.

Sam had another companion, called Arkansas for short,
Was shot by a Texas Ranger by the name of Thomas Floyd;
Oh, Tom is a big six-footer and thinks he's mighty fly,
But I can tell you his racket, he's a dead beat on the sly.

Jim Murphy was arrested and then released on bail;
He jumped his bond at Tyler and then took the train for Terrell;
But Major Jones had posted Jim and that was all a stall,
'Twas only a plan to capture Sam before the coming fall.

Sam met his fate at Round Rock, July the twenty-first,
They pierced poor Sam with rifle balls and emptied out his
          purse;
Poor Sam, he is a corpse and six foot under clay,
And Jackson in the bushes trying to get away.

Jim had borrowed Sam's good gold and didn't want to pay,
The only plan he had was to give poor Sam away.
He sold out Sam and Barnes and left their friends to mourn,
Oh, what a scorching Jim will get when Gabriel blows his horn.

And so he sold out Sam and Barnes and left their friends to
     mourn,
Oh, what a scorching Jim will get when Gabriel blows his horn.
Perhaps he's got to Heaven, there's none of us can say,
But if I'm right in my surmise he's gone the other way." [3]

Jim continued to sing, making his own selections. His
supply of songs was inexhaustible. Finally one of the listeners
shouted: "Is there an Arkansawyer in the crowd? It is a
mighty poor round-up that can't afford one Arkansawyer."

Over at one side, from two or three cowboys, came an af-
firmative reply, as they pointed to one of their associates, and
their object of designation rose to his feet. He was a tall,
loose-jointed, but rather nice looking young fellow of about
twenty-five years of age. The Texan who had first spoken
then said: "Jim, give us Arkansaw."

The singer continued:

> "I went down to St. Louis,
> I read the daily papers,
> I read them o'er and o'er
> Until there I plainly saw;
> 'Five hundred men still wanted,
> In the State of Arkansaw.'
>
> I went down to the depot,
> I saw the agent there;
> I told him what I wanted,
> Says I, 'What is the fare?'
> 'Give to me five dollars
> A ticket you shall draw
> It'll take you on the railroad
> In the State of Arkansaw.'

---

[3] There is a great difference of the wording of this song as sung upon the
range. The foregoing is the complete rendition. In many of them, however, a
number of the stanzas are omitted. There were few, if any, songs sung upon the
range which contained the exact original wording of the same. The changes came
about from the method adopted in committing them. They were committed from
hearing them sung, and were seldom ever reduced to writing.

I gave up my last five dollars,
It gave my heart a shock;
I started on the railroad
To a place called Little Rock.
I landed there next morning,
Up stepped a city chap
His hair curled on his shoulders
And he wore a coon-skin cap.
Says he, 'Good Morning, gentlemen,
The morning's rather raw,
On yonder hill stands my hotel,
And it's the best in Arkansaw!'
His bread it was corndodger,
His beef, I couldn't chaw,
He charged me fifty cents a meal,
In the State of Arkansaw.
I worked six weeks for a son-of-a-gun,
Saint Patrick was his name,
He stood six feet in his stocking feet,
He was as tall as any crane.
His bread, it was corndodger,
His beef I couldn't chaw,
He paid me fifty cents a day,
In the state of Arkansaw.
Now I'll go to the Indian Nation,
And marry me a squaw,
And bid farewell forever
To the State of Arkansaw."

When this song was completed a loud voice from another Texas cowboy on the east side of the assembled herders was heard as he said:

"I am from Concho County, Texas, and we don't sing Arkansaw that way down there." All requested that the Texas edition of Arkansaw be sung by the cowboy from Concho County. He started in a voice which was firm, but not as musical

as that of the former singer. The full wording of this rendition
cannot be given verbatim, but it ran in effect as follows:

> "When you want to go a courting,
> I will tell you where to go,
> Down here to the old-folks below
> I went down, and I must know,
> Saw the chickens in the bread-tray
> Scratching out dough.
> They ask'd me to dinner
> I thought I'd take a leave.
> Then the very first thing,
> Was a big chunk of beef,
> And it as tough as a maul,
> And an ash-cake of bread,
> Baked brand and all.
> With the old rusty knives,
> For they had no forks,
> I sawed and I sawed, but
> I couldn't make a mark.
> I sawed and I sawed
> An' I got it on the floor,
> Then I give the beef a kick
> An' I kicked it to the door.
> Along come the old man,
> With a big rusty gun,
> One old girl told me,
> I had better run;
> But I stood right there
> And fought like a bear,
> Until I got my fingers tangled
> In the old man's hair."

There might have been more of this song, but if there was,
we will never know it. Every man has a certain pride in his
native state, and this song being so applied to Arkansas had
so belittled his native state that the cowboy from Arkansas
could no longer endure it. From his dress and bearing he was a

proud, dignified young fellow. Arkansaw arose as lithe as a panther and shot across the intervening space, while Texas was still singing. The song terminated abruptly, and there was a battle to the finish for the dignity of the land of their nativity between the representatives of the State of Texas and the State of Arkansas.

The writer has traveled extensively over both of these states, and has met, associated with, and known well representative citizens of both. From his observation and association he will say that both states are above the average of the States of the Union, both in country and citizenship, and both have been unjustly and badly portrayed. The writer, like the onlookers that night, is showing no preference in the controversy. Arkansaw was somewhat justified, but Texas only meant it as a joke, which he might have applied to his own State and considered it the same. The representative of Texas was somewhat the larger, but was an older man than his adversary. They rolled down the hill, clinched in conflict. When they reached level ground, Arkansaw was seated squarely on top of his antagonist. With all the efforts possible Texas could not dislodge him. Texas would try to turn Arkansaw off of him, then he would laugh, and then try to sing more. The merriment of the crowd, and the fact that Texas was not angry, soon caused Arkansaw to see the ridiculousness of his position in the attitude he had taken, and it all ended in a good natured tussle.

Arkansaw declared that he would not release Texas until he promised that he would either forget that song, or if not, he would in the future when singing it apply it to the State of Texas. Texas laughingly promised, and all started back up the hill. One more selection was rendered by the old miner, and all parties retired to their blankets. The meeting broke up just as the first guards came in from the night herd. Men from the crowd had gone out and relieved them. The camp quieted down, the bright moonlight still poured down on the southern slope of the hillside, and a horse bell tinkled in the distance, while over the hills to the southward, breaking the stillness of the night, came the long drawn out wail of the coyote as he kept vigil over the sleeping camp, creeping closer as quiet settled over the same. Soon the activities of the day were forgotten in the sound slumbers of the night, such sleep as only active men can enjoy. This sleep was broken at sunrise, and another day ushered forth. It would perhaps be entirely different in many particulars from the one just past, but equally as interesting and exciting. Thus ended the day spent on the round-up.

CHAPTER XXI.

DAYS ON THE LONE COW TRAIL

It was a bright morning in early June in the middle eighties that, preparatory to entering into formation for their steady trek to the eastward, on their journey from their native home on the broad plains of the Panhandle of Texas, a herd of twenty-five hundred head of cattle trailed out from their bedding ground of the night before. This herd wore the brand of their native ranch burned upon their hips when they were calves. They also wore the recently affixed trail or road brand. They had journeyed east past Mobeetie and crossed the unmarked line into the Indian Territory. The trip so far had been un-eventful. The weather had been fair; they had encountered no storms. There had been no stampedes, and the herd was now "trail broke." So far it had been an ideal trip. The out-fit consisted of a boss, eight cowboys, a Mexican horse-wrangler, and a cook in charge of and driving the chuck-wagon.

As they moved out from the camp of the previous night, the cattle spread out and grazed slowly ahead, the chuck-wagon followed by the horse *remuda,* driven by the wrangler, passed on ahead of the herd. The boss rode on to survey the route ahead, two oldtime cowboys quietly took their places on either side of the points of the herd, something over one-third of the way back on the forming line of cattle two more cowboys slow-ly took their positions, one on each side; at an appropriate dis-tance to the rear two other cowobys rode to their positions, one on each side, while at the rear two youths, making their first trip up the trail, both of whom had for the first time left their Texas homes to seek adventure and to be initiated into the great ranks of cowboys of the plains, on different sides, took

Herd in formation while traveling on the trail.—McCoy.

their accustomed places. Although these boys possessed all ordinary nerve and endurance, as the distance increased between them and their boyhood homes, and as they had set on their lonely vigil on night herd, many tears had coursed down their cheeks, a fact only known to God and them. These lads were to bring up the drag, the most disagreeable place on the drive. The cattle as they grazed slowly along gradually moved closer together, the string grew longer until the herd was about one-half mile in length, and each animal had settled into its accustomed place in the line. [1] As the herd advanced, the grazing practically ceased, each rider settled into his proper location on the line, [2] and they swung into ideal speed for a good day's drive.

Not a cloud was seen in the sky, and the sun hung in the eastern heavens, foretelling that a hot day was in the making. The Washita had been left behind. The boss rode ahead, and over hills and prairie the broad winding cow trail extended before him. He complimented himself on the good fortune he had had so far in handling the herd. The wagon reached a camping place at a spring, and, long before the herd came up, stopped and prepared for the noon camp. The horses were released and grazed upon the adjacent hills, while the wrangler procured dry wood to cook the noon meal. Tying his rope around the same, and attaching it to his saddle horn, he dragged the small, dry limbs some two hundred yards to

---

[1] It is a well known fact among drivers of large herds of cattle that each animal in the herd settles into approximately the same location in the herd while on the drive each day, and that it will be found at about the same location day after day as the drive progresses.

[2] The theoretical divisions of a herd on the trail are the front, known as the "point." This is the most particular place on the drive, and is filled by the top hands, old cowboys with much experience. Next down the line is the "swing," and further down the "flank," while the rear is termed the "drag." The drag is brought up by a couple of young cowboys or less experienced riders. During a dry, still evening this is the dustiest place in the entire world, and if warm weather it is about the hottest.

the fire near the camp wagon. When the herd arrived they were released to graze during the midday stop.

This meal was only a repetition of all that had preceded, and the same as those that would follow. It was soon completed, and the cook washed the dishes and packed the wagon preparatory for the afternoon journey. The day was hot, the sun, like a great ball of fire pouring out its heat upon earthly creatures, hung in the southern sky. The wagon stood some distance apart from the campfire, and was the most available place to seek shade in which to rest during the stop.

In this outfit was a character known among his associates as "Ranicky Bill." His true name was unknown to the other members of the outfit, and should anyone have asked him what it was, the interrogator would only have exposed himself to a first class cursing. The reader may have heard of "Ranicky Bill" before, but if so, while he may be just the same sort of a fellow, he is perhaps not the same individual. The fact is that in the times referred to, it was a poor community which could not afford a "Ranicky Bill." This was, perhaps, about the worst one who ever bore this designation. On all occasions everything went wrong with "Ranicky;" at all such times he blamed someone else for his troubles and cursed them without mercy and without regard to common decency. He always, regardless of the needs of others, grabbed the best there was for himself. He was always a braggart and a bully, and in discord with all his associates, but never profited from his mistakes or cared what anyone thought of him.

Before the meal was completed, "Ranicky" had discovered the fine patch of buffalo grass immediately under the wagon and the light breeze that blew through the shade, and really cut his meal short to appropriate this position before anyone else did so. He then stretched his robust and portly form out over this shade to the exclusion of all other comers. Here

A familiar scene at meal time on the trail.—From photograph. Almost all of these men were friends and associates of the author. Note how cow-horses stand with bridle reins dropped down in front of them.

he was soon settled and fast asleep. Shortly thereafter, a couple of other cowboys came along looking for some shade in which to rest. Knowing "Ranicky's" disposition, they did not molest him, but went to the rear of the wagon, where between its wheels they found a shade sufficient to cover a portion of their bodies, and lay down.

In a few minutes after these parties had settled themselves, one of the boys at the rear of the wagon heard a familiar buzzing, and looked to see from where it came. What he saw almost paralyzed him. There, not twenty inches from the head of "Ranicky Bill," lay an enormous diamond-backed rattlesnake. This snake was coiled with its head protruding, and was sounding its warning ready to strike. Taking in the situation in an instant, and knowing that if he woke "Ranicky," he would move and be bitten, this boy reached up, quietly secured a firm hold on "Ranicky's" boot, and bracing himself, jerked with all his strength. With the force exerted in this jerk he moved his belligerent companion at least three feet. "Ranicky" was sound asleep, and it goes without saying that this process immediately awakened him. Being by nature so constituted that he was always looking for something from which to find fault, and to condemn someone else, he naturally supposed that he was the victim of a joke that someone was perpetratng on him for their amusement, and welcomed the occasion as a good opportunity to unload his pent up wrath on the perpetrator. So, dropping on his elbow, he started to pour out all the profane invectives and abusive epithets in his vocabulary. His first words were: "What the ————."

At this point, however, he heard that ominous and familiar buzzing, and knowing what it was, turned his head and saw the sight that his deliverer had seen in the first place. He saw a bunch of rattlesnake as large around as a small wash-tub coiled, thoroughly agitated, and ready to deal death to anything within its reach. He was so paralyzed from the sight which met his gaze that he could not move. "The" was the last word that he had disposed of in pouring forth his wrath, and he looked back at his rescuer, realizing what he had done, and thinking that a repetition was the only method by which he could get future relief, in a pleading voice shouted: "Jerk! Jerk! Jerk! for God's sake, jerk!"

After this snake was killed and quiet restored in camp, the performance had been so comical and so humiliating to this bully that it was taken up and "Ranicky" was reminded of it as long as he was with the outfit. At the opportune time some of the outfit would shout: "Jerk! Jerk! Jerk! for God's sake jerk!" Then everyone would yell and laugh, and "Ranicky" felt so diminutive that to the observer he seemed to shrink in size. This was really an enormous rattlesnake, and its skin was stripped from its body by cutting around the neck or back of the head and stripping it off whole, leaving the rattles on. It was then stretched and tacked on the side of the wagon box.

The saddle horses were driven up, new mounts were caught and saddled. Some of the herd was still grazing, while the remainder had lain down to rest. They were soon gathered and their heads turned to the eastward. The same formation was made and the same order taken by the riders and animals as on the morning, except that the herd was sooner in traveling formation and moving over the trail. The boss, having heard that there was another bunch of cattle a short distance ahead, crowded his horse forward, until his herd was only seen as a cloud of dust rising miles behind him.

The sun as it descended in the western sky still scorched the trail; the herd moved forward in perfect formation and in record time. The next recognized point of importance on the trail was the wide stretches of sand and crossing of the South

Canadian River, which was due within the next day or so. As the afternoon wore on, it seemed that not a breath of air stirred to relieve the monotony of the dust, which ascended in a solid cloud from the line of the cattle extending from drag to point, and trailing far behind. The two young cowboys, with fifteen feet of rope dropped down from their saddle horns and dragging on the ground, occasionally jerked this rope forward, the knot on the end of which landed with a wicked thump on the anatomy of some straggler of the herd. The dust swirled around these riders on the drag, the perspiration ran down their horses in streaks, and the lather from the same formed around the headstalls of their bridles and where the skirts of their saddles rubbed the animals. They were tired horses and riders who halted the herd at the camp arranged by the cook on a tributary of the Washita River.

This tributary ran south to the Washita from the point of the selected camp. The cook had arrived at this well selected spot about an hour before the herd. Some time after the chuck-wagon had stopped, the horses with the wrangler arrived. The cook had the camp prepared when the horses came up. The Mexican immediately began his duties of obtaining wood for the camp-fire, for use both during the evening and the morning. This was not a difficult matter. A short distance from the wagon was a drift, deposited by the water in flood time, which contained an abundance of dry wood. The Mexican was diligently tearing limbs from the same, when he dropped the stick in his hand and rushed frantically toward the wagon, where the cook was engaged, shouting repeatedly as he went: "Usted Pestola" (your pistol). The cook inquired as to what he wanted with the pistol, and the only reply he could get was: "Gato de algalia," [3] which he repeated time after time,

---

[3] This is the name applied by the Mexicans to a civet cat. These civet cats are the most diminutive-sized members of the skunk family. They are of black color with pure white spots of very small size all over their body. They are vicious little

and which the cook was not sufficiently educated in Spanish to understand.

In order to satisfy the Mexican, the cook procured his pistol and accompanied him to the brush pile. The excited son of Mexico pointed down under a good sized limb to a small black, speckled object, with its shiny little eyes peering out at them. The cook took deliberate aim, pointing between the fierce little eyes, and pulled the trigger of his Colt .45. As the smoke oozed out of the drift, there appeared the remains of the object of the man's fright, but in its demise it had left as a heritage to the vicinity a more stifling odor than an animal the size of an elephant should have possessed. This ended the matter, except from the Mexican's lamentation at being compelled to remain in that camp during the night. He claimed that this cat had a mate, and it was sure to bite someone before morning, and when it came time to retire he betook himself to the wagon, and refused to sleep on the ground.

The herd arrived, and the evening meal was prepared and disposed of. A fire of dry limbs was built to furnish light before retiring. The evening jollifications, including story telling, that were usually indulged in, were on this occasion dispensed with. All parties were tired and ready for their blankets. As soon as darkness descended the first guard on the night herd went on duty. The remaining members of the outfit one by one spread their blankets, except the Mexican, who crouched in the wagon. All were soon fast asleep. The boss, ever on the alert, having sensed the danger of a storm, when the first watch on night herd came in, roused and walked out surveying the sky to the west. As he looked, he saw ap-

---

varmints, and it is claimed they will come to the bed of a sleeper at night and bite him. It is also claimed that this bite will cause rabies the same as a dog suffering from hydrophobia. The Mexicans fear these animals very much. They claim that they go in pairs, and when one is killed they must either find the second one and kill it or move camp.

pearing a dark rolling cloud, accompanied with sharp flashes of light. He saddled his horse, which was kept ready in camp, and rode out to the herd. As he approached the guard, he pointed to the rising, boiling cloud in the west, told him that it was certain a heavy electrical storm would break before morning, that it was an ideal time for a stampede, and the proximity of the other herd rendered it bad for such to occur.

For persons who do not know the nature of these stampedes on the open range, it is well to here give a descripton of the same, to the end that some idea can be formed as to what the boss anticipated and what happened.

There is no better illustration of a panic in which the entire cause of the fright has been forgotten and absolute resignation made to do something without regard to the result than the stampede of a bunch of horses or cattle. It is simply a panic-stricken rush of animals, in which each animal runs because it is satisfied that some other animal saw something which its life depends on escaping from. Stampedes usually occur on the ranges when animals are moved from their accustomed haunts into strange surroundings. A stampede might occur at any time, but they more frequently occur soon after starting on a drive before the animals become trail broke or accustomed to the life on the same. They are caused by the fear of some imaginary danger, and they usually occur when it is extremely dark and the animals are lonely, or when it is dreary before a storm is breaking. A skulking coyote around a herd is considered one of the things which often applies the match to the powder magazine causing a stampede. Horses are much harder to handle on a stampede than cattle, because they can run faster and will run further. The theoretical way to handle a bunch of cattle on a stampede is to throw all the force of all the riders on one point of the charging herd until the point is turned, and then keep it turning until the herd runs in a circle, when they will soon jam together until they form a compact mass and cannot run further. This is called "milling" the herd. This is theory, but many times it is very difficult to work it out in practice. The herd often divides, and many things happen which are unforeseen.

The boss, after arriving at the herd, sat on his horse for some time surveying the clouds in the west and studying the temperament of the cattle. When he first came out, many of the cattle were still lying down. It was not long until they were all on their feet. The evening as well as the entire day had been exceedingly clear, the last rays of light across the long stretch of rolling prairie to the westward had shown the sun sinking like a great ball of fire beneath the horizon. Most of the cattle in the early evening had evidently lain down to rest. The horn-flies [4] had settled on the herd for a night's lodging. There had been a slight breeze in the early night. Now this heavy, black cloud, with vivid streaks of lightning shooting across it and out from it, was fast rising in the west. The wind had died down until there was not a blade of grass stirring. Everything was as tense as a tight wire. The silence seemed painful. The animals were growing uneasy and fearful of some impending danger. The boss turned his horse's head from the cattle and rode quickly to the wagon. On reaching the same he shouted: "All hands in the saddle, a storm is breaking."

No further announcement was necssary. Soon each rider had his horse saddled and was riding for the herd. When an animal fears danger it affects it very much the same as it does

---

[4] Horn-flies were small, dark brown flies. If not the regular buffalo flies, they were very similar. Especially at bedding time in the evening, and more particularly before a storm, these flies would settle on the horns of cattle. They would gather entirely around the horn, next to the head of the animal, until the horn for some distance up would be entirely covered. During the night time when they would be hungry they would drop or fly down on the animal to some convenient spot and get a lunch. This would have a tendency to make the cattle restless.

a human being, or perhaps it would be better to say that a human being, when impressed with fear, is very much animal, or that fear operates much the same on all living things. On reaching the herd and taking in the situation, all hands, including the two young men who had been reared with cattle, understood their business. The riders scattered around the entire herd. From all points sounded either the cordant or discordant notes of different songs. It was fortunate that the cattle were not expert musicians. If they had been, some of these songs might have started a stampede. Some of the songs were not exactly parlor songs. There was, however, no parlor; neither were there any frequenters of any parlors present, and the cattle did not know the difference. Some of the songs were not even complimentary to the cattle. One cowboy sang:

> "My feet are in the stirrups,
> I am seated in my saddle,
> As I ride around,
> These darned old cattle."

However, he used a more emphatic term than "darned." Even this seemed to have a soothing effect on the nervous herd.

The stillness continued, and even seemed more painful as the black cloud rose in the west until it hung in the upper sky like a huge towering mountain above the earth ready to topple over and crush everything beneath it. The shafts of lightning flashed across the heavens like searing bursts of liquid fire devouring everything in their pathway. Suddenly, at the southwest portion of the cattle, was heard a snort, as vicious and dreadful as if a bolt of lightning had been driven through one of the frightened animals. This was followed by a rush to the northeast, which gained momentum as it progressed. All available riders rushed to the point at which this charge was directed. There they crowded against the portion of the cattle which were not yet affected, driving them in a congested

A typical scene during a stampede.—McCoy

mass against the ones that were further back. Soon the portion of the herd that had started was stopped before they had the entire bunch going.

The ones that had started to run jammed together in a congested mass, but gradually extricated themselves. The stampede was, at least temporarily, allayed. Then conditions remained unchanged for some time, during which the lightning continued to play in the sky and the thunder to roll. Then, like the discharge of a heavy cannon, there came a crash and a roar that seemed to crush and stun the earth, as if it were a terrific blow dealt by some unrestrained monster. This crash was followed seemingly by a growl of vengeance, which echoed over the earth and into the very heavens. That bunch of cattle could no more be held back than could the rushing and rolling waves on the beach of the ocean. They simply swept, apparently with one accord, to the eastward, driving everything before them in their mad rush. To say that pandemonium had broken loose is expressing it in the mildest sense.

Every rider heading for the left point spurred his horse to the limit. Over the prairie, where but a few minutes before had been complete quiet, now sounded the cracking of hoofs, the clashing of horns, and that ominous roar which can emanate from nothing except a stampeding herd of wild animals. This roar came back in the vibrations of the earth as a trembling sensation. The storm had broken; the rain came down in torrents. The riders could not see four inches in front of their faces. Their horses plunged forward; neither horses nor riders knew where the next plunge would land them. If a horse's foot should land in a prairie dog hole, or any other sort of a hole, horse and rider would go down together. In such cases the horse would be struggling to rise before it struck the ground. If the rider should be fortunate enough to hang onto a bridle rein, or some other portion of the horse or saddle, he could mount and ride again, provided he and the horse were able. If the rider should be thrown clear of the horse, he would be on the prairie horseless and alone, with a fear-maddened and frenzied herd of wild cattle charging around him.

To add to all the other misfortunes of the situation, large hail stones now began to fall, like rocks hurled at the earth by some unseen enemy from his position in space. Some of these hail stones or balls of ice were larger than a hen's egg. When one of these missiles struck an animal it resounded with a dull thud, as if a rock had been hurled against it with great force. A blow on the head of a rider from one of these chunks of ice would not only severely stun him, but would cut a great gash. A blow received on the hand rendered the same numb and almost useless.

Presently, amid the flash of lightning, the roar of thunder, the pelting of the hail, the clash and turmoil of the herd, on the extreme left point, was seen the flash and was heard the sound of a heavy pistol shot, followed by many more. Presently the point began to turn to the south; gradually, slowly, but unmistakingly it turned. Most of the riders had concentrated on this point, and not a sufficient number were left farther back to protect the swing of the herd as the point turned. It was therefore soon discovered that the herd was dividing, a portion of the same passing behind the cowboys who were turning the point. The riders who were in front of the break in the herd went with the portion of the same that turned, while the ones behind the point of break went with the other portion. The point was soon stopped and held by the riders with it, but the other portion charged across the prairie for miles, leaving stragglers in its wake. The handful of men following this part of the herd were unable to check it, and it ran until compelled to stop from sheer exhaustion. When stopped, this portion was so scattered that it could not be said that it was held together.

Two of the riders had become separated from the herd during the wild charge. The horse of one of them had fallen, and he had been separated from it and compelled to seek shelter the best he could until daylight. He remained huddled up behind a bank until the light of morning appeared. The riders rode around the respective portions of the herds during the remaining part of the night. The rain continued to fall, the electrical storm continued. The lightning would flash and the chains of the same would run and play around the feet of the animals, and occasionally an electrical ball of light would gather on the point of a horn of an animal. The riders, wet, sore, and sleepy, continued with their vigil—their un-flinching duty.

When daylight broke, it revealed a drenched and dreary world. It did not appear to be the same earth that the sun had gone down upon the night before. Many of the exhausted cattle had bedded down. The riders, with their grim faces streaked from the rain, their long slickers hanging down to protect them, looked like emissaries from a foreign portion of the earth or a different age. With a brief rest and breakfast, all were in the saddles again, and the balance of the day was spent gathering the scattered herd.

The next evening was spent in the regular routine, except that everything was omitted except the evening meal. The riders who did not go onto immediate duty on night herd sought their blankets as soon as possible, and were in a short time sound asleep. The ones on night herd wore away the time as best they could, looking forward to the time their shift would terminate and they also could have a much needed rest. The weather had cooled, and sleep came to the tired men without seeking. The cattle, as well as the men, were exhausted. During the night another rainstorm passed to the south. It was not accompanied by an electric storm, and did not disturb the herd.

On the following morning the sun rose bright and cheerful. The herd was assembled, and the outfit started as usual along the trail to the eastward. During the afternoon, they came to a draw, which in ordinary times would have been no more than a waterless depression, but from the effects of the recent rains it was a wide body of water, some two hundred yards across. The herd was crowded into the same, and crossed without mishap, except that one of the riders was caught in a whirl pool, evidently caused from a submerged bank which caused the water to circle. Although his horse was a good swimmer, and rose high time and again in its efforts to withstand the whirling current, it went under several times, and the rider, who was also a good swimmer, was compelled to leave his mount. The horse drifted down with the current; when it reached land it was so exhausted that it could not stand, and would have drowned had a rider not reached it and held its head out of the water until the animal could stand on its feet.

The rider, after abandoning his horse, swam the best he could, weighted down with his boots, which is a difficult task. As he expressed himself afterward, he was making the last stroke he could possibly make in swimming when his hand pulled up a bunch of prairie grass. He knew, in his exhausted condition, if he let himself down to test the depth he could never start swimming again, so he had kept on until he had finally reached water shallow enough that he pulled up grass with his hand. A few days later, as the outfit was passing to the east of Darlington Agency on the North Canadian, some of the outfit visited the Agency, and at dinner remarked that they put up hay at the Agency for their stock. The question arose as to the price of hay, and this boy, who had pulled up the grass in his swimming efforts, stated that it all depended on circumstances; that the hay he had pulled up back of the South Canadian was worth at the rate of ten thousand dollars per ton.

The wagon was taken over this flooded draw with little difficulty. Ropes of the riders were attached to the same and fastened around their saddle horns, and it was brought across with dispatch. On these occasions everything is piled high to avoid the water, but some things usually get wet.

There was much speculation as to the condition in which the South Canadian would be found. It was not now far distant, and it was certain that the rains had raised it, but the only question was as to the extent of the raise. This question was answered late in the evening when the outfit reached the south bank of this river and looked across a sheet of water which appeared to be one mile wide. Occasional cottonwood saplings, for two-thirds of this distance on the south side of the river, protruded above the water. This established the fact that the main current was on the north side, and two-thirds of the south portion of the water was shallow. The boss ordered camp made, and the outfit to remain on the south bank until morning. This was done with the hope that the river would recede during the night.

The night was spent in a much needed rest for the men and the herd. The morning broke bright and beautiful, and the sun rose in splendor, giving promise of a bright but not too hot a day. The members of the entire outfit were happy. All the troubles and hardships of the previous days were forgotten. Such is the life of all travelers upon the trails. Such is their change in the prospective view of life. When hardships and vicissitudes crowded upon them day after day, many of them became discouraged and declared that as soon as the end of the drive was reached they would forsake the trail forever. As soon as their troubles would pass and bright days come, all would be forgotten and life shone forth bright and alluring. This was true at the time stated, even though ahead of them lay a broad flooded river. The crossing of it, though difficult, to these men was only a variation and a part of the day's work.

On investigation, it was determined that the river had fallen but very little during the night. This was not surprising. The South Canadian, which is really the Canadian, is a long river, heading in the Rocky Mountains in northern New Mexico, near the Colorado line, west of Raton. It drains a long and wide country. Preparations were made for the crossing. Two dry cottonwood logs, about twelve inches in diameter, were procured, and one lashed to each side of the wagon as low down as possible. This was done to keep the wagon from settling deep into the water. The logs were light, and would readily float and help to hold the wagon higher.

The herd was strung out. The leaders were placed in the front, and the point riders took their place on the lower side. A rider had crossed earlier in the morning, and it was disclosed that the river was not swimming except for about two hundred yards near the north bank. It might be explained here that it is well known by all trailmen, who served in the old days, that the Canadian River in this vicinity has a wide, low bottom on the south side which readily overflows. The herd trailed into the water, with the drivers crowding them on. The riders took the water in their turn, most all on the right or lower side. This is done for the reason that the most trouble in crossing cattle in swimming water is that their tendency is to drift down stream with the current, and in doing so the leaders turn until they meet the ones behind them, and thus get to "milling" or swimming in a circle. The riders on the lower side hold the herd from drifting down stream, and direct them as near as possible straight to the bank on which they are to land.

It is well known to the drovers who crossed this river, also, that this shallow portion of the river is full of holes washed out in the sand by the current. These cattle rushing forward would strike one of these holes, falling headlong, often going entirely under the water. The horses of the riders, while going forward in water less than three feet deep, would suddenly plunge into these holes, and the riders would go under. Before reaching the main channel all of the riders were completely soaked. When the channel was reached, the leaders quietly dropped into the water, until only their head and horns protruded. They were urged forward with a gusto, and soon gained the north bank. With the leaders on the bank, everything moved as regular as clock work, and the herd passed on across, following the leaders as regular as if they had been traveling on the trail. Soon the entire bunch was over grazing on the north side of the Canadian.

Following in their order the horses crossed without anything unusual happening. Then several of the riders, as is customary, attached their saddle ropes to the wagon, and with the other ends wound around their saddle horns the chuck wagon went forward with a yell and a bound. As it struck the holes in the sand it would bound and jump, and a number of times it almost turned over. The cook was seated on the spring seat, driving the team, and he bounced as if he had been riding a pitching mustang. He kept his seat, but in order to do so was compelled a number of times to grab for the side of the same. The riders, with the ropes on their saddle horns, were pulling the wagon along until it crowded the team. When the cook, to keep from going out, would grab the seat these riders would yell, "Ride him slick," and "Don't pull leather." When the deep water was reached the riders and team dropped

A very good view of a trail herd swimming a river.—McCoy.

off, and all horses began swimming. The wagon drifted down
stream, trailing behind the team. The logs held it high in the
water, and it floated gradually and slowly across on as even
a keel as a ferry boat.

The Canadian, the worst river on the entire drive, having
been crossed without any difficulty, all hands and the boss
were happy and life looked bright on "the lone cow trail."
True, every man in the outfit, except the cook, was soaking
wet, but they would soon dry, and that mattered not. In fact
this situation was taken into account as soon as everything
was on the north bank, and the riders bringing over the wagon,
not having been able to bounce the cook out of the spring seat
and get him wet, gathered him up bodily and carried him back
and threw him headlong into the river. They declared that no
"stuck up" cook could march around all swelled up with dry
clothes on when all the rest of the outfit, including "the made-
to-order cow-punchers," were soaking wet.

Soon the outfit was on the trail again, now traveling to
the north. The grass was fine, and the cattle grazed off as
contented as the members of the outfit. Water being plentiful
on the prairies, camp was made that night on the divide between the Canadian and North Canadian rivers. Anticipating
such a camp, wood had been brought along for cooking purposes.
The only trouble encountered now was the mosquitoes. There
had been much rain in this vicinity, thus, many pools of water,
and these little winged pests, with their awakening tunes, were
plentiful. A camp fire was available, and the evening not being
warm, all hands crowded around the same, for the reason that
the smoke from the fire added to the smoke from their pipes
and cigarettes helped to keep the mosquitoes away.

One of the point riders, who had been married and had
experienced domestic troubles, referring to the mosquitoes declared that they sang just like his wife's folks, and in fact he

believed that they were related. Everyone had a tale to tell, and a happy night was spent around the camp fire. The cook was joked about being ducked, and he stated that the next time they were compelled to cross a river and haul his wagon over he was going to get out before they started across and roll in the water; that he would rather get wet on the start and have the painful process over than to take the pains of going over dry and then be soaked. Finally the ones not on duty rolled into their blankets, and all spent a happy, restful, and contented night. The morning dawned bright and beautiful, and as the riders departed from breakfast to take their places in the drive even the boys on the drag were happy and full of song, and one broke forth with:

> "I will eat when I am hungry,
> I will drink when I am dry,
> If the Indians don't kill me,
> I will live until I die."

This ends the history of a few days on a cattle trail. The ones herein described are but a sample of many more that were to follow for this outfit. With this idea in mind, the reader may recall the many years of the life of this cattle trail, the many thousands of outfits which traveled over the same, and the many thousands of days that were spent by these men and boys on this lonely route threading their way across an uninhabited and uncivilized country. The reader can also realize that, especially during the early life of this trail, these days were all fraught with extreme dangers.

CHAPTER XXII.

MEXICANS AS TRAILMEN, AND THEIR HABITS

It is the purpose of the writer to set out all matters of interest affecting the life and associations of the men traveling the Chisholm Trail during all of the years of its existence. Especially in the early years of the trail, a great many Mexicans were used as drivers of horses and cattle on the same. A description of these men and their characteristics may be of interest here. This is true for the reason that few persons not in contact with these people at that time know anything of their life and habits.

A Mexican tender of stock designated himself as a *vaquero* (vakaro). This designation had the same meaning as "cowboy" when used by the English speaking people of the southwest to designate a tender, driver, or herder of stock. In its restricted sense it might refer to the herder of cattle, but in its general application it referred to the herder or driver of either horses or cattle. The driving and handling of horses was no small portion of the range industry of the Southwest. These Mexican riders were much more effective in the handling of horses than of cattle.

Inasmuch as reference has been made to the application of the name "cowboy" to the range workers of the plains country, it might be well to explain the origin of that name. The word "cowboy" was unknown prior to the time of the Civil War, and was first applied to the boys of Texas who were not old enough during the war to join the army, who remained at home, and whose principal duty was to tend and care for the family cows and cattle which were held in restraint. The word "cow-puncher" was of later origin. This word originated in the cattle country, and was used in referring to the riders and persons in charge of the cattle. This designation was applied after the shipping of cattle for the northern markets began. When cattle were driven up the trail, it was a part of the duties of the drivers to assist in loading them into the cars, and usually some of the cowboys accompanied the cars to market.

The duties of these cowboys, when accompanying the shipment to market, was to look after the cattle in the cars, and see that none lay down and were trampled under the feet of the other cattle. In performing these duties, the hands used what they termed a "prod-pole," which was a strong handle, similar to that of a pitchfork, with a spike set in the end of it, usually with a hook on it also. This was used to prod the animals and urge them into the cars, or to get them up when down. From this prodding or punching process, they designated themselves as "cow-punchers." It was a peculiar fact that anything connected with the cattle business was designated as "cow." The country was known as the "cow-country," the horses used on the range were known as "cow-horses," the camps were known as "cow-camps," the outfits were known as "cow-outfits," the owners were designated as "cow-men," the towns from which cattle were shipped were named "cow-towns"; and so without end was anything connected with the cattle business referred to.

These Mexican drovers of early days were much different from the Mexicans who are now found scattered over the country working for railway companies, most of whom are clean and intelligent. These Mexican herders of the old trail came from the cattle country and ranches of Chihuahua (Chiwawa) and Sonora in Mexico. They knew nothing but the handling of stock. Their lives had been spent with mustang horses and in handling them. They were really effective in this work. They were brutal in their treatment of their horses, but they did not fear these mustangs, and would break the spirit of the most vicious of these treacherous animals. However, a horse broken by a Mexican could hardly ever be trusted. These men had never gone to school, and were necessarily very illiterate. Some of them would come up the trail and remain over winter on the ranches in the Indian Territory.

These outfits would feed their horses ear corn during the winter. The writer recalls that some of these Mexicans were not able to count sufficiently to number the ears of corn a horse should be fed. To overcome this, the proper number of ears would be placed together, and they would be instructed to give to each horse this particular number. A Mexican would take the bunch of corn, and if he could count three he would divide it up into bunches of threes; then he would remember the number of piles of threes. Thus, if he wanted five, there would be one pile and two over, and six would be two piles, and seven, two piles and one over.

In early years many herds of horses came up the trail from the large horse ranches of southern Texas and Old Mexico. These ranches employed Mexican help in the handling and caring for their stock. Mexican labor was much cheaper than American, also these ranchmen had always employed Mexican help, and were as much accustomed to it as the people of the Southern States are to colored.

There were certain dangers which these Mexican riders feared, and to which they were constantly exposed. They were much afraid of lightning, and feared an electrical storm, the same as an animal. These men almost invariably wore high topped, broad brimmed hats or sombreros, usually made from some sort of fiber or straw. These hats were well made and very expensive. Sombrero in Spanish literally means sunshade, but it also means hat. These hats were certainly sunshades. All persons who have not seen them have seen pictures

of them. It is sufficient to say that they look just as do their
pictures. Many of these hats had a cup of bees' wax securely
woven in to the top of the inside of the high crown. It is a
well known fact that bees' wax is one of the best non-conductors
of lightning, and a Mexican always felt much more secure
during an electrical storm with this cup of bees' wax above
his head in the top of his hat.

These Mexicans were also very much afraid of snakes.
Many of them carried a *cabestros* or hair-rope, and at night
time, when they lay down on their blankets on the prairie,
would lay their hair-ropes on the ground, entirely encircling
their beds. It was generally claimed on the plains that a
rattlesnake would not go over or across a hair-rope. The writer
is not prepared to say whether this is a fact or not. He has
seen it tried, and tried it on a number of occasions, with the
result that a rattlesnake, when crowded, would run over a
hair-rope, but whether it would cross it when not, and when
taking its own course, he is not prepared to say. In any event
a Mexican felt very much more at ease with this rope encircling
him at night. These men were very panicky about civet cats.
This has been explained in another part of this work. [1]

These men from the Mexican settlements to the south, when
they can procure them, are habitual and constant users of chili
peppers. They also use much pepper even, of the strongest
kind, consisting of small peppers, in their soup. This soup
when made without meat they call *chili color-rojo,* but contracted by them into *color-rojo,* pronounced color *rojo* (*roho*),
or sometimes *row,* meaning color red, and when used with meat
as chili *con carne,* meaning chili with meat. In portions of the
country in and bordering on Mexico these small peppers grow
in abundance. They are found on small bushes. Some are
long and red, some are round and red, but the hottest ones,

---

[1]"Days on the Lone Cow-Trail," Page 345.

when completely ripe, are of a dark green color. These small peppers are not really the chili-pepper. Chili-peppers are rather large, being over two inches long, and when ripe, red or dark red in color. Peppers, especially the chili-peppers, are used in all Mexican homes. The long strings of these peppers are strung and hung around the inside walls of a Mexican house. These people become so accustomed to eating them that they have no burning sensation to the user, but it is too bad for the stranger who drifts into one of these settlements and tries to eat some Mexican soup. At one time the writer saw a boy from the north try this feat, and he promptly discovered one of these small hot peppers in his mouth. He as promptly removed the same and threw it onto the floor, when he called the waiter and warned him to get something and pick it up, as it was about to burn a hole in the floor.

From the constant use of hot pepper a Mexican's body becomes completely impregnated with the same. It is a well known fact that a Mexican being killed and left exposed on the plains or desert, neither wild animals or vultures will consume the body, and it mummifies—dries up. From this fact it can be readily determined whether remains found on the desert or plains is that of an American or Mexican. Wild turkeys in the country where these small peppers grow, feed on them, and the meat of these turkeys becomes so impregnated with pepper that persons who cannot eat the peppers cannot eat the turkeys.

Referring again to a Mexican's fear of snakes, the writer at one time was in a cow-camp where two Mexican riders were employed. In this camp were two dugouts built in the bank of a draw. The Mexicans occupied the south dugout, which was about thirty feet distant from the other. Above these dugouts was a spring, which formed a pond of water, in most of which grass was growing. This pond was well stocked with striped water snakes, about twenty inches in length. These

Mexicans, when they came into camp in the evening, would pull off their boots and walk around in their bare feet or sock feet.   One evening several of the boys, conspiring together, placed one of these water snakes in a boot belonging to one of these Mexicans.   The next morning this Mexican arose, and, while not thoroughly awake, seated himself on a log in front of the dugouts, and proceeded to pull this boot on.   He felt something interfering with the progress of his foot into the boot, and reached in with his hand to take it out.   When he withdrew his hand containing this wiggling and twisting little serpent, and saw what he had, it was the best example ever seen of a person wanting someone to help him let loose of something.   He simply could not let loose of that snake quick enough. The boot went one way, the snake another, and the Mexican jumped into the air.   Before he came down he was wide awake and swearing the most vicious Mexican oaths that could be found in his vocabulary.

In this same camp was a Texas cowboy, who would pick up large bull snakes, often five or six feet long, and carry them for any length of time in the front or bosom of his shirt.   This was not an uncommon thing on the range, as many men would do this same thing.   While the writer was County Attorney of Grant County, Oklahoma, in the early days of the Territory, a man was arrested, charged with horse stealing.   He was an old cowboy, and had a large bull snake in the front of his shirt, and the officers were compelled to take this snake away from him by force.   These Mexicans would on arising in the morning pile their blankets next to the wall in their dugout.   The snake-carrying cowboy came in with a large bull snake one day, and placed it under these Mexicans' blankets.

One of the Mexicans went into the dugout in the evening, and seated himself on the blankets, preparatory to pulling off his boots.   While engaged in this undertaking he felt something squirming under him, the snake evidently objecting to having so much Mexican weight bearing down on him. The Mexican arose and pulled back the blankets to see what there was alive underneath the same. He discovered this full-sized bull snake, and rushed from the dugout with a barrage of words belonging to all parts of speech known to the Mexican or Spanish language. The predominant parts of the same, however, were exclamation points. The only distinguishable portion of these words were, "culebra-serpiente de cascabel grande" (a big rattlesnake).

These bull snakes are the exact color of a tiber rattlesnake, and it had either made a hissing noise, as they often do, or its body dragging over the hard surface of the floor of the dugout had caused the Mexican to believe that it was rattling. In any event he rushed to the woodpile, grabbed the ax, and started after the snake. The snake in trying to escape would attempt to run up the dirt wall of the dugout, and the Mexican chopped big holes in the side of the dugout trying to kill it. It took him several minutes to accomplish this feat, during all of which time he was swearing violent oaths in Spanish, and particularly condemning the low down ancestors that would produce such a degenerate snake which would come into the house and get in his blankets.

During the eighties there were many herds of mustangs came up the trail from the ranches of wealthy horsemen of southern Texas and Old Mexico, who employed nothing but Mexican labor. The writer has bought and handled many of these horses. One of these herds was in charge of an American foreman. The herd was being held in the northern portion of the Indian Territory. Many of the horses in all these herds had been brought across the line from Old Mexico, and had burned upon them Mexican or what were usually called Spanish brands. These brands looked, more than anything else to which they could be compared, like miniature maps of Yucatan or some South American country. Some of them were very large, being as much as one foot or more in length.

The writer recalls an occasion when in company with the foreman he visited the herd above referred to. On nearing the same, and while riding up a hollow, the foreman saw the Mexican in charge running his horse across the prairie, throwing his sombrero ahead of him as he went, and then retrieving it by reaching down from the back of his horse while it was running, and picking it up. The foreman stoppel in the ravine for some time and, unseen by the Mexican, watched this process, during which time he was swearing vengeance on this son of Mexico. He stated that the backs of all the horses that this Mexican rode were chewed up by his saddle, and that he had accused him of practicing this particular performance, which he had stoutly denied. While the foreman was watching, he released his quirt from his saddle-horn; then he rushed out from his concealment toward the Mexican, with his horse running at full speed. The Mexican had just picked up his hat from the ground, and on raising up in the saddle, saw the foreman coming and remarked "Me geet hem," to which the foreman replied, "Yes, and I'll geet you." The Mexican started to run, the foreman kept at his side, and whipped him with his quirt for a full hundred yards. It was in the summer season; the Mexican had nothing on his body but his cotton shirt, and it seemed that each blow of the quirt must have cut a welt.

The most amusing part of this performance was that this Mexican's name was "Jesucristo" (Hesukristo), or in plain English, Jesus Christ. This Mexican, bearing the name of the Savior, had been chased and whipped by a common, worldly foreman of a horse outfit. It may be said in explanation that it is not an uncommon thing to see a little, black Mexican urchin or some of the stock, the property of a Mexican, possessing the name of Jesus Christ. This designation is not made by these people in a profane way, neither is it considered in that way, but is so used in reality as a matter of reverence. Most Mexicans are devout Catholics, and many of them are even fanatical. There are portions of Mexico, perhaps even yet, where it is not safe for any person to go wearing a Masonic emblem fully exposed. It is simply the difference of the ideas of the English and American race of people and of their attitude in this regard. An incident that happened in the comparatively early days of Oklahoma will well illustrate this difference in ideas.

In the early years of the Territory and State of Oklahoma, many Mexicans came to the Territory, and later to the State, to work on the railroads. These Mexicans were usually from the mining districts of Mexico, and many of them still remain here. The Mexicans here now are practically all good, quiet, industrious, and law-abiding people. Without this qualification at the present time they cannot procure or hold employment. Such was not the case in earlier days. In those times they mixed up with much bad whiskey, and it is a well known fact that a bad Mexican and whiskey do not make a good combination. They had many fights, also some were arrested for other offenses, including that of robbery. They would then appeal to their countrymen for financial assistance in employing counsel and to assist them in their troubles. This appeal was always heeded. The writer was called upon to defend many of them. At one time there were near one dozen of these Mexicans in the county jail. Among them was a Mexican possessing very little Indian blood, and who was very light in complexion. This man was really brilliant, speaking the best of English. His name was Mendosa, the most common name among Mexicans. One morning the sheriff brought into the

County Court for arraignment an unkempt, black, greasy Mexican, whose hair grew almost down to his eyebrows, and who was almost all Indian. He was charged with buglary, and could not speak one word of English. As the sheriff termed it, he could not sneeze in English.

The prisoner, Mendosa, had been acting as interpreter in the trials in court where the witnesses could only speak Spanish and could not speak English, and the judge sent for him on this occasion. When Mendosa appeared the judge requested him the first thing to find out the name of the defendant. Mendosa accordingly asked the defendant his name, and after he had replied the judge asked him what the name was, to which Mendosa replied, Jesus Christ. The judge was horrified, and looked at Mendosa in uttter astonishment. He then stated to the sheriff with disgust: "Mr. Sheriff, take this man back to jail and keep him there."

Then turning to Mendosa the judge said:

"I did not send for you expecting you to pull any foolishness on me. You will find that this court business is serious before you get through with it."

Mendosa was accordingly returned to jail. The judge recalling that the writer defended many Mexicans, and could usually get what information out of them desired, had the clerk call him, requesting his presence in court at once. When the writer arrived at the court room silence was reigning supreme. A crowd had congregated. The sheriff was there guarding his prisoner. The prisoner, as is usual in case of persons who do not know what is being said or done, sat with his eyes fixed on the floor directly in front of him, and would not raise his head. He was a bushy-headed Mexican, about twenty-two years of age, and bearing the description as heretofore stated. The judge informed the writer that this Mexican was under arrest, and asked him to ascertain his name. Turning to the defendant the writer addressed him with the few words of Spanish at his command. His head came up with a jerk, and he replied as if it was fired from a gun loaded for the occasion. The writer next asked him his name, to which he replied: "Jesucristo." The judge inquired as to what it was, and the writer replied: "Jesus Christ." The judge stared a moment with astonishment, and then said:

"I just sent one man to jail for telling me that, and I suppose I had better send you along to keep him company."

The writer assured the judge that he was not to blame, as he did not give the Mexican his name, and that this man's name was actually Jesus Christ, and that the name was not used in a profane way, but according to his native custom, it was used with much reverence and respect.

This Mexican was bound over for trial. When the case was called in the District Court, the astonishment of the County Judge was nothing as compared with that of the District Judge. When he called the docket he stopped in amazement, then finally announced, "State of Oklahoma vs. Jesus Christ. What is that? I will not try that man. He has been tried. I will not try him again. Do you want me to be a second Pontius Pilate? Where is he? Has he any attorney? If so, who is it?"

The writer answered that he was the attorney for the defendant. The judge then wanted to know what the defendant had done. The writer informed the Court that the defendant assured him that he had done nothing. The judge then asked the county attorney why he wanted to keep this defendant in jail at the county's expense when he had done nothing. The county attorney replied that he considered that he had sufficient evidence against the defendant to convict him of burglary.

The county attorney and the judge talked the matter over, and finally concluded to turn the defendant loose. The writer had stepped out into the clerk's office, and when he returned the defendant was still sitting in his usual position, looking at the floor near his feet. The judge was addressing him, saying: "You may go now. We do not want you any longer. Go on." The defendant did not move, and the judge turned to the sheriff and told him to get this man out. At this time the writer returned to the court room, and the judge asked him to get his client away, and stated that he was the first man he ever saw who, when released, would not leave. The writer turned to the defendant and stated: "Jesucristo (Hesukristo), usted, levantarse" (Jesus Christ, you stand up). The defendant immediately raised his head and jumped to his feet, when the writer continued: "Usted esta libre. Usted vamos. Poco temp. Pronto!" (You are free. You go. Immeriately. Quick!)

This man bearing the name of the Savior started without further ceremony. He did not stop as far as could be seen, but continued to run, and so far as further information goes, he may have run all the way to Mexico—he was headed that way, and the rate of speed he was making would land him there in due time.

This little circumstance illustrated the custom and usage of the two races of people in this regard better than any other that could be given. This is true of these two races, even though they are only separated by a river, across which, in most of its course, a horse can be ridden a greater part of the time. The good God-fearing people of the United States look with horror upon the use and application of the name of the Savior as it is used by the inhabitants of Mexico, and so used without any thought of profanity or taking the name in vain, but done in a well meaning way and with due reverence.

CHAPTER XXIII.

HORSES OF THE FRONTIER

The mustang horses were the first used on the cattle ranges and trails of the Southwest. These horses were the immediate descendants of the extensive herds of wild and unrestrained animals which inhabited the Western Plains before the cattle herds crowded them further to the west. In numbers these wild horses were next to the buffalo. In early days upon the frontier the capturing and breaking of these animals was a profitable business. Several methods were adopted in taking them.

One method was by running and lassoing, but this was not an easy thing to do, for the reason that they were fleet on foot, and it was difficult to approach near enough to reach them with a rope. Another method was by walking them down. This was done by following slowly on their trail and continuing without stopping. They could, when thus pursued, get no rest, and would finally cease to flee when approached. This was accomplished by having relays of horses and men, and took a long period of time.

Another method often used in early times was by "creasing" them. This was brought about by the person seeking to make the capture cautiously approaching near the herd or lying in wait until they came along. When the herd was sufficiently close for the person in pursuit to make an accurate shot he would take careful aim and fire a large caliber, long range rifle at the animal selected, striking it in the weathers, in front of the shoulder and just above the vertebrae. This had the effect of paralyzing the animal, and, before it recovered, the pursuer had it safely tied. This method was dangerous, as the bullet must be placed extremely accurately. Many more horses were killed by having their necks broken in this process than were captured. At the time of the writer's first recollections of the range, there were many of these horses in use wearing the scars where they had been creased.

These wild horses of the prairies were in turn descendants of the horses originally brought to North and South America by the early Spanish explorers. It is a fact, perhaps not well known, that there were no horses in either North or South America at the time of their discovery by Europeans. The first horses brought to this region were looked upon with wonder by the natives. Before this time, the Indians had used dogs as beasts of burden.

The writer has read an account in the history of the early Spanish explorations, where it is stated that one of the persons in command of an exploring party invited a large band of Indians to be present and witness some feats of horsemanship by his Cavaliers. While the Indians were so assembled, and the performance was in progress, one of the horsemen, who was clad in steel armor, and performing a feat with his lance, was unhorsed, and his mount left him. The Indians, thinking that the horse and rider constituted but one wondrous sort of an animal, that it had broken in twain, and that the pieces were separating, became panic-stricken and fled. This may seem strange, but it is a well known fact that upon the range cattle regard a horse and rider as one entity. They will flee from a horse ridden by a man, but they are not afraid of a horse alone, and if a man walks among them dismounted they do not know what sort of an animal he is, and will become frightened, or take after him.

Whether the statement as to the idea of the Indians and the horse and rider are true or not, it is given as a matter of history. In any event, when the Indians saw these strange animals brought to this continent by the Spanish explorers they were filled with wonder. Little did they then think that these strange beasts in future years would be their most prized possessions and their faithful beasts of burden. It is almost unbelievable that in the future these Indians would train themselves, as they did, to ride these horses, which they at first looked upon with astonishment; that some of them would train themselves until they could swing onto the sides of these animals, and send forth a string of arrows as if they were shot from a machine gun; but such is a fact.

These mustang horses were quick, wiry, and usually small in stature. There were some, however, of fair size. The most remarkable thing about these animals was their power of endurance. They were usually very nervous, and it often seemed that this fact added to their vitality. This power of endurance was beyond belief. Most of these horses could be ridden until they would stagger when the saddles were removed from their backs, and when saddled, even the next morning, would pitch and buck until they would almost break the neck of the rider. The degree to which they could be domesticated depended largely on the methods adopted by the persons handling them and the treatment given them in the breaking. Their ancestors having roamed the prairies unrestrained, they had inherited a wild disposition, until but few of them ever became perfectly gentle. It was characteristic of these horses that none of them ever did get sufficiently gentle, but when tied in a stall in a barn, and one would suddenly walk in behind them, they would jump and snort.

As heretofore observed, a mustang could not be approached or mounted except from the left side. [1] These range horses were trained to stand for any period of time without being tied. This only applied, however, while they had their bridles

---

[1] Chapter entitled "The Cowboy"—Page 274.

on. The bridle reins were simply dropped down in front of the animals, so that they would drag on the ground if they walked away. They soon learned that if they tried to travel away they would step on the reins, and it would jerk the bit in the mouth, creating pain. The breeding, rearing, and furnishing of these horses for the cattle ranges become an established business, especially in southern Texas and Old Mexico. Also the breaking of them was a business of itself. There were many professional horse-breakers. Men trained in this business had no more fear of the most vicious horse than he would have of a sheep.

A friend of the writer once told him of a ranchman in New Mexico who broke his own horses in a unique and ingenious way. This ranchman owned a number of well broken and well trained burros. All persons familiar with the habits of burros know how obstinate they are, regardless of the fact that they are well broken and gentle. An unbroken horse would be necked or tied to one of these burros with a short rope. When the horse wanted to go its way the burro would stop and brace its feet, and would not move. There would be no going unless the same was done according to the wishes of the burro. This was continued until the horse was worn out and content to travel along wherever the burro desired to go. When the burro wanted a drink, they would go to the water and drink, and the involuntary partnership was governed and managed entirely by the burro. The horse soon became very submissive, after which it was easily broken to handle and ride.

Many ranchmen would not permit a rope to be thrown on a horse in the herd, except when absolutely necessary. They claimed casting a rope among the horses had a tendency to agitate them and make them wild, which it evidently did. To obviate this, when the horses were gathered in the morning, ropes were stretched and a rope corral formed by cowboys holding the ends of the same. The horses would not attempt to force their way through or over this rope, and were soon easily caught by walking up to them. The ones which could not be so caught were roped or lassoed, but when well trained to be thus caught, a great deal of confusion and agitation among the horses were avoided.

In later years horses were imported from the eastern states for use upon the ranges. These horses were descendants of imported horses from different portions of the Old World. They were first introduced into the Northwest cattle country— Wyoming, Montana, Colorado, and the Dakotas. In time, the use of these animals spread to the Southwest until they almost crowded out the old mustangs of the plains. These horses were larger and stronger, and being bred and reared on the plains became inured to the life of the same. Also, the Government shipped Eastern horses to the different Indian tribes of the West for their use. The descendants of these animals, being bred and reared in the Western country, lost some of their size, but became adapted to the conditions, and were fine saddle horses. They had much better dispositions than the mustangs, were easily broken, and became very gentle when properly handled.

There are yet some of the descendants of these wild horses roaming in their free state in the Western portion of the plains country. In the years 1925 and 1926 the writer was in the Mesa Verde country, southwest of Durango, Colorado, and extending southwest to Gallup, New Mexico, and while he did not see them he was informed by the inhabitants that there were a few straggling bunches of the once extensive herds of wild mustangs scattered over the plains surrounding Mesa Verde Park. Some time later, the writer read an article in a magazine stating that such was a fact, and that steps were being taken whereby concerted action would be adopted to exterminate these stragglers of the plains. This was going to be done for the reasons stated, that these wild horses induced domestic animals to follow them, run away, become wild, and could not be recaptured; and for the further reason that these wild mustangs were without value, and that they consumed needed pasture which could be used by valuable domestic animals.

Referring to the complaint that these wild animals induced domestic horses to join their bands and become wild, the writer will say that this was an evident fact, and was always charged to these marauders of the plains. He has talked with many men who, when these wild herds were plentiful, made a business of capturing members of their bands. These men stated that occasionally horses with saddle marks and harness marks upon them were captured from these herds, and that they were just as wild and unmanageable as any of the rest of the bunch. One of these men stated that he once captured from one of these wild herds a horse which had shoes on, having evidently carried the same since its escape from its owner.

It is well at this time to give a few facts connected with the handling of these wild horses, either from the herds roaming the prairies at will or from the bunches of unbroken horses held in restraint.

The first necessary thing to be accomplished was to place a rope on the animal, whether done by lassoing it or any of the other methods described. When once held securely, either by throwing or otherwise restraining it, the first thing done was to place a hackamore [2] on the animal. When this was done,

---

[2] A hackamore is an improvised rope halter. It is usually made in handling wild horses. It is constructed from the saddle or lariat rope. The process followed in making it is as follows: A loop is formed somewhat larger than is necessary to go around the horse's nose. This is formed near one end of the rope. The long end of the rope is then doubled back, and a second loop is formed on the long end. This second loop is made large enough to twist around and through the first one twice, and then slip over the head of the animal, the same as the headstall of a

it could be led in a fashion. True, it would lunge and often throw itself, but with the assistance of someone driving, it was easily managed. If it was taken from a herd not held in restraint, it would be placed where, and secured in such a manner, it could not escape. It would then be taken through the regular process of breaking. First it would be taught to lead well, and then would be ridden. If it was taken from a herd held in restraint, it would, in all probability, be saddled and ridden on the spot. This was not difficult for a good rider to do. While the writer has never claimed to be or been rated as a good rider, he has performed this feat himself. Riding a wild horse was then only considered a matter of amusement.

These old-time mustangs used on the range could jump higher, kick harder, and turn quicker than the same number of pounds of bone and muscle that was ever put together in any other animal. In their wild gyrations in pitching they would side-wind, sun-fish, cork-screw, and perform all other unexpected and astonishing feats, all of which were known to no other animal or animals. The most astonishing thing about them was that some of them became worse from use, and became confirmed outlaws, and but few of them ever became entirely free from this vice.

One of the peculiar things that often happened to these range horses was that they would become "locoed." This con-

---

bridle or halter. When this is done, the portion of the rope which would be in the position of the chin strap of a bridle is pulled back and grasped tightly around the nose of the animal, and two half hitches taken close up to the back of the chin, fastening the loop first made tight around the mouth or lower part of the head. These half hitches are taken on the long end of the rope. This long end of the rope is then drawn back and run through the loop made when forming the second loop. This keeps the half hitches from slipping off, and fastens perfectly tight all the rest of the halter. Thus constructed, a very substantial temporary halter is the result. When handling very wild horses the rope was never removed from around the neck, and the hackamore was made on the same rope, so in case the hackamore should slip off, the rope would still remain around the neck of the horse. This explanation may seem complicated and vague, but it is the best that can be given without illustration. Persons familiar with the making of hackamores will readily recognize the process described.

dition is never heard of in this country at the present time, and few know of it or its characteristics. It was, however, prevalent during the days of the cattle ranges, and occasionally it affected the cattle. The writer is quite familiar with the results of this affection on horses. It is caused by eating what is known as the loco-weed, which is a small, flat-leaved, fuzzy plant, with the leaf lighter colored on the under side. In appearance it very much resembles young mullen, yet not so fuzzy. The leaf is shaped very much like the mullen, but is smaller, and the plant also is smaller. It is the first green vegetation to appear in the springtime, and animals which have gone through a severe and trying winter are induced to first eat it on that account.

The use of this plant has very much the same effect on an animal that an opiate has on a human being. When one of them acquires the habit of eating and using this plant, it will search continuously for it, will be nervous, lose flesh, and become a moral delinquent. The effect caused by continuous eating of this weed by an animal results very much the same as the condition reached by the habitual user of morphine. Horses long addicted to the use of it became and were generally known as being completely "locoed." When one of these animals was mounted, it was impossible to know just what it would do. It was liable to run into another horse, the side of a house, if there was one around, against a tree, into a wire fence, or anything else that might be in its headlong course.

The writer once owned one of these horses. It had been at one time a fine pacing horse, and when once mounted and started was still an excellent pacing animal and a fine saddle horse, but was absolutely unreliable. The only way that it could be mounted was to grasp the side of the headstall of the bridle in the left hand, and start it going around in a circle. While this process was being carried on, it was easy to step into the saddle, but the instant the headstall was released, it would either start pitching, as no other horse could pitch, or would start to run, and unless it was guided or turned away, was apt to run into anything. At one time while thus mounting this horse, it ran with the writer against an old-fashioned well curb equipped with a rope and bucket for drawing water, and knocked the curb from the well. Horses once completely locoed never entirely recover from the effects. They are apparently always scared, wild, and have no inclination to be tamed.

While many horses appeared to be much afraid, and were difficult to handle, the experience of the writer has led him to believe that much of their conduct was due to "inborn cussedness." At one time when a boy, he took a long trip helping to drive a bunch of horses to the north. On this trip pack horses were used. One of these was an old time pack horse of uncertain ancestry purchased from the Indians, which had been used by them as a pack horse to carry buffalo meat.

This old fellow was gentle, and a pitiful-looking, decrepit beast. The outfit did not use pack saddles, and the horses' backs would sometimes have small galled sores on them. If this old horse had a galled place on his back no larger than a finger nail, he would, when being packed, squirm and twist as if he were being killed, and when the pack was once on his back, he would come up to some of the outfit, and twist and squirm, and look at him with as sanctified and pity-soliciting look as was ever put out by the most consummate hypocrite. His eyes would actually fill with tears, and he would close them as if in agony, and tremble as with a chill. No human could have begged with more eloquence to have the pack loosened. This old reprobate knew just how loose that pack had to be for him to be able to turn it. If loosened, but not enough to be turned, he would start off, and as soon as he would discover that fact he would return with the same pitiful plea to have the ropes on his pack loosened. If it was again loosened, the instant he discovered that the pack was sufficiently loose that it could be turned, he would give a vicious lunge, jump, kick, and twist until the pack was on his side, when he would tear like a demon through the bunch of horses, and invariably stampede the entire herd.

We soon learned this trick of this old villain, but before we did, we had several stampedes, were compelled to gather up our horses, and retrieve pots, pans, blankets, and other camp equipment.

Horses not accustomed to crossing a bridge will almost invariably stampede when crossing one. In a stampede horses can run so much faster than cattle that it is more difficult to reach the point of the herd to turn them, but when this position is reached they are much easier to turn than cattle.

Referring to the breaking of these range horses, the persons engaged in this business often adopted various methods in riding extra vicious animals. While it was against the rules of the game, many persons used bucking or pitching straps heretofore referred to; others would hobble their stirrups. This process has also been explained. [3]

In riding these range horses when traveling—that is when not driving on the trail or riding on the round-up—there was but one gait used. This was a slow jog trot. These horses would habitually drop into this gait and keep it all day. It was peculiarly adapted to the range country, and used no other place so far as the writer knows. The few men who were in the cow country during the old range days will readily recall this adopted gait.

---

[3] See the Chapter entitled "A DAY ON THE ROUND-UP"—Page 326.

The writer has spent some little time handling horses, and spent tired and weary hours at night on night herd. Horses are more difficult to night herd than cattle. Cattle, when not agitated, are inclined to bed down at night and rest most of the time. Horses, even though they may have traveled or worked hard all day, rarely rest or cease to graze or eat until near morning. If they are tied up, they will eat hay and be active until about that time. If on grass, they will graze until about that time. When they do rest they usually stand on three feet, and sleep in that manner. They rarely lay down at night; in fact the writer has seen horses which in his opinion never laid down, unless it was to roll. It is a peculiar fact that about four o'clock in the morning, in a bunch of several hundred head of horses, they will all cease grazing almost at the same instant, and stop and rest—sleep standing up on three feet. But few of them lie down.

Even with all the faults of the old cow-horses, the men who used them and were their companions day after day, had a great affection for these animals. They were their companions in trouble and misfortune. They relied upon their riders to guide them always, and went where they directed without flinching. These mustangs, on account of their quickness and agility, were the best cutting horses on a round-up that the range ever had. When their riders once directed them to a particular animal, they would continue to dart behind it and stay behind it until it was safely lodged with the brand to which it belonged. Nothing could dodge these horses.

When the rivers were flooded, and the foam and drift swept down, these horses never flinched when their riders directed them to plunge into the red turbulent water to drive the herds across. How many men of the old range remember that peculiar and never-to-be-forgotten sensation when these faithful animals would strike quick sand? There is no other sensation like it. It can only be compared to a condition in which the entire solid earth dropped out from under the riders, and they started down, sinking into the muddy water without resistance. With a lunge, these horses would convey their riders out, and would finally bear them along in deeper water, swimming evenly, with only their heads above the surface.

When sleeping upon the prairies without a companion, except his horse, the rider always felt a consolation and a friendship in the presence of the animal. It was a rare occasion in such cases, if the rider would leave, that the horse would not attempt to follow him. In the midst of the turmoil and avalanche of the stampede, when neither man nor animal knew where his destination was, these horses, at the direction of the riders, without hesitation plunged into a surging mass of wild, crashing cattle. Considering all of these attributes and all of these facts, why should these animals go down in history with only words of condemnation written as their epitaph?

Be that as it may, as civilization took charge of the plains and western prairies, and the familiar jog-trot of the old cow-horses disappeared from the trails and their native land, these mustangs of the plains, as well as the old cow-horses of later times, were replaced by sturdy farm and fleet race horses. Now, within the memory of most of us, we have seen these other and later acquired horses cast into the discard. They have been replaced by gasoline propelled vehicles. These mediums are the universal power of transportation of the present day, and travel down and over the old Chisholm Trail, where in other days these mustangs trailed hundreds of thousands of long-horned cattle.

Now, the route followed by that old cattle trail is surfaced and covered with a ribbon of concrete—a paved highway. Over this route palatial sedans travel, with all the comforts of the parlor, while overhead huge mechanical birds, motor-propelled and man-guided air monsters, cross the country at a rate of speed much over one hundred miles per hour. Those who once traveled this highway, and thought they were making great speed at thirty or forty miles per day, look on in wonder, and so wondering they realize that all this change has been brought about within the span of a lifetime; and continuing to wonder, they inquire of themselves, "What will another generation bring forth?" This question only Time will answer.

CHAPTER XXIV.

THE FREIGHTER

To persons familiar with the parlance of the West and the Southwest, the meaning of the word "freighter," as applied in these portions of the world, needs no explanation. In case, however, that these lines should be read by persons unfamiliar with the meaning given to the same in these localities, the significance of the term should be explained. A "freighter" is a person engaged in the transportation of merchandise on the trails and highways of the West. The term is usually applied to persons engaged in such an occupation for hire, and is applied and used when articles for consumption or use are transported in wheeled vehicles drawn by animal power. In a broader sense it might even apply to the person or persons who in the mountainous regions of the West carried such articles on the backs of burros. This term, in the regions in which the business was carried on, had as well defined meaning as the term when applied to the vessels bearing articles of commerce or trade upon the waters of the world.

These old freighters of the West deserve recognition in its history. They were one of the great factors breaking the way in advance of civilization. These sturdy and fearless men perhaps encountered more hardships, dangers, and privations than any other class of persons on the frontier. Without their services, the advance on the plains and extreme outposts could not have subsisted or survived. These men were the first travelers on the Chisholm Trail. In recognition of that fact the original trail, extending from Wichita, Kansas, to Fort Sill, Indian Territory, was in early days known as "The Trader's Trail." In fact Jesse Chisholm, for whom the trail was named, was a freighter or Indian trader. In 1865 he broke this trail into the regions of the settlements of the Indian tribes, with whom he traded; carrying to them articles of traffic and commerce. Later the business of freighting supplies to the Indian agencies, frontier settlements, army posts, and all points of demand beyond the terminus of the railways became one of the great enterprises of the frontier.

In the early days of this business heavy wagons, drawn by many spans of slow, plodding oxen, bore most of these supplies. They took their slow but sure course from the termini of the railways into and across the uninhabitated portions of the country. Later these ox-teams were replaced by large and powerful mules and horses. Where any of these teams were used, generally many spans were attached to a wagon, and this wagon in turn would have one or more wagons attached to it and trailing behind. When a stream was to be crossed, or other difficult road negotiated, the trail wagons would be released and left behind, and the load thereby reduced, and as soon as the difficult stretch of road was crossed the persons in charge would return and bring up the trail wagon or wagons.

When ox-teams were used in the summer season, it was necessary to carry but very little, if any, food for the teams. They would subsist from the extensive grass along the trail. Water, however, was often a big item of necessity. Mules were much preferred to horses in this business. They would subsist on much less food and go much longer without water. While the Chisholm Trail was in all of its course the greatest cattle trail in the entire world, it was also used by these transporters of commerce. In the course of a day on the same a great number of these outfits would be met. They would be slowly taking their way along this artery of commerce. The cattle-drivers would be met pushing their beeves to market on foot, while the freighters carried their commerce in the opposite direction in their wheeled conveyances. These freight outfits varied from a lone wagon in some cases to a long string of wagons in others.

The life of a freighter might in some ways be considered a hard and lonely one, yet the men who habitually engaged in it grew to be attached to the life, and liked it. There were many trials and misfortunes connected with the business, but these men learned to take life as it came to them, and they made the best of it. The inexperienced men who engaged in the business, when they first encountered some of the difficulties and misfortunes, took them very much to heart. The writer, when a boy, spent many days in company with these wagons as they slowly wound their way over the trails of the frontier.

One of the most vivid recollections of the writer's early life occurred on one of these trips. There were many wagons in this outfit in which this occurrence took place, each belonging to a different party, all freighters on a small scale, who drove their own wagons. Among these owners was an elderly gentleman, who was intensely religious. He was well known to the writer, as were also his extreme religious manifestations. Following this inclination, he would persistently object to driving his team on Sunday. When the other members of the outfit would not consent to stop on that day, the old gentleman would growl all day, insisting that thus violating the sanctity of the Lord's day was an unpardonable sin. He would complain that he was very poor, and would not concede to such violation if such was not the case, and that he was so compelled to sin in order to live.

He drove an old style linch-pin wagon,[1] and his wagon was overloaded. It had rained, and the wheels had cut deep ruts

---

[1] A linch-pin wagon was an old style wagon, which had a large pin passing through the end of the axle to hold the wheel on. In the later styled wagons large caps, known as hub-caps, were screwed on to serve this purpose.

in the track. One of the rear wheels of this old man's wagon suddenly dropped into a rut, and the axle broke completely off just inside the wheel. The entire outfit congregated around the disabled wagon to give counsel and assistance. The writer to this day, not only remembers, but plainly sees, that old gentleman as he stood in his sad bereavement by the side of his wrecked wagon. He was the possessor of a long flowing beard. He would raise up the wheel that was broken off and hold it in a perpendicular position, and would then with all the force he possessed slam it down onto the ground. This he did repeatedly.

During all this performance the most vicious torrent of profanity that was ever heard, poured forth from his lips. His art and effectiveness in swearing would have put to shame the worst "cussing" pirate who ever sailed the Seven Seas. A large portion of the life of the writer up to that time had been spent among men on the frontier, and he was accustomed to hear profanity in all its most vicious forms, but this old gentleman with the deep religious profession out "cussed" them all. The writer had always looked upon him as a religious example, and as a man who would suffer himself to be executed rather than utter an oath of any kind. Boy, as the writer was, he stood and looked upon the scene with open-mouthed wonder, and too astonished to move. One of the party afterward, joking the old gentleman, said that he swore by note, while another added that he needed no notes, but could swear without them.

Everyone was willing to lend a helping hand to a person in distress. The old gentleman's load was divided up on the different wagons. A long pole was run back under the broken axle to keep that corner of the wagon clear of the ground, and dragging that corner of the same the wagon was conveyed to a point where another axle could be made by hand to replace the one broken. This was done by members of the party while they all waited until it could be finished. The party then journeyed on. The misfortune was turned into a source of merriment, and the old gentleman never again objected to driving on Sunday. If the writer should live the span of several lifetimes, he will never forget his astonishment at the job of cursing that old gentleman did. He simply swore until his long whiskers trembled and vibrated with the terribleness of the same, rendering emphasis to his emotions.

When high waters were encountered on the trails, the freighters, as well as other travelers on the same, were compelled to often lie for days behind swollen rivers. These men grew to consider these things as necessary events of their lives, and would remain quietly in camp until the waters receded, apparently happy and contented. In those days men did not go through the world with the rush and bustle that they do at the present time. This mode of life rendered them happier and more contented. After these floods in the rivers, one of the greatest difficulties in crossing them was the quicksands, encountered in all of them in the plains country. When it was possible to do so, a herd of cattle would be first driven over the river after a high water. These cattle would not bog in the quicksand, and in going over the same would settle it, so that horses and wagons could easily go through.

A wagon is the most difficult of all things to handle in quicksand. Once stopped or slowed down, it rapidly settles deeper in the sand. In such cases it is often necessary to remove and carry out the load from the wagon, and also take the wagon apart and remove it piece at a time. When several in an outfit were crossing these rivers they would assist each other by attaching several teams to a wagon, hurrying it across rapidly to keep it from settling in the sand. When a horse or mule would drop into a pocket of quicksand, the balance of the draft animals would drag it out, and they would all rush on. When oxen were drawing wagons through these rivers containing quicksand the ox-whips would be brought into service, and the locality would resound with the crack of the driver's whip, which echoed like the report of a pistol. These cracks of the whip would punctuate the string of profanity which poured forth both emphatic and long, in volume sufficient to wake the dead. It was said that oxen became so accustomed to drivers swearing at them that it was impossible for anyone to drive them without cursing them. It has been also said of one driver that his oxen considered his favorite cuss-words as being their names, and responded to them when thus summoned or called.

After traveling through the dust and heat with a freight outfit all day, camp would be made in the evening, the animals watered, and either lariated on long ropes or released to graze upon the luxuriant grass along the trails. A number of freighters usually traveled together, and would congregate in camp. A hearty meal would be enjoyed, and the drivers would relax with the utmost satisfaction. The cares of the day would be completely forgotten. In the colder portions of the year a fire would be built according to the temperature. An evening of entertainment would be spent, which would not be surpassed even by an evening in a cow-camp, after which these nomadic wayfarers of the plains would spread their bed upon the ground and enjoy a night's repose and sleep which could not be surpassed.

The writer can give a better idea of an enjoyable evening spent in a freighter's camp by giving, as well as he can now recall, a reminiscence of one of these evenings.

At the time of the writer's first knowledge of the trail, oxen had almost entirely been discarded for draft purposes, and mules and horses had superseded them. There was one old member of the party, whose whiskers had grown long and bushy in the service as a freighter on the trail. He had, after spending most of his life driving oxen, very reluctantly given up the use of the same in his business. After this old traveler of the trail had settled himself for the evening, reclining in utter contentment and satisfaction, he broke forth with the following rambling discourse:

"This ere thing of usin these overgrown burros in draggin frate over this country is not at all to my liken. It is not accordin to the Scripters and is not right. In the days of the Bible they rode their mules, but did not frate with them. It was never intended that man should work behind a mule. If it had been, God would not made him so handy with his hind legs and heels. Besides that, a mule is not a socible critter. All that he ever thinks about is cussedness and about doin jist what you don't want him to do. He spends his whole lifetime studyin up deviltry and some way to kill you or cripple you for life. A mule has but one note in his whole language, and that is in complete discord with everything else in the world. As a piece of cussedness a mule is the greatest success of all the works of Nature. If he starts to go through a piece of quicksand, he will go just far enuf to git out himself and then turn round and laff at you. I had a little runt of a mule one day, when I touched him up in the flank with the whip, kick my hat plum off my head, and me settin up on the wagon seat. To do this he must jumped off the ground for he couldn't stood on his front feet and reached as high with his hind heels as he did. Nothin of that kind is a socible act by any animal. An ox wouldn't done anything like that.

"If you start to love a mule, make friends or get socible with him, he will just watch a chance to get a good kick at you with his heels and knock you into 'kingdom cum.' When I drove cattle it was altogether different. I learned to love my oxen. I made pets of them and sociated with them until it seemed they was a part of my family. Think of adopten a mule into your family. The nearest I ever come of tryin it was after I was married when I took my mother-in-law to live with me.

"You know, I once had an old ox; I called him Samson because he was so strong; but I had just as well called him Solomon 'cause he was the wisest critter I ever seen. I could talk to that ox and he knowed everything I said to him. He would come and stick his head under the wagon in the mornin and lick me in the face to wake me up, as if to say: 'It is time to get up and go to work.' When it was time to hitch up, old Samp would just walk up and stick his head through the bow of the yoke as if to say to all the other oxen: 'Come on, it is time to hit the trail.'"

Then a younger man of the party, being a farmer from Kansas, who was freighting to earn enough to tide him over the winter, took up the conversation, saying:

"That is about the best advertisement that I have ever heard for the old time oxen. That is but the ox's side of the argument. We had better call a convention of the mules and take this matter up with them. These oxen are not half as near angels as my friend thinks they are. Only today as we came along the trail a big, fat steer near the road stopped eatin long enough to raise his nose, look us over and nod his head as much as to say: 'Go to it, mules. I am glad you took the business over before I was old enough to be put into the yoke.' These oxen are not half as docile as you make them out; besides that, they are cowardly beasts. I knew an old fellow who had an ox that was afraid of snakes. A snake had probably made a face at him some time in his life and scared him to death. This old man drove this ox in a team to Wichita with his family once. There had been a big show in town, and they had left a large poster on the side of a building by the road where they went along. This poster had the picture of a great big snake on it, and you know that cowardly old ox saw it, got skeered at it, and run off, thinking it was after him, turned the wagon over, scratched them all up, and mighty near killed them."

Then spoke up an old timer of the party, a bewhiskered westerner, who had been at one time a miner in the mountains:

"You all say that a mule is an oversized burro. Now, I am always for the burrough. The burrough has found and carried more gold out of the moutains than any man or other animal. I come just as near bein a member of the burrough family as the brother over there is of the ox. Now, these oxen are not the simple critters you might think they was. I know of a trick that one of them deceitful varmints pulled off once, that for pure down right crookedness not only took the cake, but walked off with the whole banquet. This is what he did: When I was out at Virginia City durin the boom days, they had to frate everything in from Californy. There was an old Jasper by the name of Dodson, who had a string of ox-teams and frate wagons. He trailed several wagons, and had several yokes of oxen for each lead wagon. He had a wise old ox he called Buck. Now, you talk about bein wise. If other oxen are dumb, it is because ol Buck got all their sense. When this outfit that old Buck was with unloaded their frate at Virginia City, they went out to the edge of town and camped.

The next day when they got ready to start back to Cala-forny, they brought all the oxen up to inspan them to the big, high-topped, covered wagons. They used these tops to protect the frate from the weather. All the oxen was standin there, but suddenly old Buck was missin. He had been seen there just a minit before, but now he had disappeared, and as com-pletely as if the ground had opened and swallered him up. They searched the whole town and country for him, but could not find him. Finally they started back without him, leadin his mate. All went well until two days after that; when they was crossen a crick they heard an awful racket at the back end of the rear trail wagon.

"On investigation they found that old Buck had been ridin in that trail wagon, and had fell out, and was tryin to get back in. The fact waz that contankerous old cuss, when they brought him up with the rest of the oxen, he seen that he was goin to have to help pull the wagons back, and seein the end-gate of the trail wagon down, had walked right into that trail-wagon, and rode there for two days. He had got along fairly good, but almost perished for a drink, and when they was crossen that crick with lots of water in it, he reached down to get a drink, and fell out into the water, and then tried to get back in. This old villan of an ox just figgered out that it would be better to ride back to Calaforny in that trail wagon than to help pull the outfit. If it hadn't been that he had to have somethin to eat and drink he would have rode all the way, too. He never thought of that or he would have taken some feed and water in the trail wagon with him. Now if anyone ever heard of a mule or burrough that pulled off an onrier stunt than that, I want to hear from him and I will give up and let the ox have it."

Freighting the necessary supplies to the various cow-camps on the cattle ranges of the Southwest, far from the terminus of any railway, was a part of the services performed by the freighters. All of these different points required supplies in order to subsist, no matter how far they were from the lines of any railway. These must be furnished regardless of the distance, condition of the weather, or of the roads over which they must be transported. This required the freighter to be on the job regardless of conditions. Often severe blizzards blew down from the north, making it impossible for anyone to survive on the open trails.

On these occasions all persons on it were compelled to seek the nearest shelter, even though it was only some friendly bank which would protect the traveler and his animals from the violence of the storm. Often they would be compelled to lie there for days while the bleak winds whistled above their heads and the drifting snow swirled and sifted down upon them. On these occasions both men and beasts suffered extremely. The writer recalls one occasion on which a freighter bearing supplies to a cow-camp, and following a dim trail which branched off from the main one and led to the camp sought, was caught in a blizzard. It swept down on the freighter so that he was unable to follow the dim road, and was compelled to stop and make camp. A few days thereafter, when the storm had subsided, his camp was discovered. His horses had broken loose and fled; the man had made a bed and covered himself with all his bedding, and had drawn a tarpaulin over it all, but when found was dead—frozen stiff.

On these trips during the winter season the freighter was compelled to cross all the water courses on his route, including the large rivers of the plains. It will be borne in mind that none of these rivers were at that time bridged. It was seldom that any of them were frozen sufficiently solid for a wagon and team to pass over on the ice. When this condition was met the freighter was compelled to cut a pathway through the ice, after which the animals drawing the heavy wagons would plunge into the icy river, which often came up around their sides, and drag the wagons across the stream.

During the extreme rainy portions of the year and after snows had melted and soaked the soil, the unimproved dirt roads became almost impassable. Over long stretches of the same it was necessary to leave trail wagons behind and return for them; or for teams to be doubled and several attached to one wagon. Travelers on the trail were always ready to help other wayfarers, whether they knew them or not. A man was never left in trouble, regardless of the time or effort necessary to relieve him.

During the early days of the frontier, the dangers from Indian attacks were the worst obstacles faced. In this regard, when Indians in the vicinity were on the war path, the freighter exposed himself to extreme danger. His protection was almost always totally inadequate. Such was the case of Pat Hennessey, who in transporting his freight wagons over the Chisholm Trail was seized by a body of Cheyennes, perhaps a marauding detachment of old Stone Calf's contingent of these Indians. Hennessey was captured and murdered—gave up his life in the line of duty.

The freighters, with the other pioneers of the West, served their purpose, and theirs was not by any means the least. Their deeds are now history, much of which has never been recorded, but in any event, it has all gone into that of the frontier; the deeds constituting which paved the way for the civilization which followed—the civilization of today.

CHAPTER XXV.

THE POND CREEK RANCH AND GRAVES
NEAR THE SAME

It is usually the case that persons living in the vicinities of historical points know less about them than persons living further away.   Some time ago the writer was stopping in a county seat town in Texas.   The county bore a Spanish name, and in conversation with a group of citizens, some of whom had lived there all their lives, it was discovered that none knew the meaning of the name of their own county.   These men did not lack in intelligence, but had been too busy with other affairs of life to think of or investigate this matter; neither did they know of several historical events that had taken place in the early history of their community.   Upon the writer informing them of these facts, they were all deeply interested.   These people, as is usually the case in such matters, became the most interested students in these historical facts.   They did not know that their community had any historical significance, but when they found it had, they were eager to learn more of the same.

The writer grew to manhood in close contact with this old trail, and it is with a purpose to attempt to preserve some of the early history of it that this book is written.   Much of its earliest history has now been lost.   How thankful we would be if some one had preserved it for us.   This history would have been very interesting to us and to future generations.

The fact that persons living in the immediate vicinity of historical points usually know least about them is especially true with reference to the people living in the vicinity of the location of the Old Pond Creek Ranch.   Few persons now living

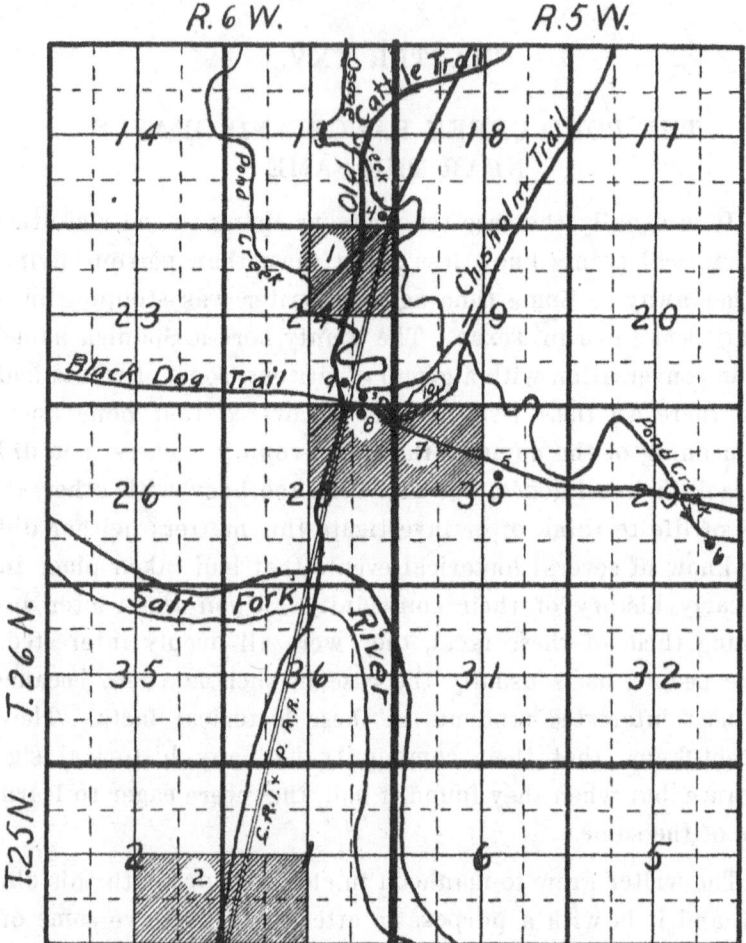

Plat showing location of Old Pond Creek Ranch, or Sewell Stockade, and historical points near the same.

1. Present City of Jefferson.
2. Present City of Pond Creek.
3. Location of Old Pond Creek Ranch or Sewell Stockade.
4. Point where Tom Best was killed.
5. Point where Ed. Chambers was killed.
6. Location of Indian graves on Green Homestead.
7. Original location of County seat, from which it was removed **prior to** opening.
8. Graves of Tom Best and Ed. Chambers.
9. Water tank on railway near Jefferson.
10. Semi-circular pond, for which Round Pond was named.

near this location even know where the old ranch stood, and many do not know there ever was such a place. This is true, even though it was one of the historical points in the Indian Territory, and one of the most important points on the Old Chisholm Trail between Abilene, Kansas, and San Antonio, Texas. All the life and activity of this old ranch is now gone, and nothing, not even a stone, marks the spot where it stood. The men who made it famous are now stilled in death. Likewise, the memory of the ranch itself has succumbed to the change in the activities of a busy world; and both have been forgotten.

This old land mark stood about fifty yards south and one hundred yards east of the present water tank of the Chicago, Rock Island, and Pacific Railway, and about one mile south of the town of Jefferson in Grant County, Oklahoma. A few broken pieces of glass and crockery turned up by the plows in a field are all that remain to mark the spot where it stood.

In 1865, when Jesse Chisholm made the first recorded trip over this trail from his trading post at Wichita, Kansas, to the Cimarron River, he doubtless passed within a few hundred feet of the point where this ranch was afterward located. When the first herds of cattle came up from Texas in 1867, they passed not over two hundred yards to the west of it. This ranch stood a short distance south from the bank of the stream of Pond Creek, where it makes the bend to the east. About one mile to the south and a short distance west, the trail crossed the Salt Fork River.

The Salt Fork River is generally known as the Salt Fork of the Arkansas, while the Cimarron during the cattle days was known as the Red Fork of the Arkansas. Both of these streams were very appropriately named. The waters of the Cimarron are usually very red, being colored from the red hills through which it flows, while the Salt Fork is extremely salty, being in its upper course impregnated by the beds of rock salt beneath its surface and over which it flows. The Salt Fork, by the Indians and early explorers, was known and so designated on early maps as the Nescatonga, and the head waters of the stream are still known by that name. This name is of Indian origin, and refers to the salty condition of the water. This being the case, the only change made in the name is the change from Indian to English, as they both mean the same. The stream of Pond Creek and the Salt Fork River in their course first come into close proximity at this point, and then run parallel to each other to the east for about fifteen miles, where Pond Creek empties into the river. In this course the two streams are from one to four miles apart. The land between them is a level bottom, with the exception of a string of sand hills, which skirt the river on the north side. This bottom contains some of the best land in the state. In the cattle days, it was considered the best grazing ground to be found.

When the writer first knew this country in the vicinity of the Pond Creek Ranch, he was just a boy, but a vivid recollection of the same remains in his mind. He thought it to be the most beautiful country he ever saw. Both in the bottom between the river and the creek, and on the hills on both sides, the broad prairies stretched away as far as the eye could see. In the springtime beautiful flowers of all colors could be seen in every direction. Over these prairies were in those days seen the most beautiful mirage ever seen in any land. These beautiful productions are now seldom seen in any form, and never with all their beauty as seen in this country fifty years ago. Even nature has rebelled and refuses to produce in the atmosphere the beautiful scenes which once it did, when the country remained in its primitive state. Once the traveler over this country looked upon views of beautiful lakes, extensive jungles of tropical woods, towering structures of magnificent cities, and followed the shores of receding water ways as they dropped back before his advance. These, like the original travelers over these prairies, have departed to an unknown land.

It is difficult to state, with any degree of certainty, who built the first structure or habitation at the Pond Creek Ranch, or when it was built. This is some of the lost history. The first authentic history we have as to the same is in the early seventies. At this time a man by the name of Sewell maintained a stockade at this place. It was then known as "Sewell's Stockade," and was evidently constructed for protection of the nearby inhabitants and travelers on the Chisholm Trail and on the Black Dog Trail[1] against the Indians, most of whom were in a wild state at that time and caused a great deal of trouble to all persons stopping or traveling in this part of the country.

It is well to note here that in addition to the Chisholm Trail, which was a wagon and cattle trail, and ran practically

---

[1] This particular trail, known as the "Black Dog Trail," will be distinguished from the Osage War Trail proper, which ran east and west, crossing about ten miles south of this point. From as far back as 1840, and perhaps further, this Black Dog Trail had passed over this route along Pond Creek. It was traveled more by the Osages than the other trail. It was an Osage trail, and was named after Black Dog. He was the leading war chief of the Osages. He was quite a historical character. There was another trail named after him, which was located in the southeastern portion of the state, and which crossed Little River about ten miles below Three Forks. There was a common council ground for many years used by the Osages and a number of Plains Indians near the Salt Plains, some twenty miles almost due west of the Pond Creek Ranch, and this trail was established by Black Dog as being a shorter route for the Osages in reaching this portion of the country.

Black Dog was a conspicuous figure at these meetings. He was a giant in stature, standing almost seven feet tall, and it is claimed he would consume from eight to twelve pounds of beef each day. He was considered untrustworthy and treacherous. He headed a party of Osages at one time who ambushed and killed a number of Creeks, and had other depredations charged up to him. He died March 24, 1848, and was succeeded as chief by his son Young Black Dog. A contest for leadership of the Osages arose between this son and another leading Osage character known as The Wolf. As a result of this contention, The Wolf and his faction withdrew from the Osage tribe, and removed to the Cherokee Nation. Here under the observation of John Ross, The Wolf made a very creditable citizen. The Osages were really divided into three clans or factions.

north and south, there was another trail running east and west on the south side of the creek of Pond Creek, known as the Black Dog Trail. This trail was named after an Osage chief, and was primarily an Indian trail over which the wandering tribes of Indians drove their ponies and drew their traverses. In later years, it was also doubtless used by other travelers taking this route. This Black Dog Trail crossed Pond Creek some few miles below the ranch, and continued east on the north side of the creek. The exact location of this crossing is not now known.

In the early history of this place there was also a man by the name of Hopkins, who owned a ranch a short distance below the Sewell Stockade on Pond Creek, and he evidently later maintained the Pond Creek Ranch itself. The ranch in early times was often known as "Hopkins," and was so designated on many of the maps up to the time of the opening of this country to settlement in 1893. In the seventies, we have authentic information of at least three ranches east of the Pond Creek Ranch and along the Salt Fork River and Pond Creek. The names of the owners of these different ranches were Hopkins, Col. Dean, and Luke Short.

In these early times, the Osage Indians were considered the most troublesome of all the tribes in this locality. They were accustomed to making forays into the vicinity of the Pond Creek Ranch, and killed many people on these raids. At the time stated, these expeditions were much talked of, and were generally known as "mourning parties," or "funeral parties." This name was given by the white settlers and travelers on account of a peculiar custom among this particular tribe of Indians which brought about these excursions. Among the Osages, as well as most of the other Indian tribes, it was the custom when a warrior died to bury him with all the scalps of enemies taken by him during his career. This was done by these simple-minded people feeling the assurance that the deceased would march on into the "happy hunting ground" loaded down with scalps and, among those who had gone before, would be welcomed with open arms; and that his prowess as a great warrior would crown him with glory.

In later years, when the mortality was lessened in the Indian wars and the wars with the pioneers, scalps became scarce with the surviving warriors, and they were about to be driven to the extremity of being buried without this very necessary equipment. In this case, a warrior would be compelled to proceed into the Great Beyond scalpless and disgraced, and to live through eternity with the other warriors who had gone before dangling their numerous trophies of battle in his presence, to his chagrin, and humiliation. This was an awful predicament, not only to the departed and disgraced warrior, but was humiliating in the extreme to his many friends and relatives whom he had left behind, and they could hardly bury him realizing this condition.

The friends of these scalpless warriors conceived the idea that if they could go forth and procure a scalp and bury it with the deceased that he could carry this scalp on his departure, and thus deceive his associates on the Other Side into believing that he had peeled it himself from the head of some luckless antagonist. With this idea in view, on the death of a warrior who was not the possessor of a scalp lock, his friends whom he left behind, to prove their friendship and loyalty, would start out to procure a scalp from any possible victim. This would be used for the fraudulent purpose stated, even if the parties attempting to procure the same were compelled to die and be buried scalpless themselves. The parties going out to procure these scalps grew to be known as "mourning parties" or "funeral parties." These were usually the parties who swooped down upon and caused so much consternation among the scattered population in the vicinity of the old Pond Creek Ranch. The fear of the inhabitants for these marauders can be easily excused when they realized that their scalps were about to be lifted to be buried with and borne through the Great Beyond upon the person of some Osage warrior who had failed to procure one himself during his lifetime. These parties actually procured many scalps for this purpose.

The writer as a lad first visited the Pond Creek Ranch in 1881, was familiar with, and traveled this trail often from that time up to the time of the opening of the country for settlement in 1893. At the time of his first association with the trail, the route of the same at Pond Creek, as well as many other places, had been changed. Where the City of Enid is located the trail at that time ran a considerable distance to the east of the original location. At the Pond Creek Ranch, instead of running north from the ranch, the travel on the wagon trail, and much of the travel on the cattle trail, ran east from the ranch, passing around the south side of the pond on the south side of Pond Creek, and crossing the Creek almost three-quarters of a mile east and between a quarter and a half of a mile north of the old ranch. This point of crossing was just below the mouth of Osage Creek, which runs into Pond Creek on the north side, and was at the point where Pond Creek runs the farthest to the north, being about a half mile east and a quarter south of the present town of Jefferson. In crossing at the point where the trail was first laid out, it was necessary to cross both Pond Creek and Osage Creek. Both of these streams had steep banks and were difficult to cross. The banks at the east crossing were steep and difficult to negotiate with loaded wagons, especially when coming from the south, but there was but one creek to cross. The herds continued for some time to cross on the old route, but finally when fences were built they were compelled to take the eastern crossing. The original trail passed over the present townsite of Jefferson.

The banks at this eastern crossing have been washed out until they are now perpendicular. The old marks, however, are still plainly visible where the many wagons marked their course down the bank, and many deep cow-paths still remain as evidence of the thousands of hoofs that scarred the same. After the trouble with the boomers began in the early eighties, a camp of soldiers were usually maintained in the timber on the east side of this trail and on the south side of this east crossing. The writer has spent many jolly and happy days and nights with these boys of the United States Army. Much time was spent hunting prairie chickens in the sand hills on the Salt Fork to the south of this camp. These chickens would be cooked and served in army style. The last time the writer visited this point, he stood on the cow-path marked hill on the north side of the creek and looked down to the south. Apparently he could see again the large bell-shaped government tent to the east of the trail, with the smaller government wall tents around it, and could see the horses of the cavalry tied to the long rope stretched between the trees. While looking upon this scene, the memory of the past was so vivid as to be almost lived over again.

This pond on the south side of Pond Creek and east of the ranch, which has been referred to, is now, except in extremely wet weather, nothing more than a dry depression. Upon the writer's first knowledge of the same, it was a broad, deep lake. When Pond Creek would be flooded it would flow over the entrance to this pond, and when the water would recede it would leave it full. The water was then so deep that the cattle and horses could not wade it. This pond was then full of fish. The writer remembers one occasion when, in the dry portion of the summer, the pond became so low that the cattle and horses would wade across the same and rile the water until there could be seen many large fish swimming to the top. Some years before the opening, several parties came down from Kansas with plows, cut a ditch at the lower end of this pond, and lowered the water until they could take their seines and catch the fish. This they did, taking wagon loads out of this pond. This, however, left the pond permanently low, and it never was the deep lake that it was before. Now it has either been completely drained or by natural process, it has filled until this pond of the early history of the Pond Creek Ranch is only a memory.

In the *Chronicles of Oklahoma*, a quarterly publication, issued in magazine form by the Historical Society of Oklahoma, in the issue of December, 1925, will be found an article written by James C. Henderson of Jay, Delaware County, Oklahoma. This was written in about 1917, and details the life of Mr. Henderson for several years during the middle seventies in this locality. He was stationed for some time at a point which he states was east of the Pond Creek Ranch, at a point where the Salt Fork River was about one mile from the Creek. This would place the location about six miles east of the Ranch. This is an extremely accurate and truthful article. It came to the writer like a voice from the past, speaking to him from the days of his boyhood, from the days when he traveled these prairies before a plow had marred their surface.

Mr. Henderson reveals the fact that he was present in the Territory until well into the eighties. His picture accompanies the article, and the same is familiar. The writer remembers him very well, and has met him many times. The writer also knew personally most of the parties mentioned by him. He gives some information which the writer did not know, and which he is satisfied is quite authentic. He states that Polecat Creek, which empties into Pond Creek on the north side,

James C. Henderson, Range Rider at Old
Pond Creek Ranch or Sewell Stockade.—
Courtesy of Oklahoma State Historical So-
ciety.

some miles below the Pond Creek Ranch, was known by the
Osage Indians as Ne-wheh-ka-ha Shinga, which meant "Little
Stinking Creek." As the creek has been known in later years
as Polecat Creek it is quite evident that the aroma spread
by these bright colored and beautiful little animals caused the
Indians to apply this name to the same. It also sounds as if
the Indian who did so, and proclaimed the same to the world,
had just escaped from an encounter with one of these little
creatures.

Referring to Mr. Henderson's article we can get a clear
idea of the impression that this locality would make upon a

person at that time. On page 285 of the Chronicles we find the following in this article:

"We first camped on Pond Creek in the fall of 1874. There was something wild and weird about this creek and this something seemed to be lacking with the other numerous creeks upon which we had camped. It looked like a deserted village. There were numerous signs of its having been a great camping place for the Indians. There were old ash heaps and the remains of old tepee frames and many burying grounds. On the bank of the creek, near where the Black Dog Trail crossed it, was a lonely grave. A chief's daughter had been buried there. The remains of these Indians lay in these graves for many moons undisturbed and unstartled by the yell of the fierce Pawnee, but it was not to be forever thus."

Continuing on page 286 he states the following:

"There were several human skulls lying around in different places. These skulls seemed to be of two kinds. One kind had a seam running from the front, or forehead, to the back. The other had the same seam, only it forked and made two seams near the back of the head. We supposed that one kind was that of an Indian man and the other that of an Indian woman."

Beginning on page 266 of the *Chronicles* we desire to quote Mr. Henderson in reference to a circumstance which happened when one of these mourning parties came to Hopkins' Ranch and tried to get the scalp of the negro cook, as follows:

"About nine or ten o'clock that day the Indians reached Hopkins' dug-out on Pond Creek, about four miles below the old Sewell Stockade. The men had all gone to look after the cattle, but a negro cook was in the dug-out. (I have forgotten the Osage name for negro, so I have substituted the Ponca word for black man, which is probably the same, as the languages of the two tribes are of common origin, and many, if not most of the words, are identical.) This wau-ka Sabba heard someone say 'Hello' in plain English, and thinking it was someone from our camp he said, 'Come in.' But no one came, so he opened the door to see who it was, and there were three Indians standing in the door. He tried to close the door but the Indians caught it and began to push, and as he threw his weight against the door in an endeavor to shut it one of them reached in and cut off a large bunch of his wool, but did not reach his scalp. There was a loaded revolver lying a few feet away, but the negro was afraid to let go the door to get it. After this struggle had lasted a few moments, Wau-ka Sabba saw that he could not shut the door, so he jumped back and let the Indians fall inside. Before they could get on their feet again, Wau-ka Sabba had grasped the revolver and began shooting, and thus succeeded in driving the Indians out, when he closed the door. He did not kill an Indian, although he said his weapon was within two feet of their faces when he was shooting. The rest of the Indians were hidden in the brush about a half a mile away and the three Indians at the dug-out began to signal for them to come by setting fire to the dead grass and throwing it up in the air. Wau-ka Sabba was watching them through the crack in the door, and when he saw the main band of Indians coming he thought it was time to move. There was a rear door that opened out down under the creek bank, and the negro ran out this door and through the woods, but the Indians saw him, and the three that were already at the dug-out jumped on their horses and took after him, shooting as they ran. The rest of the Indians were coming in full cry, but the negro had some advantage as there was lots of grape vines and green briar thickets which he could run through, but the Indians, being mounted, had to go around these. Also, whenever he came to the creek he would run down and up the banks, while the Indians had to ride around the big bends. The Indians ran him within a half a mile of the stockade (Sewell's), and they shot at him every time they caught sight of him. He said afterward that when he reached the stockade there was a tired nigger there. He certainly made a great run, as the Indians put him through under whip and spur for almost four miles. Had his shooting been as good as his running he might have given a better account of himself."

The writer remembers well the location of this dug-out, and could go to it yet. The distance, as stated, from the Pond

Creek Ranch is about correct. However, had any of us traveled it under the circumstances that Wau-ka Sabba did, it might have seemed much longer. Henderson later held a bunch of cattle on the Chikaskia River, above the mouth of Bluff Creek, at which place the writer saw him many times.

At some time in the early eighties, the Pond Creek Ranch was taken over and operated by Anderson Hance. Hance's mother was remarried to Mr. George Hanes, who conducted a store at Caldwell, Kansas, for many years. Mrs. Hanes spent much time with her son at the Pond Creek Ranch. She was a very large, dark complexioned, jolly woman. She often told of a circumstance of being on a stage coach going south over the Chisholm Trail. Among the passengers were a couple of officers from Texas. These officers had a couple of bad prisoners whom they were returning to Texas for trial. These prisoners had in some way concealed some pistols in the stage coach, and when they came to Buffalo Springs, near the present town of Bison, they procured these pistols and took charge of the officers. The stage coach was drawn by mules. The outlaws desired to ride these animals and leave the stage coach behind, but they did not know whether the mules could be ridden or not, so they required the driver of the stage coach to mount them and ride each of them around in a circle until they were convinced of the fact that they could be ridden by them in making their escape. This circumstance was very ludicrous and extremely amusing in the way she described the same.

Anderson Hance operated this ranch for many years, and did a profitable business in so doing. It was a very important post on the trail; there were always many people coming and going, and many stopped at the ranch for their meals. The writer can recall numerous occasions, during storms in the winter season, when not only the ranch house was crowded, but the park along the creek was an extensive camp ground. At the time of the breaking up of the cattle business in the Cherokee Strip, Anderson Hance moved to Glazier, Texas, where he operated a cattle ranch and prospered. He came from there for many years to attend the old cowboys' annual reunions held at the 101 Ranch.   He died at Glazier in 1926.

Across Pond Creek, to the northeast of the ranch, is located a beautiful large grove, which is now known as Rock Island Park. This is one of the most beautiful parks in the State. It is thickly timbered, and was a jungle of underbrush. This brush was cleared out following the opening, and a special act of the Territorial Legislature having been passed authorizing the same, Rock Island Township, in which it is located, purchased it, and it is still owned and operated as a public park.

In the act of Congress opening the Cherokee Strip, it was provided that certain of the members of Cherokee families could select at such place in the Outlet as they desired allotments of eighty acres each. One of these allotments was located at the Old Pond Creek Ranch, and included the park referred to. This allotment was purchased by the Rock Island Townsite Company. While this Company bears the name of the railway, it had no connection with it. The portion of this allotment west of the railway was divided into lots and sold. The portion east of the track, where the old ranch stood, was not sold in lots. A flourishing town existed for some time at this point and on adjacent land, but after the railway station was established at Pond Creek, or the Government townsite of Round Pond, the county seat of the county, the town was moved to a point about one mile to the north, where it is now located as the town of Jefferson. On account of the acts of the persons in charge of the location of these county seats, such strife arose over the location of the same, that it destroyed the prospects of building a large city in this county, until the other towns in adjoining counties had gained such a start that no town of any size has ever been built in this, Grant County, even though it is one of the best counties of the State. The people of this county, although in no wise to blame for these things, will suffer from the effects of this mismanagement for all time.

The first county seat, selected by the Government agents locating the same, was just to the south of the old ranch. The north line of it was less than one hundred yards from where the old ranch house stood. The allotment above referred to having been located, and two more eighty acre allotments having been selected to the west of the location of the townsite, the Government agents moved the Government Townsite and made that as their excuse for so doing. Instead, however, of moving it to the north where the best land in the county could be found on which to locate it, and thus bring it nearer the center of the county, these parties, in all their wisdom, moved the same two miles to the south, within four and one-half miles of the south line of the county, and to the south of the Salt Fork, the worst river in the outlet. This county was twenty-eight miles wide north and south.

About one hundred and fifty yards to the south of the site of the old ranch, and across the public highway from the same, on the top of a small, sandy mound only a few feet high, are two graves. The remains of two men rest here who gave up their lives in the winning of the frontier to civilization. The poet, whose name the writer cannot now recall, described in the following elegant words the death of Robinhood who threaded the green forests of England:

> "Give to me my bent bow in my hand,
>   And an arrow I'll let flee;
>   And where that arrow is picked up,
>   There shall my grave dig be."

The men of the frontier, whose graves mark the lines of the western trails, did not know where their last resting place would be, nor did they have time to designate the same. These men were surrounded by dangers by which they were usually cut down in the prime of life and without warning. Their deaths were almost always instantaneous and unforeseen.

Much discussion has arisen as to the death of these men, whose graves were located at the Old Pond Creek Ranch. The writer has talked with men who declared emphatically that they died from fever, and others claimed that they were outlaws who were killed and buried there. None of these parties knew anything about the matter other than some rumor they had heard, and some of them upon inquiry had confused these graves with others. In one instance in particular it was discovered, on further inquiry, the party had the location entirely wrong. In another case it developed that the party was thinking of the graves at the Red Fork Ranch, where two outlaws were killed and buried. The writer has known these graves at the Pond Creek Ranch since 1881, and has investigated, perhaps, more than any other person, the history of the same. He knew personally and very well one party who was present when one of these men was killed by the Indians, and talked with many more who knew the circumstances of the killing of the other.

When the writer first looked upon these graves, each grave was marked with a board at the head of the same. On one of these boards was marked in a legible hand as follows: "Tom Best, killed by Kiowas in 1872." On the other, in the same manner, appeared the following: "Ed. Chambers, killed by Osages in 1873."

In time these boards decayed and fell over. They were picked up and replaced by friends who shared the fortunes of the frontier, until they became so badly decayed and worn that they were barely legible; but many were the men who remembered the words on the same. When the railway was built to this point, in 1889, Anderson Hance, who was operating the ranch, procured some of the best and largest rock that he could obtain from the railway company, and had the same inscription as had been on the board carved on a stone to place at the head of each grave. These stones are still at the graves. The lettering on one has been somewhat marred by the marks of a plow, but the lettering on both is clearly legible. When the town was located at this place, this land was covered by buildings, but the graves were preserved.

The same lettering as is now on these stones has been retained at all times since the remains of these men were laid there to rest. This point was then on the far frontier. It is hardly fair to accuse the companions of these men, whose lives went out on the plains—whether from violence or disease—of having placed a diabolical falsehood above their remains to deceive future generations as to the cause of their demise or doing so as a simple prank and joke on the dead men. Men of the frontier did not deal with their companions in that way. There may be men in the world who are depraved and ruthless enough in their dealngs with their fellow man to be guilty of doing or permitting such things, but they were not found among the pioneers of the West. Life, in this locality at that time, was too precarious to make a joke of it. Men who had interest enough in a companion to leave a marker and inscription above his last resting place certainly would not place a false statement on the same. These men fought for life and existence side by side; and when a companion fell, he was laid to rest with all the reverence and solemnity possible, and the truth was reported as to the cause of his death. The written inscriptions left upon these graves by their comrades carry the information to future generations that these men died at the hands of the Indians. Why should this not be the case? Death at the hands of the Indians was the greatest danger that beset these men at that time. In the article written by James C. Henderson, heretofore referred to, the facts of the killing of both of these parties by the Indians are verified to a certain extent. Henderson refers to the frequent incursions of the Osage funeral parties into this locality at that time. Also the positive information furnished the writer by Bedford Wood, who was present when Tom Best was killed, would place the fact of his killing by the Kiowa Indians beyond doubt. Further reference to Henderson's article, being had on page 260 of the *Chronicles,* is the following:

"These Indians then went west, up the Salt Fork, and they killed a man near where the Black Dog Trail crossed Pond Creek. This man belonged to an outfit that was coming up the trail from Texas with a herd. Some of the cattle had strayed off, and he was hunting for these strays when the Indians found him."

It is true that Henderson fixes this time in May, 1874, instead of 1873, but he states positively that these Indians were Osages. Henderson was familiar with this tribe of Indians, and was satisfied as to their identity. He knew that these Indians frequented this locality more than any other tribe. The discrepancy of one year in time is easy to make after a lapse of forty-five years, and it was in this case. If any person detailing events that happened forty-five years ago can come within one year of the correct date, he is doing extremely well. The other facts as to the killing referred to by Henderson correspond exactly with the facts as hereinafter stated as to the killing of Ed. Chambers.

Further, this statement of Henderson's shows that a man was killed in almost the exact location where it is claimed Ed. Chambers was, and why should it not have been he? Also, the party killed must have been buried some place, and why should the Pond Creek Ranch or Sewell's Stockade, which was the most public place in the country, not have been selected as the place of such interment? The natural course of events would affirm this as being the logical place of burial.

The only method we have of ascertaining the history of these early events is from the statements of those who either knew personally by being present at the happening of the same or from the statements of those who were in position to know most about the facts. The information of the writer in reference to the killing of Tom Best, the first man laid to rest in these lonely graves, was obtained from Bedford Wood. Bedford Wood was related to, and as the writer remembers, a brother of, S. T. Wood. S. T. Wood was a man of considerable prominence in southern Kansas in the early history of the same. He was a surveyor who assisted in surveying much of the western country. He helped to survey and make a map of all the cattle ranges in the Cherokee Outlet. He was for many years County Surveyor of Sumner County, Kansas, a position of considerable importance at that time.

Bedford Wood was a cowboy in the earliest times of the cattle industry in the Indian Territory. He worked with some of the companies in what is now Old Oklahoma, and later for many years was connected with the Snow Cattle Company, or Snow and Rannels, who operated a ranch on Red Rock, south of the present City of Perry, in the Cherokee Outlet. He was afterwards one of the deputy marshals of the City of Caldwell, Kansas, and was for many years a member of the police force of the City of Wichita, Kansas. He was later connected with a private detective agency in Kansas City, Missouri, where he died in the early part of the present century.

In 1872, the cattle coming up the Chisholm Trail came from central and the south central portion of Texas. The cattlemen on the north end of this trail, who intended driving cattle up from Texas, would start as soon as the grass was sufficiently advanced to furnish subsistence for their horses in early spring, and would drive a portion of the horses they took with them and ride the remainder. At least a portion of the cowboys who intended to accompany the herds back would go with them on these downward trips.

In April, 1872, one of these outfits started south to Texas. Among the cowboys accompanying the same were Bedford Wood and Tom Best. The names of others have been given to the writer, but time has eliminated them from his memory. When they reached the Pond Creek Ranch, it was learned that the Salt Fork River just beyond the ranch, which lay in the course of their travel down the trail, was swollen until it was impossible to cross. This was a frequent occurrence at this season of the year. The outfit was compelled to lie over at the ranch until the flooded condition in the river would subside. They remained in camp there for three days. On the fourth day one of their number, who made frequent trips to the river to ascertain its condition, reported that the water had fallen until it could be crossed.

The horses of the outfit had at this time grazed to the north about a mile and a half, and several of the cowboys went after them. Among this number were Tom Best and Bedford Wood. They traveled north over the present townsite of the town of Jefferson, and headed toward Osage Creek, a quarter of a mile north of the same, advancing to the creek just east of where the bridge on Government Highway 81 crosses it. When they reached a point about fifty yards south of the creek, a puff of smoke arose from the south bank. This puff of smoke was accompanied by the report of a rifle. Tom Best fell from his horse. His companions went to him and ascertained that he was dying. They rushed on toward the creek to apprehend his slayer, and as they did so they saw two Indians crossing the bend in the creek to the east. They pursued these parties, but they took refuge in the thick timber and underbrush in the region of the park, and thus escaped.

The members of the outfit ascertained that these Indians were members of a Kiowa raiding party then in the vicinity. These raiding parties usually numbered from ten to twenty, or more, and they would send out scouting parties of two or three, and the rest would keep concealed. In any event, the companions of the slain cowboy learned enough to satisfy them that the slayers of Tom Best were Kiowa Indians. This being the case, according to their own standard, Tom Best died in vain, as these Indians failed to recover his scalp as a hereditary trophy. Tom Best was laid to rest in a grave on the top of a sandy mound south of the ranch, and a wooden marker was placed at his head, giving his name and the brief fact that he was killed by the Kiowa Indians, and the year of his death. His companions journeyed on down the trail, taking an empty and ownerless saddle along.

At the time of the opening of the Cherokee Strip for settlement, the writer took and proved up a claim three-quarters of a mile west of the Pond Creek Ranch. There was no depot at the present City of Pond Creek for some time after the opening. There was a considerable sized town around where the old ranch had stood, and the writer had his office there. In 1894, Bedford Wood, who was well known to him, stopped at his office. He had heard him tell many times before of the facts as heretofore set out. Wood requested then, as he had on several occasions, that the writer at some time reduce these facts to writing, and it was fully intended by both parties that such would be done, but as is usually the case in such matters, it was considered there was no hurry, and it was delayed until the opportunity passed. There were many facts told him as to this killing which he cannot, on account of the lapse of time, recall.

The writer has never talked with anyone who was at the Pond Creek Ranch or Sewell's Stockade when Ed. Chambers was killed, neither has he known anyone who helped bury him. It must be remembered that in 1872-3 there were really no well established cow-camps in the vicinity of the Pond Creek Ranch. The Indians roved over this part of the country unrestrained. They traveled east and west past this point over the Black Dog Trail. The cattlemen traveled north and south over the Chisholm Trail, and at the junction of these trails the old Sewell Stockade had been established, evidently keeping a supply of necessaries to sell to the travelers or to trade to the Indians. The writer has heard detailed all the information, authentic and otherwise, in reference to the death of Ed. Chambers since he first knew these graves. He has adopted the portion which he deems most authentic, and which he is satisfied is the true information as to the same. These facts he will here relate.

Ed. Chambers was a Texas cowboy, and, in 1873, was staying at a camp of a transient cattle outfit near the Sewell Stockade. It was a notable fact, in those times, that cattle drivers coming up from Texas would often drop off of the trail a short distance and lie over, permitting their cattle to rest. It seems that Ed. Chambers was a member of one of these outfits. His duties called him several miles to the east of the Pond Creek Ranch. Henderson says he was looking for strays, and while he was traveling in this bottom between the creek and river he was discovered by a large band of Osage Indians, who immediately started to pursue him.

Chambers started west, running his horse, attempting to reach either his camp or the Stockade. He kept ahead of the

Indians until he reached the heavy sand in the sand hills, about
one mile southeast of the Stockade, when his horse soon became
exhausted or was wounded, and the Indians began to crowd
upon him. He dismounted and took refuge behind a sandy
knoll. The Indians, adopting their usual tactics in such cases,
began to circle him. Chambers was armed with a Henry rifle.
This was the most formidable weapon in use at that time for
this sort of fighting. The sandy condition of the soil made
the progress of the Indians slower, and they were a fair target
for Ed. Chambers' rifle, and he took advantage of the opportunity. It has been told the writer that he killed many Indians before they killed and scalped him. When found, there
was a pile of empty shells of cartridges lying by his side, a
mute reminder that he had sold his life dearly.

Chambers was found and picked up tenderly by his companions, and laid to rest on the sandy knoll south of the Pond
Creek Ranch, by the side of the grave of Tom Best, who had
preceded him to the Great Beyond by one year. His last resting
place was marked by a small slab, leaving to future visitors
the information that his name was Ed. Chambers, and that he
had fallen at the hands of the Osage Indians in the year 1873.
There were no newspapers in the country at that time to publish the circumstances of his killing. There were no historians
in the land to chronicle the history of these events. For that
history we must depend on the traditional history of the times.
In any event, he had given up his life contributing this as his
share to the winning of the West. His companions were compelled on their return to Texas to make that trip with their
ranks fewer by one. This one still rests where he was laid
in 1873.

It will never be known how many Indians Ed. Chambers
killed before he gave up his scalp to his pursuers. It is a well
known fact that in all Indian warfare, the Indians never leave

a fallen companion on the battlefield.   A warrior will risk his life as quickly to retrieve a fallen associate as he will to rescue a live one.   They performed this feat by two warriors riding their horses side by side and reaching down from the same, one grasping a fallen Indian by the arm and the other by the leg, thus carrying him between their horses from the field of battle.

In 1893, at the time the Cherokee Strip was opened, D. R. Green, who was generally known as "Cannonball Green," and for whom the Cannonball Highway running west from Wichita, Kansas, was named, from the fact that he designated his stage line operated over this route as the Cannonball Stage Line, and for whom the City of Greensburg, Kansas, was named, took a claim on Pond Creek, about three miles down the river east from the Pond Creek Ranch.   In the spring of 1894, while excavating in the edge of the timber near the creek, they found an Indian grave, and upon examination it was discovered that there were many more in the vicinity.   This was about the natural distance from where Ed. Chambers was killed for these Indians to bury their dead.   The graves were of comparatively recent origin, and the time of the burial of Ed. Chambers, which was twenty years before, would indicate that it was near the time of this circumstance.   The dead, from the point where Ed. Chambers was killed, could not have been carried a much greater distance.   It is only conjecture, but is it not fair to presume that the Indians who occupied these graves fell before the Henry rifle of Ed. Chambers?

To all the travelers on the Chisholm Trail past the Pond Creek Ranch, these graves were always held in the greatest reverence and respect.   Most any old cowboy or freighter traveling the trail would have fought at any time to preserve them. The ranks of these men have now been so depleted that a few years ago, when the writer attempted to raise a subscription to have a monument placed at these graves, it was impossible to find a sufficient number of the old guard to raise the necessary funds.

In the winter of 1888, the writer made a trip into the southwestern portion of the Indian Territory. On this trip he visited a number of cow-camps and many cowboys, with whom he was well acquainted. At that time the Rock Island Railway was building from Caldwell south to the Pond Creek Ranch. It was known that the line of this railway would run near these graves. The report had been brought to these cow-camps that the survey of the railway crossed and would destroy the graves. It was remarkable, the interest that was manifested in that fact. It was universally declared by the cowboys with whom the writer talked that if these graves were molested, no line of the railway, if built over the same, would be permitted to remain. A cowboy seldom made an idle boast, and it is the firm opinion of the writer that had the line been built over these graves that it would have been torn up. The writer was requested to investigate as to the location of the railway on his return and report to one of the parties with whom he talked. This he did, and discovered that the railway was located about one hundred yards to the west of the graves.

These graves are now unmarked, except for the stones referred to. There is no monument erected to mark the last resting place of these men. There is no history recording the deeds they did except this brief account of the circumstances under which they were cut down. These men who rest here were boys who went out from their youthful homes and their native communities in civilization to lend their aid and contribute their part to the civilization of the West. They were cowboys who once sat their saddles well as they traversed the broad prairies and the limitless open spaces of the then Great

West.   In carrying out the enterprise in which they had enlisted, they were stricken down in the prime of life.   Theirs were the fortunes of war, and the lines here written are the only ones recording the information that they ever lived.

CHAPTER XXVI.

THE DEATH OF PAT HENNESSEY

The writer finds this subject very difficult to deal with. This is not the fact for the reason that it is any more laborious to record the authentic and known facts connected with the same, but so much has been written, printed, and placed in circulation—much of which is purely imagination—purporting to set out the details of this matter, that in writing the authentic facts constituting this event, it is not only necessary to set out the facts, but also to set them out in such manner and with such verification that the reader will know they are true. It is, also, necessary to set out these facts in such a way as to eliminate from the mind of the public the erroneous statements that have been made and published in reference thereto.

The writer will not be understood, however, as claiming that all that has been written and given to the public in reference to the death of Hennessey is fiction or unauthentic. Many correct statements have been published as to the same, but on the other hand, much has been written and published which has no foundation in fact. Much of this writing has been done without any claim on the part of the writers that they had any authentic information as to the matter about which they wrote. These articles are purely visionary and, while highly colored or set forth in flaming and extravagant language, they are nothing more than flowery fiction. The writing of such articles is excusable on the part of anyone who is imaginative, given to reflection, or visionary.

The lonely grave of Pat Hennessey was, prior to the opening of Old Oklahoma for settlement in 1889, only a few feet from the main track of the Chisholm Trail, the principal highway running north and south across the Indian Territory. The travelers along this trail in stage coaches or other conveyances suddenly and unexpectantly came face to face with death; not ordinary death, but death by violence of the most barbarous sort, and that in a land so far removed from civilization that the primitive surroundings had not been in the least removed. This situation was romantic in the extreme, so much so, that simply gazing upon this lonely grave was sufficient to arouse in the mind of a person possessed of any degree of imagination the material "to point a moral or adorn a tale." Any fairly effective writer who passed by this grave, upon reflection, had a wealth of stock in trade to write a long and interesting article. This was especially true, if the party on making inquiry as to the facts, happened to fall into the hands of someone who was verbose and prolific in dealing out information which had come to him after having been magnified and distorted by having passed down from several thousand different informants before him.

There is in truth but a brief and plain statement of facts connected with this matter. These facts have been detailed before. For this reason, another difficulty arises in writing this article. That is, in setting out the known facts, it is necessary to almost copy what has been written. This is true for the reason that all the authentic information as to this circumstance is derived from the same sources.

A very accurate and detailed account of the facts connected with this matter are given by Mr. George Rainey in his very interesting book entitled "The Cherokee Strip." The writer of this article is able to add nothing to Mr. Rainey's account, except a few small details. These matters came to him from his old friend, W. E. Malaley, who has usually been credited with being the first person to find the slain Hennessey. It is quite apparent, however, that the other two members of the party who were killed with Hennessey had been removed and buried before Malaley's party appeared upon the scene. It was some seven years after the death and burial of Hennessey, that the writer first stood by and looked upon this grave a few feet to the west of the main track of the Chisholm Trail.

In 1871, the main line of the Atchison, Topeka, and Santa Fe Railway reached Newton, Kansas. This was the first point on any railway to shorten the route of the Chisholm Trail from Abilene. Newton is some sixty-five miles south of Abilene. In the spring of 1872, a branch line extended down from Newton to Wichita, Kansas, thus lopping off another twenty-six miles of the length of the trail. From 1872 to 1880 all freight and supplies going to the country south of Wichita were hauled from that point over the Chisholm Trail. The transporting of these supplies developed an extensive industry. The men engaging in this work were denominated "freighters." Their sturdy teams of mules, horses, or oxen wound their slow and laborious course to the southward, drawing their heavy conveyances.

Pat Hennessey was a professional freighter. His home was really on the trail. He spent much time, however, about Caldwell, Kansas, where he had many friends. Most of his time, when not on the trail, must have been spent at Wichita, as that was the terminus of the railway. He often stopped at the home of a Mr. Hartop, who lived upon a farm and operated the Alton post office five miles east and one mile south of Caldwell. Pat was a congenial, inoffensive, bewhiskered Irishman. Nothing is known of the antecedents of Hennessey before engaging in the business of a freighter. When a small boy, the writer lived with his parents but one mile from the Alton post office. Hartop came from Cleveland, Ohio, and for some reason the writer gained the idea that Hennessey came from the same place.

There is no inference, from the fact that nothing is known of the prior life of Hennessey, that there was anything dishonorable to conceal in the same. From the character and disposition of the little Irishman, it would be extremely rash and unjust to him even to imagine that there was anything of the kind existed. Persons on the frontier in these days were not interested in the past lives of their associates, and rarely ever made any inquiry as to such. In fact this was not a good practice to adopt or pursue. The writer lived for years among the persons who had been friends and associates of Hennessey, and none of them knew much more about him than has just been stated. He was a true friend, an honorable man, and recognized his obligations. When this was said of a man in those days, he was entitled to full fellowship in the highest society of the frontier.

When a small boy, in about 1879, the writer made almost daily trips to the Alton post office after the mail. He recalls very distinctly that on one of these occasions there was a lady visiting the Hartop family, who they stated was either a Mrs. or Miss Hennessey, and that she was either the wife or sister of Pat Hennessey. George Rainey, in his book dealing with the matter, makes reference to a statement made by Agent John D. Miles to the effect that he had received a letter from a sister of Hennessey, and this may have been the sister.

The information given as to the death of Hennessey, which has been adopted by the writer as the correct facts connected with the same, came from W. E. Malaley and from William Matteson. Mr. Rainey states that he talked to Mr. Matteson, and received his statements first hand. While the writer never saw Matteson, he has been informed by several persons who did talk to him that he stated substantially the same as he did to Mr. Rainey. The facts given by these parties constitute

all the authentic information that comes down to us relative
to this matter.

In the latter days of June, 1874, Pat Hennessey, George
Fant, and Thomas Calaway started from Wichita, Kansas, each
driving a wagon loaded with freight to be taken down the
Chisholm Trail and drawn by one or more teams of mules.
Fort Reno at that time had not been established, but there were
some soldiers in or about the Darlington Agency, beside many
other persons, and a horde of hungry Indians at this and other
points down the trail to be fed.   The destination of these
freighters was at some of these points.   There has been much
contention as to the exact date of the killing of Hennessey.
The writer had always understood that it occurred on July
5th, but Mr. Rainey states that it occurred on July 4th, and this
is doubtless the correct date.   In any event, the exact date is
not of any great importance.   The evening prior to the date
of the killing, this outfit arrived at the ranch at Buffalo Springs.
This was located near the present town of Bison.

The condition that existed at that time, so far as the Plains
Indians were concerned, was agitated and very dangerous.   This
had been the condition for some time.   It is unnecessary to
go into detail in reference to this, but it is sufficient to say
that a portion of the Cheyennes under Stone Calf had been in
open hostility, and many marauding bands were traveling over
the country.   Conditions had grown so bad at the Darlington
Agency that it was ordered by the Agent, John D. Miles, that
a party accompany him to Kansas.   The object of this trip
was two-fold.   One was to remove the women and children
from the agency on account of the dangerous condition from
the Indians; and the other was that Miles should go on to
Fort Leavenworth and procure more soldiers for the protection
of the agency.

In carrying out the arrangement stated, it is a question whether this party left Darlington Agency on the morning of July 4th or 5th. It is about thirty-five miles from the Agency to the Red Fork Ranch, and about twenty-four miles from Darlington to the station at Kingfisher. It is uncertain whether this party stopped over night at Kingfisher, but it is hardly probable, as it is certain that they arrived at Red Fork Ranch on the evening of July 5th. This party consisted of Agent Miles, J. A. Covington, Agency Clerk, Mrs. Sara Covington, wife of J. A. Covington and daughter of Brinton Darlington, Katie Covington, infant daughter of the Covingtons, W. E. Malaley, United States Marshal, one or more other ladies from the agency, a lieutenant, and two or more soldiers, including the driver of the ambulance in which the ladies rode. On the morning of July 6th, they started on their journey to the north from Red Fork Ranch, and after traveling about nine miles they came to the scene of the recent massacre.

When Hennessey and his party left Buffalo Springs on the morning of the killing, the keeper of the ranch counselled them not to go on down the trail, advising them that it was extremely dangerous, but Hennessey and his companions did not heed his advice, and continued on their journey. When they had proceeded about six miles, they approached the bluff which rises from the bottom of Turkey Creek on the east side. Some distance on down the trail and at a point which is at the south side of the present City of Hennessey, a draw intersects this bluff, coming from the east. This draw has rather steep banks, and the old trail veered to the east to cross the same.

Suddenly a bunch of horsemen, consisting of fifty or more, rode out onto the trail, coming out of this ravine and approaching the Hennessey party. The wagon driven by Hennessey was in advance of the others. There is some evidence that the rear wagons turned and started to run back toward Buffalo Springs. This was borne out from the fact that empty crates and cartons which had contained merchandise were found off of the trail and to the north of where the wagon driven by Hennessey was found. It was often the case on the frontier that persons pursued by Indians would throw out from their wagons all they could of their load. This served two purposes. It lightened the load, and the Indians would often stop to recover the merchandise and let the pursued gain time or escape.

William Matteson and his companion, who were carrying the mail, had advanced on south down the trail from Buffalo Springs until they were within two miles of the conflict. They could see the trouble, and turned and made their way back to Buffalo Springs. Matteson states that he and others from the ranch returned and recovered the bodies of Fant and Calaway, and took them back to the ranch, where they were buried in shallow graves. These graves must be entirely lost, as the writer never saw them.

When Miles and his party came upon the scene in the forenoon of July 6th, they found Hennessey tied to a wheel of his wagon and dead. The wagon had been set on fire, and was partially destroyed. It was so badly burned that one wheel had dropped down, and some oats which had been carried for feed for the mules had run out and was still burning. It was presumed that Hennessey had been tied to this wheel, the wagon burned while he was still alive, and he burned to death. This was judged to be the case, as they found no other marks of violence on him, but it appears that his body was so badly burned that it is not probable that such evidence would have been found even if it existed.

Matteson states that it was on July 4th that the killing took place, and that he left soon thereafter for Caldwell. This being the case, Matteson was gone on the forenoon of the 6th, when the Miles party arrived. It was presumed by Malaley and his associates that the killing had taken place the day previous, which was on July 5th. This was very vividly impressed on their minds, for the reason that they thought if they had started one day sooner on their trip, they would have reached this point on the forenoon of July 5th, and would have been ambushed and slaughtered instead of, or as well as, Hennessey. Hennessey was buried by the Miles party. Malaley did most of the work. The grave was shallow, but the interment was carried out in the best possible manner under the conditions. There were not sufficient implements available with which to dig the grave.

It is a wonder that as shallow as the body was buried, and being buried without any protection in the way of a box, that the wolves did not dig out the remains, but it was not done. It was in the direct pathway of the cattle coming up the trail, and the grave was tramped by them, in fact so much so that the buffalo grass finally grew close around the same. When the writer first saw it in 1881, the dirt was still loose on the top of the grave, and there was a slight elevation there. There was one or more rocks lying flat on it. On one of these rocks was carved Hennessey's initials and the year of his death. Malaley stated that he made an examination in the vicinity to ascertain the facts connected with the killing. He was at the time United States Marshal, and it was his duty to make a report of this happening.

His investigation revealed, in addition to what has been stated, that just below the bank where the draw entered from the east there were many pony tracks, indicating that they had stood there for some time. From appearances, the Indians had been concealed at this point to ambush parties coming down the trail, as the tracks continued from there to the place of the attack. Malaley stated there must have been fifty or more ponies in this bunch. He further stated that when they approached the ranch at Buffalo Springs there were a number of persons waiting there and standing out watching. These must have been parties who had arrived at this point from the north and, being afraid to proceed, had stopped. There was evidently very much agitation at this place at that time, and it is no wonder that there was some confusion as to the exact facts. Here were stranded this handful of people; far removed from any assistance, they did not know at what minute a band of these ruthless warriors would descend on them and they would be left as Hennessey was, mute evidence of what had happened.

These people were more interested in saving their scalps than remembering what had taken place. The Wichita Eagle, which was then a small weekly paper, in its issue of July 9, 1874, reported the killing as having occurred on Pond Creek.

Hennessey and his companions were killed by a roving band of young warriors who had detached themselves from Stone Calf's contingent of the Cheyennes. This was the conclusion reached within a short time after it happened. It is a well known fact that an Indian is the most difficult person to obtain information from. This is especially true when he does not want to impart it. The writer was well and intimately acquainted with many men who were closely associated with the Cheyennes, and it was only through cautious observation in seeking information that they fully determined the fact stated. They never were able to learn with any degree of certainty the number or identity of any members of this Indian band.

It has been claimed that Hennessey and his companions were killed by white outlaws. No motive has ever been shown for such a killing. It has been asserted that Charley Hasbrooks, who was hung at Wellington, Kansas, some time after this happening, took part in the killing and was hung for it. Charley Hasbrooks was a young lawyer. He never took part in any acts of violence. That was not his method of doing business. His offense was in manufacturing testimony and obtaining the release of outlaws through legal proceedings. He maintained offices at both Caldwell and Wellington. He was arrested in the old City Hotel at Caldwell, held in custody with two of his former clients at Wellington, and all of them were hung just south of Wellington, on Slate Creek, by a body of vigilantes who cleaned out southern Kansas of horse thieves and other outlaws.

Hennessey was buried by the side of his wagon, where found. When Old Oklahoma opened for settlement in 1889, a town was located on this beautiful site, overlooking the valley of Turkey Creek, which lay to the west. This town was named for the man who had died upon its site and had been buried within its borders some fifteen years before. In making the survey of the town, it was found that the grave was in the street. It was removed to a nearby lot, and a little park established around it. The fence has now been removed, and nothing marks the spot to which the grave was removed, nor does anything mark the spot of its original location.

After the opening of Old Oklahoma for settlement, W. E. Malaley settled at Hennessey, living there for many years. Shortly after the opening of the Cherokee Strip in 1893, the writer maintained an office in the City of Pond Creek, which was then the county seat of Grant County. On frequent occasions Mr. Malaley visited the office of the writer, and many hours were spent conversing as to the days on the frontier which had passed. On one of these occasions, in about the year 1900, when Mr. Malaley was in the office of the writer, Temple Houston, who was also a friend of the writer, came to his office, and met Malaley. The writer remarked that Malaley was the man who first found Hennessey after he was killed. Houston then stated that he had a gun which was presumed to have belonged to Hennessey. He did not describe it, as to whether it was a revolver or rifle. All firearms are known as guns by western people. The conversation turned upon the question as to the location where it was found. Houston stated that it was only a supposition that it was Hennessey's gun, and that he understood it was found some distance to the southwest of the grave. All parties present knew well the lay and condition of the ground in this locality, and it was presumed that the distance must have taken it over the bank going down into the bottom of Turkey Creek.

In this discussion between the parties mentioned the following argument on both sides of the proposition was presented as hereinafter set out: It would have been impossible for a gun or a pistol as this was to have remained undiscovered at any point near where the grave was located. The ground in this locality was covered by short buffalo grass, and a pistol could have been seen for a great distance; also, a gun was one of the first things that an Indian availed himself of when he killed a man. Had this one belonged to Hennessey, it is very probable that it would have been carried away by the Indians. Hennessey may have been captured some distance from his wagon, and taken back to the same, and might have lost this gun far away from the wagon.

This pistol was afterward presented to Dave Leahy by Houston, and is now in a collection in the Court House at Wichita. No one knows whether it was Hennessey's pistol or not. It may have been. In any event, regardless of the fact as to whom it belonged, it is a valuable and prized relic. In days gone by it belonged to some wanderer on the plains.

Mr. Rainey in describing this killing of Hennessey quotes a statement made by Mr. R. C. Williamson, in which he says that he was not in the country at the time the killing happened, but received the current information afterward as to the same. The statement as set out by Mr. Williamson is in effect the general statement told along the trail of the circumstance. He was well known to the writer, and spent much time on the trail. In this article he also states that he had a conversation with an Indian at Relay Creek, between Ft. Reno and Cantonment, in which the Indian informed him that he was shot by Hennessey at the time of this killing. Mr. Williamson says that this Indian was lame from the effects of this bullet. This is very valuable information, and in fact the only authentic information there is as to any resistance on the part of Hennessey. Mr. Williamson was a very reliable man, and this fact is important for the reason that it was so seldom that an Indian could be induced to talk, but when he did, he rarely, if ever, boasted and very seldom misrepresented.

In arriving at the facts as to what happened at the time of the killing of Hennessey, it must be borne in mind that the only information we have is that given by Matson and the party to which Malaley belonged. This tells us nothing as to the actual killing aside from the circumstantial evidence. This makes the information given by Mr. Williamson more valuable.

Some of Hennessey's close friends have advised the writer that he was not a gun-man, never carried a Winchester rifle, and was a very poor rifle shot. They further stated that he usually kept a pistol about his wagon, and also carried an army musket, which he used to kill prairie chicken with.

It has been stated heretofore as to Malaley having seen the pony tracks under the bank from where Hennessey was killed. In early days, when persons on the frontier found horse or pony tracks, the first thing they did was to examine them. It could be easily determined what sort of an outfit had left the tracks from such examination. Indian horses were always barefooted; cavalry horses wore what was known as government plates on their feet. Cowboy's horses were also unshod, but they never were found together in any great numbers.

Mr. Rainey in his article states that it has been claimed that tracks showing high-heeled boots were found at some point. Mr. Malaley has informed the writer, however, that a short time prior to the killing of Hennessey, some shots were fired one night around the Red Fork Ranch, and that on the following morning tracks were found in the sand near the house showing high heels. The fact that Hennessey was killed by a body of Cheyennes belonging to the dissatisfied element then at large is so well settled that the fact is no longer a debatable proposition.

Regardless of all the uncertain items entering into the details of this important and historical happening, the fact remains uncontroverted that Hennessey died—was killed—and buried at the time and place heretofore stated. He went down in the battle of life on the broad plains which he loved. He was buried by the side of the trail along which his wagons had so often traveled, on the beautiful landscape which he had viewed with admiration, little thinking that in future time his grave would be the principal landmark on the same.

CHAPTER XXVII.

A ROMANCE AND TRAGEDY OF THE PLAINS

That facts can be stranger and more tragic than fiction is truly exemplified in the life and death of Clement Bothamley. That the history of the events of the Chisholm Trail, which threaded the broad plains of the Western wilderness, should claim and include in the same a portion of the life and the death of one of the nobility of Old England, would seem at least peculiar; but such is the case.

Clement Bothamley was born in England in about the year 1852. He was a member of the English nobility. It is said that he was a lineal descendant of John Churchill, Duke of Marlborough. His family stood high and prospered through many generations. Their wealth had been great, but maintaining the dignity of their position had proven expensive, and through later generations the family fortunes waned. The statements herein contained are according to the information of Bothamley himself, and are doubtless in the main correct. Allowances may be made, however, in these statements, and consideration given to the fact that he was, as far as possible, advancing such as would either excuse or mitigate the apparently inexcusable acts and conduct of himself as a transgressor.

On account of the elevated position of Bothamley's family, and also of the depleted condition of its exchequer, it became imperative that Clement should marry some lady of his class, who not only had the class, but also possessed therewith a sufficient fortune and income to maintain his family in its normal position and standing.

As is usually the case, instead of following the prescribed and urgent course outlined in the matter, Clement proceeded to become much enamored of a very beautiful girl, who, while otherwise satisfactory, was minus the fortune. This fortune being consideration number one in the requirement which should be possessed by his companion in this matrimonial adventure, his family opposed the same, and the affair was broken off. The lady of his choice reluctantly but gracefully retired from the scene, and married a soldier by the name of Captain Millick. Clement, in obedience to the wishes and dictates of his family, married an elegant lady of high standing. She possessed the attribute of great wealth, but was minus the beauty. It seemed to be very difficult to find a lady who had all the qualifications, and the fortune being paramount, it was given preference. It may be said for this newly acquired Mrs. Bothamley that she was well educated, highly respected, and proved to be a very sensible woman.

As was customary in such cases, immediately upon the marriage of Bothamley, his newly acquired wife delivered to him all her family fortune. All the property which she possessed thus passed into his hands and into his keeping, except that he did not keep it, but proceeded as far as possible to spend it immediately. This marriage, as usual in such cases, did not prosper well. Mrs. Bothamley was a patient and loving wife. No charges, which would tend in any way to bring about the results and the matters and things which subsequently occurred, were ever made against her. Two children, a boy and a girl, were born to Bothamley and his wife, and the family, under all normal rules of the game, should have been prosperous and happy. Clement Bothamley was a handsome young aristocrat, and lived up to his standing and reputation. He spent lavishly, and was away from his home, his wife, and family, most of the time. Even in that day and age of the world, his dissipation mounted to the high water mark—to the limit. His wife, with only her children as associates to console her, went through a dreary and forsaken world without complaint. She was a victim of Fate and of a brutal wretch of a husband.

These conditions continued until the year 1877, at which time Captain Mellick, the husband of Bothamley's first infatuation, died, leaving his widow with two children, and no means whatever. This widow, in order to earn a living for herself and children, was soon compelled to seek employment, while her mother cared for the children. In the fall of 1878, while Clement Bothamley was traveling through distant portions of England, he unexpectedly again met Mrs. Hattie Mellick. Without hesitation and without one thought for the sorrow of his wife and family, Bothamley sought to renew with this lady the association which had been dashed to pieces on the rocks years before on account of the lack of a financial navigator to guide it. In justice to Mrs. Mellick, it may be said that she was a conscientious woman, and that she at first refused to consider again the attentions of Bothamley, but through his persistent efforts, and using the same charm in this affair which characterized his life and dealings with women, and which eventually brought him disaster and ruin, he finally again won her favor.

Mrs. Bothamley became aware of conditions, and did all she could to prevent the result that followed, but when all hope was lost, she bowed her head to the inevitable. This she did with a grace befitting her long line of noble ancestry, and proved herself a soldier in defeat as well as in victory. Clement Bothamley sold the remnant of the fortune which he had acquired through his wife, and as appeared later, made arrangements whereby after his departure remittances and payments on the same would be sent to him across the ocean. The full particulars in reference to this part of the affair have never been divulged, but after he settled in America he made repeated trips to the East, and, on account of some prior arrangement, always returned with considerable sums of money.

In the year 1879, Bothamley, taking with him a large portion of the remnant of his wife's fortune, in company with Mrs. Hattie Mellick, took passage from Liverpool to New York City. They sailed under the name of Mr. and Mrs. Mellick. On arriving in New York City, they departed for points in the West. They visited Chicago and other places, then in the early part of the year 1880 appeared at Florence, Kansas, and finally in March, 1880, settled at Newton in that state. At this place at that time were residing a number of English families, and Bothamley and his companion, passing under the name of Clement Bothamley and wife, settled among and associated with the members of this English settlement. They built at Newton a large and commodious house, which was considered a mansion in those days.

These new members of the English colony were reputed to be quite wealthy, aristocratic, and to belong to the nobility of England, and the English colony accepted them as such. At this time Life spread out its beautiful broad vista before these transgressors, exposing one continuous bed of roses. This apparently was the fruit of their treachery, deception, and transgression of the laws of God and man. Fate, however, with a cruel and relentless hand, brings its day of reckoning. In June, 1880, suddenly appearing over the bed of roses, came the all conquering monster of Death and bore away Mrs. Hattie Mellick, otherwise known as Mrs. Hattie Bothamley. She was buried in the cemetery at Newton under the name of Mrs. Hattie Bothamley. Fate had spread this beautiful view before these parties as if to make their disappointment more acute.

However, the disposition of Clement Bothamley seemed to even defy the normal characteristics of men. After the death of his companion, it would seem that the future would have appeared dark and dreary to him. It did not affect him in the least; a few days after the death and burial of this woman, who had left her children, family, home, relatives, friends, and native country, and crossed the ocean to a strange and distant land with him, only to locate her own grave at the end of the trail, he was visiting at the home of another English family in Newton, when he met Nellie Bailey. She was the wife of Shannon Bailey, a wealthy and prosperous business man formerly of Newton, Kansas, who had located in northern Kansas, where he was engaged in the banking business. Mrs. Bailey was stopping a short time in Newton, her former home, before joining her husband. Clement Bothamley, upon meeting her, immediately set forth to make a new conquest in the person of Mrs. Bailey. She was at that time a young and beautiful girl, being only seventeen years of age.

Here, it will be necessary for the present to leave Clement Bothamley and take up the antecedents of Mrs. Nellie Bailey.

Nellie Bailey's maiden name was Nellie C. Benthusen. She was born at Algonquin, Illinois, on September 19, 1863. Her parents in 1871 moved with their two children, Nellie and her brother, from their former home to Harvey County, Kansas. There they settled on a farm near Halstead. Nellie obtained a fair education, being much above the average for the time. She was sent East, and attended a seminary at Rockford, Illinois. While she was attending school at this place, her parents moved from their home on the farm to the City of Newton, which was then and still is the county seat of Harvey County. There seem to have been strewn many boulders in the pathway of Nellie Bailey, similar to those found in that of Clement Bothamley.

While Nellie Bailey was attending school at Rockford she met a young man by the name of Alvin Lakeside. With full faith in the correctness of their own judgment, these two young people concluded that they were well suited to each other, which they may have been, and they agreed that they would be married as soon as convenient. Lakeside came to Newton and built a residence, which was to be occupied by them after their marriage. The weather was fair and the sky was clear for these two young people, but as many times happen, there were unforeseen breakers ahead. Nellie was barely sixteen years of age at that time, and the match she had planned, from a financial view, did not appeal to her parents.

About this time Shannon Bailey, a wealthy, prosperous, and intelligent business man of Newton, appeared on the scene. Although he was much older than Nellie, the handsome, sixteen-year-old girl suited him, and he proceeded to drive his suit for her with the same effectiveness that had made him successful in the business world. He was a man to whom no one could find any objection, and he suited Nellie's parents. The date of the wedding had been set for Nellie and Lakeside, but the engagement was broken, and immediately thereafter, in the year 1879, Nellie and Shannon Bailey were married at Newton. Had Shannon Bailey known the result of this marriage, he would perhaps never have appeared for the ceremony.

Although Shannon Bailey was well established, had a prosperous business, had the best of standing, and was well liked at Newton, after his marriage his wife desired that they move away and establish themselves at some other place. In order to comply with her wishes, in 1880 Shannon Bailey went to northern Kansas, where he purchased a controlling interest in a bank, and prepared a desirable home for himself and wife. He had gone to look after his business at this place and arrange things to receive her, while his wife had remained behind for a short time to visit among their friends and acquaintances, when she was soon to follow.

While so preparing for her departure she visited at the home of an acquaintance, an English lady, and it was here that she first met Clement Bothamley. This is the meeting to which we have heretofore referred. Had Clement Bothamley and Nellie Bailey been able at this time to have foreseen the ultimate result of this meeting, they would both certainly have agreed never to meet again. To anyone observing the relentless hand of Fate and the unerring blows that it deals to those in this world who transgress the laws of right, justice, and equity, and the reward that persons usually reap for such transgressions, even on this side of the grave, it would seem useless to inflict upon them further punishment in the World to come.

At this time Clement Bothamley was a man of about twenty-eight years of age, but even though he was young in years, during the portion of this twenty-eight years since he was a youth, he had burned the candle at both ends, and even at this time his constitution was undermined from dissipation. While he was still handsome and dashing in appearance, the marks of his past life were being written upon his face; his physical being had begun to yield to the growth of the seed that had been sown years before, and pointed to the breakdown that was soon to come.

Nellie Bailey soon departed for the home prepared for her by her husband, but from that time on she was evidently in communication with Clement Bothamley, and all the wealth and all the favors bestowed upon her by a kind and devoted husband failed to satisfy her. She was restless and discontented. For this reason her husband soon sold his business in northern Kansas, although it was prospering, and he and his wife entered upon a tour of protracted travel. This they continued during the next several years. During this time they visited most points of interest in the United States. Also, during this time Mrs. Bailey doubtless met Clement Bothamley a number of times by pre-arrangement, at different points. In the year 1882, she left her husband while they were traveling in the East. She first went to the home of a cousin at Newark, New Jersey, and from there to the home of an aunt in Wisconsin. When she left her husband she took with her a vast amount of expensive jewelry and other movable possessions which he had bought for her.

During the time the Baileys were traveling, Clement Bothamley sold his home in Newton. With the proceeds of this sale and other money he had acquired from the East, he had purchased a ranch of four quarter sections of land near Sedgwick City, located in the southwestern portion of Harvey County. This portion of the country at that time was largely unsettled, and in addition to his section of land which he had purchased, he had a large grazing range around the same. Through his experience in the United States, Bothamley had grown to be a shrewd and prosperous business man. He was reckoned as a good trader and dealer in stock, of which he bought and sold a great amount. He bought southern cattle brought up the Chisholm Trail, wintered, and sold them, and in all his stock trading transactions he made money. He had a well-equipped ranch, with cow-hands and servants, and was considered prosperous.

In about June, 1883, Bothamley announced to the persons living with him on his ranch, and to other friends, that his sister Bertha was coming from England, and was going to live with him. In the month of June of this year, Nellie Bailey left the home of her aunt in Wisconsin, traveling on the train, passed through her old home town of Newton without being recognized or observed, and went on to Valley Center, about twenty miles beyond Newton. There she was met by Clement Bothamley, and they traveled from there to his ranch near Sedgwick City, about twenty miles distant. Here he introduced her as Bertha Bothamley, his sister, who had just arrived from their old home in England. She lived at this ranch, passing under the name of Bertha Bothamley, for about sixty days. During this time she remained as much in seclusion as possible, and was never recognized, although her parents and childhood friends lived at the City of Newton, the county seat of the county.

From about the time that Nellie Bailey came to the Bothamley ranch, and up to the latter part of August, Bothamley was preparing for a trip to the South, where he could procure a larger and more extensive range for his stock, his destination being at some point in Texas. In his preparation for this trip, he built a house on wheels, which was drawn by a number of spans of oxen, and in the latter part of August, 1883, he departed on this journey. His outfit consisted of from twenty-two to twenty-five hundred head of sheep, a number of oxen, saddle horses, a spring wagon drawn by a fine team of horses, and one or more milch cows led behind the wagon on which was borne the house. The persons going forward with this aggregation were Clement Bothamley, his sister Bertha, otherwise Nellie Bailey, a lady who was being taken along as her companion and whose name was Mrs. Lacey, and two boys, one of whom was to drive the ox teams drawing the home on wheels, or car, and the other to drive the herd.

Thus they started with this equipment, traveling by slow stages southward toward the Indian Territory, and to make connection with the Chisholm Trail. Almost immediately, they encountered bad weather; it rained almost incessantly. Clement Bothamley was unfitted physically from the effects of his past life to stand the rigors of such a trip. He had been for some time past the victim of sciatic rheumatism. From exposure, this ailment rapidly grew worse, and he suffered excruciating pain. When the outfit reached Mount Hope, only a short distance from his ranch, he was unable to proceed further, and he was compelled to remain there in the care of a doctor, while the rest of the party journeyed on with the outfit.

They went south, striking the Chisholm Trail and crossing the state line between Kansas and the Indian Territory at Caldwell. They followed this trail southward, past the Pond Creek Ranch, and forded the Salt Fork River. A short distance south of this river, at a point near the present City of Pond Creek, they turned to the southeast. They traveled some three miles in this direction, camping on Wild Horse Creek. This was done in order to make a camp where their stock could have grass for grazing and to avoid the extensive herds traveling up the trail. From this point Mrs. Bailey returned to Mount Hope to bring on Clement Bothamley. Mrs. Lacey had stopped at Caldwell as they passed through that town. She did this to visit some persons with whom she was acquainted, and was to return with Mrs. Bailey and Bothamley as they came back, and go with them to join the outfit.

On arriving at Mount Hope, it was discovered that Bothamley's condition was not improved, and it was with difficulty that he could even walk, but he was placed in the spring wagon, and they started back to the camp on Wild Horse. On reaching Caldwell it was learned that Mrs. Lacey had been sick and was not able to return with them to the camp. Arrangements were made to leave her at Caldwell, with the understanding that she would subsequently take the stage running south over the Chisholm Trail, and meet the rest of the party at Fort Reno, some hundred and twenty-five miles down the trail.

Mrs. Bailey and Bothamley went on to the camp, and the outfit moved on its journey down the trail. Bothamley's condition was such, however, that they made little progress, and were compelled to remain in camp for days at a time. Bad weather was again encountered, and all the members of the

outfit bore a very dejected and discouraged appearance, which
appearance was not deceiving. Bothamley lay in his bed in
the car; he was scarcely able to move, and in extreme pain.
He was continuously taking morphine to alleviate the same.
The herd must be looked after both day and night, and Nellie
Bailey and the boys were compelled to attend to this, which
they did during all kinds of weather. During the rains they
were much of the time soaking wet and exposed to all the
elements.

In this condition the outfit reached Hackberry Creek, about
nine miles south of the present City of Enid. They arrived
at this place on the evening of October 7, 1883. It is thus seen
that they had made but very little progress, not being over one
hundred and sixty miles from where they had started, and
having been on the road about two months.

Hackberry is a small creek, having only pools of water
standing in the same, except in flood time. It flows into Skeleton Creek, which was then often known as Ephraim Creek,
which in turn flows into the Cimarron River. The clouds hung
low, the night was dark and dreary, with a drizzling rain.
The boys caring for the stock were young and inexperienced in
such work, especially under the conditions that existed. Nellie
Bailey had been compelled to assist them during the day and
early night in handling the stock.   She was weary and exhausted from her exposure and the rigors of her care. She
left the boys to guard and care for the herd as best they could,
sleeping and watching in turns, and she retired to the car for
rest. Bothamley was in agony from his ailment, and lay upon
his couch in a bewildered condition. Nellie Bailey had gone
to sleep upon a cot in the car. Above the head of Bothamley,
on his couch or bed, hung an ivory handled Colt .45 six-shooter,
one of his prized possessions.

Suddenly, just before the break of day in the morning, a loud explosion and roar was heard in the car, and Nellie Bailey leaped from her cot to find the lights extinguished and everything in utter darkness. The night outside of the car was intensely black, being just before daylight, and a mist being over the landscape. She attempted to arouse Bothamley, was unsuccessful, and rushed from the car to seek the boys who were attending the herd.

One of them went to the car, and returned in fear, stating that he could get no reply from the interior, and that he did not want to further endanger his life. The other boy, being older, then went to the car and succeeded in lighting a lantern. When he did so, he found Bothamley lying on the couch with one arm dropped across his breast. His pistol was by his side, where it had fallen from the other hand. A large hole was observed just below the right eye, where a bullet from his gun had entered his head. Bothamley was dead, and his blood had saturated the immediate part of the bed surrounding his head. There these parties were, in the midst of terrible weather, in an uncivilized country, with this stock to care for, and a dead man on their hands.

Had the past life of both Clement Bothamley and Nellie Bailey been laid before a stranger, and he could have looked upon this scene, he would have remarked at the true reckoning that Fate brings. In this condition they remembered that a couple of wagons had passed them going north just before dark the previous evening. They knew that these men and wagons could not have gone far before nightfall, and were doubtless camped a short distance up the trail, and one of the boys started to find them. These wagons were found about daylight, still in camp. The parties with the wagons consisted of two men, who returned with the boy to the camp on Hackberry Creek. One of these men was Ralph P. Collins, one of the owners of the Red Fork Ranch, located some twenty-five miles to the south on the trail, the location being at the present City of Dover, Oklahoma. The other man was a rancher in the same vicinity, whose name was Donaldson.

These two men immediately took in the situation, and rendered the parties all the assistance possible. The dead man was taken to the Skeleton Ranch, located back up the trail at a point now on the eastern portion of the townsite of the City of Enid. A coffin was prepared from such scraps of lumber as could be found at the ranch. One party has informed the writer that a portion of the stable door and a part of a goods' box were used in making this casket. There Clement Bothamley, an English nobleman, claimed to be a direct descendant of John Churchill, Duke of Marlborough, was laid to rest in a shallow grave a short distance from the Skeleton Ranch. His grave was made near several other graves of persons who had preceded him in death, and who had died from violence.

After the interment of Bothamley, the parties started on south down the trail. On the evening of about October 12th they reached a point about twelve miles north of the Red Fork Ranch. This location must have been on Turkey Creek, near the present City of Hennessey. While in camp at this place, four officers came down from Caldwell, Kansas, and arrested Nellie Bailey and the two boys for the murder of Clement Bothamley. The officer in charge in making this arrest was Chris Hollister, Deputy United States Marshal, having jurisdiction in the Indian Territory. He was accompanied by a detective from the East, who had been following Clement Bothamley. The other two officers accompanying him were Hendry Brown and Ben Wheeler, marshal and deputy marshal respectively of Caldwell. These prisoners were returned to Wichita, Kansas, and placed in jail. The remains of Clement

Bothamley were disinterred, removed to Newton, Kansas, and there buried at the side of Hattie Mellick or Hattie Bothamley.

Soon it was discovered that the girl traveling under the name of Bertha Bothamley, and posing as a sister of the dead Englishman, was no other than Nellie Bailey, once the wife of Shannon Bailey, who had been one of the most influential and prosperous men of the City of Newton, located only twenty-six miles north from the City of Wichita where she was held in jail. It was further discovered that Nellie Bailey, before they started on their fatal journey, had received deeds from Clement Bothamley for all his property. The detective from the East had followed Clement Bothamley, and his entire life, both before and after he left England, was bared. The entire life of Nellie Bailey, from her girlhood to the time the prison doors at Wichita closed on her, was exposed to the world.

This offense being charged to have been committed in the Indian Territory, the United States District Court of Kansas had jurisdiction of the case. The prisoners were presented for preliminary examination before a United States Commissioner, and Nellie Bailey was held on a charge of murder, and the two boys were held as witnesses. Hon. J. W. Ady, a lawyer of Newton, Kansas, who later was well known to the writer, and who was an able criminal lawyer, with a wide reputation as such, was employed to defend Nellie Bailey. W. E. Stanley and T. B. Wall joined as attorneys for the defense. Both of these men were eminent lawyers. W. E. Stanley was later Governor of the State of Kansas, and T. B. Wall was later District Judge.

Nellie Bailey was indicted by the grand jury, and her case was called for trial in the United States District Court at Wichita on the 15th day of January, 1885. The case was tried before C. G. Foster, then United States Judge for that district. It was prosecuted by Col. James R. Hallowell, who was an able lawyer and United States District Attorney at that time.

He was assisted by Charles Hatton, Assistant United States District Attorney. Col. Hallowell was the same person who was afterwards known as "Prince Hal," and who is famous in the campaign in the early nineties, in which he was defeated for Congress by the alleged "sockless" Jerry Simpson. This case was tried over a period of some five days, and at the end of the trial the jury within a few minutes returned a verdict of "not guilty."

On this trial there was really little difference in the testimony of the witnesses. The undisputed evidence appeared substantially as heretofore set out. The only damaging testimony against the defendant was the fact that Bothamley had turned much money and property over to her before his death, but taking into consideration their relations when he did so, he must have desired her to have the same in case of his death. The writer has understood that this property was not retained by Nellie Bailey, but was turned over by her to the rightful wife of Clement Bothamley in England.

The evidence further showed that Bothamley had suffered from sciatic rheumatism for several years, that it had gradually grown worse, and that he had become a morphine addict. The doctor who treated him at Mount Hope testified that Bothamley was not rational much of the time, that he was a chronic user of morphine, and that he had stated repeatedly in the presence of the doctor and his wife while being treated by him that he was going to commit suicide. The two boys accompanying the outfit testified that Bothamley repeatedly threatened to commit suicide, and on at least two occasions they had been compelled to restrain him by force from so doing, at which times they had taken his gun away from him. Nellie Bailey at the time of this trial was twenty-one years of age and beautiful, but had evidently overestimated the result of her powers over men, and was a victim of her own folly.

It was a curious co-incidence in connection with this case, that of the four officers who made this arrest of Nellie Bailey none of them lived to see the case tried; all of them died violent deaths. All of these parties, except the detective, were well known to the writer. The detective, who followed the case from the East, it is said, was killed in some encounter. Chris Hollister, who was a brave and respected Deputy United States Marshal, was killed in attempting to arrest a horse thief near Hunnewell, Kansas. Hendry Brown and Ben Wheeler were both killed by a mob at Medicine Lodge, Kansas, while attempting to escape after their capture following the killing of two officers of a bank while attempting to rob the same.

In this trial at Wichita the history of the life of Clement Bothamley was published to the world. It told of the deeds of the man who had battled with Fate in two continents, and whose life and deeds had left behind him a trail of misery. Nellie Bailey, leaving her associations with Clement Bothamley behind her, soon departed to some unknown portion of the West. The history and life of the Chisholm Trail continued on for almost six years after that fatal night in October, 1883, when Clement Bothamley, racked with pain on the lonely prairies near the little branch of Hackberry Creek, nine miles south of the present thriving City of Enid in the then Cherokee Strip on this trail, sentenced himself to death, and sent a bullet through his own brain.

During these remaining years the herds continued to travel up this ancient trail past the scene of the termination of the trip of this caravan to the South. It was traveled by all classes of people, including the missionaries of the West, wandering over the land with their Bibles in their saddle pockets, and the most dangerous outlaws of the times, who lived and died beyond the law. The history of the deeds of these men make up the history of the trail. The actors in this romance and tragedy of the plains played their part in this great drama of revolving events constituting the history of this great thorough-fare of the West. It is not for us to say whether it was good or bad; suffice it to say that it is a part of the history of the trail.

CHAPTER XXVIII.

KILLING OF ED. SHORT AND CHARLEY BRYANT

In the preceding pages the writer has set out principally the acts of men performed within the law, and a brief outline of the lives and works of men connected with the Chisholm Trail, who made the world better by their living. The recording of such does not constitute all of the history of any enterprise, country, or portion of the same. All history is crowded with deeds of lawlessness, and without recording such, the complete history of the subject dealt with cannot be written. It is not done to perpetuate the infamy of the men who transgress the law, but for the purpose of setting forth the correct and full history as it exists. We do not make the history; we only record it. Further, the final result almost invariably illustrates that crime does not pay, and preserves the history of the gallant acts of the men representing the legal side of the controversy. In view of the foregoing explanation, the writer, in this chapter, and in a number of the succeeding chapters, will deal with subjects involving men who lived, for a portion of their lives at least, beyond the law and died as a result of such transgression.

The matter herein recorded happened on the Chisholm Trail shortly before the track of the same was obliterated by the plow of the homesteader. The date was in the early days of August, 1891. In order to more clearly appreciate the facts as herein set out, and the location where the same happened, it is necessary to make a brief explanation as to the surroundings and the location.

The traveler going northward up the Chisholm Trail from the Red Fork Ranch on the Cimarron River passed through a succession of glades and openings in the blackjack trees, which skirted the river on the north for many miles on either side of the trail. This journey took him to the grave of Pat Hennessey. This point was in the portion of the country known as Old Oklahoma, which had been opened for settlement in 1889, and on this August day, 1891, the City of Hennessey had been established near this grave. Journeying on northward seven miles further, the traveler came to Buffalo Springs, the last named point being just north of the line of Old Oklahoma and in the Cherokee Strip. The Cherokee Strip at that time had not been opened to settlement, but the trail south of the same had been divided up on the farms along its route. Buffalo Springs, prior to the opening of the Cherokee Strip to settlement, was only a camping place along the route of the trail. Now near the same stands the City of Bison.

The Chicago, Rock Island and Pacific Railway had been built south across the Cherokee Strip and Old Oklahoma in the summer of 1889, and a station known as Waukomis established at a point seven miles south of the present City of Enid. The traveler on the old trail, going north, passed over unbroken prairie after leaving Buffalo Springs. Six miles north of this point, after the building of the railroad, was located this station of Waukomis, which at that time consisted of a section house, a box car on the siding, which served as an office, and cattle pens, which were used for loading small bunches of cattle. At this point now stands the prosperous little city of Waukomis. Past this station at the time of this happening, as if waiting for the long herds of cattle to appear again and travel over the same, stretched the Chisholm Trail.

During the few years immediately preceding the happening of this event, which occurred on the evening of August 3, 1891, an organization of outlaws, known as The Dalton Gang, had infested a large portion of northern and eastern Oklahoma.

This organization, in addition to the Dalton Brothers, included Bill Doolin, Dick Broadwell, Bill Powers, Charley Bryant, and at times, others. Among the deeds of outlawry committed by this band was the robbery of the train on the Atchison, Topeka, and Santa Fe Railway at Red Rock, Oklahoma, in June, 1891. Both the passenger and express cars were robbed at this time. However, only a small amount of money was procured. During the robbery Charley Bryant observed the telegraph operator in the depot sending a message over the wire, giving notice of the hold-up, and he fired upon the operator, killing him instantly. Bryant was sometimes known as Black Faced Charley, on account of certain black spots on his face, said to be powder burns, and he has also been designated as Black Eyed Charley.

After this robbery the participants scattered, and a wide search was being made for the various members of the gang. At this time Ed. Short was a Deputy United States Marshal, and was also marshal of the City of Hennessey. During the memorable county seat war in Stephens County, Kansas, he had been marshal of the city of Woodsdale in that county. It was during this war that it had been necessary to send out the state militia to quiet the contention and violence, and it was as a result of this war that Sam Woods was killed. Short had filled many positions as a peace officer, and was considered a fearless and effective man. He had spent much time at Caldwell, Kansas, prior to the opening of Old Oklahoma to settlement, and the writer knew him well.

About the first of August following the Red Rock robbery, information was brought to Short that there was a man with a saddle horse sick near Buffalo Springs, and it was surmised by Short that he might be one of the train robbers wanted. There was in Hennessey at that time a boy by the name of George Baldwin, who had removed to Hennessey from Caldwell, Kansas, after the opening of that country for settlement. Baldwin was procured to go out and see the sick man and persuade him to come into Hennessey for treatment. This was desired by Short so that he could ascertain if possible the identity of the stranger. Baldwin went out and found the party, and it was learned that he was suffering from malaria, had had a chill, and was rolled up in his blanket on the prairie near Buffalo Springs. Baldwin prevailed upon him and induced him to go into Hennessey, where he could receive medical treatment. The sick man on going into town took and occupied a room at the Rock Island Hotel, a two-story frame building.

Short satisfied himself, after the stranger came into town, that he was one of the persons engaged in the Red Rock robbery, and arrested him. He did this after using strategy in getting into the room when food was brought to him and getting the drop on the suspect. When the stranger saw that resistance meant sure death, he surrendered. He proved to be Charley Bryant, one of the worst members of the Dalton Gang.

After the capture was made, the most serious question arose. This question was as to what disposition could be made of the prisoner. There were but few jails in this new country at that time, none of which were located on the line of the railroad which passed through Hennessey. To take the prisoner across the country to the jail at Guthrie meant sure delivery by the other members of his gang. Short remained awake and guarded him all night on the night of August 2nd. It was finally concluded to take him to the Federal jail at Wichita, Kansas, some hundred and forty miles north of Hennessey.

A Mr. Overton, who was a Deputy United States Marshal and agent of the railway at Hennessey at that time, assisted Marshal Short in looking after the prisoner during the next day, which was Sunday. The north bound passenger train arrived at Hennessey about five o'clock that evening, and Short took passage on the same with his prisoner, bound for Wichita. The marshal had at first handcuffed the prisoner's hands behind him, but he complained so much about this position hurting him that Short changed the handcuffs before starting on this journey, placing the prisoner's hands in front of him. This change afterward cost Ed. Short his life.

On this journey Marshal Short carried the Winchester rifle taken from the prisoner at the time of his arrest. It was a well known and realized fact that the members of Bryant's gang, who were still at large, were as desperate characters as were found in the West, or that ever had been in any country, and that they would take any chances to rescue the prisoner. For this reason, instead of taking the prisoner into the coaches, he was placed in the baggage car. This car was used as a combined baggage and mail car. It was equipped with a set of pigeon holes for the sorting of letters. Into one of these pigeon holes had been stuck a .45 caliber Colt six-shooter, the same either belonging to the express agent or being the pistol taken from Bryant when arrested.

The first stop of the train on its journey northward was at Waukomis, thirteen miles from Hennessey. It was realized that if an attempted rescue of the prisoner was to be made by his associates, that Waukomis was the logical place for such attempt. On nearing this station Marshal Short left his prisoner in the baggage car, directing the agent to keep an eye on him while Short went out onto the platform to watch for any attempt at rescue. The marshal then went out onto the platform, continued to the bottom of the steps, and leaned out, looking up and down the track to see if anyone was in sight.

As soon as the officer stepped from the baggage car, Bryant, unnoticed by the baggage agent, reached into the pigeon hole, and seized in his two handcuffed hands the pistol placed there. He then ordered the agent at the point of this pistol to open the door for him, and to say nothing. This the agent was compelled to do. Charley Bryant then stepped out onto the platform of the car with this pistol seized in his two handcuffed hands. As Marshal Short turned from his observation along the track, he faced his prisoner with this pistol pointed at him. The marshal was quick to act. He whirled, and the Winchester rifle in his hands sent forth missles of sure death to everything in front of it. The pistol in Bryant's hands roared repeatedly until all six of the loads in the same were discharged. In this affray Marshal Short fired eight shots from his Winchester rifle.

It is a question as to which fired first, the outlaw or the officer. In all probability, however, the first shot fired by each of the parties was the fatal shot. Marshal Short was on the east side of the car during this shooting, and before he ceased firing at the prisoner, Bryant fell to the west and died instantly. The marshal survived long enough to help place the prisoner back on the train, and then lie down on a couch, but in a few minutes he was also dead.

At the time of the happening of this deplorable affair, the writer was at home in Caldwell, Kansas, being home on a vacation from school. The information of these killings was immediately sent out over the wire, and the further information was sent to Caldwell that the bodies of the officer and outlaw would be taken off the train at that point and arrangements should be made to care for them. The writer, being well acquainted with the marshal at Caldwell, was requested with other available parties to help render this service. This was done, and the body of Marshal Short was taken to the Schaeffer Undertaking Parlors, and the body of Charley Bryant was temporarily removed to the City building. An examination was made as to the wounds on the dead bodies.

There was but one fatal wound on each of them. A bullet from the pistol fired by Bryant had entered the marshal's shoulder and ranged down, evidently reaching vital organs of his body in its course. Outlaw Bryant had a bullet hole drilled by the Winchester rifle held by the officer squarely in the center of his breast, about even with the heart. This wound must have completely severed the spinal cord. The bodies of both the marshal and the outlaw were prepared by the Schaeffer Undertaking Parlors, and the body of Short was delivered to his mother in the East, and that of the outlaw was turned over to relatives. There was one thousand dollars reward for the capture of Bryant, and this sum was paid to the mother of the slain officer.

The writer having known the marshal in his lifetime, and having helped in caring for the slain desperado, remembers very well the impression created by each of these men. Marshal Short was a blond man, of large and robust physique and commanding appearance. He had the appearance of a fearless and effective officer, which he was. He had come from the State of Indiana, but the West was his adopted home, and he sought employment where his services in the interest of law enforcement were desired.

Charley Bryant was a Texan born and raised, coming from Wise County, Texas. He was insignificant in appearance. He was not only small, but very slender, bearing the characteristics of a man who had spent his life in the saddle. He had served as a respected cowboy in Texas for many years, but the last eight or ten years of his life had been spent in Oklahoma, and mainly in association with outlaws. His companions during this period had been desperate characters, and he grew to have no superior among men beyond the law. He had been sick for some time before his death, which may have caused his diminutive appearance to be more pronounced after his death.

In the exchange of shots during this episode another passenger on the train, John Dobson, a citizen and resident of Caldwell, Kansas, was shot in the arm by a ball which passed through the car.

This was one of the last tragedies to occur on this ancient trail in this vicinity, and the old trail, together with its scenes of violence, its usefulness and services rendered to humanity, has passed away.

CHAPTER XXIX.

THE TALBOTT RAID

The Talbott Raid is the usual designation of a battle upon the streets of Caldwell, Kansas, between the officers and citizens on one side and four Texas men, who sought to take the town, on the other. A recital of this affair might not be considered as having any place among historical matters connected with the Chisholm Trail. Caldwell, Kansas, however, was located on this trail as originally established. After the railway reached Caldwell it was for years the terminus of the same, and these Texans after escaping traveled down or near it in making their escape. Further, the entire history of Caldwell is, in fact, a part of the history of this trail.

This battle took place on December 17, 1881. The events in detail leading up to the same are not well remembered by the writer or anyone else. This is especially true for the reason that these events were not, for the times when they occurred, out of the ordinary, and were such that there was nothing to impress them upon the mind of anyone.

In the fall of 1881, there appeared in Caldwell a man representing himself to be a Texas cowboy. He had, in all probability, come from the South with one of the later drives of the season. He gave his name as James Talbott, and his general appearance showed him to be from the southern cattle country. Soon after the appearance of this man in Caldwell, he was noticed to be in company with a woman, whom he represented to be, and who may have been, his wife, who had come there to join him. Talbott and this woman settled down to keep house in the northeast portion of town.

Soon thereafter there appeared in the town three other men, each of whom was accompanied by a woman who was represented to be his wife. These men also all claimed to be from Texas, and all claimed to be cowboys, and all had the appearance of being typical men of the southern cattle country. These men, together with their women companions, were all close associates of Talbott and the woman accompanying him. These three men gave their names and were known as James Martin, Bob Munsin, and Bob Bigtree. These parties all settled down to housekeeping in the vicinity of Talbott's residence. They had the appearance of being cowboys who were simply resting up with their wives from the season's work on the range.

The four men and their companions soon entered upon a life which they would perhaps designate as, "one continuous round of pleasure." They all visited and spent much time at the dance hall and bar connected with the same, and they visited the saloons and gambling halls; in fact they spent most of their time at these places. None of them went long without a drink of some kind, and on various occasions they became very drunk.

People generally did not inquire into the affairs of these four men and their women companions. In fact it was not uncommon at that time for this class of people to settle down in that community for a few months and then pass on. Also, in those days, it was not considered polite to attempt under such circumstances to inquire into a stranger's antecedents.

Various ones of these four men were arrested for drunkenness or disturbing the peace on different occasions, and James Talbott was at least one time detained in the city jail to sober up. This interference by the authorities with what these people considered their inalienable prerogative caused an overgrown feeling of resentment in their whisky-befuddled brains.

It is also probable that the finances of these parties grew low. The life that they were living evidently required a great amount of capital to maintain. Like most men of their kind, they were liberal spenders, and did not appear to know the value of money. The condition of their finances was perhaps the cause of their arrangement for departure from the city, and this increased their feeling of resentment. This resentment, so far as anyone could ever ascertain, was the sole cause of the trouble that followed. No one has ever been able to learn of any other motive for the outbreak.

The City of Caldwell, prior to the event herein dealt with, had had many marshals or chief peace officers, most of whom had died violent deaths in the line of duty. The City had shortly prior to this time procured and placed at the head of its police department a man specially qualified and adapted to fill the position. His name was Mike Meagher (usually pronounced Mayor). Mike came from Wichita, Kansas, and was a brother of John Meagher, who had served as mayor of the City of Wichita. This new marshal was a man of high standing as a peace officer, and had a reputation for coolness and deliberation in the face of danger. He was possessed of an unusual amount of nerve combined with shrewdness and strategy. Mike's brother John was engaged in the livestock and cattle business, and was a man of considerable means and financial ability. We shall notice later as to the part that John Meagher played in this tragedy of the West.

A recital as to the matters occurring in this affair will be better understood if, before entering upon the same, a graphic description is given of the portion of the City involved in this battle.

The Meridian Highway, being Government Highway 81, at the present time, as the traveler goes north, passes along the main street of the City of Caldwell until it reaches a point due west and two blocks distant from the depot of the Chicago, Rock Island, & Pacific Railway. The highway turns due east at this point, passing on the street immediately north of the depot to which we have referred. At the time involved in this recital, the depot at this point was not built, neither was the line of the Rock Island Railway built to Caldwell. The business portion of the City at that time was principally in two blocks, running north and south. One of these blocks was north and the other south of the street running east on the north side of the present site of the Rock Island depot.

The brick building known as the Danford Building, which played an important part in this battle, was and is located on the right side on the corner where this highway turns east. To the north of the present site of the depot referred to, and across the street from the same, was the Red Light Dance Hall. This was a large notorious place of ill repute, which was well patronized. One block south of where this highway turns east, and on the corner on the east side of the street, was the Hubble Store. This was a large, well-stocked store, being a general outfitting establishment for the cattle country trade. Just to the east of the Hubble Store, and across the alley from the same, was a brick blacksmith shop, operated by a tall, good-natured blacksmith known as "Lengthy Jones." To the east of the south side of the Danford Building and across the alley from the same was a small, square frame building used as a storehouse. The houses occupied by Talbott and his associates were something over one block north of the street where this highway turns east.

It was subsequently learned that Talbott and his associates had been making arrangements for days to leave the City, and it was their further intention to commit the depredation they did commit, and incidentally kill Mike Meagher. In carrying out their arrangement they had saddled their horses and tied them to the hitch-rack in front of the Red Light Dance Hall. Bob Bigtree had also gone to the harness shop in the south side of the Danford Building and ordered and was having made a cartridge belt with two rows of loops for cartridges on the same. When the battle started at about ten o'clock in the morning, Bigtree was just completing the purchase of this belt, and he immediately put it on and joined his companions.

The writer will attempt to set forth the happenings of this event as they were talked over and generally understood by the citizens immediately following the same. The writer was but a small boy at that time, but these matters were so vividly impressed upon his mind that they may have had a more lasting effect than had he been older.

At about ten o'clock on the morning referred to, Jim Talbott appeared in the middle of the street about thirty yards north of the corner where the highway turns east. He drew his pistol from its holster and took aim, and fired at someone in the middle portion of the block to the south of him and on the west side of the street. It was presumed that it was Mike Meagher at whom he was shooting, as he was in that vicinity, and it was the evident intention of the party to kill him. This shot was immediately returned by someone in the vicinity of where it had been aimed. Talbott was then joined by his three companions, and they took their stand in the middle of the street, near where Talbott had fired the first shot.

The parties on neither side of this controversy had had time to procure their rifles, and a severe pistol battle took place at this point, during which it does not appear that anyone was seriously injured. Talbott and his men were, however, crowded back down the street to the north, but retreated slowly and deliberately, firing as they went. After they had retreated a short distance, Talbott, who was the leader, commanded his men to get their Winchesters. All four of them then rushed to their homes and returned with their Winchester rifles. The battle then continued with them using these guns. They fought their way back down the street until they reached the street where the highway now turns east.

Martin, Munsin, and Bigtree followed this street to the east, toward where they had left their horses, while Jim Talbott turned to the right, going behind the Danford Building and taking position behind the small, square building across the alley behind the same. He did this, perhaps, thinking that Meagher would follow him down the street and pass the northeast corner of the Danford Building, when he would be in the open, in clear view, and would be a good target for his rifle. Meagher did come down this street on the sidewalk just as Talbott had expected, but exercising the precaution and shrewdness which was characteristic of the man, instead of passing around the corner, when he reached the rear of the building, he cautiously looked around the corner, and discovered Talbott looking around the corner of the other building, fifty or seventy-five feet away.

It was the evident intention of these parties to kill Mike Meagher and then rush to their horses and make their escape. In order to carry out this end, Talbott had evidently adopted this plan to get the job done. From their positions stated, a duel took place between Mike Meagher and Jim Talbott, in which they used their Winchester rifles. When one of them would peer around the corner of his building the other would attempt to snap-shoot him before he could get his head back. Meagher was on the rear corner of the Danford Building, next to the street.

In 1892 the writer returned to Caldwell, and remained there awaiting the opening of the Cherokee Strip, which opened for settlement in 1893. While he remained there, he had his office in the Danford Building, and at that time there remained several large places where the bricks were shot out on the corner at the east or rear end of the building next to the sidewalk. This was near where Mike Meagher had stood, and these holes were made by bullets from Jim Talbott's rifle, and were made near where Mike Meagher's head had been. This building was later extended east to the alleyway.

This duel continued for some time. Finally Meagher concluded that he would go back to the main street of the town, down the south side of the Danford Building, which was some fifty or seventy-five feet wide, would go around the small building, behind which Talbott was concealed, come up behind him, and thus easily capture or kill him. Meagher took this course and went around the building. Talbott possessed the same shrewdness as did Meagher, and when he missed the marshal from behind the building where he had been concealed, he immediately suspected that his antagonist had taken this course.

In order to avoid the result that Meagher had contemplated, Talbott stepped out in the open, some distance from the building which had concealed him, and to a point where he would have a full view of both corners of the same, and was watching the corner of the building where Meagher came around. Mike Meagher for once did not use his ordinary precaution, and rushed around this corner to come up behind Jim Talbott, supposing that he was where he had last seen him, and lost his life. Talbott fired at him, killing him instantly.

Caldwell at that time was a western frontier town where most all of its citizens bore arms and knew how to use them. By the time Meagher was killed, the citizens had gathered in great masses, and most of them carried a gun of some description. Talbott, immediately after shooting Meagher, started and ran to the northeast, toward the point where their horses had been left at the racks in front of the dance hall. His escape was one of the most spectacular ever witnessed. Dozens of men were shooting at him with all kinds of firearms. His course was over open ground, a distance of about one hundred and fifty yards down a gradually sloping hill, and in covering this distance he would zigzag, run, fall down, and roll over. This was done in order to confuse the men who were shooting at him and to make it more difficult for them to hit him. He accomplished this escape successfully and without a scratch, and reached the point where their horses had been left.

At this time in the recital of the occurrences, it is necessary for us to leave the four outlaws and observe what had been taking place in another portion of the City. Hubble, who operated the store to which we have referred, shortly after the shooting began, discovered that the outlaws had left their horses, on which they expected to make their escape, saddled and hitched to the rack in front of the dance hall. These horses were perhaps three hundred yards from the rear of the Hubble Store. After taking in the situation, Hubble took his Winchester rifle and went back through his store, crossing the alley to the Jones blacksmith shop. Going to the east door of the shop, he had a full view of these horses. He took rest with his rifle against the side of the door of the shop, and with as much deliberation as if he was shooting chickens' heads off, he killed most, if not all, of these horses.

When Talbott and his companions reached the point where their horses had been left, they found all of them either dead or dying. They immediately seized upon the first available animals that they could procure, and left the town riding two on each horse. There was an old settler living east of Caldwell at this time. He resided on and owned the farm adjoining where the writer lived as a boy. His name was Moses Swaggart, and he was generally known as "Uncle Mose." He was the father of Frank Swaggart, whose capture by the Indians is described in a later chapter. Uncle Mose was a big-hearted, harmless citizen, and one of the best friends and neighbors whom anyone ever had. He was a man of peace, knew nothing about firearms or their use, and did not care to acquire any such knowledge. He had an unexplainable habit and peculiarity. When traveling around the country with his team hitched to his wagon, no difference how long or how short the journey to be taken was, he always led a horse tied behind his wagon.

Uncle Mose on this day was coming into town from the east with a small load of hay on his wagon box, which he was taking to town for his brother Mack, and had the indispensable horse trailing behind his wagon. As Talbott and his gang rushed out of town, riding two on a horse, they met Uncle Mose at the east side of town, on what is now the Meridian Highway. Talbott and his companion riding a single horse rode up to the side of the Swaggart wagon, and seeing the extra horse, Talbott's companion dismounted from his seat behind his leader and started to untie the led horse. Uncle Mose slowly raised up on his load of hay and, seeing what was being done, informed the parties that this was his horse. Talbott raised his Winchester rifle, and pointing it at Uncle Mose said: "Sit down, old man! You see that crowd of men with guns coming. They are all after us, and you had better be quiet." It is needless to say that Uncle Mose, as any other man would have done under the circumstances, obeyed this order implicitly. He dropped down into the hay, out of sight, and his only regret was that the hole he was sitting in was not deeper.

Bar BQ Campbell was a cattle man known all through the West. He owned large cattle interests in the Indian Territory and also in Western Kansas. He was designated as above for the reason that his brand was a bar, B, and Q, made thus —BQ. He was the owner of a palatial home, where he resided, some two miles southeast of Caldwell. He also owned several very reputable race horses, one of which was tied at a rack in front of his home. When Talbott and his men came along the road in front of Campbell's house, headed to the south toward the Indian Territory, not far distant, they discovered this horse. One of the two remaining men riding one horse immediately dismounted and took possession of Campbell's race horse. Campbell joined the pursuing party, and was later shot through the hand in the fight.

Charley Moore, at this time, was the owner of a horse ranch on Deer Creek in the Indian Territory. This ranch was located about eleven miles southeast of Caldwell, and the ranch house at this time was unoccupied. It stood on the south side of Deer Creek in a thick bunch of timber. To the south of the same was a steep bank or bluff rising from the creek bottom. It was very difficult for a man to scale or climb over this bluff unaided, and it was impossible for a horse to pass over the same. To the north of Deer Creek at this point was a small creek, which would be properly designated as a draw or ravine, which, when it had water in it, drained into Deer Creek. This draw or ravine extended to the north for a long distance, and at places had steep banks.

When Talbott and his men left Caldwell, crowds of men on horses, and well armed, followed them. When the raiders had reached this draw or ravine in their flight, they were so closely pursued that they took refuge behind the steep banks on this draw. They were almost surrounded, and a crowd of citizens was advancing on them, and from all appearances it would not be long until they were captured. At this point there were many citizens engaged who narrowly escaped death or severe injury. A number of the pursuing party had bullets pass through their clothing, or very near them. One young man, of whose name the writer is not sure at this time, but who, to his best recollection, was Charley Hall, had a bullet fired by the fleeing desperadoes pass through his hat, very near his head.

Bar BQ Campbell, in his eagerness to capture the escaping outlaws, advanced close to the top of the bank of this ravine, distant about one hundred yards from the hollow in which the fleeing party had taken refuge. Campbell raised up and was peering over the hill to take a shot when a ball from the rifle of one of the desperadoes struck the side of his Winchester and passed directly through his hand, and missed his head but a short distance. The word immediately passed down the line that Campbell was shot. All the members of the pursuing party left the positions where they were stationed to hold the outlaws, and rushed to look after Campbell, with the result that during the excitement and confusion, Talbott and his men, taking advantage of the opportunity, escaped and ran south into the timber surrounding the Moore ranch house.

Firing was kept up by the pursuers and answered by the fleeing parties until dark. For years afterward these trees bore the bullet marks of the rifle balls fired into them during this evening and night by this pursuing party. When darkness settled over the scene, the pursuers, to prevent an escape of the outlaws during the night, placed guards around this timber and ranch house. They expected at daylight on the coming morning to capture the refugees easily. The citizens did not think it possible that anyone could escape over the steep bank to the rear of this timber, and knew that the horses of the escaping party could not be taken over the same.

For that reason they did not take extra precaution to guard this particular point. During the night Talbott and his men discovered that this portion was not well guarded, and they climbed upon each others' shoulders, and by such means the top man, who was carrying a rope, after reaching the level ground pulled his associates up. The four men thus surrounded escaped on foot. This escape was not discovered until the following morning, when the pursuers firing into the timber received no shots in response. An investigation was made and the escape discovered. The four horses which had been taken by these parties the previous day, and on which the outlaws had effected their escape, were all left in this timber, and were returned to their owners.

After this escape nothing was heard of Talbott and his companions, and nothing was known of their trip south to Texas, except that it was reported that some horses were taken from freighters near Wild Horse, which was some thirty-five or forty miles down the trail. These parties evidently rode these horses back to Texas.

It was later learned that James Talbott shortly after this battle drifted out to California. His full name was James Sherman Talbott. The Sherman was his mother's family name. After this trouble, he dropped the Talbott and went under the name of James Sherman.

In 1894, Talbott was discovered living under this name on a ranch in California. The writer is not able at this time to give the exact location of this ranch, but it was near a small town at the foothills of one of the mountain ranges. Talbott was immediately arrested for the killing of Mike Meagher and brought back to Wellington, Kansas, for trial, Wellington being the county seat of Sumner County, in which county the City of Caldwell is located.

It had been so long since the killing of Meagher, and so many of the persons who were present at that time had either disappeared or died, that it was almost impossible to find the necessary witnesses to show that Talbott killed Meagher or had anything to do with it. It was also difficult to show that the prisoner was actually engaged in the fight. Some of the men who dressed and cared for Meagher's body after his death, on account of the lapse of time, were unable to state the exact location of his wound or on which side he was shot. Talbott was tried several times for this killing, and a hung jury was the result each time. He was finally released. The writer has before him at this time a certified copy of the original information charging these four parties with the murder of Mike Meagher, and on which Jim Talbott was tried. James Martin, Bob Munsin, and Bob Bigtree were none of them ever heard of after their escape over the bank at Moore's ranch on Deer Creek.

The writer has heretofore referred to John Meagher, the brother of the slain marshal. John Meagher, as stated, was a prosperous and influential citizen, and a man of considerable means. It is claimed, and the writer understands it to be a fact, that after the killing of Mike Meagher and the escape of Jim Talbott that John Meagher sold most of his possessions in Wichita and southern Kansas and started to travel in a light buggy, drawn by a team of ponies. The object of his journeys was an unlimited search for Jim Talbott. On these journeys he was armed appropriately for the occasion of a meeting with the party sought. It was stated that his travels were to be ended only when he found Talbott. It is claimed that John Meagher spent a large portion of his fortune in this search, all of which was without result.

The matters and things that the writer has detailed up to this time in this chapter were matters of general knowledge at the time of this happening, and he has given the source of his information. The occurrences following the trial of James Talbott he has gained from general reports and newspaper articles, and has no personal knowledge of the same. The newspaper information is as follows:

After the release of Jim Talbott at Wellington, Kansas, he returned to his ranch in California, where he had resided prior to his arrest. He made frequent trips of several miles to the small town where he did his trading. On these trips he journeyed on horseback. A few months after his return he made one of these trips as usual, but did not arrive home that night, and on the following morning, upon investigation being made, his body was found lying at the roadside riddled with buckshot. Thus ended the life of the two principal actors in this tragedy. Jim Talbott's trial was thus passed on to a court where the memory of witnesses could not be dimmed or clouded by lapse of time.

It is impossible in the happening of any matter similar to the one described herein to take place without many humorous things occurring during the same. This is true without regard to the seriousness of the occurrences or how tragic are their results. This happening is no exception to the rule. It is worthwhile to enumerate some of these occurrences.

There was a boy well known in Caldwell at the time of this event who was similar to characters found in most towns. The high point of his proclivities was that he wanted to be the first to investigate any unusual occurrence, and his presence was indispensable in the midst of everything. When Talbott fired his first shot, this lad rushed to the spot to make his usual investigation, but by the time that he arrived at the point to be investigated, the bullets were flying thick down the street and singing like bees. The inquirer beat a hasty retreat to the north. As he fled he yelled for help and that they were killing everyone in town. He reached a point in his travels north about one block from where the first shot had been fired, and on the west side of the street, near where the old school building stood. At this point the wooden sidewalk had a step where it raised several inches. This young man having run far enough and being unable to fly sought safety by crawling under this sidewalk. After he started under he continued to crawl back to where the room was not so spacious; there he remained for the reason that he could go no further forward. After matters had quieted down and he sought to back out he discovered that he could go neither way. Later in the day his shouts were heard, and he was released by kindly hands raising the sidewalk.

On the west side of the main street of the City, at about the center of the block south of where Talbott had fired his first shot, and in the vicinity of where the bullets he fired were aimed, there was a grocery store. One of the clerks working in this store, at the time this first shot was fired, was out in the street. This clerk immediately had urgent business back in the building, but when he turned to make his run for the same, the bullets were coming thick, and the distance was too long for him to negotiate. He had to pass a pine box sitting at the curb of the sidewalk. This box was made of soft pine, and was not over a quarter of an inch thick. This enclosure, however, looked very inviting to him, and he leaped into it for shelter. Here he remained during all this pistol battle, with the bullets riddling everything around him. He felt very secure in his retreat, and after the battle was over he emerged, a happy man without a scratch, complimenting himself on his wisdom and good judgment.

On the east side of the street, where Talbott fired his first shot, upstairs, and almost opposite to the same, there roomed an old gentleman. This old gentleman had been a soldier during the late war. He had but one eye. The writer never knew whether he lost this eye in the service or not. He drew a large pension, and was comfortably fixed financially. With nothing to bother about and nothing to do, he spent most of his time with anyone he could talk to, and the principal topic of his conversation was the many catastrophies he had encountered while in the service of his country. He always loved to relate the various encounters he had engaged in during the war. This old gentleman was one of the best of citizens and one of the nicest men possible to meet, but he had an exaggerated idea as to his fighting ability. He was the possessor at this time of a .32 rim fire pistol, the composition of which was cast iron, commonly known as pot-metal, covered with a poor grade of tin, represented to be nickel or silver, and which pistol carried five cartridges.

When this shooting began, he was in his room. He immediately seized this trusty implement of destruction, and rushed down stairs. There he saw Talbott and his men in the middle of the street shooting to the south. When the old gentleman arrived at the foot of the stairs bearing his trusty five-shooter, he considered the range too great to start a battle with these men in the middle of the street, so in order to get a shot at closer range and thus insure their immediate destruction, he dropped flat on the sidewalk, rolled out to the edge of the same, and into the gutter at the edge of the street, which was quite deep at this point at that time.

Having sought and gained this favored location for carrying on his offensive and defensive operations, he raised himself up, peered over the embankment, as if he was shooting Indians from a buffalo wallow, or soldiers of the opposing ranks over the breast work at Cold Harbor, and fired every load out of his pistol, while the men in the street were so engaged that they did not see him and did not know he was there or that he was shooting at them.

The writer has read many articles descriptive of the Talbott Raid. Some of these were extremely erroneous and were written on the dime novel plan, and from their painted and extravagant language branded themselves as not being correct.

Others have been correct in the main, but none have contained a complete and correct statement of the occurrence. There may be errors in the recital of this matter as herein set out, but if there are they are matters of small consequence. The material facts as herein stated are as near correct as it is possible to make the same. It must be borne in mind that this event has long since passed into history. Fifty-four years have come and gone since this memorable occasion, years that have swept all of the actors in the same into Eternity. This is written in an attempt to preserve the history of this affair for future generations.

Hendry Brown.

CHAPTER XXX.

HENDRY BROWN

The Atchison, Topeka, and Santa Fe Railway extended south to Caldwell, Kansas, in the spring of 1880. A spur was built on south a couple of miles to the line of the Indian Territory, now the north line of the State of Oklahoma. Here, just east of the Chisholm Trail, extensive loading pens, chutes, and long wings were built for the handling and loading of cattle coming up the trail. Caldwell was then the northern terminus of the Chisholm Cattle Trail.

In the late years of the seventies, the wild Indians of the plains of the Panhandle of Texas had been subdued and placed on reservations. The Panhandle was immediately taken over by cattlemen and the entire country divided into ranches. This became the greatest breeding ground for cattle in the entire world. Railways had been built into eastern Texas, and the cattle which formerly came up the trail from that country were handled by these railways. The Panhandle was overrun with cattle, and the herds poured across the plans east past Mobeetie, meeting the Chisholm Cattle Trail south of Fort Reno and following it northward. During the summer season these herds followed each other in rapid succession. This trail became one of the busiest arteries of commerce in the United States.

The Panhandle of Texas was the great source of beef supply for the country. Millions of hoofs trod this ancient highway. Its course was tramped for hundreds of yards in width. Through it wound deep paths where the cattle had followed each other. During the busy season, from it at intervals, rose great clouds of dust where the herds took their course over the same as they were urged on by the spectacular and dust-coated drivers. Over this route also daily, each drawn by several spans of horses or mules, rushed in both directions numbers of Concord Stage Coaches. These coaches plunged forward, pitching and rolling as if they were making a race for life. Wagons drawn by plodding animals and loaded with freight, or returning empty, wound their way along this course. Long strings of wagons of Indian freighters moved in either direction, going to the terminus of the railroad for freight or returning loaded. Occasionally a lone horseman, mounted on his cow-pony, headed for town or returning therefrom, moved slowly along in a familiar jog-trot.

Caldwell had developed into the principal cattle shipping point in the West. It was also the busiest and toughest town on the frontier. Here drifted the worst characters to be found, men who lived violent lives and died violent deaths, and here also congregated the wildest women to meet them.

As these conditions existed, it was in the year 1882 that a lone horseman rode north up the trail. His horse's head was directed toward this frontier city. From a casual observation, there was nothing to attract attention to this man more than other cowboys who daily rode up or down the trail. His appearance was anything but striking. He was small in stature, and slender, very much under size, and the lines of his body were not a model by any means. The only distinguishing feature of his face was a square set jaw, not unlike that of a bull dog. A handkerchief knotted together at the ends hung loosely around his neck. He wore a white hat, the brim of which was much narrower than that worn by most cowboys, and in all he was well covered with dust.

If the observer had occasion to speak to or enter into conversation with this rider, he would have immediately discovered marked peculiarities of the man. His words were few and were parted with reluctantly. His disposition impressed one as being surly, that he did not care to be bothered, did not appreciate one's company, or felt bored by one's inferiority. In fact his disposition seemed very much reserved; not only reserved, but made one feel easier after parting with his company.

There was, however, little in the appearance of this man to reveal his past or the history of his turbulent career. This was just as he wanted it to be. Little did he reckon what the history of his life would be in the country into which he was then riding, or what would be his untimely end. It is well to observe here, that never into the soul of this man entered a feeling of remorse, pity, or love for his fellow man. He possessed the most stoical disposition that could be crowded into a human being. No exhibition of grandeur or beauty, or any scene of suffering or horror, ever changed the expression of his face.

As this traveler journeyed north over the trail, he came to the bluff near the state line that overlooks the City of Caldwell. This was his first sight of civilization perhaps for many months, and was the point that he had traveled many days to reach. He and his horse were travel-stained and travel-worn, for it is said that he had ridden all the way from Old Tascosa.

At this time, it is well to observe the conditions that existed in the little city that he was riding down upon. He knew these conditions well, and these were what caused him to make this journey.

At the time of the building of the railway on to Caldwell in 1880, George Flat was marshal of the town. He incurred the displeasure of many persons living in and out of the same. It was claimed that he was overbearing and arbitrary, and finally, that he drank too much whiskey. The opposition to him, whether justified or not, grew so great that he was removed from office. He had antagonized so many men who never forgot, and had made so many enemies during his tenure in office, that he refused to lay aside his guns when he retired from it, but increased their number to three. In justification for this conduct, he claimed that from his service as marshal and enforcement of the law, his life was in danger, and that it was necessary that he be able to defend himself. This claim was doubtless justified. One night after his retirement from office, as he journeyed home, he passed an implement yard. From this ambush, many guns blazed, and before he could draw a weapon he was riddled with buckshot and bullets. This was the end of the trail for one marshal of Caldwell.

Mike Meagher was installed as permanent marshal of the town. He was instantly killed in the line of duty in the Talbott Raid. George Brown was then selected as chief peace officer. Brown was a man of fine judgment, and one of the best business men of the town, but it required more than this qualification to prosper as marshal of this frontier city. He had served but a short time when he was notified one night that there was serious trouble at the Red Light Dance Hall. He fearlessly started to subdue it. As he ascended the stairway, just as he reached the top, a pistol shot roared through the building, and George Brown, one of the best citizens of the town, fell with a bullet through his brain, while his blood flowed out over the floor.

Conditions had grown such that it seemed a useless sacrifice of human life to install an officer as chief of police who would attempt to subdue or cope with the lawless element that swept into the town. The persons whose inclinations were to violate the law took advantage of this situation. A lady was not safe to walk down the sidewalk. She would in all probability be insulted or crowded into the street by a set of hood-lums. The officers of the town were at a loss to know what course to pursue to solve the problem that faced them.

Such was the situation and the dilemma when, at the time stated, this lone horseman rode onto the streets of Caldwell. Riding up in front of a saloon just north of the Hubble General Supply Store, he tied his horse to a hitch rack, and going into the saloon followed the custom of law-abiding cowboys who did not seek trouble. He handed his pistols and Winchester to the man in charge for safekeeping. He then astonished the bar tender by walking out without taking a drink. Be it said for this man, that as long as he lived in the town he was never seen drunk in public, and if he ever drank to excess, he did it in private. The stranger made inquiry for the office of the mayor of the town. The writer has heard it said that some other party had spoken to the city authorities in reference to this man prior to his arrival. This may be true, but the writer doubts it very much. This man did not want his antecedents and record examined into, and knowing the character of the man, it would have been his method to ride into town un-announced and ask for what he wanted.

In any event, when he appeared at his office, the mayor did not know him. With his handkerchief hanging loosely around his neck, and with the trail dust upon him, he walked into the office of the chief executive of the city. He then bluntly stated that he understood that the officers and citizens of the town desired to obtain a marshal who could hold things down and handle the existing situation. He was informed by the mayor that such was the case, but the task seemed hopeless. The newcomer then stated that he had a man who could get the job done, and as a guarantee he would give them a trial without pay. The mayor asked him where his man was, and when he could enter upon his duties. To which the stranger replied that he was the man, and that he could enter upon his duties immediately. The mayor, who was a large, portly man, looked down upon the insignificant form of the applicant with astonishment. The chief executive stated that if the newcomer was sure he could fill the bill, he would call the city council together and see what they could do for him. "But," said the mayor, "what is your name?" The reply simply was: "My name is Henry Brown." It will be observed that the only disguise that this man appeared under was in the spelling of his first name, the correct spelling of the same being "Hendry." The council was immediately called together, and the conclusion reached was, that whether the stranger made good or not, the situation was as bad as it could be and it would do no harm to try the applicant. Henry Brown was employed by the City of Caldwell and took a position on the police force, first as deputy. He was designated as a deputy, but was in fact the head of the force, and was soon named as such.

At this time, it would be well to understand who this stranger was and what his past life had been.

The first authentic information we have of Hendry Brown is when he appeared as a cowboy at the South Springs Ranch of John Chisum, south of Roswell, New Mexico. This was at the beginning of the active hostilities of the Lincoln County War in New Mexico. His nativity and family he never discussed. The time was in the late years of the seventies. The principals in this war were John Chisum and Alexander McSwain on one side and a faction controlled by Major L. G. Murphy on the other.

During the war, Brown served as a companion of the indomitable William H. Bonney, better known as "Billy the Kid," a lad then only eighteen years of age. This was a time and place when every contender truly wore his life on his pistol belt. He rode at the side of Billy the Kid at *Agua Negra*

Canyon, when Morton and Baker, who were their prisoners, were shot down by this boy of the frontier, and McClaskey, who was one of their own companions, was shot to death by a bullet from an unknown source when he tried to protect the prisoners. He was also with Billy the Kid when he rode into Lincoln in July, 1878. In this party were, aside from these two, Charlie Bowdry, George Coe, Tom O'Folliard, Jim French, Doc. Shurlock, Harvey Morris, Francisco Somora, Ignacio Gonzales, Vincent Romero, Jose Chavez, and Ighenio Salazar. These men were all warriors of the Chisum and McSwain clan, ready and able to shoot it out with anyone. They took quarters in the store and home of their leader, Alexander McSwain. Here they were set upon by about seventy-five or more of the Murphy men, and then took place what is known as the famous "Three Days Battle." In this battle many men were killed, and the McSwain house burned. In this encounter also was killed the leader, McSwain. McSwain was a deeply religious man, who was forced into this war by the patent justice of his cause, and who never fired a shot in this battle or in the war, and who died fleeing from his burning house and clutching his Bible to his breast.

Billy the Kid, Brown, and most of their followers escaped after killing many men. In this war, Brown, assisting the Chisum faction, fought on the side of recognized justice and right. After the termination of the war, Billy the Kid organized from his old associates a gang of freebooters, who preyed upon the country. Their principal source of revenue was the taking of cattle which legally belonged to someone else. This practice had been engaged in so long in that country, and by men who considered themselves within the law, that it did not seem a serious transgression by the members of this band. These parties did not consider themselves outlaws, as they claimed their acts were from practice half legalized. The mem-

bers of this band were by some considered as the worst kind
of cut-throats, and by others, which included a large part of
the population, they appeared like unto Robinhood of old—
friends of the down-trodden, oppressed, and poor. It was the
overdoing of this cattle taking by Murphy which brought on
the Lincoln County War. Billy the Kid's band was composed
of himself, William H. Bonney, Hendry Brown, Charlie Bowdry, Tom O'Folliard, Jim French, John Middleton, Fred Wayte,
and Doc. Shurlock. Shortly before the death of Billy the Kid,
Hendry Brown parted company with this organization, leaving
them at Tascosa, Texas. This is the last we know of him until
he appeared at Caldwell at the time stated.

When Brown was installed as marshal, he was authorized
to select his own deputy, and he chose and imported as such
a tall, stalwart Texan by the name of Ben Wheeler. In quieting the town, Brown did all that he agreed to do. When a
question of difference arose, he shot first and argued afterward. Caldwell soon had a reputation which was as much
of a terror to the lawless element as it had had an attraction
before. Those with lawless inclinations made a detour when
they came to the city limits, and all bearing firearms either
parked them outside the town or carried them in muzzle-re-
versed and sought a place to deposit them. These officers
furnished somewhat of a comical sight as they walked down
the street together. Brown, small and insignificant, strolled
along with his tall, broad-shouldered deputy looking down upon
him. The ponderous dimensions of Wheeler made the small
body of Brown look even smaller. However, what Hendry
Brown, like his old associate Billy the Kid, lacked in size, he
made up in disposition and spirit. He killed several men in
the beginning of his term of office. Many of these killings
now are and ordinarily would be considered wanton and without cause, even cowardly. Among those killed was an old

Indian Chief, whose name was "Spotted Tail." This killing was unnecessary. When Brown began to shoot at him, the Indian did not even know that Brown was an officer, and thought that it was an attack by some private individual.

Brown's identity was not generally known in Caldwell at this time, nor until after the raid at Medicine Lodge, Kansas, as a result of which raid he lost his life. Brown was considered as the deliverer of this frontier cattle town from the wild men of the West. The City Council passed resolutions expressing their thanks for this deliverance. They bought and presented to Brown a gold mounted and engraved Winchester Rifle, with his name and the names of the donors cut upon it. The stock of this gun was inlaid with ivory and pearl. They also presented to him a saddle mounted with gold, and to Wheeler one mounted with silver. This gun was laid down by Brown when he surrendered to the authorities at Medicine Lodge, and the saddles of both Brown and Wheeler were taken by their captors at the time of their surrender at that place.

While things went well on the surface, and the lawless element drifting into Caldwell had been subdued, yet after the lapse of a short time, there was a secret organization under cover which infested the community. The full extent of this organization was never discovered until after the killing at Medicine Lodge. The facts were that there were certain parties in league with the officers who robbed drunken men and anyone available in back alleys or any other out-of-the-way place. On all these occasions the officers were at some other place and never could make contact with the persons committing the depredations. It was also learned that arrangements had been made by these parties at one time to rob the Santa Fe train coming into Caldwell.

Finally, the true character of these men was exposed to view and a revelation made to the world in general. On the morning of the 30th day of April, 1884, Hendry Brown, Ben Wheeler, William Smith, a cowboy, formerly employed on the T5 Range, and John Wesley, also known as Harry Hill, an ex-cowboy, rode into the City of Medicine Lodge, Kansas, the county seat of Barber County. Medicine Lodge is west and north of Caldwell, distant some fifty miles. These parties made their way direct to the Medicine Valley Bank, one of the largest banking institutions in the country, and one which always had plenty of available money on hand. They dismounted, leaving their horses in charge of one of their number. The other three, which included Brown and Wheeler, entered the bank. E. W. Payne, President of the bank, was on duty in the same, and also George Geppert, Cashier, was filling his position in the bank. Brown was well known to these men, and it is said that when he came into the bank, these officers little surmised any trouble and asked him what they could do for him. This question was answered by the stern command to raise their hands and hand over the cash in the bank. The officers of the bank first considered this demand as a joke, but they were soon to discover that it was a stern reality. A battle ensued, in which both Payne and Geppert were killed. It is uncertain who killed Payne, but it is claimed that Ben Wheeler killed Geppert.

After the shooting began in the bank, the city marshal and other citizens of the town rushed to the scene and opened fire on the man holding the horses. The three in the bank seized what money they could and rushed to make their escape. They fled safely from the town, but as they crossed the Medicine River, south of the same, Ben Wheeler's horse bogged in the quicksand, and he was compelled to abandon it, and they left with him and one of the other members of the party both riding one horse. While this robbery was in progress, and the news was spreading over the town, there were nine western characters, principally cowmen and cowboys, sitting together at a table in a saloon playing cards. When the news of this holdup was carried to this saloon, these nine men started in a body to enter the battle. They all procured their Winchester rifles and other firearms, then congregated, and made the chase together. The pursuers pressed the fugitives, who, after they crossed the river and proceeded as stated, with Wheeler (a very large and heavy man) and another of the party on one horse, all being unfamiliar with the country, ran into a blind canyon.

Here a battle ensued, which lasted for a long time. The robbers were finally, however, driven back into this canyon. There was a large pond of water in the same, and the fugitives were waist deep in the water as they fought their way back. Late in the day they surrendered, laid down their arms, and were taken back into Medicine Lodge. Here all four of these parties were placed under guard in the jail. When night came, a mob was organized to seek vengeance on the killers of the officers of the bank. This mob proceeded to the jail and broke down the door. Brown had concealed a small pistol in his boot, but this was taken away from him, and his last hope of escape vanished. He, attempting to escape, rushed out of the door first. He turned to the left, received a charge of buckshot in his back, and went down about twenty feet from the door and died. Wheeler came out about the same time and turned to the right. A pistol was fired at him at such close range that it set fire to his shirt. This fire was a target at which others shot. He ran about one hundred and fifty yards and fell, severely wounded. He then begged for his life, informed his captors that there were things he could tell which were of much interest to them, and he would reveal them if they would spare his life until morning. Smith and Wesley did not get an opportunity to run, but were seized and taken in charge by the mob. All the three living members of this gang were taken to Elm Creek, about one-half mile east of Medicine Lodge, and there hanged.

Thus ended the career of Hendry Brown, a man whose energies and ability rendered him capable of being a very useful citizen, and whose name might have been written high among men had it not been for his inherent desire to violate the law and live a life beyond the same.

In Caldwell, during the time that Hendry Brown served as marshal of the town, was but one man who knew him or of his past life. That man was Charles A. Siringo. Charley Siringo was an old-time cowboy, a strictly law-abiding citizen, and a man who attended to his own business. Charley came from Matagorda, Texas, where he had first served as a cowboy in the old days when they drove the wild long-horns out of the chaparral thickets, where they had lived until moss had grown on their horns. He later served as a Pinkerton detective, and wrote a number of books, including "Riata and Spurs."

Siringo had served as a boss for many years for the LX Company, and had met and knew Billy the Kid and his band, including Hendry Brown. Charley Siringo, who was well known to and was a friend of the writer, was one of the greatest and most efficient cowboys who rode the plains; he feared no man. Hendry Brown knew that Siringo knew him, and after Brown's death he freely told of his knowledge of Brown, and that he had been called upon by certain parties in the interest of Brown while he was marshal, and threatened with sure and certain death should he ever reveal Brown's identity. Anyone who knew Charley Siringo knows that it was not through fear that he did not make public this information. Siringo said that it appeared that Brown was making good and had permanently forsaken his evil ways, and he felt sure that he would continue to do so. For this reason he thought that it would not only be an injustice to Brown, but also to the people he served, to reveal the facts as to his past.

CHAPTER XXXI.

CAPTURE OF FRANK SWAGGART BY THE INDIANS

In the early years of the decade beginning with 1870, the course of empire was fast drifting to the westward. The homes of the settlers were growing more numerous and dotting the western prairies. The men with the plows were following and crowding the buffalo from the plains. Joining in this march were two brothers, Mose and Mack Swaggart. They loaded their wagons, and, leaving their boyhood home in the East, joined the white-topped caravans moving to the west. These brothers both had families, Mose having a wife and six children, and Mack a wife and four children. The children of these families were small, the youngest of each being only a few years of age, and the oldest being far below maturity. These emigrants journeyed westward with the rest across the Mississippi River, through the settlements of Missouri, crossed the Missouri River, and pushed their way past the homesteads of eastern Kansas. Their destination was uncertain, but they sought a location where each of them could file on, acquire title to, and establish a home for the future on one hundred and sixty acres of Government land.

The life of these families was similar to that of all other settlers in their location at that time. Their hardships herein stated were most of them the same as of all other early settlers in southern Kansas. These families, like others around them, were destined to perform their part in the early settlement of this frontier country.

They traveled as far as they could travel and still remain in bounds of an organized state government. They landed on the south boundary of what was then known as the Osage country. They settled about forty-six miles south and ten miles west of Wichita, Kansas. Here each homesteaded a claim five miles east of the little settlement at Caldwell. These claims joined. The claim of Mack Swaggart was on the south line of the Osage country, which at that time was the south line of the settlement in the State of Kansas, and the claim of Mose joined it on the north. This location was, however, two and a quarter miles north of the line of the Indian Territory. This resulted from the fact that there was a discrepancy in the surveys of Kansas and the Indian Territory. In Kansas the survey is reckoned from the 6th Principal Meridian and in the Indian Territory from the Indian Meridian. The survey in the Indian Territory was being run at that time, and was not completed. After it was completed this strip between the two surveys at this place constituted this two and a quarter mile strip which was not settled for many years later.

At the time of the settlement of these brothers in southern Kansas, and for many years thereafter, the bones of the departed buffalo marked the prairies with white spots as far as the eye could see. The country was half civilized, and neighbors were usually far apart. Occasionally the tidings of an Indian uprising, either actual or imaginary, was carried throughout the country, and the inhabitants would flock to a general center for mutual protection. Existence was a struggle on this frontier. Then, in 1874, came the ravages of the grasshoppers. These pests came down in clouds, darkening the sun. They consumed everything that should be eaten by a grasshopper, and many things that should not. The writer has heard old settlers relate that they even ate holes in and chewed on fork handles and other things that no normal grasshopper would be presumed to bother. This was strictly an open prairie country, without timber, and the only available fuel that could be obtained was from the little timber that grew along Bluff Creek and Deer Creek, several miles distant in the Indian Territory. Had it not been for this timber, the early settlers in southern Kansas could not have survived these pioneer days.

As the trouble with the Indians subsided and grew less, the cattle industry in the Indian Territory crowded further to the south. No better grazing country could be found. In 1878 this industry was flourishing, and it was the ambition of every boy on or near the border to join the ranks of picturesque cowboys, who lived and worked in the Indian Territory or any other point to the southward. Also, it was necessary that all members of the family should do their best, render all assistance possible, and earn every dollar they could for the support of the family.

Frank Swaggart was the oldest child in Mose's family, and in 1878 was a well developed, handsome, auburn haired boy of seventeen years. About seventy miles almost due south across the Indian Territory line was an extensive cattle ranch known as the Hughens Ranch. This ranch was located in a portion of the country which was later known as Old Oklahoma, and near the present site of Guthrie. One of the persons employed in the operation of this ranch, and who was one of the bosses on the same, was a man named Bedford Wood. Wood was a northern man, but he had traveled the trails ever since the Chisholm Trail had been opened in 1867.

Some of Bedford Wood's relatives lived in southern Kansas, near the Swaggart home, and he and the Swaggarts were well acquainted. In the fall of 1878, Bedford came to Kansas to visit his relatives and old friends, and while there Frank Swaggart was employed by him to assist in taking a bunch of horses to the Indian Territory ranch of Hughens. They left in the month of November of the year stated. They journeyed with this bunch of horses down the Chisholm Trail. They left

this trail at some point near Skeleton Creek, and cut across
the country to the southeast to the Hughens Ranch.

These horses having been delivered, Frank prepared for
his return journey to his home, which he was to make alone.
At daylight on the morning of a day in early November, he
mounted his horse, which he had brought along to ride back,
and started north on his return. It was necessary that he cut
across the country to meet the Chisholm Trail. There was
quite a fog that morning as he traveled in the valley of the
Red Fork or Cimarron River.   He became confused in his
journey and lost his way. At about ten o'clock in the morning
he saw what he thought was a number of men, and started
to them for the purpose of making inquiry as to his whereabouts.   When he reached this party, he discovered that it
consisted of about ten young Indian bucks.

After the Indian uprising of 1874 up to the time stated,
and for many years later, dissatisfied members of the Cheyenne
warriors who had gone with Stone Calf's contingent, caused
trouble at every opportunity.   This was true from the time
of the killing of Pat Hennessey up to the time the cattle were
removed from the Cheyenne and Arapaho Country in 1885.
The Indians who had thus met Frank Swaggart were doubtless
a party of these Indians.

These young bucks at this time had been on a hunting
expedition, and were carrying a bunch of about six wild turkey which they had killed. They were arrogant.   The full
meaning of this word under these circumstances has been described in another chapter of this work.

After Frank came up to this party, they compelled him
to dismount from his horse. They then required him to strip
off all his clothing, except his underwear. They even took his
hat from his head and his boots from his feet. Then one of

these Indians deliberately mounted his horse; they handed Frank the bunch of turkeys they had been carrying, and compelled him to accompany them carrying them. They traveled for miles, their captive trudging along with them bearing the burden of their load of game. He was without his clothing, bareheaded, and barefooted. He knew not where he was going, where they were taking him, or what his fate would be when they reached their destination. Finally, just before sundown, they came to the general camp of the Indians. This camp had a permanent appearance, and the opinion formed by the captive was that there were several hundred Indians in the same. However, knowing these Indians as the writer afterward did, and the numbers who usually went on these trips, his judgment would be that the number was much less. It must be remembered that this was only four years after the killing of Hennessey by the Indians, and the reader can well surmise what revolved through the mind of this captive during this journey and during all the time of his restraint.

These Indians as usual had a large band of horses grazing near their camp. In subsequent years the writer traveled over this portion of the Territory, became quite familiar with the same and the regular camping grounds of the Indians, and his judgment is that this camp was located on the north side of the Cimarron River, between the mouth of Skeleton Creek and the Old Red Fork Ranch, on a spring branch running into the river on the north side in what was then the first open space through the blackjack timber east of the ranch named, being north and across the river from Campbell Creek. This was several miles east of the ranch, and a favorite camping ground for the Indians. Beside the fine spring water in the creek, there was an abundance of large trees, furnishing shade in the summer, and protection and wood in cold weather.

The Indians in this camp at that time had a good supply of game of various kinds, were well supplied with food, and were apparently having a celebration or banquet of some character. But even having this abundance they would not allow their captive to have anything to eat, but they would eat and tantalize him with the food. The Indians would then gather around him in bunches, and have all sorts of amusement from his predicament. The captive had a good supply of long, auburn hair, and the Indians would catch him and twist it up on the top of his head, and then take a large butcher knife and run it around his scalp, going through the performance of removing the same.

At last they tired of their amusement with their captive, in which they had handled him much the same as a cat would a captive mouse. At about dark they took him to the outer edge of the camp and commanded him to leave. He was much relieved that they had spared his life, but his predicament at this time can well be imagined. It was sixty-five miles north in a straight line to the nearest settlement, and that over a wild and barren prairie, without a roadway or trail. It was growing colder every minute, and from all appearances would be a cold, frosty night, and freeze considerable. There he was in this wild country, with only wilder men about him. He had had nothing to eat since morning. He had no clothing on except his underwear, he was barefooted and bareheaded, and had no protection from the freezing temperature, nor did he have any matches or other means of starting a fire.

As he left the Indian camp, he observed that the weather had cleared and the stars were shining brightly. He could now at least know his course. He, like all other boys of the frontier in those days, could easily ascertain his direction by the stars. As he went out of the Indian camp traveling north he observed a bunch of the Indian ponies enclosed in a temporary corral near the camp. To keep the Indians from seeing that he was noticing the ponies, he bore off in another direction. With the sight of these horses there arose and developed in the mind of this captive an idea as to his only means of escape from the disaster which had beset him. In his course of travel from this camp, he soon came to a bunch of bushes and grapevines near the edge of the timber. He carefully concealed himself in this cover, and huddled up to keep as warm as possible, and remained there until all the merry-making was over in the camp.

Finally, long after dark, when every sound had ceased for some time among the Indians, he, knowing his life depended on the success of his escape, stole from his hiding place with much caution. During the time that he had remained in his place of concealment, he had selected and procured a small, strong, stout grapevine, and broken it off about six feet long. Taking this grapevine, he proceeded silently and stealthily over to and among the corralled ponies. Frank knew that Indian ponies were usually very gentle. In fact most of them were ridden by young Indians from the time they were young colts, but it was necessary that he be very cautious, and be sure to start no commotion that would arouse the sleeping Indians.

He stated that it took him at least one-half hour to select and catch one of the ponies, but he finally was able to approach and put his grapevine around the neck of one of the gentlest of the bunch. Had he had daylight and all the time needed, he could not have made a better selection. The one selected was round as a dollar, and almost entirely white. The father of the writer, in the spring of 1879, purchased and the family moved upon the homestead above described, formerly owned by Mack Swaggart, and the writer, together with the Swaggart boys, for many years used this pony in herding cattle. The little fellow was the gentlest and most likeable

animal that anyone ever possessed. He was simply a delight
for boys to handle and ride. They named him "Injun," and
he knew his name very well.

Frank led this pony away from the Indian herd and away
from the corral. As soon as he had gotten a sufficient distance
from the camp of the Indians, he mounted the pony and started
on his northern journey. Indian horses, used by them at that
time, were taught to be guided by swinging or leaning the
body of the rider, indicating the course that was to be taken.
Frank, guiding this Indian pony in this manner and with the
grapevine, rode north across an unmarked prairie during the
entire night. Near morning he grew so cold that he could not
guide the pony, but the rider sitting straight on his mount
perhaps indicated to the horse that it was desired to go straight
ahead. In any event, the pony kept his course well.

The night was bitter cold, and had it not been for the
heat from the pony's body, which was made warmer from the
rate of speed that he was traveling, Frank would have doubtless frozen. He traveled in a lope during the entire night.
In his course he had kept to the east of the Chisholm Trail.
He struck the trail which branched off from the Chishlom
Trail below the present site of Waukomis, thence running northeast to Arkansas City. This trail was used generally as a
cattle, freighters', or traders' trail. He followed this trail for
a short distance, and about sun-up he came to the wagons of
a bunch of freighters who were camped at this point, bound
for Arkansas City. The occupants of these wagons had not
stirred from their night's repose when Frank rode up and
hollowed.

He was so cold and so nearly frozen that he did not know
whether he had traveled along this trail or had just struck
the same. When these freighters were aroused, they investigated and found that Frank was so nearly frozen that he could

not dismount from his pony. They were compelled to lift him to the ground, and he could not stand when they did so. His feet and legs were badly frozen. These freighters took him and cared for him, taking him to Arkansas City with them. It was two days before they could remove him to his home. In those days there were no telephones or telegraph lines. They took Frank to his home, which was west from Arkansas City, some twenty-six miles distant. They also took the Indian pony along. Frank did not recover from this experience until the next spring. The writer first saw him the next February, and he was then confined to the house a portion of the time suffering from the effects of his frozen limbs.

He did fully survive this experience, however, and the writer knew him well in after years as a typical cowboy, and one of the most effective and handsome men who rode the range. He traveled the trails from Wyoming and Montana to Mexico, and in later years grew to be quite wealthy. He lived to be fifty-eight years of age, but he was always well impressed with the fact that he could not have come any nearer losing his scalp and still have retained the same than he did on that evening in November, 1878, on the banks of the Red Fork or Cimarron River.

CHAPTER XXXII.

THE COWBOY CAPITALS

At all times during the cattle drives from the south, from the time the first long-horned, fleet-footed, stampeding herd of southern cattle was guided across the unbroken and unmarked course over the prairies to the northern market in 1867 up to the time the Chisholm Trail was closed forever by the onward march of the homesteader in 1889, there was some town at the north end of these drives, where the cattle trail and the steel rails met, that was recognized as the principal shipping point. Robert M. Wright in his interesting and instructive book, "Dodge City—The Cowboy Capital," has adopted the very appropriate name of "Cowboy Capital" for Dodge City during the period of its reign as the principal cattle shipping point at the end of the trail. This is perhaps the most appropriate designation that could be made for these points, and they will here be referred to as such.

Dodge City, Kansas, well deserved this recognition during the years of its supremacy. It held this position during some of the best years of the cattle business. It was, considering the entire history of the cow-towns, by no means, however, the only pebble of its kind on the beach. We will deal with these towns in the order of their existence as such.

It will be borne in mind that there was no shipping point in Kansas or west of Kansas City, Missouri, until 1867, and hence no cowboy capital. The facilities for handling the southern cattle had been established at Abilene in Dickerson County, Kansas, it having been selected as the most accessible point on the then newly established line of the Kansas Pacific Railway for such purpose.

Abilene as a Cowboy Capital.

When the first herds broke the trail across the prairies of Oklahoma and Kansas, and drifted down upon the little settlement at Abilene, this town was, in truth and in fact, the first Cowboy Capital. It held this position without opposition for several years thereafter. The cowboys who drove these herds had, most of them, recently returned from service in the armies of the then late war. They were young men—boys of spirit and activity. For weeks and months they had crowded on their herds during the day and stood guard during their allotted shifts during the night. When the elements were at their worst, and all Nature seemed to conspire against them, they had ridden with the cracking hoofs and clanking horns in the mad stampedes. Their entire lives had been one continuous exposure to danger and death, and they had become accustomed to a life of fearlessness.

When these boys reached the terminus of their drives, this little settlement was a metropolis to them, and they sought to enjoy themselves as best they could with such means as were available. One of the things to which they were exposed was cheap whiskey, which had been made for profit and not for consumption. They drank the same as any other class of men drank. Some took one drink and some took many. The ones who took too much told the world not only what they were but what they claimed to be. Few of these boys caused any trouble, but the ones who did had their iniquities charged up to all the rest.

When these cowboys reached the end of their drives, they were dusty and dirty, their clothes greasy and ragged; they were unshaven and their hair was long, and they then, perhaps, received the first money that had been paid to them since they started on their long drive. In twenty-four hours after their entry into town, no one would recognize the trim, well-dressed and handsome boys they met as being the travel-stained and travel-worn cowboys who had arrived in their midst only a few hours before. A new and expensive Stetson hat sat at a rakish angle on each head. In later years an expensive, thick silver or gold roll encircled the crown of the same where the band might have been. The clothes they bought were the most expensive and attractive that could be had, and their feet were incased in tight-fitting boots with small heels, three inches high, with quilted tops that came to their knees. These boots were equipped with large Spanish spurs, which kept up a constant jingle. This jingle was music to the ears of all westerners. These boys spent their money freely, and many of them left on their return trip without a cent.

This description of the cowboys and their habits is given for the purpose of showing the advantages to these towns and the vast revenue that poured into the Cowboy Capitals. Also each outfit was replenished with provisions and all necessaries for the return trip to Texas. Herds during the summer season were constantly arriving and outfits departing. Each herd had a number of cowboys, depending on the size of the same. The men who bought and sold these cattle, and the men who shipped them, made much money, and spent it in these towns freely.

When Abilene was established, and the cattle shipping begun, there were at this point no settlements to the south of the railway. Soon thereafter, however, the homesteaders with the plows and the hoes dotted the prairies between these herds and the railway. Arrangements were then made for a couple of years, whereby the settlers were paid satisfactory amounts for the privilege of driving over their lands. Some of the herds finally went some seventy miles further west on the same line of railroad to Ellsworth, south of which the settlers had not yet established themselves. Many cattle were shipped from Ellsworth. The close of the shipping season of 1871 saw the last herd arrive in Abilene, and also in Ellsworth. The reign of Abilene was for five years, with Ellsworth sharing the title with it during the last portion of the same.

In the year 1871, more cattle came up the trail than in any other one year during its operation. In this year over six hundred thousand head went north over the same. A few of these cattle went west to Great Bend in order to avoid the settlement, and also a few late herds were shipped from Newton. All the rest of that number were handled at Abilene and Ellsworth.

In the year 1871, the Atchison, Topeka, and Santa Fe Railway built west from Emporia to Newton, reaching Newton after the shipping season, except for a few late drives. Newton was on the Chisholm Trail, about sixty-five miles almost due south from Abilene. Thus the first sixty-five miles was cut off of the trail and plowed under by the homesteaders. Joseph G. McCoy, who in conjunction with others, had established the shipping yards at Abilene, immediately built shipping pens at Newton, from which a few herds were shipped in the late season of 1871 and most of the drives of 1872.

The life of Newton as a Cowboy Capital was brief, but what it lacked in time it made up in activity. It is said that as a result of one misunderstanding at this point, in one evening eleven men lost their lives. Newton at this time was a small town, and was not prepared and equipped to handle the situation of so much energy and activity of hot-blooded, belligerent men from the South. Newton, during its reign as a frontier "cow town," had more men die violent deaths in the same length of time than any other frontier cattle town.

Wichita, Kansas, in 1872, was a town of about two thousand inhabitants. It is located about twenty-six miles south of Newton. The main line of the Atchison, Topeka, and Santa

Fe Railway continued on west from Newton in 1871, but in the spring of 1872, a branch line was run from Newton south to Wichita, and it being located on the Chisholm Trail, another twenty-six miles was cut off of the north end of the trail, and Wichita became the Cowboy Capital of the West.

Before the rails were laid on this railway to Wichita, Joseph G. McCoy, the pioneer cattle shipper of the West, together with his associates, built shipping pens at Wichita. In the season of 1872 many herds stopped at Wichita and waited for the road to be completed in order to ship from that point. Wichita continued in its supremacy as a cattle shipping town until 1876.

It is fifty miles straight south from Wichita to the north line of Oklahoma, then the Indian Territory, and the point where the trail crossed the state line at Caldwell, Kansas, is about fifteen miles west of Wichita. In the early years of the seventies the homesteaders were rapidly crowding westward and were settling southern Kansas. These settlements were interfering very much with the cattle on the trail reaching the shipping point at Wichita. This matter was handled satisfactorily to all parties concerned for a time. This was done by compensating the land owners for their damages sustained by the trespassing herds. With the increase of settlers the trouble increased, and finally, with a few herds going through in the early drives of 1876, they ceased, and Wichita as a frontier cattle town passed into history.

Wichita, profiting by the experience of other towns, prepared itself well to receive and handle the worst element that came in with the cattle trade. While a number of men were killed during the period of its supremacy, the average was not nearly so large as in most of the towns handling the same sort of visitors. Wichita not only handled the cattle trade well, but on losing the same, instead of sitting down in despair, it renewed its efforts and energy, which eventually has made it the first City of the Southwest.

As has been stated, the railway in 1871 built west from Newton. It had reached Dodge City, Kansas, in 1872. Dodge City is the same distance north from the north line of Oklahoma, then Indian Territory, as Wichita, but being something over one hundred and fifty miles west of Wichita, the country south of the same had not at that time been settled. In 1876, when the trail was closed to the south of Wichita on account of the settlements, the country between Dodge City and the Indian Territory line being open and no obstruction to the herds reaching the shipping point on the railway at that place, the southern cattle drives turned to Dodge City, and it became the Cowboy Capital of the West.

In the year 1876, the herds from the south poured into Dodge City. This result for some time had been foreseen. Mr. Wright in his book heretofore referred to, quoting a newspaper article published in Dodge City during the year 1872, states:

"In the future, situated as it is upon one of the best railroads traversing the country from east to west, the Atchison, Topeka, and Santa Fe, it will probably occupy an enviable position as a cattle market."

Dodge City, ever since the railway arrived in 1872, had been a thriving western town. It was contiguous to Fort Dodge, and being nearer the hunting grounds, it had been the principal outfitting town for buffalo hunters and for the purchase and shipping of buffalo hides, which at that time was a thriving business.

Most of the drives over the Chisholm Trail up to this time had reached the trail at the crossing of the Colorado River near Austin, Texas. Here many trails from the south converged. Taking this route, however, it was necessary to travel back west to reach Dodge City, a distance of almost one hundred and fifty miles. In the year 1877, to shorten this distance, a well-defined trail was laid out and followed. It started in the vicinity of San Antonio, Texas, and took a northward course, crossing the Red River north and a short distance west of the present city of Vernon, Texas. J. Doan, in the spring of 1878, established a store on the south or Texas side of the river at this crossing. At this store he made a specialty of cowboy supplies and general outfitting for cattlemen and cowboys.

During the summer of 1878, J. Doan was joined by his brother, C. F. Doan and his family. C. F. Doan had formerly been in the West, but had returned to his home in Ohio, but now came back to join in this enterprise with his brother. These brothers enlarged their store and increased their supplies until they built up the business to a high standard. This store became one of the landmarks of the Southwest. The crossing of the Red River at this point was known as "Doan's Crossing," and the store was known the entire length of the trail and over the plains as "Doan's Store." This trail was known and designated on the maps of that period as the "Western Cattle Trail" and "Texas Cattle Trail." It will be observed in the article heretofore set out, taken from the *Cheyenne Transporter* in 1884, they refer to this trail as the "Western Trail."[1]

The Chisholm Trail was closed in Kansas on account of the settlements from 1876 until 1880. Well has Wright said during this period of time that Dodge City was the "Cowboy Capital." It was not only the "Cowboy Capital" of the West, but of the entire world. Dodge City at this time was a typical western and frontier town. It, like Newton, was not large, but what it lacked in size it made up in frontier life. During its reign it had for its protection some of the best peace offi-

---

[1] See *Indian Tribes Familiar to the Trail*— Page 179.

William (Bill) Tilghman, one of the greatest peace officers the West ever had.

cers of that period. Among these men were W. B. (Bat) Masterson, who was also Sheriff of the county, William Tilghman,[2]
and Edward Masterson, brother of Bat Masterson. Edward
Masterson was killed in the performance of his duty in Dodge
City on April 8, 1878. There was also among these officers
Ben Daniels who, Theodore Roosevelt has said, was the bravest
man he ever knew. There were also many other noted western peace officers who served this town.

---

[2] William Tilghman was afterward a resident of Oklahoma and one of the greatest
peace officers of the Old West. He had jurisdiction over the country once crossed
by the Chisholm Trail. He arrested and brought in some of the worst outlaws the
West produced. He served as marshal of many towns and cities, as sheriff, and was
at all times deputy United States Marshal. His life was devoted to law enforcement,
and he died in the line of duty.

During the time of the supremacy of Dodge City as a frontier cow-town, although it had some of the best peace officers there ever were in the West, it was for some time designated as the wickedest town in the United States, if not in the world. There was never a mining town of the mountains with a worse reputation. A short extract from a poetical effusion of the time will illustrate the general reputation of the town:

"Society bans me a savage from Dodge;
And Masons would ball me out their lodge.
If I'd hair on my chin, I might pass for the goat
That bore all the sin in the ages remote."

The extensive industries which helped to advance Dodge City were, in their order of time, the great amount of buffalo hunters making that their headquarters, next, the great cattle trade during the years it was the principal shipping point, and after the settlers took possession, the bone industry, being the shipping of buffalo bones, was no small item. Wright, in his book referred to, states in reference to this:

"One of Dodge City's great industries was the bone trade. It certainly was immense. There were great stacks of bones piled up by the railroad track—hundreds of tons of them. It was a sight to see them. They were stacked up way above the tops of the box cars, and often there were not sufficient cars to move them. Dodge excelled in bones like it did in buffalo hides, for there were ten times the carloads shipped out of Dodge than out of any other town in the state, and that is saying a great deal, for there was a vast amount shipped from every little town in western Kansas."

It established a famous "Boot Hill" cemetery, where none were buried except those who died with their boots on. A school building was afterward erected on the site of this burying ground. Dodge City continued as the principal cattle shipping point until 1880. Then, like Wichita and the other Kansas

cattle towns, the homesteaders crowded in on the some fifty
miles intervening between it and the line of the Indian Territory.
Wild, stampeding Texas cattle were not conducive to the well
being of growing crops. While a route was kept open to some
extent across this intervening country, and the cattle shipping
business in Dodge City did not immediately die completely, it
eventually decreased to a minimum. Dodge City is located in
a fine cattle rearing country, and there are still many local
cattle shipped at that point.

In 1880, the Atchison, Topeka, and Santa Fe Railway
extended south from Wichita and reached the north line of
the Indian Territory at Caldwell, Kansas. Two years later a
branch line was run south from Wellington, Kansas. This line
was known as the Leavenworth, Lawrence, and Gulf Railway.
The town of Hunnewell was established on the line of the Indian Territory at the point where this road reached the same.
Hunnewell is about twelve miles east of Caldwell. It really
required two shipping points at this time to handle all of the
cattle which came up the Chisholm Trail from the south. Most
of the cattle, however, were handled at Caldwell, and this
little city on the state line, which in days gone by, before it
possessed a railway, had seen so many herds pass on, now became the greatest cattle shipping point in the West or Southwest. From 1880 until the Chicago, Rock Island and Pacific
Railway extended south from Caldwell in 1889, Caldwell grew,
flourished, and its name went forth to the world as the greatest
frontier town of the West. It adopted the name of the "Border
Queen." The booted, spurred, and sombreroed cowboys crowded
its streets, walking with their characteristic and dramatic
strides.

Like other frontier towns, many were its brave officers who
went down in the performance of their duty. A noted Kansas
lawyer, while defending a man for murder at Wellington, dur-

ing this time, made the statement, "that all the citizens of Caldwell who are not here as witnesses have died violent deaths and have been laid away in the cemetery north of town." The result of the situation was the installing of Hendry Brown, a western gun-man, as marshal, with the result as stated in a former chapter. He was so successful and possessed so much extra energy that he took on bank robbery as a side line.

In 1877, Charles Goodnight and his brothers-in-law, the Dyer Brothers, came to the Panhandle of Texas. In 1878, they established a great cattle-raising industry in that country, which was also taken up by others, and all of that vast country was appropriated to that business. Large syndicates were formed by Eastern and foreign capitalists who acquired ranches, many of which would include an entire county.[3]

By the year 1883 the Panhandle was crowded with cattle. They were driven east past Mobeetie and joined the Chisholm Trail, and reached Caldwell for shipment on their journey to market. A few of these cattle were shipped from Kiowa, a town on the Kansas line some sixty miles west of Caldwell, but Caldwell remained the principal shipping point for the vast herds coming up from the Panhandle. Caldwell was the home of the Cherokee Strip Live Stock Association, and boasted of the largest and best opera house west of Kansas City. Money was plentiful and everyone prosperous. Gambling halls were open day and night. Twenty dollar gold pieces clinked on the floors of the hotels as men wagered them on a throw at a crack.

---

[3] A story is told of these times as follows: An Englishman belonging to one of these ranches invited a cowboy to take a drink with him in a nearby saloon. The Englishman, on going up to the bar, produced an English coin, saying: "You see the likeness of his Majesty, the King, on that coin, he made my grandfather a Lord." The cowboy, quietly laying on the bar a copper penny, said: "You see the likeness of that Red Indian on this penny, he made my grandfather an angel."

As the cattle were holding the frontier, and the home-steaders were gradually fighting their way further westward, there was much rivalry between these two classes. This was evidenced by a poem, a parody on Sheridan's Ride, which went the rounds at this time. It is worthy of reproduction here, and we quote it as follows:

"Up from the South, comes every day,
 Bringing to stockmen fresh dismay,
 The terrible rumble and grumble and roar,
 Telling the battle is on once more,
 And the granger but twenty miles away.

 And wide still, these billows of war
 Thunder along the horizon's bar;
 And louder, still, to our ears hath rolled
 The roar of the settler, uncontrolled,
 Making the blood of the stockman cold,
 As he thinks of his state in this awful fray,
 And the granger but fifteen miles away.

 And there's a trail from fair Dodge town,
 A good, broad highway, leading down;
 And there, in the flash of the morning light,
 Goes the roar of the granger, black and white
 As on to the Mecca they take their flight.
 As if they feel their terrible need,
 They push their mule to his utmost speed;
 And the long-horn bawls, by night and day,
 With the granger only five miles away.

 And the next will come the groups
 Of grangers, like an army of troops;
 What is done? what to do? a glance tells both,
 And into the saddle, with scowl and oath;
 And we stumble o'er plows and harrows and hoes,
 As the roar of the granger still louder grows,
 And closer draws, by night and by day,
 With his cabin a quarter-section away.

And, when under the Kansas sky
We strike a year or two that is dry,
The granger, who thinks he's awful fly,
Away to the kin of his wife will hie;
And then, again, o'er Kansas plains,
Uncontrolled, our cattle will range,
As we laugh at the granger who came to stay,
But is now a thousand miles away."

The days of glory of all things and all locations must eventually fade and leave its glory as only a memory. So it was with Caldwell. In 1889, Old Oklahoma was opened to settlement, the railway extended on south, and into Texas. The Chisholm Trail in all its length was closed forever. This great thoroughfare, over which millions of heads of cattle had traveled, and along which so many hundreds of picturesque cowboys had trailed their herds, was henceforth to remain as only a memory. The remaining men who rode this trail are few, but its memory will always linger with them and grow more sacred as the years increase.

CHAPTER XXXIII.

GOVERNMENT OPENINGS FOR SETTLEMENT ALONG THE TRAIL

While it is generally known that the land lying along the Old Chisholm Trail in Oklahoma was acquired from the Government by homestead entry, and the Government had procured this land from the various Indian tribes, yet the facts in reference to the former ownership and interests in the same and the method of acquisition by the Government are not generally known. It is not the purpose of this article, and space will not permit going into detail as to the various treaties involving this land entered into by the Government and the various Indian tribes having an interest therein, yet it is the purpose to give a general outline and idea as to such acquisition by the Government and the conditions which brought about the openings for homestead settlement of the various portions of the same. While the reader may not think this information will be interesting, if he or she will follow carefully the history of the title to this land, the writer feels that the result will be gratifying.

It has been observed in previous chapters that the Cherokee Indian tribe owned a strip of land fifty- eight miles wide lying immediately south of the State of Kansas, and extending westward from the Arkansas River as far as the possessions of the United States extended. This was known as the Cherokee Strip or Cherokee Outlet. This was given to the Cherokee Indians in addition to their reservation proper in the eastern portion of the Indian Territory. This land was acquired by the treaty of 1836. This treaty provided, after the grant made for the land in the eastern portion of the Territory, the following:

"In addition to the seven millions of acres of land thus provided for and bounded the United States further guarantee to the Cherokee Nation a perpetual outlet west and a free and unmolested use of all the country west of the western boundary of said seven millions of acres, as far West as the sovereignty of the United States and their soil extend."

The foregoing grant, it will be observed, covered the Osage reservation as well as the Outlet. The Osage Indians were not settled on this reservation until 1872, at which time a portion of the Cherokee land was ceded to them.

In the treaty made with the Creek or Muskogee Indians in 1825 it is stated:

"It is further agreed between the contracting parties that the United States will give, in exchange for the lands hereby acquired, the like quantity, acre for acre, westward of the Mississippi, on the Arkansas River, commencing at the mouth of the Canadian Fork thereof, and running westward between said rivers, Arkansas and Canadian Fork, for quantity."

Further provision is made in this treaty for an inspection, selection, and survey thereof. A portion of this land was subsequently set over to the Seminoles, who were in fact a part of the Creek. In the treaty made with the Government and the Choctaw Indians at Dancing Rabbit Creek in 1830, the following grant is made to the Choctaws:

"The United States under a grant specially to be made by the president of the U. S., shall cause to be conveyed to the Choctaw Nation a tract of country west of the Mississippi River, in fee simple to them and their descendants, to inure to them while they shall exist as a nation and live on it, beginning near Fort Smith, where the Arkansas boundary crosses the Arkansas River, running thence to the source of the Canadian Fork; if in the limits of the United States or to those limits; thence due south to Red River, and down Red River to the west boundary of the Territory of Arkansas; thence north along that line to the beginning. The boundary of the same to be agreeable to the treaty made and concluded in Washington City in the year 1825. The grant to be executed so soon as the present Treaty shall be ratified."

By virtue of a treaty concluded March 24, 1837, between the Government and the Choctaw and Chickasaw Indians at Doaksville, near Fort Towson, in the Choctaw Nation, a portion of the land ceded to the Choctaw Indians was turned over to the Chickasaw for use and occupancy, to be known as the "Chickasaw District of the Choctaw Nation." The provisions of said treaty as to said grant read as follows:

"It is agreed by the Choctaws and Chickasaws that the Chickasaws shall have the privilege of forming a district within the limits of their country, to be held on the same terms that the Choctaws now hold it, except the right of disposing of it, (which is held in common with the Choctaws and Chickasaws) to be called the Chickasaw District of the Choctaw Nation; ————"

The description of the land thus granted is set out in article two of the treaty as follows:

"Beginning on the north bank of the Red River, at the mouth of Island bayou, about eight or ten miles below the mouth of False Washita; thence running north along the main channel of said bayou to its source; thence along the dividing ridge between the Washita and Low Blue rivers to the road leading from Fort Gibson to Fort Wachitta; thence along said road to the line dividing Mashu-la-tubbe and Push-mata-haw districts; thence easterly along said district line to the source of Brushy creek; thence down said creek to where it flows into the Canadian river; ten or twelve miles above the mouth of the south fork of the Canadian; thence west along said Canadian river to its source, if in the limits of the United States, or to those limits; and thence due south to Red River, and down Red River to the beginning."

It is thus seen that the land entirely across the Indian Territory in the central portion thereof was held by the Five Civilized Tribes, the Cherokee, Creek or Muskogee, Seminole, Choctaw, and Chickasaw. This status of ownership continued until the close of the Civil War.

In 1865 the members of the five civilized tribes were informed by the Government that they, having entered into treaties with the Confederate States and accepted the authority of the Government of the Confederacy, had all dissolved and forfeited all allegiance to and protection of the Government of the United States, and that all treaties theretofore entered into with the United States Government were abrogated and forfeited and all their lands reverted to the United States Government, and that it was necessary that new treaties be made. Accordingly, in September, 1865, there was called and held a council at Fort Smith with the representatives of the Government and representatives of all the different members of the Five Civilized Tribes, and also with the Osage, Seneca, and Quapaw. An extract from the terms presented by the Government and accepted by the Indians at this meeting will show the condition of affairs better than any general statement. This extract reads as follows:

"Whereas the aforesaid nations and tribes, or bands of Indians, or portions thereof, were induced by the machinations of the emissaries of the so-called Confederate States to throw off their allegiance to the Government of the United States, and to enter into treaty stipulations with said so-called Confederate States, whereby they have made themselves liable to a forfeiture of all rights of every kind, character and description which had been promised and guaranteed to them by the United States; and whereas the Government of the United States has maintained its supremacy and authority with magnanimity with all parties deserving its clemency, and to reestablish order and legitimate authority among the Indian tribes; and whereas the undersigned representatives of parties connected with said nations or tribes of Indians have become satisfied that it is for the general good of the people to reunite and be restored to the relations which formerly existed between them and the United States, and as indicative of our personal feelings in the premises, and of our several nations and tribes, so far as we are authorized and empowered to speak for them; and whereas questions have arisen as to the status of the nations, tribes, and bands that have made treaties with the enemies of the United States, which are now being discussed, and our relations settled by treaty with the United States commissioners now at Fort Smith for that purpose:

"The undersigned do hereby acknowledge themselves to be under the protection of the United States of America, and covenant and agree that hereafter they will in all things recognize the government of the United States as exercising exclusive jurisdiction over them, and will not enter into any allegiance or conventional arrangement with any state, nation, power, or any sovereign whatsoever; that any treaty of alliance for cession of land, or any act heretofore done by them, or any of their people by which they renounce their allegiance to the United States, is hereby revoked, cancelled, and repudiated.

"In consideration of the foregoing stipulations made by the members of the respective nations and tribes of Indians present, the United States, through its commissioners promise that it will re-establish peace and friendship with all the nations and tribes of Indians within the limits of the so-called Indian Country; that it will afford ample protection for the security of the persons and property of the respective nations or tribes, and declares its willingness to enter into treaties to arrange and settle all questions relating to and growing out of former treaties with said nations, as affected by any treaty made by said nations with the so-called Confederate States, at this council now convened for that purpose, or at such time in the future as may be appointed."

Following this council at Fort Smith, there were, in 1866, treaties entered into by all the members of the five civilized tribes in the City of Washington. In the treaty with the Creek Nation we find the following provision:

"In compliance with the desire of the United States to locate other Indians and freedmen thereon, the Creeks hereby cede and convey to the United States, to be sold to and used as homes for such civilized Indians as the United States may choose to settle thereon, the west half of their entire domain to be divided by a line running north and south; the eastern half of said Creek lands, being retained by them, shall, except as herein otherwise stipulated, be forever set apart as a home for said Creek Nation."

By virtue of the foregoing and by a similar treaty with the Seminole, all the land comprising Old Oklahoma or that portion included in the opening of 1889 had been conveyed under the same terms to the United States Government. This was the basis of the contention of Captain David L. Payne and his Oklahoma Boomers, by which they claimed this land was subject to entry as Government land.

In their treaty made the same year, the Choctaw and Chickasaw ceded to the United States all that portion of their domain known as the leased district, this being all portions of their lands lying west of the 98th Meridian. The Choctaws and Chickasaws also agreed by this treaty to receive into their tribes and share their lands with not to exceed ten thousand Kansas Indians.

The Cherokee by virtue of the treaty of 1866 released no land to the Government. They did, however, agree to the location of certain other tribes of civilized Indians on the Outlet on certain terms.

After these treaties the Five Civilized Tribes settled down to recuperate from the disastrous effects of the Civil War. Southern cattle poured up over the Chisholm Trail. Various tribes of Indians were settled by the Government on portions

Capt. David L. Payne, Leader of the Oklahoma Boomers.—Courtesy of the Oklahoma State Historical Society.

of the lands acquired from the Creek and Seminole Indians. The portion so settled upon by other Indian tribes constituted but a small portion of the entire amount thus acquired by the Government by the terms of these treaties. The remaining portion was undisposed of, was unoccupied, except by intruding cattlemen, and was roamed over by hunting parties of Indians and whites generally.

In 1879, E. C. Boudinot, who was a member of the Cherokee Tribe of Indians, being a member of the famous Cherokee family of Boudinots, checked up the situation as to the rights of the Government in the lands involved in these treaties. The following statement issued by Boudinot sets forth his claim in detail:

"The United States, by treaties made in 1866, purchased from Indian tribes, in the Indian Territory, about 14,000,000 acres of land.

"These lands were bought from the Creeks, Seminoles, Choctaws and Chickasaws; the Cherokees sold no lands by their treaty of 1866.

"The Creeks, by their treaty of 1866, sold to the United States 3,250,560 acres, for the sum of $975,168. The Seminoles, by their treaty of 1866, sold to the United States 2,169,080 acres, for the sum of $325,362.

"The Choctaws and Chickasaws, by their treaty of 1866, sold to the United States the 'leased lands' lying west of 98 degrees of west longitude, for the sum of $300,000. The number of acres in this tract is not specified in the treaty, but it contained about 7,000,000 acres. (See 14th Statutes at Large, pages 756, 769 and 786).

"On these ceded lands the United States has since appropriated for the use of Sac and Foxes 479,667 acres, and for the Pottowatomies 576,877 acres, making a total of 1,055,544 acres. These Indians occupy these lands by virtue of treaties and acts of Congress. By an unratified agreement the Wichita Indians are now occupying 743,610 acres of these ceded lands. I presume some action will be taken by the United States Government to permanently locate the Wichitas upon the lands they now occupy. The title, however, to these lands is still in the United States.

"By executive order Kiowa, Comanche, Arapahoe and other wild Indians have been brought upon a portion of the ceded lands, but such lands are a part of the public domain of the United States, and have all been surveyed and sectionized.

"A portion of these 14,000,000 acres of land, however, has not been appropriated by the United States for the use of other Indians and in all probability never will be.

"These unappropriated lands are situated immediately west of the 97th degree of west longitude and south of the Cherokee Territory. They amount to several millions of acres, and are as valuable as any in the Territory. The soil is well adapted for the production of corn, wheat and other cereals. It is unsurpassed for grazing, and is well watered and timbered.

"The United States has an absolute and unembarrassed title to every acre of these 14,000,000 acres, unless it be to the 1,054,544 acres now occupied by the Sac and Fox, and Pottowatomie Indians. The Indian title has been extinguished.

"The articles of the treaties with the Creeks and Seminoles, by which they sold their lands, begin with the statement that the lands are ceded 'in compliance with the desire of the United States to locate other Indians and freedmen thereon.'

"By the express terms of these treaties the lands bought by the United States were not intended for the exclusive use of 'other Indians' as has been so often asserted. They were bought as much for the Negroes of the country as for Indians.

"The Commissioner of the General Land Office, General Williamson, in his annual report for 1878, computes the area of the Indian Territory at 44,154,240 acres, of which he says 17,150,250 acres are unsurveyed, the balance of the lands, amounting to 27,003,990 acres, he announces, have been surveyed; and these lands he designates as 'Public Lands.'

"The Honorable Commissioner has fallen into a natural error; he has included in his computation the lands of the Cherokees west of 96 degrees west longitude, and the Chickasaw nation which, though unsurveyed, can in no sense be deemed 'public Lands.' The only public lands in the Territory are those marked on this map, and amount, as before stated, to about fourteen million acres.

"Whatever may have been the desire or intention of the United States government in 1866 to locate Indians and Negroes upon these lands, it is certain that no such desire or intention exists in 1879. The negro, since that date, has become a citizen of the United States, and Congress has recently enacted laws which practically forbid the removal of any more Indians into the Territory. Two years ago Mr. Mills of Texas caused a provision to be inserted in the Indian appropriation bill, prohibiting the removal of the Sioux Indians into the Indian Territory; a project at that time contemplated by the Interior Department; and by a similiar provision in the Indian appropriation bill of last winter, the removal of any Indians from Arizona, or New Mexico, into the Indian Territory is forbidden. These laws practically leave several millions of acres of the richest lands on the continent free from Indian title, or occupancy, and an integral part of the public domain."

Following the disclosures of Boudinot, in the early eighties, the agitation for the opening to homestead settlement of the undisposed of ceded lands was taken up by Capt. David L. Payne. Payne was an energetic western character of remarkable ability. He had been a soldier in the late war, an Indian fighter on the Western plains, in which he served as captain, a member of the legislature of Kansas, and had been in the Government service at Washington City. Payne made several excursions with colonists into the Indian Territory, and was on each occasion seized and retained for indefinite periods of time and then released. His principal object was to obtain a hearing before some civil tribunal whereby he could determine in a legal way the question as to whether the undisposed-of lands were the property of the Government or belonged to the Indians. He at one time started a settlement at Rock Falls on the Chikaskia River south of Hunnewell, Kansas. This was on a portion of the Cherokee Outlet, in which the Cherokees in any event held the right of possession as against any intruders. The Government was under obligations to enforce that right. This not being a portion of the ceded land, it is difficult to ascertain the real object of this settlement.

Payne's activities were suddenly brought to a termination by his untimely death in November, 1884. He died while sitting at the breakfast table in a hotel at Wellington, Kansas. His place was taken immediately by his lieutenant, Capt. W. L. Couch, who carried on the agitation by following the same methods adopted by Captain Payne. The writer at this time resided at Caldwell, Kansas, and while only a boy, he knew very well a large number of the boomers, including Captain Payne, Captain Couch, Col. Sam Crocker, and many others, and visited the settlement at Rock Falls.

For several years prior to the first opening in 1889, there were many people who had come from foreign localities waiting for the opportunity to homestead in the country to be opened for settlement. Some of these parties had rented farms near the border, some lived in towns, and others camped along the streams, procuring employment whenever available. Many of them were members of the invading parties who made many excursions into the Indian Territory. They were as often removed by the soldiers, and their leaders held in custody for a short time and then released. As long as the soldiers seized these parties, and the power of the regular army and military was used, no judicial determination could be obtained as to the status of this land. The leaders of this organization even procured persons to sell whiskey in the country sought to be opened in order to induce the Government to arrest them for so doing on Indian land, and thereby procure a ruling as to the status of the land. The Government, however, met the contenders by such authority that the matter could be tested.

These agitators were known generally as "boomers." For years they supported a paper known as the Oklahoma War Chief. It did not appear regularly, however, but was printed first at Wichita, Kansas, and afterward in turn at Geuda Springs, Arkansas City, Rock Falls, south of Hunnewell, Kansas, in the Indian Territory, South Haven, and last at Caldwell, all of said points, except Rock Falls, being in southern Kansas. The paper, as well as the leaders of the colony and the editors, were taken charge of by the United States soldiers in August, 1884. The equipment for publishing the paper at this time was destroyed. It is said that the press and type were dumped by the soldiers into the Cimarron River on their return trip to Fort Reno. Col. Sam Crocker was the last editor of the paper. Crocker was a brilliant man and a great organizer and agitator. He was an experienced lecturer, editor, and printer. He never lacked for words, either in writing or speaking, that would burn his adversary up. He was arrested while editing this paper at Caldwell. The arrest was made under a charge of "seditious conspiracy and inciting insurrection and rebellion." This is an offense defined by the United States Statutes. He was taken to the Federal jail at Wichita, and kept for several months. During this time he edited the paper from his cell. He was finally released without trial.

The last issue of the *Oklahoma War Chief* was published at Caldwell in the fall of 1886. The reason for abandoning this paper at that time perhaps was that Crocker was the power behind the same, and he devoted most of his time from that period on in lecturing for the boomer cause and in lobbying for the same in Washington City. Col. Crocker, Captain Couch, and Sidney Clark, another important figure among the boomer colony, spent much of their time during the two years immediately preceding the opening of 1889 in Washington City, lobbying in the interest of legislation for the opening for settlement of the undisposed-of ceded lands of the Indian Territory. On one of these lobbying enterprises, Dr. Munford of the Kansas City Times, and an important national figure at that time, accompanied these parties to Washington City, and remained there for some time assisting in this work. In the subsequent opening, Sam Crocker took a claim, which is now included within the corporate limits of Oklahoma City. He lost the same in a contest for the reason that he was on the right-of-way of the railroad in the opened country prior to and at the time of the opening.

Finally, through the efforts of these parties, a rider was attached to the Indian Appropriation Bill of 1889, providing for the opening of this portion known as Old Oklahoma for settlement. This bill became a law. On March 21, 1889, President Harrison issued his proclamation fixing April 22, 1889, at twelve o'clock noon, as the time for the opening.

This country was opened without further provision, except that the first man on the land after the time fixed by the proclamation was entitled to 160 acres of the same by prior settlement. This devolved the matter down to a proposition that the man who could transport himself with the greatest speed to a valuable tract of 160 acres of land was the winner. In other words, it was a horse race or any other kind of race that would move a homeseeker from one point to another in the shortest space of time. This was the greatest diversion in such a matter that had ever occurred in the history of the world. It was brought about from the mere fact that such a great mass of people each had the same objective which could only be settled and determined by a trial of speed.

Never before in the history of civilization had such a gigantic body of people rushed pell mell into an extensive country, by one swoop torn the entire land from the public domain, and reduced it to private ownership. Before the sun set on the evening of the 22nd day of April, 1889, almost every acre of the millions of acres opened for settlement was appropriated by private owners. This county, while one of the best portions of the Indian Territory, was one of the wildest. The soldiers who had so long guarded this land against the homesteader, sounded their bugles as a signal for the entry upon the same, then stepped aside, abandoned their vigil, and watched the throng pass by them into the promised land. In the space of three hours this land was transformed from a howling wilderness into a well-settled and thickly peopled country. The deer fled before the advancing throng, the wild turkeys sought shelter in the trees, the wild wolves dashed into cover, and then out of cover before the advancing horde. The elements of the wilds were subdued, and darkness fell over a land appropriated by the homesteaders.

This paved the way for subsequent openings for settlement in the Indian Territory, which followed in rapid succession. This tract first opened for settlement lay near the center of the Indian Territory. In the year 1891 the Iowa, Sac, and Fox, and Kickapoo reservations, aggregating over three-quarters of a million acres, were opened for homestead settlement. In 1892, the Pottawatomie reservation, consisting of over one-quarter of a million acres, was also opened. These lands all lay to the east of the portion included in the first opening. The same year the Cheyenne and Arapaho country lying to the west of Old Oklahoma was also thrown open for settlement.

This last named land consisted of over three and one-half million acres.

On the 16th day of September, 1893, the greatest opening to occur in the history of the world took place. The Cherokee Strip or Cherokee Outlet, consisting of six million acres, including some of the best land in the Indian Territory, was thrown open to homestead entry. There had been so much complaint charging that persons entered the other lands opened before the appointed time that the Government devolved a method which was intended to overcome this trouble. They established booths at convenient points on the borders of the country to be opened. By this arrangement each person who intended to enter a tract of land was compelled to visit one of these booths, and the officer there would issue to such person a certificate to the effect that the settler had been present and obtained this certificate, which must be presented at the land office when the applicant appeared to file on his land. Without one of these certificates the applicant would not be permitted to file on a tract of land. Whether this arrangement relieved the situation is very questionable. These persons who entered prematurely were denominated "sooners," and it was generally recognized that it would take more than a stop to procure a certificate to delay a sooner in his unlawful course, and he cared nothing for the false statement he made to procure the same.

Completely encircling this land, for days and weeks prior to the date for the opening, there were vast throngs congregated, gazing across into the promised land. In the towns bordering on the Cherokee Strip were contrived, set up, and operated every conceivable device and scheme that the mind of man could invent to separate the members of this throng from what money they had. This is an inevitable evil that follows all such congregations of people, and never did it flourish to a greater extent than immediately preceding and following this opening. This was true from the fact that perhaps never before in civil life in this country did more people congregate with one purpose than did to participate in or witness this opening and race.

The persons who viewed this opening witnessed one of the greatest scenes that ever occurred in any land or country. The writer took part in this run to the extent of a twenty-mile ride. Just preceding the appointed hour of twelve o'clock high noon on the day of the run the line was formed and stood at attention and ready, as if awaiting the command to make a charge long anticipated on an enemy long sought. Looking in either direction down this line, it stretched as far as the eye could see. Not only was it a line, but a line of masses of people. These included every sort of conveyances that had been invented up to that time. The writer has often in later years wondered what would have been the result if automobiles and airplanes had been in use at that time. It was truly an assembly of variegated humanity, ranging from the most refined to the worst degenerate; one in which they all met on one level and upon equality. If there was any exalted member of society on this occasion, it was the one who was mounted on the most likely horse or was best equipped to pass over the surface of the ground for a considerable distance in the shortest period of time.

In this aggregation were parties on foot, on bicycles, in two-wheeled carts, parties with the two front wheels on their farm wagons, with the tongue fastened so it would not tip, and a box on it like unto a chariot, with two horses attached thereto, others in heavy farm wagons, and the majority mounted on horse back. Some of these parties rode high-spirited race horses, and others, cow-ponies or cow-horses. The race-horse riders usually ran their horses down in a few miles, and were compelled to land where their mounts gave out. Some had a relay of horses, one which was ridden and the other led. When the one ridden gave out, the led horse was saddled and completed the race.

The ones which usually made the best long race were the ones who rode the horses accustomed to be ridden over the prairies for long distances. These horses, when not crowded on the start, kept a steady gait for several miles. The day was hot; they perspired freely in the first few miles, then the strong wind, which was blowing, dried the perspiration, and they stretched out with a good speed seemingly for an indefinite distance. It was really remarkable the time that some of these horses made.

Trains were run into the country on the railways running into the same, but by regulations they could travel only fifteen miles per hour. This was a handicap to the persons entering thus. From the point where the train entered the Indian Territory south of Caldwell, the Rock Island Railway ran southwest. Round Pond, now the City of Pond Creek, was the first county seat in the opened country south of Caldwell. It was about twenty-one miles due south of the Kansas line, and in this distance the railway ran about ten miles west. The train on this railway did not reach the vicinity of Pond Creek for over one-half hour after most of the first horsemen had reached that locality. A foot racer, equipped with spiked running shoes, came out to the claim of the writer, over one-half mile from the railway, stopped, and sat down. When the writer rode up to him and advised him that that particular claim was taken, he was so exhausted from his race that he could not at first answer, but when he could he said that he did not suppose there were any objections to him sitting down on the claim. The next morning after the run, the writer, while riding along the trail, met a man walking north on the same, who said that he was going back to God's country. The writer inquired why he did not go back on the train. He answered that he would not ride on a train on a railway where a horse could outrun the train thirty minutes in a thirty-mile race.

After the run most of the settlers erected some meager evidence that the tract on which the settlement was made had been appropriated, and then rushed to the land office in the district in which it was situated to file a homestead entry as required by law. This caused a congestion at the land offices. The settlers formed in line, awaiting their turn to file. These lines extended for long distances and included thousands at each land office. It required months to dispose of all these applicants.

The parties in these lines formed themselves into companies of one hundred each, and elected a captain for each company, then each man had a number assigned to him. He took this number, returned to his home or to his claim, and awaited his turn. The newspapers printed these numbers, showing the last number that was filed each day. By this means the parties were enabled to keep track of the time when they would be reached in the process of filing. This same practice on a smaller scale had been followed before the run at the registration booths. Where there were two or more settlers on a quarter section of land, the one failing to get the filing was compelled to file a contest against the entryman. In this contest the party would allege a prior settlement on the land.

As soon as the filings were completed, the trial of these contests began. The testimony was all reduced to typewriting.

and this testimony read, and a decision as to who was the prior settler was then, at some time in the future, made by the register and receiver of the local land office. The party who lost in this decision had a right of appeal to the General Land Office. The case was then tried there on the same record, and a decision rendered by the Commissioner of the General Land Office. This decision either affirmed or reversed the former ruling. The party who lost in this decision had a right of appeal to the Secretary of the Interior, where the trial was had on the same record, and which decision was final. Most of these contests were taken to the Secretary of the Interior, or the tribunal of last resort.

It required years to adjust all of these contests. This was finally done, and the country settled down into the ordinary routine of a prosperous agricultural land. These contests further drained the meager purses of the settlers. This land and country finally grew and prospered into one of the richest and best improved regions in the world. In those days it was little dreamed that vast oil fields would extend over large portions of this land, that the bristling derricks of many gushers would rise over the country thus opened, millions of dollars of wealth would pour out from beneath the surface of these homesteads, and that Oklahoma would become one of the richest oil-producing districts in the world. Many who made this famous run have lived to see this condition, and have seen many of these men and women who rode in the race on that memorable September 16, 1893, become millionaires from such production. Looking back over these years with meditation, we can hardly realize the changes that the last forty years have wrought. Further, taking a full comprehensive view of the situation, we can but join in the declaration of the poet when he said:

"So dwelt the wild Indian by Ontario's side,
Nursed hardy on the brindled panther's hide;
As fades his swarthy race, he with anguish sees
The whiteman's cottage rise beneath the trees.
He leaves the shelter of his native wood,
He leaves the murmur of Ohio's flood,
And plunging forward with indignant grief,
Where ne'er foot has trod the fallen leaf,
Be bends his course, where twilight reigns sublime,
Through forests silent since the birth of time." [1]

---

[1] Scenes of Infancy—Quoted by Sir Walter Scott in *Guy Mannering*, Chapter VIII.

CHAPTER XXXIV.

COUNTY SEAT FIGHTS AND RAILWAY WARS

The Government Townsite of Round Pond, now the City of Pond Creek, is located five miles from the south line of Grant County. It will be borne in mind that Grant County is the first county in the State of Oklahoma on the north side. The original town of Pond Creek, now known as Jefferson, was located two and one-half miles north of the present City of Pond Creek, and seven and one-half miles from the south line of the county. The City of Medford, the present county seat of the county, is located six and one-half miles north of the original town of Pond Creek. Grant County is and always has been twenty-eight miles across the same north and south. This makes the City of Medford near the geographical center of the county.

The original Chisholm Trail crossed the Government Townsite of Round Pond and the Townsite of Jefferson, or Old Pond Creek. It originally passed approximately two miles to the east of the City of Medford, but, in the process of straightening, it gradually dropped back west until at the time of the opening of the country to settlement, it crossed the eastern portion of the townsite. This original trail also crossed the townsite of Enid and that of North Enid in Garfield County, the next county to the south.

This description of the locations is given in order to convey a better understanding of what subsequently took place. All of these towns are and were located on the line of the Chicago, Rock Island, and Pacific Railway Company. There were at the time of the opening of the country, in 1893, depots located on this railway at Medford, Jefferson, and North Enid, but there were none at Enid or Round Pond, now the City of

Pond Creek. The representatives of the Government sent out to locate the County seats in these counties, immediately preceding the opening of the country to settlement, first located the county seat in Grant County near the old site of the Pond Creek ranch, or the first town of Jefferson, at which point there is now no town, but only the water tank of the Railway Company. The original location of the Government Townsite in Garfield County was at North Enid, which station on the railway was then known as Enid. At each of these townsites there were reserved and set apart for townsite purposes three hundred and twenty acres of land.

Departure will here be made from the course of events to state that the writer had known and traveled this trail since 1881, and that among the persons familiar with the country, it was always presumed that when the country was settled, a county seat would be located and a city built on the hill just east and across Osage Creek from the present town of Jefferson. This location slants down to the south with a gradual decline over rich, fertile land to the excellent grove which now constitutes the magnificent park owned as such by Rock Island Township. This should have been the natural and logical result. Had this been done, one of the best cities in the State would now stand on this location.

After the selection of the Government townsites as stated, and before the opening of the country, three Indian allotments of eighty acres each were located adjoining the primary location of the Government Townsite at Old Pond Creek or Jefferson, another Indian allotment was selected at Medford, and four Indian allotments were located adjacent to the townsite located at the present site of North Enid. These were selected in accordance with the treaty with the Cherokee Indians allowing certain members of their tribe a right to select allotments of eighty acres each in the land opened to settlement. These were evidently selected at these points on account of the proximity of the townsites.

After the allotments were selected, on account of their location near the Government townsites, immediately prior to the opening, these original locations which had been made by the Government officials were changed by them, new locations selected, the new townsites surveyed, and at Enid a land office building was constructed on the public square. In Grant County the location was moved two and one-half miles to the south. This location, as stated, was only five miles from the south line of the county, and is on the south side of the Salt Fork River. This river is a wide, sandy stream, and while in low tide there is not a large flow of water on the surface; at high stages it is filled with quicksand and is a very dangerous stream to negotiate.

The Rock Island Railway considered these changes and the moving of the towns to points where they had no depots unwarranted. It refused to recognize such towns, and refused to establish any depots or railway accommodations for the new townsites so located. This brought about what were known as the railway wars in both Garfield and Grant Counties.

It has been stated, argued, and seriously contended that the Chicago, Rock Island, and Pacific Railway Company was interested in the allotments and property other than their depots and right-of-ways at these old townsites. The Townsite Company operating at the station of Old Pond Creek was named and known as the Rock Island Townsite Company. The writer was intimately associated with this Company, and was one of the legal advisers of the same. He desires here to state that the Rock Island Townsite Company had no connection whatever with the Rock Island Railway Company. This Townsite Company was incorporated prior to the opening, and not only had no connection whatever with the Railway Company, but no person interested in the Railway Company, either as officer or otherwise, so far as the writer knows, had anything to do with the Townsite Company. This was the only town that the Rock Island Townsite Company was interested in, and this name was selected simply because its holdings were on the line of the Rock Island Railway. The incorporators were citizens of Wichita, Caldwell, and other towns along the railway in Kansas and Oklahoma. This Townsite Company, immediately after the selection by the Indian of the allotment just north of the west portion of the Government townsite first selected, bought the same, and also purchased an option on the other two which lay just west of the original Government townsite.

When this first location of the townsite was made by the Government official at Old Pond Creek, it was named Round Pond. This name was given it on account of the location of the large pond which then encircled the park or grove of timber, and which ran along the north side of the townsite. When the townsite was removed to a point south of the river, the name was taken with it, and this townsite was platted and recorded as Round Pond, and so remains. Immediately after the opening, the town located on the townsite of Round Pond was incorporated under the name of Pond Creek. When the post office at the old townsite or depot of Pond Creek was established, W. J. Hicks was appointed postmaster. Hicks had formerly lived at Jefferson, Texas, and when he was requested to suggest a name for the new post office, he presented the name of his old home. Thus the post office was named Jefferson, and when the town was incorporated, in order to make the corporate name correspond with the name of the post office, it was incorporated as Jefferson. The town was subsequently moved one-half mile to the north of the original location, where the townsite was platted as Old Pond Creek, but the town was incorporated as Jefferson.

From the foregoing recital, we can readily see the conditions well set, not only for the railway war, but also the county seat fight which followed in Grant County. In both of these controversies all parties concerned were acting in absolute good faith. Neither party was at fault, and both parties were imposed upon. The Railway Company had secured a grant of land when they constructed their line through the country, which was done long before the country was opened for settlement. In procuring this right-of-way, they had selected it to accommodate their conditions at the points where the stations were built. In order to comply with the requests of the new towns the Railway Company was not only called upon to erect new improvements at the new locations only a few miles away from their regularly established depots, but these new locations lacked the facilities for operating a depot and improvements connected therewith. It also not only rendered the old location practically useless, but if they retained the same it added the extra expense of operating another station and the stopping of trains at intervals only a few miles apart.

The foregoing was the argument of the Railway Company, while on the other hand the towns were suffering from the lack of railway facilities. They had the inconvenience of a railway running through their limits and trains roaring over the road, but no advantages. Their condition was deplorable and needs no comment to be well realized. At Pond Creek the railway crossed the main street near the center of town. It happened that every few days, after these conditions had existed for a considerable period of time, some party crossing the railway suddenly became unable to get his conveyance, which he happened to be taking over just before a train came along, off of the track. The trains did not attempt to stop, disregarded the obstructions, and scattered them over the adjacent townsite. At one time a wagon was stalled on the track, but when the train passed on someone was minus a wagon. At another time a house was being moved over the track, and the train made kindling wood out of that particular habitation.

As early as the fall of 1893, steps were taken to procure Congress to pass a law requiring trains to stop at all county seat towns in Oklahoma, but relief from this source was slow. Meanwhile, during the spring and summer of 1894, things were happening almost daily near these county seat towns along the lines of the railway. The writer saw bridges on the railway sent skyward in broad daylight, with clouds of dust ascending from the same like lava hurled from a volcano. Bridges on the Railway were blown up north of Pond Creek, one was burned south of the same, and piles were sawed off on others. The same conditions existed and similar acts of violence took place near Enid. Still the Railway Company refused to stop its trains. At Pond Creek, in June, 1894, the joints on the track of the railway were broken and the track to the south of the break turned over for about two blocks. A train of Texas cattle approached from the south, and some of the citizens of the town tried frantically to stop the train before running into this torn-up portion of the track.

The engineer paid no heed to their demonstrations, but threw the throttle further open to destroy the obstruction which he thought was on the track. The fireman on this train reported that the engineer, who was looking out of his window and trying to determine what sort of an obstruction was on the track ahead, seeing the ties and track sticking up and recalling the fact that a house had been placed on it before, informed the fireman that the citizens had now placed a windmill on the track. He proceeded to annihilate that windmill, with the result that the engine and several cars left the track, and Texas cattle were scattered promiscuously over the country. The strangest thing imaginable is that during this entire railway war and county seat fight, while several persons were severely injured, no fatalities occurred. Finally, late in the summer of 1894, Congress passed an act requiring the trains to stop at all county seats on their lines in the Territory. The Railway Company complied with the conditions, and the railway war was at an end, but not the county seat fight.

In these county seat fights the same conditions existed as in the railway wars. As stated, while none of the parties interested were to blame for these conditions which precipitated the entire counties into these county seat controversies, still the people were the ones who were compelled to suffer the consequences. They suffered these at a time when they could least afford to do so. The country was new, the people were poor and striving for an existence. Most of them had come to the new country after reversed circumstances, and to recuperate their fortunes or make a new start in life. Drouths had swept the country, crops had failed, and to add to all this misfortune, they found themselves engulfed in the bitterest sort of controversy with the people whose interests should have been entirely in accord with their own.

Persons who never were involved in a county seat fight cannot realize the bitterness of the feelings that such a controversy engenders. This feeling is not only bitter in the extreme, but also lasting. The settling of the matter only makes the feeling more bitter with the ones who lost. These are not all the difficulties; the controversy itself diverts the energies of the persons whose interests are to build up the county, and directs them to tearing portions of it down. It also deters and keeps away desirable citizens, and causes persons of influence and energy, who would strengthen and bring wealth and prosperity into the country, to move away.

Grant County is a fair sample of these results. It is considered, and statistics show it to be, one of the first counties of the State. All the towns of this county have been ruined by the early strife in the same. From this effect they will never recover. On the other hand, who has benefited by this strife? To this question we are compelled to answer, "Not one person interested in the same." It is a sad fact that these experiences teach a lesson that apparently no one will heed. These controversies are all a delusion and snare. If the writer could compel the people generally to heed this lesson and follow his advice he would be one of the greatest benefactors of mankind.

No action was taken in the county seat matter in Grant County until the early part of the year 1899. At this time a petition was circulated calling a county seat election. This petition was circulated and presented to the Board of County Commissioners by the citizens and supporters of Medford for the county seat. Two of the three commissioners were Medford sympathizers. It was incumbent on the commissioners, in any event, to call the election. This they did on April 5, 1899. The writer at that time was County Attorney of Grant County. A petition, requesting the writer as such officer to appeal from the order made, was signed by fifteen persons, as required by law, and presented to him. The law directed the County Attorney to take such appeal. This was done.

An application for injunction was then made, and presented to Judge Jno. L. McAtee at Enid. This he denied, and an appeal was taken from his decision to the Supreme Court, which was later decided sustaining the lower court. This opinion was rendered by Judge Irwin for the Court, in which it was held that such an election could be held under the law while the territorial government was in force, regardless of the fact that the county seats were located by act of Congress. Subsequently, in a mandamus suit brought to compel the placing of a location north of Jefferson on the ballot to be voted for in this election, Judge B. T. Hainer for the Supreme Court rendered another decision, in which the matter was discussed at length, and authorities cited, holding that no election could be held to remove county seats located by act of Congress while the territorial form of government was in force, and that the provisions of the Organic Act governed.

In view, however, of the ruling on the application for injunction, the citizens of Pond Creek were placed in a peculiar position. The only way they could extricate themselves was to raise a question of fact, which would necessitate a trial. This was done. Before the matter came up for trial the writer had gone out of office as County Attorney, and was employed and served as one of the Attorneys in the trial of this case. One of the contentions, which was made in utter good faith in this case, was that the petition did not contain a sufficient number of legal signers. This matter was by Judge McAtee referred to W. E. Cogdal, an Attorney of Enid, for finding of facts and conclusions of law, as well as a contest filed by Medford as to the result of an election which had been held and in which it was alleged that Pond Creek had cast too many votes for the citizens actually in the town. The late Judge A. M. Mackey and the writer represented Pond Creek in this trial. This referee court and retinue, consisting of attorneys, bailiff, reporter, and an array of deputy sheriffs, traveled from town to town in the county, taking testimony, for a period of sixty-three days. This testimony, when transcribed, filled a good-sized dry goods box. The referee rendered his opinion, but before the matter could be presented, Judge McAtee was removed from office, and Judge Beauchamp took his place. When the matter was presented to Judge Beauchamp, he, in accordance with the decision of Judge Hainer, held that no election could be had while the Organic Act was the supreme law.

This decision was not appealed from. The question was

temporarily settled, being thus put to rest until after statehood. A long fight was made before the Constitutional Convention by both parties to control the provisions of the instrument being prepared so far as it dealt with county seat propositions and elections. Finally, after statehood, in the spring of 1908, an election was called and held. In this election, as in the previous election, Medford, Jefferson, and Pond Creek were candidates. Medford received the majority of votes, and was declared to be the county seat. An appeal was taken to the Supreme Court, and decided against appellant, and the county seat matter in Grant County was forever settled in favor of Medford.

In Garfield County there never was any election nor any county seat fight. Enid, being near the center of the county, and having the Government land office, after the railroad trouble was terminated, gained such a prestige that no question was ever raised attempting to change the county seat. In Kay County, which lies immediately to the east of Grant County, there was also a severe fight for the location of the county government. This was not, however, brought about by the fact that the county seat was too far from the center of the county, but arose from the fact that there were three large cities in the county, each of which wanted to be the county seat. The result was that when one of the towns was eliminated, it threw its support to the City of Newkirk, the original county seat. This influence permitted Newkirk to hold the county seat. Kay County then built at Newkirk one of the most magnificent Court Houses in the State, and that county seat was settled for all time.

One of the most lamentable things that ever happened in Grant County took place during the trial of this county seat case. That was the killing of George Smith, the deputy sheriff in charge of the officers accompanying the referee court. While this killing was not brought about by the county seat controversy, as stated, it occurred during the trial of the same. The circumstances of this killing are as hereinafter set out.

The writer went out of office as County Attorney of Grant County the first Monday of January, 1901. He was then hired by the citizens of Pond Creek to represent them in the county seat controversy, and carried and paid out all the money necessarily paid out by the City of Pond Creek in this trial. This included the witness fees, which must be advanced. These witnesses were all subpoenaed by the deputy sheriffs accompanying the Referee Court. On Saturday, the 11th day of May, 1901, this Court was held at the Town of Wakita, which is in Grant County, and some sixteen miles northwest of Medford. Court adjourned at noon of this day, and the members accompanying the same all departed to their homes. This was before the days of automobiles, and almost all of these parties were traveling in buggies. The deputy sheriffs were all mounted on horses. When the parties left Wakita after the noon meal, George Smith rode in the buggy of the writer and led his horse. In this manner the writer and the deputy reached Pond Creek late in the evening. This now seems strange, in as much as with the present method of transportation this distance would be covered in not to exceed forty-five minutes.

The writer directed Deputy Smith to return to his office later in the evening and assist him in matters which he was checking up as to the witnesses who would next be subpoenaed. The deputy returned just before dark, and stated that he was going to the depot to meet the train, and would return in a short time. The writer asked him to go to the printing office before making this trip, and bring him more receipts to be signed by the witnesses, which were printed for his use; and asked him to do this at once as the printing office would close, and he must have the receipts before leaving Sunday evening.

The writer stepped out to the barber shop, and on his return, found the receipts on his desk. He then departed for his home two miles north, and did not know of the killing of Smith until the next morning when he returned to Pond Creek.

Deputy Smith, after delivering the receipt books, went directly to the depot. His purpose was to meet the train and attempt to find thereon a criminal whom he desired to arrest. The depot was some three blocks west of the office of the writer. In the first block east of the depot, and between the depot and the office of the writer, were at that time some three or four saloons. A darky, who did not reside in Pond Creek, but who often stopped in the city and was well known there, and who was known under the name of "Nigger Bill," was proceeding to get thoroughly intoxicated, and the keepers of the saloons referred to had refused to sell him any more whiskey. Bill was a big, burly darky, and when drunk was quarrelsome and dangerous. He concluded that it was on account of his racial affiliation that he was thus discriminated against, and proceeded to "cuss" out everyone he met. In doing this, he called them "white trash" and all kinds of names.

There was a Texan by the name of Fisher who resided in Pond Creek, passing by, and heard Bill's vindictive utterances. Fisher, thinking that the darky was talking to him in particular, and it being against the dignity of a Texan to be talked to in that manner, especially when the talker was a colored man, drew from his waist-band a .45 Colt pistol, and struck Bill over the head with the same. The blow was administered with such force and Bill's head was so hard that the gun flew out of the Texan's hand. This lick, while it stunned him, did not even stagger Bill; he immediately drew a thirty-two pistol from his pocket, and gazed around for some adversary to shoot. Fisher immediately retreated, and took refuge behind a wagon which was standing at the edge of the street.

At this time Deputy Smith came along, returning from the depot, and seeing the pistol lying on the sidewalk, and the darky standing there with a gun in his hand, he called Bill by name and asked him what the trouble was. The deputy, not thinking that the colored man had any intentions toward him, kicked over the pistol which was lying on the sidewalk, and reached down to pick it up. As he did so, Bill fired with his thirty-two pistol. Smith being in a stooping position the ball struck him just above the right ear and ranged forward into his brain.

Bill, after the shooting, seized both pistols and backed down the street to the east. A crowd was assembled on the sidewalk on both sides of him. As he backed away, he pointed his pistols first at the crowd on one side and then on the other, all the time admonishing them to stand back or he would shoot. There were no electric lights in those days, but there was a bright light in a restaurant in the next block to the east, and a number of parties had taken a position across the street from this bright light. They were armed with shotguns loaded with buckshot, and intended to riddle the colored man when he came in view between them and the light. In the crowd on the east side of Bill was J. C. McClelland, who operated a bank in Pond Creek at that time. McClelland was a powerful man physically. He had been Sheriff of Kingman County, Kansas, for years, and knew how to handle desperate men. He knew "Nigger Bill," and shouted to him, asking him what the trouble was, and telling him that he wanted to talk with him. While doing this, he was getting closer to Bill, and as he turned to look at the crowd on the opposite side, McClelland rushed up behind him and held both of his arms until he could get assistance, when the darky was disarmed and rushed to the County jail.

In a couple of hours a messenger came from the Barkley Hospital located in the north part of town, to which Smith had been immediately removed after the shooting. This messenger brought the information that the deputy was dead. Smith had been raised in the old Town of Jefferson. His mother had died before his father moved there. His father was poor. The lot of this family had been extremely hard. George had been a puny little lad when he played around the streets of Jefferson, but on reaching the period of young manhood he grew stout and robust, and was looked upon as a very trustworthy and reliable young man. J. D. Butts, the then Sheriff of Grant County, had placed him in his office as a deputy. George had made good in this position, and was well liked.

When the news came that he was dead, a sadness fell like a dark shadow over the entire town and community. There was not a word said, but soon men, singly and in pairs, were seen to join a crowd at the jail. They demanded of Under-sheriff Robinson the keys. He refused, and was dragged from the jail. He broke away from his captors and ran, and as he did so, he threw the keys into the grass, where they were soon found. Bill was led from the jail with a rope around his neck. He slipped this rope off and started to run, but the crowd fell on him, and he was tied more securely and led down the main street of the town to the spot where he had shot Smith. There he was drawn up to the cross arm on a telephone pole. The rope was too short to reach over the cross arm, but another piece was procured, the rope lengthened, and the prisoner was lifted up from the ground with his hands tied behind him. In this manner he died, and remained hanging there until near noon the next day, when he was cut down and buried on the top of the high bank on the south side of the Salt Fork River, at a point about one-half mile east of Pond Creek.

CHAPTER XXXV.

SUNDRY MATTERS OF INTEREST

There are several matters of interest connected with the Chisholm Trail, which will be grouped in this chapter.

One of these is the many trails branching off from the main Chisholm Trail. It has been observed that all of the trails from southern Texas met at a common crossing of the Colorado River, near the City of Austin. North of this point, and just north of Red River, a trail branched off to the northeast. This was the trail followed by the cattle drives of 1866. This trail passed up over the land of the Five Civilized Tribes, including that of the Cherokee. It was little used as a cattle trail after the main trail was broken in 1867.

There were many other minor trails which branched off at intervals along the main line. Most of these went to the cattle ranches various distances from the main trail. Some distance north of Buffalo Springs, in the Cherokee Outlet, there was a trail which bore to the northeast, crossing the Salt Fork River at the mouth of Pond Creek, south of the present prosperous little city of Lamont in Grant County. This trail bore to the northeast, going to Arkansas City on the south line of Kansas.

Perhaps the most important branch bearing off from the main trail was what was known as the Cantonment Trail. This trail left the main branch immediately after crossing to the south side of the Salt Fork River. It bore to the southwest, crossing the present paved highway known as Government Highway 81 in the hollow about one-half mile south of the large cement bridge now spanning the Salt Fork River, and a little less than one mile north of the present City of Pond Creek.

This trail wound its way to the southwest, crossing Coldwater Creek, Wagon Creek, sometimes known as Wagon Wheel Creek, Turkey Creek, Indian Creek, sometimes known as Walnut Creek, and the Cimarron River at the mouth of Indian Creek. Some two miles north of this crossing was located the Quinlan or X— (X Bar) Ranch, on Indian Creek. It still continued southwest, passing near the present City of Fairview, county seat of Major County, Oklahoma. It then passed on more south than west to Cantonment, now known as Canton, in Blaine County, Oklahoma. In its course south, at a point about nine miles north of Cantonment, it passed a short distance west of what was then known as Cedar Springs.

Cedar Springs, just east of the highway, was an important camping spot on this line. After 1884, just east of the trail at this point, there was for a number of years an Indian's grave, if such is the proper designation of the same. This Indian had been, not exactly interred, but disposed of after death by sewing him up in a heavy rawhide, and after so doing by hanging the rawhide up on a large limb of a tree by strong strips of rawhide. Then his horses, dogs, and other chattel property of which he was possessed, except his wives, were taken under the tree and killed, so that they could accompany him to the Happy Hunting Ground.

This rawhide, as is natural, grew smaller each year, until it had shrunk to a small portion of its original size. This was said to be the last resting place of Running Buffalo, a Cheyenne Chief. He had been killed near Cantonment in May, 1884, while extracting without permission some horses from a herd passing over the country en route to Kansas. This happening is dealt with elsewhere herein. Buffalo had been a bad Indian, and it was generally supposed that there were scalps and other relics of frontier Indian wars interred with him in this rawhide. Buffalo and his rawhide disappeared in a few years, and the writer has been informed that it was cut down by a bunch of eastern hunters, who were curious as to its contents, but that no scalps were found, and that nothing but beads and simple trinkets shared the rawhide with him.

At this grove at Cedar Springs was a frontier contrivance, a description of which might be interesting to people of the present day. This was a primitive turkey trap, made for the purpose of trapping wild turkeys, many of which were then found in this locality. The construction of this trap is interesting. It consisted of a log pen, some sixteen or twenty feet square, about five feet high, and covered on top with poles. On one side, the bottom log was some little distance from the ground, and there was a ditch about two feet wide dug from a sloping bank back under this log to a sufficient depth that a turkey walking along with its head down eating could pass under the log without touching the same.

There were no openings in this pen large enough to permit a turkey to crawl through except the place at the bottom of the log, to which reference has been made. The operator would then take corn or some other commodity that would interest a hungry turkey, scatter it on the ground out for some distance, and up along this path or ditch running into the pen, placing a generous amount in the pen. The turkeys would walk along with their heads down, interested in gathering up the food scattered for them. After they were inside the pen, they would raise their heads, look around, wondering how they got into the enclosure, and try frantically to escape through the small cracks, but would never think of lowering their heads and crawling out under the log. The lack of such crawling-under instinct was fatal to the turkeys once inside, and a sad lesson to them.

At Cantonment this trail turned west, going in that direction until it connected with the Western Cattle Trail, crossing the Red River at Doan's Crossing. At Cantonment it was said that there were living about six hundred Indians, most of them Arapahoes. Part of their houses were built in stockade style, constructed of small cedar logs procured in the canyons of the nearby Gloss or Glass Mountains. Others were built in ordinary log-house style out of the same sort of material. All of them had the cracks filled with cement obtained from the same mountains. These mountains at the present time are a large cement producing district.

At the Red Fork Ranch, the present site of the town of Dover, in Kingfisher County, Oklahoma, the trail divided. The cattle trail followed the river for a mile and one-half and crossed the Cimarron River at the mouth of Kingfisher Creek, while the old trail, or what was known as the Trader's Trail, went south, crossing the river where the present highway and railway crosses the same. This trail continued south and a little west to Caddo Springs, the site of the old Cheyenne School, now known as Concho, and then on to Darlington Agency, Fort Reno, Anadarko, and Fort Sill.

Another item of interest that deserves consideration is as hereinafter set out. This matter, while the same was well known to the writer, had been overlooked until reading the *Chronicles of Oklahoma,* published by the State Historical Society. In the issue of September, 1934, appeared an article written by Martha Bunton, entitled "The Murder on Turkey Creek." The writer was an old friend of D. W. Jones, more familiarly known as Dan Jones, who figured prominently in this matter. Dan Jones was one of the early keepers of the Red Fork Ranch. He sold the ranch in about 1880, and removed to Caldwell, Kansas. He was engaged in business there, and incidentally was a peace officer, serving as Deputy United States Marshal for many years. At the opening of Old Oklahoma in 1889, he took a claim near where he had kept the Red

Fork Ranch, and was for many years in the Sheriff's office of Kingfisher County, being the county in which his claim was located. At such times as the writer was attending Court in that County, Jones would always hunt him and they would talk over the events of the Old Trail and the history of the frontier, with which both were familiar. The circumstances in the happening referred to in this article have many times been discussed, and the facts of the same related by Jones to the writer.

This article so appearing in the *Chronicles* is a very graphic portrayal of the facts of this matter as they were related by Jones. In fact the writer had forgotten the names of the parties and the dates until reading the same. There are but a couple of very minor matters in this article as published that the writer would seek to vary. One of these is that the ranch of Mr. Jones is stated therein to have been about ten miles northeast of the place where this murder occurred. His ranch was about seven or eight miles southeast from this location. The ranch of Mr. Harris, who also assisted in this matter, as the writer recalls, was some miles northeast of the scene of the killing. This is very minor in importance, and might happen in any recital, especially after the lapse of so many years. The article itself really shows, however, that this ranch was southeast of this location, as it states that Jones was going back from the direction of his ranch, and he was facing a northwest wind.

In reciting the facts of this occurrence the writer will largely follow the article referred to. In the fall of 1876, Richard Wannamaker, a German, of about fifty years of age, and a man well experienced in the West, having spent years of his life, not only in the middle West, but in California, was preparing to cross the Indian Territory to Texas. He was then at Medicine Lodge, Kansas, and had about thirty head of ponies or horses, considerable personal property, and a moderate sum of money, the exact amount of which was never learned. He was a dentist by profession, had a small dental outfit, and contemplated opening an office in Texas.

Wannamaker was looking for one or more companions to accompany him across the Indian Territory. He met Frank Kilborn, who had a wife and three children, and was possessed of a wagon and harness, but had no horses. Kilborn also was desirous of crossing the Indian Territory to the State of Texas. Both of these parties desired to locate in Texas and make that State their future home. They agreed to associate themselves together and use their joint property in making this journey. It was also necessary for Wannamaker to procure a couple of extra men to accompany them to look after his stock and drive the same. He finally secured the services of two transient parties, Dick Simpson and Monroe Kipinizer, to accompany them and perform these services.

On November 11, 1876, this group of newly made friends set out on their journey to Texas. They left Medicine Lodge, Kansas, where the outfit had been organized, and the parties had met. Medicine Lodge is about fifty miles northwest of Caldwell, Kansas. They struck the Chisholm Trail at Caldwell, and took their course south, heading toward their destination in Texas. On November 24th this party reached a point on Turkey Creek some eighty miles down the trail from Caldwell. This was the first timbered country that the parties had reached. With the exception of glades, this timber came down to the creek. Wild turkey and deer were in abundance there at that time, and the parties concluded to stop for a short time and kill some of the game.

It is here well to observe the different individuals making up this outfit. As stated, Wannamaker had long been in the West, and had much experience on the frontier. The Kilborns were honest, ordinary people, with three small children. Their only object was to reach the Southern country and prepare them a home. Simpson was about twenty-six years of age, and had been employed as a roustabout or horse wrangler with various outfits. Kipinizer was an illiterate lad of about eighteen. He had no education whatever, but was honest and trustworthy. All of these parties before this meeting had been total strangers to each other.

Wannamaker, Simpson, and Kipinizer all started out hunting. Wannamaker and Simpson were equipped with double-barreled shotguns, and Kipinizer carried a Winchester rifle. Simpson and Wannamaker were hunting on one side of Turkey Creek, and Kipinizer on the other. Kipinizer heard shots fired in the vicinity of where his companions were, and crossed over the creek to see whether they had killed any game. He soon met Simpson, who stated to him that he had killed Wannamaker. Kipinizer thought the older man was simply joking, as he was given to such extravagant statements. The two, however, soon returned to their camp. Simpson then began to express anxiety about Wannamaker, stating that he was afraid that he was lost and would not find his way back to camp.

Later in the evening Simpson suggested that the members of the party had better go back along the creek and try to find Wannamaker. Kipinizer had become suspicious of Simpson, and refused to go with him. Kilborn, however, started out with Simpson on the search, but soon also became suspicious of him, thinking that he had killed Wannamaker and now intended to kill the entire remaining members of the party. For this reason, Kilborn soon returned to camp and reported his suspicions. Leaving the herd of ponies and going without waiting for the return of Simpson, who never did return to the camp, the parties took the wagon and other belongings and started for the Darlington Agency, which was on down the trail about fifty miles from their camp.

On arriving at the Agency they immediately reported to Agent John D. Miles the facts as far as they knew them. Agent Miles had the parties composing this outfit remain there, procured a detachment of soldiers from the nearby Fort Reno, and sent Ben Clark, who was long a trusted employee at the Agency, and who was one of the editors of the *Transporter* published at the Agency, with the soldiers, as his agent and representative.

There was a hunting party of Sac and Fox Indians camped on Turkey Creek, near where the Wannamaker outfit had stopped. These Indians met a Mr. Harris, who happened along, and informed him of the facts connected with the party of white travelers, that they had departed leaving these horses and one of their party behind, and that it was probable that the one left behind had been killed. Dan Jones, the keeper of the Red Fork Ranch, some seven or eight miles down Turkey Creek, was the recognized leader among the scattered inhabitants of white men in this portion of the country. Harris knew Jones, and went to see him and consulted with him about the matter.

These two men started out to investigate, and soon struck the wagon tracks of the departing Wannamaker party, followed it back, and found the herd of horses grazing where they had been left. They started to drive these animals to the Red Fork Ranch. The Indians who were camped nearby, seeing the parties taking the horses away, sent two of their number to inform them as to what they knew about the occurrence. The statement of Dan Jones in reference to this matter was published in the *Transporter* at the Darlington Agency, and this article copied in the Arkansas City Traveler, and we here set out the same, beginning when they had traveled about four miles on their journey to the Red Fork Ranch with the horses:

"After we had traveled about four miles we saw two Indians coming behind us at full speed, and I rode back to meet them. When they came near I saw they were Sac and Fox Indians. To the inquiry as to what they wanted, they replied in broken English, 'See white man dead, squaw find him.' Leaving Harris to take the stock to the ranch, I turned back with the two Indians, who said they would guide me to the dead white man. Just as we descended into the bottom, after a ride of four miles, the sun was setting. A cold wind from the northwest blew in our faces and the tall waving grass made specters of the long shadows that fell across our path as we sped along the stream. We passed down a steep bank into the timber and I found myself in the midst of an Indian camp where everything was in confusion. At a word from my guides, they all uttered something which was unintelligible to me, but quiet was restored. My guide dismounting, signalled to me to do the same, saying, 'Come.' Then on foot I followed the Indian who went stooping and dodging through the brush some four hundred yards, when he halted and pointed ahead, said, 'See,' and in the growing darkness I beheld the body of the dead man. Upon approaching the body I found it to be of a man about fifty years of age. He was lying on his back, his right arm across his breast, his left arm thrown out. He had been shot with a shotgun, the charge entering the left side of the face and many of them coming out on the right side of the ear. The left pocket in his pants was wrong side out, showing that he had been searched."

Jones returned to his ranch without further examination of the body. On arriving, he found Ben Clark and the soldiers there. This was on November 29th. The next morning the parties, including Clark, the soldiers, and Jones, went to further investigate the remains of the dead man and the surroundings. On such examination they found that all the papers and personal belongings of the deceased had been removed, and that some animal had eaten a portion of his face away. None of the parties present were able to identify the dead man, and it was necessary to bring a portion of the members of the deceased's outfit from Darlington Agency to identify him. He was then buried on the east side of Turkey Creek, near where the remains were found. The article referred to states that the grave was unmarked. The writer will say in that regard, that such statement is correct so far as any name being left on the grave was concerned, but from Mr. Jones he understood that stakes were driven around the grave, and that the grave was near the Bull Foot Stage Ranch. If this is true, the writer has seen this grave many times. There was no name to determine whose body was interred there so far as the writer ever saw, but the stakes around the grave were kept intact for many years.

A detachment of soldiers was sent out from Fort Reno to search for and capture the murderer Simpson, who had fled. He was subsequently arrested at Jacksborro, Texas, and brought back to answer for the murder of Wannamaker. The writer has, however, been unable to ascertain the result of such trial. There was found among the personal effects of Simpson when arrested the billfold of the deceased, which had evidently contained his money. This billfold also contained numerous papers of interest, some of them dating back as far as 1861, and most of them dated at locations in California. It also con tained a letter writen in German by the brother of the deceased, at a point in Switzerland, in June, 1875.

This billfold and its contents, and the other effects of Wannamaker, were turned over to Agent Miles, who was compelled to settle the estate of the deceased. The property of this estate consisted of thirty head of horses, only two of which were branded, a double-barrelled shotgun, ammunition, six pairs of dental forceps, various articles of dental equipment, and sundry other items of minor importance. This property was sold as provided by law, and in the absence of any known heirs the proceeds were turned over to the Secretary of the Interior. This letter from the brother of deceased was so badly worn that only a small portion of it could be read and translated.

The Kilborns, on account of the death of Wannamaker, were left in a very bad condition. Their relations with Wannamaker had been very congenial and satisfactory. They liked the deceased very much. On account of his sudden death, they were left in the midst of a wild and unsettled country with limited means, a wagon, and their personal effects, and no horses to draw the same. This matter was solved by the authorities permitting them to take a team of the Wannamaker horses and depart for their destination in Texas. This was done with the understanding that the horses were to be returned within a stipulated time. This was carried out, and this team was returned long before the time expired.

This circumstance is but illustrative of the characteristics of men in every walk of life. One man, with perhaps a born criminal mind, who could not nor would not act along the legal lines of organized society, at the first opportunity broke out with his lawless proclivities, committed one of the most cowardly and dastardly crimes imaginable, not only killing his friend for a paltry few dollars, but placing a cloud, horror, and grief over the lives of the balance of the party, which doubtless remained with them the balance of their lives, and also placing them in a most helpless condition. This inoffensive man was shot down in cold blood.

The situation in this country at that time rendered it very difficult and awkward to handle these cases, and after a man's guilt was fully, fairly, and satisfactorily established, he was usually dealt with in a more summary manner. Justice was the watchword of most of the men on the frontier, and a man transgressing these laws according to their code usually received justice, whether he wanted it or not. The Agent and members of the official family at the Darlington Agency were Quakers, and lived up to the letter of the law, so this murderer fell into the hands of the United States Army, and he was protected by the soldiers. Had it not been for these conditions, he would probably have been apprehended before he ever reached Texas, and would have answered for his crime in the land where it was committed. This was the temper of the body of men on the frontier, and they lived up to their convictions.

CHAPTER XXXVI

PRESERVING THE NAME AND LOCATION
OF THE TRAIL

As heretofore observed, the Chisholm Trail acquired its name on account of the connection of Jesse Chisholm with the early history of the same. Jesse Chisholm at this time lived at Wichita, Kansas, and is given credit for permanently locating the trail from Wichita to Anadarko and then on to Fort Sill. By this trail is meant the Trader's Trail, he having only traveled the Cattle Trail to the Cimarron River. There can be no controversy as to the location and name of this trail, nor that the cattle trail extending on to Texas acquired its name from the association with and from the fact that it was an extension of this trail, the north portion of which was used in common with it.

Within the last few years a claim has been advanced and agitated, which was unheard of before, and that is to the effect that the Western Cattle Trail, running from near San Antonio, Texas, crossing the Red River at Doan's Crossing, the old location of Doan's Store, north of Vernon, Texas, and south of Altus, Oklahoma, and running north to Dodge City, Kansas, was the correct Chisholm Trail. It is understood that this claim was started as a joke, but was then taken up by persons who knew nothing about the location of the Chisholm Trail, and while it really had no foundation in fact, the claim gained such momentum among people living in the portion of the State where the western trail crossed until they were really serious about the matter. There is not and never was any question as to the importance of the Western Cattle Trail, and no one, much less any of the old frontiermen, desires in the least to detract from the importance of the same.

The old cowboys, freighters, and other persons who had traveled the old Chisholm Trail, many of whom had spent years of their lives upon the same, held the name, designation, and location of this trail sacred.   Most of these men were growing old; the farther they advanced in life the more they cherished the scenes of the most active portion of their lives, and the men who started this claim can well realize the agitation and worry that the same caused these kind-hearted old frontiersmen.

After this claim was going good, these old friends of the Chisholm Trail, recognizing the injustice of the same, called a meeting, which assembled at Enid, Oklahoma, in the spring of 1930.   The survivors and remnant of the old guard of the frontier, who had traveled the Chisholm Trail, met at this meeting.   The claim which had gained circulation was at this meeting condemned as absurd, resolutions passed denouncing the same, steps taken to advertise the error and injustice of the claim, and to record the facts to be preserved for future generations.

At a meeting of the Old Time Cherokee Strip Cowpunchers Association, of which the writer is a member, and which meeting was held at Cowboy Hill at the 101 Ranch on the 31st day of August, 1930, a resolution was passed in reference to this matter, in which the correct route of the Old Chisholm Trail was set forth.   This resolution reads as follows:

"Realizing that there has been considerable discussion as to the true location of the old original 'Chisholm Trail' and as many of our members have driven cattle up over the old original 'Chisholm Trail,' we feel that we are justified in designating the true location by living witnesses here and we do recommend to the State Highway Commission that they place suitable markers on the Chisholm Trail as designated by the Committee on Resolutions and this assembly of living pioneers who are here gathered.

"Beginning at Caldwell, Kansas, the Chisholm Trail passed through or near Pond Creek Stage Ranch. Passed the Skeleton Stage Ranch on through the present townsite of Enid. 'Buffalo Springs' or now Bison, through Hennessey, to Red Fork, now Dover, and after passing Dover the Chisholm Trail passed to the Southwest through Kingfisher and Caddo Springs and on to Darlington Indian Agency, thence to Fort Reno and in a southwest course to Fort Sill. The Chisholm or freight trail ended there.

"After leaving Dover the Cattle Trail left the Chisholm Trail, passing to the southeast, thence bearing south passing east of El Reno and crossing the South Canadian River near Union City, thence Chickasha and Rush Springs, passing near Marlow and crossing Red River east of the mouth of Cache Creek."

This resolution was printed in the roster and proceedings of the Association, and a copy of the same preserved in the State Historical Society at Oklahoma City.

A letter written by a citizen of Western Oklahoma, setting forth the claim stated and advanced by them, was published in the *Daily Oklahoman* at Oklahoma City in October, 1930. J. B. Thoburn, who was at that time Curator of the State Historical Society of Oklahoma, and who was and is without question the best-advised man and best authority on historical matters connected with the old Indian Territory and Oklahoma, prepared a reply to this letter. This reply was published in the *Daily Oklahoman* on November 2, 1930. This reply, not only coming from so eminent an authority, but being so apt in detail and explanation, should be and is set out herein as follows:

"My attention was called to the letter in the Sunday *Oklahoman* from George O. Hopkins at Elk City, relative to the

Chisholm Trail. I decided to break my silence on the subject and try to close the needless dispute.

"No one doubts the good faith and sincerity of Ackley and other old time trail drivers who, after having helped to drive herds up from Texas on the Chisholm Trail proper, and who, when sent up the new trail to Dodge City a year or two later, merely assumed that the name of the Chisholm Trail was a general term that could be applied to any northern bound cattle trail, because some of the songs, ballads and traditions of the earlier trail had been carried along.

"But the spirit of contentiousness which blinds its eyes to the historically established fact that the Chisholm Trail became recognized as an Indian traders' road more than two years before the first herds of Texas cattle ever trod its path and still insists that Jess Chisholm had as much to do with the trail that passed northward across western Oklahoma as he did with the original and only Chisholm Trail is not entitled to very much consideration.

"The facts are that Jess Chisholm died in March, 1868, only nine or ten months after the first herd from Texas passed northward on the wilderness highway which had come to bear his name, while the trail through the western part of the Territory from Texas to Dodge City was not even broken by the first herd that passed over it until more than eight years later, in the late spring and early summer of 1876.

"Mr. Hopkins' amazing statement as to the reason why the later trail was established through the western part of the Indian Territory to Dodge City proves his resourcefulness in the elements, even though his knowledge of local history is manifestly limited. This pronouncement is as follows:

" 'The former trail came across Red River near Terrell, Okla., going up near Enid. Near Enid a group of easterners rented a large tract of land, on which they placed fine-blooded cattle. The Texas cattle were not allowed to go through this tract because of the danger of transmitting the Texas fever to the fine-blooded cattle. Consequently the trail was shifted westward. The Enid trail was used by a cattle man by the name of John Chisholm. A half breed Indian by the name of Jesse Chisholm was famous on the trail through western Oklahoma, hence the Chisholm trail.'

"The only thing wrong with the statements in the paragraph just quoted is that they each and all lack a foundation in fact, so it is unnecessary to reply to any of them in detail. However, it is not out of place to review briefly the history of the two trails after 1875.

"The close of the war saw changed conditions in the overland cattle drivers' industry for two reasons, namely (1) there were too many homestead settlers between Wichita and the Indian Territory line to make possible the continuance of that place as a shipping point for cattle that had been brought up the trail from Texas, and (2) the close of the last great Indian war on the southern plains and the final retirement of all of the Indians of the Comanche, Kiowa, Cheyenne, and Arapaho tribes to their reservations had made possible the development and use of a new trail through the western part of the Indian Territory with its first railway shipping point at Dodge City.

"From 1876 to 1879 inclusive Dodge City was the general destination of trail herds and for the time being the Chisholm Trail was little used, save by freighter and stage driver. Early in the spring of 1880, however, the Santa Fe railway extended its line from Wichita to Caldwell, near where the Chisholm trail intersected the boundary line between Kansas and the Indian Territory. Straightway the trail drivers of Texas resumed the use of the Chisholm trail to the new shipping point at Caldwell. Both trails were in use and both Caldwell and Dodge City continued to be live 'cow towns' during the ensuing four years.

"Homestead settlers were still pushing westward, however, with the result that after 1884 no more trail herds were driven to Dodge City market because there were too many settlers between that point and the Indian Territory line.

"The abandonment of the Dodge City trail through part of its course in western Oklahoma and the diversion of its herds to new shipping points on more recently constructed railway lines kept part of that trail still in use for several years longer. Meanwhile, trailing herds continued to be marketed each year at Caldwell until 1889, after which the settlement of Oklahoma and the southward extension of the Rock Island line, from that point, put a period to the story of the overland cattle trade in what is now Oklahoma."

In referring to the article of the gentleman who wrote the publication referred to by Mr. Thoburn, it is not necessary, or the intention of the writer, to question his sincerity, but his statement made in reference to the Old Chisholm Trail is badly at fault. The writer was personally familiar with this trail and the conditions along the same at all times after 1878, and traveled this trail after 1881. Not at that time, nor at any time prior thereto, had there been any blooded cattle kept in the Cherokee Strip along this trail. The entire Cherokee Strip had been for years held by ranchmen, and Texas cattle grazed all along the trail to the Kansas line. It is true that after 1876, these cattle could not pass to Wichita through the settlements in southern Kansas from the Indian Territory, but it was not on account of any blooded cattle being kept on the ranches in the country south of Kansas.

Further referring to this article, the writer will say that there was no John Chisholm. There was a John Chisum, heretofore referred to in a chapter devoted to him and his activities. John Chisum never drove cattle north over this trail. He settled in New Mexico, establishing the *Bosque Grande* ranch north of Roswell in 1867. We have it direct from his associate and contemporary at all times after that date, Charley Goodnight, that John Chisum never drove a herd north across the Red River. His home had been for years, prior to going to New Mexico, in Concho County, Texas. So far as Jesse Chisholm is concerned, his history is well known, and anyone can inform himself as to the same by examining any history of the early days of this country, being the period in which he lived. He never traveled either of these trails, except the traders' portion of the original Chisholm Trail. He died in 1868, long before the establishment of the Western Cattle Trail, and certainly could never have traveled it. This being the case, the statement made by the writer of that article to the effect that "Jesse Chisholm was famous on the trail through western Oklahoma" could not be correct, unless departed men traveled it. Furthermore, the men driving cattle north from Texas in these days did not let anyone in the Indian country stop them and say where they should go through, much less a "group of Easterners." There was no railway or shipping point at Dodge City until 1872, almost five years after Jesse Chisholm died.

After the interest had been taken in preserving the location and name of the Chisholm Trail by the old timers as above stated, the members of the State Legislature coming from the districts along the trail, when that body met in the session of 1931, took up the matter. They assembled the facts and concluded to present a bill finally establishing the location and designating not only the Chisholm Trail, but also the Western Cattle Trail. This was done, recognizing the fact that the routes and names of these old important trails should be truly located, designated, and perpetuated before they were lost and while living witnesses of these routes could be found. This was not unusual, as many of the States through which passed the old Oregon and Santa Fe Trails had been called upon and passed acts settling controversies as to the routes of the same. This was done in order to finally put to rest any future controversies, when all persons having actual knowledge of the same had passed away.

On behalf of the members desiring this action, Senator Clark and Representative Thornhill, members of the legislature, called upon the writer and asked him to frame a bill in line with the acts passed by former legislatures of other States designating old trails. This he did. This bill, carrying an emergency clause, passed the Legislature of the State of Oklahoma, and was signed by the Governor, and became a law on the 31st day of March, 1931. This act is found in Session Laws of Oklahoma, 1931, at Page 217, being Chapter 65, Article 5, and reads as follows:

"AN ACT PROVIDING FOR LOCATING, TRACING, MAPPING AND FILING PLATS OF THE LINES OF THE OLD ESTABLISHED CATTLE TRAILS ACROSS THE STATE OF OKLAHOMA, AND PROVIDING FOR THE EXPENSES OF SUCH WORK, AND DECLARING AN EMERGENCY.

BE IT ENACTED BY THE PEOPLE OF THE STATE OF OKLAHOMA:

SECTION 1. It shall be the duty of the State Highway Department of the State of Oklahoma, and the said department is required to immediately locate the correct line of the old established Chisholm Trail across the State of Oklahoma, showing as near as possible the exact location that the same crossed each section of land in said State in its course from the point where said trail crossed the south line of said State in southern Jefferson County, Oklahoma, to where it crossed the north line of said State in northern Grant County, Oklahoma, and said Highway Department shall also locate in the same manner the correct line of the old established Texas Cattle Trail crossing Western Oklahoma from where it crossed the south line of the State of Oklahoma, crossing the Red River at what is known as Doan's Store or Doan's Crossing, and following the line of said trail north to where it crossed the north line of said State of Oklahoma south of Dodge City or Fort Dodge, Kansas. The said department shall cause maps to be made of the said locations so determined by them, which said maps shall show the location of the main line of the Rock Island Railway running across said State to Dallas, Texas, and shall show the location of the present Meridian Highway, being Government Highway No. 81, across said State, and the proximity of said railroad and said highway to said trail.

SECTION 2. At least one copy of the said maps above referred to shall be retained in the office of the State Highway Department and one copy shall be furnished to the State Historical Society to be preserved in the office of said society, and that similar copies of the same shall be prepared, either by drafts or by printing, and shall be by the said Highway Department and by the said State Historical Society furnished to all known map makers, who are making and placing upon the market maps of the State of Oklahoma, so that the same may be copied and inserted on said maps.

SECTION 3. That all expenses connected with the carrying out of this provision shall be defrayed and paid by the State Highway Department out of any available funds in their hands; provided, that in no event shall the expense exceed five hundred dollars out of the general revenue fund." [1]

In this act the Legislature did justice and gave due credit to both of these old trails, and detracted nothing from the importance of either. Both of them are and were historical landmarks, and are two of the important thoroughfares of the Old West. If this act is carried out, in the future the traveler on the modern established automobile routes across the State of Oklahoma can see and know where once existed these famous

---

[1] We are informed and understand that the prior members of the State Highway Department of Oklahoma, or a majority of the same, subsequent to the time of the passage of this act, located a highway in the vicinity of this Western Cattle Trail, marking it as the "Chisholm Highway," or "Chisholm Trail Highway." It is difficult, in the face of this act of the Legislature and the uncontrovertible facts, to find any excuse for such action. Such action can benefit no one, and will only have the effect of confusing the location of the Chisholm Trail. It cannot even be claimed that any person by the name of "Chisholm" had any connection with this Western Cattle Trail. We also understand that the excuse was made by one of the members of the board that they could not designate the true Chisholm Trail by this name, for the reason that it was known as the Meridian Highway, and they wanted to perpetuate the name of the "Chisholm Trail." If this was the theory, to say the least, it is a peculiar method of reasoning, and if it is correct, we would suggest that we perpetuate the name of Plymouth Rock by locating it in Florida. Action should be speedily taken by the Highway Department to correct this error and save confusing the location of the Chisholm Trail.

ancient highways, over which millions of Texas cattle wound their tedious way, and can see and know the routes where once the picturesque cowboy, wearing his broad-brimmed sombrero, with chaparajos encasing his legs, with spurs jingling, and with all his other frontier equipment, crowded on these vast herds of long-horned cattle; but as they do so they can realize the changes that time has brought about and the swath that its cycle has cut, and they can say of this army of hardy and fearless pioneers—this advance guard of civilization on the frontier—that "The knights are dust and their good swords are rust." [2]

---

[2] This quotation from Coleridge is quoted by Sir Walter Scott in *Ivanhoe*, Chapter VIII.

CHAPTER XXXVII.

ROUTE OF THE TRAIL ACROSS THE CHEROKEE STRIP

It has been observed that the route of the early trail south of Kingfisher, or south of the point where the same struck Kingfisher Creek near the present City of Kingfisher, changed so much between the time the first drive came over it until it eventually settled to a point approximately the same as the line where now runs the track of the Chicago, Rock Island, and Pacific Railway, that it is difficult to give an exact location of the correct line of the same during this period the change was taking place. [1]

It has been further observed that from the point where it struck Kingfisher Creek on to the mouth of that creek, it always followed the east side of that creek to the Cimarron River. It then crossed the river, going northwest on the north side of the same for about one and one-half miles to the Old Red Fork Ranch, from which point it ran north on the east side of Turkey Creek to Buffalo Springs, or the present City of Bison. This portion of the trail has always kept the same route from the time of its establishment, or the first drive over the same, up to the time it was abandoned and closed by the settlements.

---

[1] The writer has herein persistently refrained from giving an exact location of the Chisholm Cattle Trail on south to the Red River after leaving Kingfisher Creek. There is a reason for this. Regardless of where the writer would locate this portion of the trail, it would stir up an unlimited amount of opposition; and the facts would be that all parties would be right. The route of this trail changed so much, especially during the early years of the life of the same, that it is impossible to give an exact location of the same over this portion. First, it ran very much to the east to avoid the Indians to the west, and later it varied very much in places on account of water and grass. The best we can do is to give a general course.

At Bison, or Buffalo Springs, the trail entered the Cherokee Strip or Outlet. The line of the trail from that point on north to the Kansas line was in about 1872, when the land along the same was surveyed, marked by the United States Government, and appears on the plat book in the United States Land Office at Washington City. It is the purpose of the writer to designate each quarter section of land over which the trail at that time took its course. This will be interesting to persons who now own farms along this route. Persons who will not be interested by this information can omit the reading of this description, and pass on to the closing.

Inasmuch as the sections in the townships begin to number from the north side of each township, it is best to commence this description at the north line, that is, at the point where the trail entered the Cherokee Outlet, southeast of Caldwell, Kansas. The first tier of townships in Oklahoma is only four miles wide. This is true from the fact that the survey was made on the south side first, and the last tier was only that wide. This would make it begin with section thirteen, being the first numbered section in this tier of townships in Oklahoma. The trail, however, entered the Outlet in section fourteen. First will be given the township and range, and below it each quarter section over which the trail ran, as follows :

TOWNSHIP TWENTY-NINE (29)   NORTH OF RANGE FOUR (4) WEST OF THE INDIAN MERIDIAN:
Northwest Quarter (NW¼) of Section Fourteen (14),
East one-half (E½) and Southwest Quarter (SW¼) of Section Fifteen (15),
West one-half (W½) of Section Twenty-Two (22),
Southeast Quarter (SE¼) of Section Twenty-One (21),
East one-half (E½) of Section Twenty-Eight (28), and
North one-half (N½) and Southwest Quarter (SW¼) of Section Thirty-Three (33).

TOWNSHIP TWENTY-EIGHT (28) NORTH OF RANGE
FOUR (4) WEST OF THE INDIAN MERIDIAN:

West one-half (W½) of Section Four (4),
East one-half (E½) of Section Eight (8),
East one-half (E½) of Section Seventeen (17),
East one-half (E½) of Section Twenty (20),
Near Center Line between East one-half (E½) and West one-
half (W½) of Section Twenty-Nine (29), and
West one-half (W½) of Section Thirty-Two (32).

TOWNSHIP TWENTY-SEVEN (27) NORTH OF RANGE
FOUR (4) WEST OF THE INDIAN MERIDIAN:

East one-half (E½) and Southwest Quarter (SW¼) of Section Six (6).

TOWNSHIP TWENTY-SEVEN (27) NORTH OF RANGE
FIVE (5) WEST OF THE INDIAN MERIDIAN:

Southeast Quarter (SE¼) of Section One (1),
East one-half (E½) of Section Twelve (12),
North one-half (N½) and Southwest Quarter (SW¼) of Sec-
tion Thirteen (13),
Northwest Quarter (NW¼) of Section Twenty-Four (24),
East one-half (E½) and Southwest Quarter (SW¼) of Sec-
tion Twenty-Three (23),
Northwest Quarter (NW¼) of Section Twenty-Six (26),
East one-half (E½) and Southwest Quarter (SW¼) of Sec-
tion Twenty-Seven (27),
East one-half (E½) and Southwest Quarter (SW¼) of Section
Thirty-Three (33).

TOWNSHIP TWENTY-SIX (26) NORTH OF RANGE FIVE
(5) WEST OF THE INDIAN MERIDIAN:

Northwest Quarter (NW¼) of Section Four (4),
East one-half (E½) and Southwest Quarter (SW¼) of Sec-
tion Five (5),
Northwest Quarter (NW¼) of Section Eight (8),
Southeast Quarter (SE¼) of Section Seven (7),
North one-half (N½) of Section Eighteen (18).

TOWNSHIP TWENTY-SIX (26) NORTH OF RANGE SIX (6) WEST OF THE INDIAN MERIDIAN:

East one-half (E½) of Section Thirteen (13),
East one-half (E½) of Section Twenty-Four (24),
East one-half (E½) and Southwest Quarter (SW¼) of Section Twenty-Five (25), and
West one-half (W½) of Section Thirty-Six (36).

TOWNSHIP TWENTY-FIVE (25) NORTH OF RANGE SIX (6) WEST OF THE INDIAN MERIDIAN:

East one-half (E½) and Southwest Quarter (SW¼) of Section Two (2),
West one-half (W½) of Section Eleven (11),
West one-half (W½) of Section Fourteen (14),
West one-half (W½) of Section Twenty-Three (23),
Northwest Quarter (NW¼) of Section Twenty-Six (26),
East one-half (E½) of Section Twenty-Seven (27), and
East one-half (E½) of Section Thirty-Four (34).

TOWNSHIP TWENTY-FOUR (24) NORTH OF RANGE SIX (6) WEST OF THE INDIAN MERIDIAN:

East one-half (E½) of Section Three (3),
East one-half (E½) of Section Ten (10),
North one-half (N½) and Southeast Quarter (SE¼) of Section Fifteen (15),
North one-half (N½) and Southwest Quarter (SW¼) of Section Twenty-Two (22),
West one-half (W½) of Section Twenty-Seven (27), and
West one-half (W½) of Section Thirty-Four (34).

TOWNSHIP TWENTY-THREE (23) NORTH OF RANGE SIX (6) WEST OF THE INDIAN MERIDIAN:

East one-half (E½) of Section Four (4),
East one-half (E½) of Section Nine (9),
East one-half (E½) and Southwest Quarter (SW¼) of Section Sixteen (16),
West one-half (W½) of Section Twenty-One (21),
West one-half (W½) of Section Twenty-Eight (28),
Northwest Quarter (NW¼) of Section Thirty-Three (33), and
Southeast Quarter (SE¼) of Section Thirty-Two (32).

TOWNSHIP TWENTY-TWO (22) NORTH OF RANGE SIX (6) WEST OF THE INDIAN MERIDIAN:

North one-half (N½) and Southwest Quarter (SW¼) of Section Five (5),

Northwest Quarter (NW¼) of Section Eight (8),

East one-half (E½) of Section Seven (7),

North one-half (N½) and Southwest Quarter (SW¼) of Section Eighteen (18),

Southwest Quarter (SW¼) of Section Thirty (30), and

Northwest Quarter (NW¼) of Section Thirty-One (31).

TOWNSHIP TWENTY-TWO (22) NORTH OF RANGE SEVEN (7) WEST OF THE INDIAN MERIDIAN:

East one-half (E½) of Section Twenty-Four (24), and

Northeast Quarter (NE¼) of Section Twenty-Five (25).

TOWNSHIP TWENTY-ONE (21) NORTH OF RANGE SEVEN (7) WEST OF THE INDIAN MERIDIAN:

East one-half (E½) of Section one (1),

East one-half (E½) of Section Twelve (12),

East one-half (E½) of Section Thirteen (13),

Eats one-half (E½) of Section Twenty-Four (24),

East one-half (E½) of Section Twenty-Five (25), and

East one-half (E½) of Section Thirty-Six (36).

TOWNSHIP TWENTY (20) NORTH OF RANGE SEVEN (7) WEST OF THE INDIAN MERIDIAN:

East one-half (E½) of Section One (1),

East one-half (E½) of Section Twelve (12),

East one-half (E½) of Section Thirteen (13),

East one-half (E½) of Section Twenty-Four (24),

East one-half (E½) of Section Twenty-Five (25), and

East one-half (E½) of Section Thirty-Six (36).

There has just been given to you the exact official route followed by the Chisholm Trail in 1872. At some locations along this line now rise prosperous and progressive cities. The rest has been plowed under, and beneath the fields of waving grain,

> So prone and still this trail does lie,
> As it would if trails could die.

Annually the plows of the husbandmen stir this soil; they sow and reap their grain to prepare food for the Nation, but for many years to come these plows will turn up the hard, packed, and glistening earth tramped as hard as stone by the thousands of hoofs that trod the same as their owners took their tedious way along this ancient thoroughfare. When the last herd progressing up this trail reached its destination, and the last cowboy turned to bid it farewell he waved his broad-brimmed *sombrero,* and in a solemn voice exclaimed, "A DIOS!" [1]

---

[1] *A Dios* is Spanish and means farewell or adieu. The "a" is a preposition, meaning from, by, with, or according to. It is pronounced with a very short sound. "Dios" is pronounced Deos, and means God, Deity, or any person or thing passionately beloved. This was universally the cowboy's address of a fond and affectionate farewell.

INDEX

G.

H.

I.

J.

K.

L.

M.

S.

T.

V.

W.